Philosophy, Social Theory, and the Thought of George Herbert Mead

SUNY Series in the Philosophy of the Social Sciences

Lenore Langsdorf, Editor

Philosophy, Social Theory, and the Thought of George Herbert Mead

Edited by

Mitchell Aboulafia

State University of New York Press

Published by
State University of New York Press, Albany

© 1991 State University of New York

Printed in the United States of America

For information, address State University of New York
Press, State University Plaza, Albany, N.Y., 12246

Library of Congress Cataloging-in-Publication Data

Philosophy, social theory, and the thought of George Herbert Mead/
edited by Mitchell Aboulafia.
     p. cm.—(SUNY series in the philosophy of the social
sciences)
     Includes bibliographical references.
     ISBN 0-7914-0359-9 (alk. paper).—ISBN 0-7914-0360-2 (pbk.:
alk. paper)
     1. Mead, George Herbert, 1863-1931. I. Aboulafia, Mitchell.
II. Series.
B945. M464P55   1991
191–dc20   90–30134
                                                       CIP

10 9 8 7 6 5 4 3 2 1

For Matthew Aboulafia

Contents

Preface

Were it not that George Herbert Mead has been well known in sociological circles for much of our century, I might have titled this anthology, "An Invitation to the Thought of G. H. Mead." There is little doubt that certain audiences require an invitation, given the rather peculiar reception Mead has encountered for the better part of half a century. Although he is viewed by many as one of the giants of classic American philosophy, the interest he has generated and the impact he has had outside of the school of symbolic interaction simply cannot compare to that of James, Peirce, or Dewey. Although he is hailed as the progenitor of a school of sociological thought, the relative scarcity of monographs about Mead stands as compelling testimony to his failure to achieve philosophical renown or to shake the popular imagination.

Both Dewey and Whitehead praised Mead as "a seminal mind of the very first order."[1] Several of his ideas, for example, role taking and the generalized other, have the ring of accepted wisdom; and a number of philosophers, primarily in the pragmatic tradition, have addressed his thought over the years. So why has Mead not received the critical treatment that a figure of his stature deserves? Why should this key figure, a veritable storehouse of interesting ideas, have been overlooked by so many for so long? Why have some of the implications of his most seminal ideas only recently begun to see the light of day? Why have a number of highly respected German thinkers—for example, Habermas, Tugendhat, Joas—sought of late to highlight the insightfulness and unique untapped potential of Mead's work? Why is now the time to turn to Mead?

These questions are clearly historical as well as philosophical. They presume, of course, that there is considerable depth to Mead's thought and that it has only begun to be fully mined. Ample support for these assertions, I believe, will be found in the work of the authors in this anthology. We might speculate here as to why Mead has not received his due in the past, although such speculation may tell us more about Mead than about "objective" historical conditions. In so doing, we could begin by noting that he drew upon diverse and often warring traditions. His ideas, for example, encompass the seemingly antithetical camps of the Enlightenment and Romanticism, and he utilizes the perennially American languages of behaviorism and functionalism to develop an idealistically inspired dialectic of the self and the other. But this in itself explains little, for being received as a synthetic thinker might just as well enhance one's reputation as detract from it.

Mead was an interdisciplinary thinker at a time when disciplinary lines were deepening into active fissures, and his apparent fence straddling well could have appeared monstrous to those engaged in "rigorous" philosophical, sociological or psychological investigations. Needless to say, Mead's hybrid philosophy, his mode of thought, and the nature of his writings would not have offered themselves in a very positive light to analytic philosophers in the heyday of analysis. At the same time, continental thinkers, be they phenomenologists, critical theorists, existentialists, or orthodox Marxists, for the most part, had little use for pragmatists. Mead was so classed by one and all. And this is especially unfortunate because many of those attuned to continental thought would have found his dialectic of the self and the other rather congenial, had they been inclined to look beyond this appellation and the jargon of behaviorism.[2]

It also is worth noting that, on the one hand, Mead was something of a systems theorist, whose ideas would have appeared insufficiently systemic for those inclined to grand models. On the other hand, although he saw himself as a supporter of novelty and individual agency, his claims regarding agency were such that they would have appeared too weak for the existentialists and their anti-systemic protégés. Finally, whereas his good friend Dewey would produce enough volumes to fill a small library, Mead never wrote a contemporary classic: no *Being and Time*, no *Tractatus*, not even an *I and Thou*. His most famous book, *Mind, Self, and Society*, is a compilation of notes—as such it gravitates to the imprecise and repetitive—and many who have read it have never bothered to consult the limited number of more carefully argued articles he saw fit to publish. Mead, it seems, for the better part of half a century, was in the wrong place, with the wrong approach, with the wrong sort of publishing record, for both professional philosophers and those who followed their lead.

Yet Mead's place is one that many now find themselves turning to, whether they know it to be Mead's or not. As modernity strives to come to terms with the challenges of postmodernity, as the walls between analytic philosophy and continental thought show signs of decomposition, as philosophers either yield to or strive to confront the extreme cultural relativism of our times, as many question the very future of philosophy as a separate discipline, Mead stands out as theoretician whose views directly address or bear on these themes, and as one who merits our concerted attention. He is a philosopher whose thought is attuned to the profound philosophical issues at stake in the myriad of contemporary challenges to foundationalist and transcendentalist assumptions. He is a social psychologist and sociologist who understands the importance of genetic and developmental approaches, while, for the most part, avoiding the reductionism from which these approaches often suffer. He is a thinker who understands the key role language plays in the development of the self and self-consciousness, but who also understands that there is a world from which language emerges, and that practical activity informs and nurtures linguistic interactions. He is a theoretician who strives to account for the way in which the social can generate and nurture the individual without producing an overly socialized self in the process. And, even if he does not succeed in deciphering this puzzle, he presents us with numerous intriguing leads; for example, his concept of sociality, for breaking the code. His thought in many ways is compatible with important currents in both continental and Anglo-American theorizing, once these orientations are set free from their often parochial pasts. (It is here, by the way, I would locate some of the reasons why a number of contemporary German theoreticians have found Mead to be a thinker worthy of intensive study. Mead has aroused interest in a postwar, postanalytic, post-Americanized Germany, but nevertheless a Germany in which there are still thinkers who have imbibed the tradition of German idealism that nurtured Mead's own thought.) Last but not least, Mead is a behaviorist whose thought inherently transcends behaviorism. As Habermas aptly notes, "If we want to release the revolutionary power of the basic concepts of behavior theory, the potential in this approach to burst the bounds of its own paradigm, we shall have to go *back* to Mead's social psychology."[3] But, as Habermas knows, one can never *simply* go back to Mead's social psychology, if for no other reason than that his social psychology breaks the bounds of its own discipline.

The accuracy of these rather breathtaking claims for Mead's thought can be assessed only by coming to terms with his work. Some important thinkers already have attempted to do so. In part, this book is being offered to bring their work on Mead before different audiences. In selecting elements to be anthologized I have kept several goals in mind. First, I wished to introduce readers to Mead's thought or reinforce existing interest by publishing some of the best recent expository and historical material on him. Hence, I have attempted to select pieces that cover many of the fundamental themes of Mead's approach, placing them first in the order of articles in the book. Second, I wished to show the potential of Mead's thought for addressing some of the more compelling present-day issues. To this end I have sought pieces that both critique Mead's ideas and develop them. And, although I have not attempted to cover in depth every aspect of Mead's thought—for example, his intriguing ideas on the nature of the physical thing— the cornerstones of his social thought indeed are presented here. I hope that, in reading this work from cover to cover, a reader with little background in Mead's thought will find a congenial and sophisticated introduction to Mead and the avenues that his thought opens up. Those already familiar with Mead should be delighted and intrigued by the breadth and originality of insights offered. Mead surely does not have the answers to all our questions, but he can assist us in approaching them from a fresh angle; and the articles in this volume begin to show us how.

However, these ends do not exhaust my hopes for the book. I also wish to place before a wider audience several dimensions of Mead's thought that have not been given their due. One of these is the political dimension. Whereas few would hold that Mead is a major political theorist, considerable evidence demonstrates that political concerns and interests were crucial in the development of his ideas; and far too little has been written about this aspect of Mead. Hans Joas—whose work, along with Dmitri Shalin's, leads off this book—stakes out this territory when he tells us that in his opinion, "the development of Mead's [social] theory ... was made possible by the positive relationship of the American pragmatists to the ethical implications of a categorical notion of democracy and to the emancipatory prospects of progress in technology and the natural sciences."[4] The pivotal importance of specific progressive ideals in Mead's personal and intellectual development is documented in Shalin's contribution to the volume.

This is not to say that Mead's political ideas would be of interest only to antiquarians. Although we may smile affectionately at the naivete of certain of his claims, his vision of dialogue, rationality, and democracy as the triumvirate necessary for the good society appears to gain in authority as the years pass. This is in spite of all that we know about the difficulty of defining and achieving rational discourse. Although Mead was more than willing to criticize American society for the excesses of its capitalism and for its denial of community, he also was an ardent defender of the transformative power of democracy, especially the grass-roots variety. Mead, of course, shared his desire for a truly democratic and just social order with other noteworthy thinkers of his generation; for example, Dewey. If Mead were with us today he, no doubt, would be looking for ways to support those who, from Eastern Europe to China to the Philippines to grass-roots movements in Western Europe and the United States, are struggling to assert control over their own lives.

What makes Mead interesting here, of course, is not so much his political positions, which have been admirably defended and critiqued from many quarters, but the manner in which his own support of them was related to his arguments about the development of the mind and the self. If we are the sort of social beings that Mead thinks we are—and if our capacities, including rationality, are linked to our interactions with others in the manner that Mead argues—then there indeed are good reasons for defending dialogue and democracy. There would be good reasons even for believing that a much (and often justly) maligned strategy for interpreting and grappling with our world, namely, the belief in social and economic progress, would have its merits. Such a belief merits reconsideration to the extent that growth in the density of human interaction and communication leads us not to an inevitable iron cage of anonymity, but to new modes of interaction that enhance the likelihood of democratically inspired dialogue and negotiation.

Habermas, that contemporary dreamer of rationality and democracy, is no doubt a more sophisticated political theorist than Mead. Yet, it is no accident that Mead turns out to be one of the central figures in his *Theory of Communicative Action.* Although Habermas clearly criticizes Mead—for his lack of development of a theory of language, for his failure to come to terms with the phylogenetic, and utlimately for his lack of systemic model of social and cultural organization—Mead is a seminal figure for him, in part because of his insights into the capacities that we must nurture if we are to create the good society. To understand the conditions necessary for developing and living in a democratic society, both Mead and Habermas would have us look to the sources of communicative competence and foster those institutions that would develop its rational components.

Mead was commited to actively searching for ways to improve the lot of humankind. He believed in the promise of science; and he believed that if the scientific sensibility were properly understood and employed, it could assist us in eradicating misery and in improving our lives. He believed that progress in human affairs is not only possible but the likely result of our active endeavors to achieve it. These are not new themes. They are in some ways the dominating icons of our (Western) culture. They have been seriously challenged from several directions, of course; and numerous critiques have made it clear that it is neither prudent nor acceptable to take them as they have been passed down to us by previous generations. Indeed, given the persistent dangers of living in a world in which instrumental reason thinks it is entitled to run amok, it behooves us to ask if we can and should adhere to these icons at all. Mead, however, would ask us not to throw out the baby with the bath water.

Although many of the authors gathered here are critical of important features of his thought, by and large, they are—as most Mead scholars have been—sympathetically disposed to what we might call Mead's ameliorationist vision. Several explicitly direct themselves to themes related to it. For example, Shalin takes up Mead's progressive political agenda; Joas discusses the emancipatory potential of Mead's nonpostivistic approach to science; Swanson suggests the importance of collective experience in the development of our skills and powers, among them reflective intelligence; and through a reading of Hegel informed by Mead, I address the stunting of potentialities and the deformations of character that can occur in relationships of domination.

Invoking Hegel's name provides an opportunity for noting an additional concern of the book. In my view, Mead's indebtedness to German idealism, specifically Hegel, has not been addressed in the depth it mertis; hence much of what is subtle and unique about Mead has been missed or misconstrued. This is not to say that scholars have been unaware of Mead's early interest in Hegel, rather that the usual approach has been to mention it as just that, an early interest, and then to move on to more important topics at hand. A second strategy has been to acknowledge idealism's impact, but to see it as so pernicious that it must be avoided at all cost in developing the more valuable sides of Mead.[5]

It appears that with few exceptions most of those who have written on Mead simply were not well-versed in, or hostile to, the Hegelian tradition. For those with only limited familiarity with Hegel's work, it makes admirable sense to see him as the quintessence of much that Mead actively opposed: a conversative political vision and the denigration of the empirical sciences in the name of a higher rationality. But there is another Hegel; viz., the unrivaled dialectician who gave us the dialectic of recognition. Hegel the organic thinker, like Hegel the theoretician of the development of the self through the other, left an indelible imprint on Mead. To what degree this was a diret imprint and to what degree it came through Josiah Royce is a question worthy of further investigation. In any case, not only should Hegel's influence not be sidestepped, it should be acknowledged and explored. But aside from the question of influence, a dialogue between Hegel and Mead has much to offer, for they are admirably suited as foils for each other. So, for example, Tugendhat, a thinker well-versed in German idealism with commitments to analytic philosophy, confronts Hegel with Mead in his *Self-Consciousness and Self-Determination*.[6] As will be apparent, a number of our authors are quite knowledgeable about Hegel, and their approaches to Mead reflect this fact.

Lest the reader think that the readings at hand are all committed to extravagant Hegelian ruminations, let me explain without further ado that most of the pieces either fail to mention Hegel or expend little energy in directly discussing him. In addition to seeking articles that exhibit the political and dialectical sensibilities of Mead, I have sought material that would juxtapose Mead with a number of thinkers who traditionally have not been associated with him, hoping that such material might suggest new lines of research. And, as previously mentioned, I also have sought articles that would address a number of trends in 20th century thought.

The book opens with the aforementioned pieces by Shalin and Joas that locate Mead within specific intellectual and political traditions. Joas connects Mead with a number of important continental theoreticians, for example, Fichte and Dilthey, in addition to exploring the more well-worn path of Darwin's impact on Mead. The next part, Functionalism and Social Behaviorism, begins with Cook arguing for the importance of reading Mead as a functionalist to understand the development of his social psychology and takes up the evolution of Mead's ideas where Joas's contribution leaves off. Cook is followed by Lewis's reading of Mead as a social behaviorist, in an article that summarizes various interpretations of Mead's view of the "I." These two papers have been joined together because of the historical and conceptual connections between functionalism and behaviorism and because they provide valuable alternative interpretations of Mead's distinction between the "I" and the "Me." Their conjunction in the same section is not meant to suggest that functional and behavioral readings of Mead do not differ in significant respects.[7]

Drawing on the work of Habermas and Tugendhat, the third section takes up one of our century's most enduring obsessions:

Language. Both thinkers are well-versed in continental thought and both have spent a good deal of time studying analytic philosophy. Coming to Mead with this background has yielded some intriguing results, including Habermas's striking attempt to augment Mead with Wittgenstein and Tugendhat's relentless critique of what he considers Mead's failure to come to terms with important distinctions; for example, that between practical and theoretical inner dialogue. Tugendhat also presents us with the rather interesting option of reading Heidegger and Mead as supplements to each other. In addition, joining Habermas and Tugendhat in one section highlights important features of a dialogue they have had with each other over the years. The final section brings together Swanson's article and my article under the rubric of the Interpersonal and Intrapersonal. These pieces are concerned with demonstrating how Mead's dynamic conception of the self as a social self contributes to our understanding of its capacities. Swanson refers to a number of empirical studies and discusses his own work in this area, whereas I proceed by analyzing Hegel's master and slave text in light of certain basic Meadian and Freudian assumptions. Both articles suggest that Mead and Freud might be used to augment certain weaknesses in each other's views.

Several important perspectives in 20th century thought are addressed in the book: behaviorism, functionalism, linguistic analysis, socialism, and psychoanalysis. Nevertheless, given the constraints of space and availability of material, an anthology by its very nature must be plagued by certain gaps. Here, phenomenology and Marxism are discussed far too briefly, and structuralism is left totally by the wayside. Mead's potential contribution to feminism also is not addressed; and this is especially regrettable given Mead's lifelong commitment to women's rights.[8] The source of these defects, in certain instances, can be attributed as much to a dearth of appropriate material as to criteria for inclusion. Still, not only have certain approaches been given short shrift, but a number of respected scholars have been excluded. It will be immediately obvious, for example, that I have not done justice to those writing as symbolic interactionists, especially given the quantity of material they have written on Mead over the years. In defense I can plead that their work already is closely associated with Mead's name, whereas one of my goals has been to show Mead's potential for connecting with those in different traditions. (I do expect that the papers anthologized here will be of interest to symbolic interactionists.[9]) I have made a modest attempt to redress some of these omissions by including a wide-ranging bibliography of recent material on Mead.

There always is the undeniably idiosyncratic and circumstantial in the genesis of anthologies. I focused on material that could heighten interest in Mead among a variety of different audiences, but even in this regard certain hopes were deferred. Perhaps this book will assist in kindling interest in Mead among those attuned to the current debate between proponents of the so-called postmodernist and modernist perspectives. In general, far too little has been written on Mead and recent intellectual currents; for example, on Mead and those dedicated postmodernists, the deconstructionists.[10] Mead, after all, is a thinker of novelty, one who would tell us that we can give the novel its due without descending into, or being absorbed by, an endless play of signs. But these and other movements will have to await another day and another book, a day and a book that ideally this book will help to realize.

The contributions to this volume have been collected from a wide variety of publications. I have sought to adhere as closely as possible to their original formats. Explanatory notes and references have been added to several of the selections. They are designated by superscripted lower case letters in the text.

Acknowledgments

I had been forewarned by the wise: anthologies have little heart and they actually enjoy devouring an editor's time and peace of mind. My experience will be different, I retorted. Besides, I had an obligation to assist in promoting George Herbert Mead's thought after he had so kindly assisted me with mine.

Having now joined the camp of the wise—at least with regard to anthologies—I feel genuinely entitled to the luxury of an acknowledgments page. A number of colleagues and friends have been particularly supportive during the trials of this project: Steven Crowell, Michael M. J. Fischer, Kirk Harlow, R. Lane Kauffmann, Mark Kulstad, John J. McDermott, Tullio Maranhão, Elliot Pruzan, Denny Schmidt, Curt Smith, and Richard Wolin. A special word of thanks is due Patrick Heelan and Thomas McCarthy for their generous advocacy of the project, and John Gorman for the keenness of his editorial eye. I would also like to thank the members of the Rice (University) Circle for intellectual sustenance in the outlands of Houston. A word of appreciation must go to my graduate students at the University of Houston-Clear Lake for their willingness to grapple with Mead (and with me on Mead). One student in particular, Raimundo Gonzalez, stands in need of special recognition. Raimundo passed away early in 1989. He was 66 years of age and had recently begun a second career teaching philosophy at a local community college. He bequeathed a love of philosophy—which he pursued year after year while working full time—to those who were fortunate enough to have studied with him. I must not forget to thank my editor at SUNY, Rosalie M. Robertson, for her labors on behalf of this project, Sharon S. Bennett and Gnomi Goulden for their copy-editing, and Margaret Simpson for her typing and good cheer.

My deepest gratitude is once again reserved for the companionship of Barbara Ellman, my wife, and for my two young daughters, Lauren and Sara, who have assured me that Mead's optimism regarding the human condition was not misplaced.

The Faculty Research and Support Fund of the University of Houston-Clear Lake assisted this project through two grants. A sincere word of thanks to all of the authors in this volume for their willingness to allow their work to be reprinted, and to the following publishers and journals for granting permission to reprint:

Dmitri N. Shalin, "G. H. Mead, Socialism, and the Progressive Agenda," first published in the *American Journal of Sociology*, Vol. 93, No. 4. Copyright © 1988 by the University of Chicago.

Hans Joas, "Mead's Position in Intellectual History and his Early Philosophical Writings," excerpted from *G. H. Mead. A Contemporary Re-examination of His Thought*, trans. Raymond Meyer. Copyright © English translation 1985 by Basil Blackwell (Polity Press). Reprinted by permission of Basil Blackwell. Published by MIT Press in the U.S.A.

Gary A. Cook, "The Development of G. H. Mead's Social Psychology," first published in the *Transactions of the Charles S. Peirce Society*, Vol. 8, No. 3, Summer 1972.

J. David Lewis, "A Social Behaviorist Interpretation of the Meadian 'I,'" first published in the *American Journal of Sociology*, Vol. 85, No. 2. Copyright © 1979 by the University of Chicago.

Jürgen Habermas, "The Foundations of Social Science in the Theory of Communication" and "Mead's Grounding of a Discourse Ethics" excerpted from *The Theory of Communicative Action, Vol. II*, trans. Thomas McCarthy. Copyright © English translation 1987 by Beacon Press. Reprinted by permission of Beacon Press. British Empire rights granted by Basil Blackwell (Polity Press).

Ernst Tugendhat, "Mead I: Symbolic Interaction" and "Mead II: The Self," excerpted from *Self-Consciousness and Self-Determination*, trans. Paul Stern. Copyright © English translation 1986 by MIT Press. Reprinted by permission of MIT Press.

Guy E. Swanson, "The Powers and Capabilities of Selves: Social and Collective Approaches," first published in the *Journal for the Theory of Social Behavior*, Vol. 15, No. 3, October 1985. Reprinted by permission of Basil Blackwell.

Mitchell Aboulafia, "Self-Consciousness and the Quasi-Epic of the Master," first published in the *Philosophical Forum*, Vol. 18, No. 4, Summer 1987.

Introduction

Having delineated the goals and themes of this book in the Preface, I would like to set the stage for the expository and critical pieces that follow by offering an account of Mead's social thought. My aim is by no means to provide a definitive scholarly reading of Mead's mature thought, which, even if possible, would require a substantial work unto itself.[1] Rather, my goal is to orient readers who are unfamiliar with Mead's thought (or have not read him for some time) through an account that avoids detailed criticism and shuns claims to comprehensiveness, but does highlight many of the ideas and topics discussed, criticized, and developed in this book.

Mead perhaps is best known as a theorist of the self, and there is good reason for this. Even when he does not directly address the issue of selfhood, one can see how deeply his thought has been informed by the analysis of the self, and through this analysis we will approach Mead. In following this course, we must begin with his concept of the mind, for without the mind there can be no self for Mead. As a thinker deeply indebted to the Darwinian turn of the late 19th century, he conceives of mind, both ontogenetically and phylogenetically, in terms of evolutionary development; that is, in terms of emergence.[2] To explain how mind emerges, Mead has recourse to the *gesture*.

Mead tells us that animals gesture to one another and that in so doing communicate. When a dog bares its fangs at another dog, it makes a gesture; and a second dog may respond by running away or perhaps by baring its fangs. A gesture may be thought of as a stimulus that calls out a response. It also may be thought of as that feature of an action that can stand for or symbolize that which follows the gesture. For Mead, the meaning of a gesture is to be understood in functional terms, so that in our example the baring of fangs by the first dog means run or bare fangs (back), which is the response of the second dog. In this sense, meaning is objective and can be observed and studied, for it is defined in terms of the responses of organisms to each other.

For human beings, however, meaning is not simply a function of objective responses that can be noted by a third party, because human beings are aware of meanings and have the capacity to point them out to themselves, even in the absence of others. How does this capacity arise? Human beings make use of vocal gestures. As we cross a busy street I turn to a friend and yell, "Stop!" to prevent her from stepping in front of an oncoming car. In so doing, we both hear the word *stop*, and there is a tendency to respond to it in me as there is in my friend, because I hear the same word my friend hears. *Stop* is a vocal gesture. Mead tells us that, "In the case of the vocal gesture the form [the organism] hears its own stimulus just as when this is used by other forms, so it tends to respond also to its own stimulus as it responds to the stimulus of other forms."[3]

The vocal gesture provides a mirroring or reflective dimension to our responses to stimuli. This dimension can be employed to distinguish the vocal gesture from the gesture or, in alternative terms, the *significant symbol* from the symbol. "Gestures become significant symbols when they implicitly arouse in an individual making them the same responses which they explicitly arouse, or are supposed to arouse, in other individuals, the individuals to whom they are addressed."[4]

In using significant symbols or vocal gestures, I respond implicity as the other responds explicitly to my gestures. I say to my friend, "Open the window," and I can feel a tendency in myself to respond as my friend does, even though I do not overtly do so. We have both learned to react to the same symbols in a similar fashion; and we both are aware of the responses that these symbols call out in us. "The critical importance of language in the development of human experience lies in this fact that the stimulus is one that can react upon the speaking individual as it reacts upon the other."[5] Unlike animals, human beings are aware of meanings because they can hear their gestures as the other hears them, and can respond to them as the other has responded. How do I learn the meaning of a vocal gesture? I become aware of what it means by "viewing" it from the perspective of the other; that is, by being aware of alter's (potential) response to my vocal gesture. I "see" my own gesture in light of this response.

A relatively sophisticated nervous system is required in order to be able to discriminate the kinds of stimuli that the vocal gesture demands. The genesis of this nervous system, in terms of both the evolution of the species and the development of the individual, owes much to the capacity of the hand to grasp and manipulate objects. In his *Philosophy of the Act*, Mead divides experience into perceptual, manipulatory, and consummatory phases; and this division is predicated on the importance of physical contact with objects, specifically the unique sort of contact accessible to human beings because of the hand.[6] The world of immediacy, to which the animal is confined, gives way to a realm of mediation as human beings extend the "distance" between the perceptual and consumma-tory stages of the act—for example, seeing the plant as food and eating it—through the increasing complexity of the manipulatory stage. The latter stage allows us to treat objects in different ways, and hence see them as means to different ends. Only with the use of significant symbols, however, is the full potential of the manipula-tory stage of the act realized, for then direct contact can be superseded by the innovations of language.

Given Mead's sensitivity to the importance of the hand, it is no surprise that he is well aware that the hand allows us to develop sophisticated sign languages. We can see the hand as the other sees it, in a fashion analogous to the manner in which we can hear the vocal gesture as the other hears it. The hand can be used to produce significant symbols. Nevertheless, Mead argues that the vocal gesture holds a unique place in the genesis of the mind for both the species and the individual; and he investigates significant symbols in light of our ability to produce vocal gestures.[7]

For Mead, significant symbols allow us to be aware of mean-ing; and meaning is defined in terms of the similarity of responses; that is, in functional terms. This understanding of meaning is criticized by both Tugendhat and Habermas as conflating the similarity of responses with the identity of meaning; and both point to the source of this confusion in Mead's failure to grapple with the intricacies of language.[8] Be this as it may, when one is aware of a meaning, for Mead, one is "self-conscious." This designation stresses that the awareness of meaning rests on the reflective character of significant symbols.[9] However, it should be noted that the term *self-conscious* in this context does not imply a consciousness of self; that is, an explicit awareness of having a self, a self-consciousness. (I will address the relationship of the self to self-consciousness later.) Significant symbols go hand in hand with (self-conscious) meaning, and from their use mind emerges.

> Mentality on our approach simply comes in when the organ-ism is able to point out meanings to others and to himself. This is the point at which mind appears, or if you like, emerges.... It is absurd to look at the mind simply from the standpoint of the individual human organism; for, although it has its focus there, it is essentially a social phenomenon; even its biological functions are primarily social.[10]

To develop a mind one must learn to anticipate the response of the other to specific symbols, and this task of anticipation can be spoken of in terms of "taking the attitude of the other." In responding as the other has responded to gestures, I learn to take the attitude of the other toward these gestures. This means that I am prepared to respond as the other has responded to them, even if I do not overtly do so.[11] Eventually I am readily able to respond to my own gestures in the absence of the other; that is, I am able to talk to myself.[12] There is an ambiguity in Mead's use of the term *response*, however, which should be mentioned here; and in this ambiguity we can catch a glimpse of how Mead's model begins to transcend ordinary behaviorism in the direction of a theory of communication. Mead does indeed use the term *response* for the simple reaction to a stimulus, but he also uses it to suggest the answer—that is, the response—one receives in addressing the other.[13] As such, the term *response* comes to connote something more than a mere reaction to a specific stimulus; it comes to suggest the ability address another in a fashion that shows a communicative intent. We address ourselves as we address the other; and in so doing, we do not simply wait for a reaction, but expect an answer, a response. We behave as speakers and listeners.

Human beings learn to respond not only to specific signs or behaviors of others, but to complex groupings of these behaviors; and in so doing, they learn to take roles. The child learns various roles by playing the self and the other, so to speak. He or she learns these roles by taking over the behaviors associated with these roles; for instance, father, nurse, or police officer, and by also learning to take the roles of child, patient, or bad guy. "The child says something in one character and responds in another character, and then his responding in another character is a stimulus to himself in the first character, and so the conversation goes on."[14] The child responds in certain ways that call out other responses, and these networks or integrated sets of responses are what we call *roles*. We might think of roles as selves, but, for Mead, they are only nascent selves.[15] A role or even a number of roles in themselves cannot produce a fully developed unified self.

There is a unity or wholeness to the self that transcends the specific roles any of us might play. How are we to understand this unity? The self, for Mead, is a phenomenon of cognition, and as such, self-consciousness is intimately connected with the possibility of having a unified self.[16] We need, then, a way of being aware of ourselves that transcends the specific "seeing" of ourselves from the perspective of a particular other, which is merely a seeing that takes place in relation to specific behaviors or roles. We must be able to view ourselves from the perspective of an other that is more general and abstract than those previously mentioned, an other that can frame the various "facets" of the self—its behaviors, gestures, and roles—and from whose perspective we can be aware of them as elements of a greater whole. This other, for Mead, is the *generalized other;* and it arises as we take the perspective of a social group.

> The organized community or social group which gives to the individual his unity of self may be called the "generalized other." The attitude of the generalized other is the attitude of the whole community. Thus, for example, in the case of such a social group as a ball team, the team is the generalized other in so far as it enters—as an organized process or social activity— into the experience of any one of the individual members of it.[17]

Mead turns from individual roles to his notion of *the game* to clarify how a self comes into being. Take, for example, the game of baseball. To play first base, I must be able to take the attitudes of all of the members of the team and experience them as an integrated system. Games contain implicit rules of behavior that we often seek to make explicit—in the case before us, not only the rules of baseball, but of a particular team's manner of dealing with other teams. To have a self under these circumstances I must be attuned to the rules and attitudes that organize and constitute my self as they do the community of the team. Needless to say, Mead's rather notorious example of a baseball team providing a generalized other, which in turn gives rise to a self, has left quite a few commentators rather cold. The self appears, after all, to be more than a mere set of behavioral dispositions, learned in relation to some social group.

In spite of Mead's example, concentrating on his phrases "whole community" and "organized process or social activity" may be of some value in dealing with this most slippery of Meadian neologisms. For Mead, there are systemically organized spheres of activity; and when we participate in these spheres we learn to "see" ourselves from their perspective, so that our own behaviors are integrated because those of the social group are integrated. We view ourselves from the perspective of the group/system when we follow the rules that make the group possible. In this respect, for example, a family may be viewed as a system, for there are implicit rules that organize the behavior of the group as a group, and individual interactions within the group are comprehensible because of the overall organization. The self, then, is the constellation of responses that I cognize as me, because of a certain social group; and I can be aware of this object—this me—because I can view it from the perspective of an other, that is, a generalized other, that frames and integrates what I see.[18]

But this still seems a bit unsatisfactory, for even if we accept this definition of the self—which, as we shall see later, Mead qualifies—we appear to be left with a multitude of selves rather than a self. And Mead himself provides support for this view. He tells us that there are a multitude of social groups, and each appears to give rise to its own generalized other.

> Some of them are concrete social classes or subgroups, such as political parties, clubs, corporations, which are actually functional social units, in terms of which their individual members are directly related to one another. The others are abstract social classes or subgroups, such as the class of debtors and the class of creditors, in terms of which their individual members are related to one another only more or less indirectly.[19]

So, if we are to follow Mead here, not only is the self a cognitive object—one that we can be aware of because a generalized other frames and demarcates as we take its perspective—but there are a multitude of such cognitive objects. We have looked for a unified object to call the self and instead have found a multitude of unities, as poor Meno was able to find only a multitude of virtues when Socrates asked for merely the definition of virtue. Mead's position, however, actually is more intriguing than this rather contemporary vision of a multitude of selves might lead us to believe: (1) because he expands the notion of the generalized other in an interesting direction, and (2) because of the manner in which his notions of novelty and sociality account for transformations of the self. I will turn to the former point first.

There is a sense in which a society as a whole can be spoken of as having a generalized other; and, if so, it follows that one could have a self that corresponds to this generalized other. Where might we look for such a generalized other? A turn to the normative and the notion of a moral community will prove fruitful.

> There are what I have termed "generalized social attitudes" which make an organized self possible. In the community there are certain ways of acting under situations which are essentially identical, and these ways of acting on the part of anyone are those which we excite in others when we take certain steps. If we assert our rights, we are calling for a definite response just because they are rights that are universal—a response which everyone should, and perhaps will, give.[20]

The scope of what is referred to as a community can extend far beyond the subgroups that produce generalized others. A society, a culture, or even a global community can give rise to a generalized other that has as its source shared normative standards. This generalized other would allow individuals to transcend the so-called subgroups and have selves that are integrated on a "higher" level of abstraction, selves that depend on norms that permeate the whole of a society or a world community. Under these circumstances, similar responses to ethical issues pervade the entire society or global community. Mead tells us that,

> We all belong to small cliques, and we may remain simply inside of them. The "organized other" present in ourselves is then a community of a narrow diameter. We are struggling now to get a certain amount of international-mindedness. We are realizing ourselves as members of a larger community. The vivid nationalism of the present period should, in the end, call out an international attitude of the larger community.[21]

Although sharing a kinship with Freud's superego, the generalized other is inherently more rational and consciously accessible than the superego. It is not simply an external power that infiltrates our more primordial id, but, in a basic sense, it is us.[22] We are rational beings, after all.

> What we term "reason" arises when one of the organisms takes into its own response the attitude of the other organisms involved. It is possible for the organism so to assume the attitudes of the group that are involved in its own act within this whole co-operative process. When it does so, it is what we term "a rational being." If its conduct has such universality, it has also necessity, that is, the sort of necessity involved in the whole act—if one acts in one way the others must act in another way.[23]

Given this view of reason, and his claims concerning community and the generalized other, we can conclude that, for Mead, the scope and growth of the self is intimately connected with its capacity for the universality of the rational. The explicit linkage of the development of the self to the growth of a community highlights the importance of the political and normative in Mead's scheme. His views on these matters must be addressed if we are to fully understand his social psychology; Dmitri Shalin's and Hans Joas's contributions are of considerable assistance in this regard. I should also mention Guy E. Swanson's article here, for it addresses the importance of community in the development of certain capacities.

Having invoked Freud's name, I should at least note in passing Mead's position on the notion of instinct. Mead argues that human beings possess impulses, but he views impulses as having greater plasticity than instincts. "An impulse is a congenital tendency to react in a specific manner to a certain sort of stimulus, under certain organic conditions. Hunger and anger are illustrations of such impulses. They are best termed 'impulses' and not 'instincts,' because they are subject to extensive modification in the life-history of individuals."[24] Mead does not dismiss the impulsive from his analysis of human development and behavior. However, he does have a tendency to see impulses, and the conflict that they may engender when met by societal or parental demands, in terms of alternatives for growth. It can be argued that he does not sufficiently consider the range of psychological consequences that conflict may bring in its wake.[25]

There is a tension between the particular and the universal in Mead's concept of the generalized other, and this tension can be placed in the context of a more pervasive friction in his thought, one that can be spoken of in terms of the Enlightenment and Romanticism.[26] Mead is dedicated to the Enlightenment's notion that science, empirical science, and progress truly go hand and hand. In general, his political and social vision exhibits a profound kinship with Kant's enlightened cosmopolitanism. Yet, we also can see elements of the Romantic in Mead; he is deeply committed to honoring the particular and the unique, in an almost Herderesque fashion. This comes through in his awareness of the multiplicity of subgroups and generalized others and in his understanding of the limits history places on reason; it also comes through in his claims regarding novelty, which will be addressed later. We can see another feature of the Romantic sensibility, actually a quasi-Hegelian sensibility, in his concept of the self, a self that develops as it encompasses otherness and yet gives otherness its due. Nevertheless, as important as the particular and the unique are for Mead, he is dedicated to the goal of internationalism, which is linked directly to our capacity to take the roles of others. There is a deep commitment in Mead to the notion that our actions will become ever more rational as we have ever greater contact with the perspectives of others. Rationality, universality, and the experience of taking other perspectives all are intimately tied together for Mead, although universality must be understood in functional, not Platonic, terms.

Mead's appreciation for the unique can be seen in his metaphysics of the novel, which claims, for example, that time itself would have no direction if it were not for the upsurge of (novel) events.[27] Without the novel, the universe would be lost in the perpetual present of a closed system, in which elements of the system would merely exchange places in the eternal now of an eternal recurrence. Darwin put an end to any such fantasies for Mead. Even if we wish to bypass Mead's metaphysical speculations on emergence and time, we cannot bypass the novel, for we cannot understand Mead's concept of the self without it. In my view, Mead's famous "I" and "me" distinction should be viewed as an attempt to clarify the novel's place in human experience, although as J. David Lewis's article so aptly documents, there indeed has been much debate on this subject.

We have spoken of how the self comes into being as one views the constellation of our responses from the perspective of the (or a) generalized other. The self in this respect is a cognitive object; and this object can now be spoken of as the "me." What then is the "I"? The "I" is that which is both aware of the "me" and the "initiator" of responses; and its responses exhibit varying degrees of novelty. "The 'I' is the response of the organism to the attitudes of the others; the 'me' is the organized set of attitudes of others which one himself assumes. The attitudes of the others constitute the organized 'me,' and then one reacts toward that as an 'I.'"[28] In being the seat of awareness and activity, the "I" might be spoken of as the transcendental ego; the "me" would be its empirical counterpart, the objective ego. This said, it is important to emphasize that Mead wished to have the "I" and "me" interpreted "from the point of view of conduct itself."[29] He wanted them to be understood in functional, not metaphysical, terms. Mead was even willing to refer to an "I" as fictitious[30] and as a presupposition.[31] Gary Cook's article is of considerable value here, for it is one of the finest accounts of Mead's functionalism to date; and it specifically addresses to the "I" and "me" distinction from this perspective.

The "I" is never immediately found in experience. It acts, or reacts, and then one becomes aware of its actions. "If you ask, then, where directly in your own experience the 'I' comes in, the answer is that it comes in as a historical figure. It is what you were a second ago that is the 'I' of the 'me.' It is another 'me' that has to take that role. You cannot get the immediate response of the 'I' in the process."[32] For this reason we often are surprised by our own actions; that is, the 'I' reacts and we become aware of its actions only after they are transformed into the "me." That which becomes aware of the "me" is not the "me" itself, but a new "I" hidden from view, which now allows us to be aware of the previous "I's" responses, responses that have been transformed into the "me."

We can resort again to baseball for an example of what Mead has in mind. A player may anticipate how he or she will react when making an upcoming play, but then be surprised by what actually happens in the situation. The awareness of the play is not due to the "I" that acted, but to a new "I," one that is aware of the objectified action, an action now seen in terms of the "me." "The 'I' gives a sense of freedom, of initiative. The situation is there for us to act in a self-conscious fashion. We are aware of ourselves, and of what the situation is, but exactly how we will act never gets into experience until after the action takes place."[33] Mead does not deny that we can predict responses based on prior behavior, but he does claim that because of the element of novelty we can never be absolutely certain that we will respond in a specific fashion. It is not that the "I" always responds in absolutely novel ways—such a claim would destroy any possibility of understanding human behavior—but that it acts in ways that exhibit varying degrees of novelty.[34]

Although the "me" is presented as "the organized set of attitudes of others," it must serve the additional function of being the "site" at which we become aware of the "I's" novel responses as *my* own responses. In other words, the "me" has a personal and unique dimension because the "I's" novel responses modify the "me" as they become integrated into the prior organization of the "me," and it is this new organization that I become aware of as (the new) "me." With Mead's "I" and "me" distinction we have before us a self that contains a seat of novelty as well as a set of organized prior responses, a set of responses that comes not only from others but also results from one's own past novel reactions. I should note here that Mead's language of the self can lead to a good deal of confusion. At times Mead restricts the term self to the "me"; that is, the self is an *object.*[35] At other times, the term *self* includes both the "I" and "me" functions.[36] I will follow the latter course, using the term *object-self* exclusively for the "me."

How Mead integrates these two aspects of the self is a key question, which I will turn to later by employing Mead's concept of sociality to assist in articulating the relationship. First, I would like to address one of the more interesting anti-Cartesian implications of Mead's "I" and "me" distinction. One might criticize Mead's distinction by suggesting that it leaves out the fact that we seem to have an immediate awareness of the "I." Thus, I can be aware of both initiating and observing my actions, so that I have a sense of myself prior to reflection; that is, prior to the arrival of the "me." I have an immediate intuition of myself as a self-conscious subject who acts. Mead's model suggests that the belief in such a pre-reflective self-consciousness actually is due to a confused analysis of our own mental processes.

Mead argues that we can be conscious of the "I's" actions only on reflection; that is, after the transformation of its activity into an object-me. He does acknowledge, however, that we often feel as if there is a "running current of awareness of what we do which is distinguishable from the consciousness of the field of stimulation."[37] How is it that we often feel as if we are immediately aware of our own observer consciousness? What we call the *observer consciousness* is "not the actual 'I' who is responsible for the conduct in *propria persona*—he is rather the response which one makes to his own conduct."[38] I speak. In speaking, I respond to my own words, in that my words call out a response. Now this response may seem as if it were made by the "I" that originally spoke. In fact, what I am aware of is the response to my first words, a response that I can be aware of because it has been objectified, and as such is now the object of a new "I." "The action with reference to the others [or to oneself] calls out responses in the individual himself—there is then another 'me' criticising, approving, and suggesting, and consciously planning, i.e., the reflective self."[39]

I say to myself, "I hate to go to bed early," and I hear, seemingly at the same instant, the response: "But it's bad for you to stay up late." I naively take this response to be a product of the original "I" that spoke the words, "I hate to go to bed early," when actually these words are a commentary of the "me"; that is, of prior learned responses on the "I's" original words. The action, the speech, of the original "I" has been converted into an object, and is joined to a network of prior attitudes that serves as a commentary on it. The speech becomes part of a network of relations that provides a context for interpretation and action.

For Mead, I can be confused about my own mental processes; although my awareness of the "commentary" on my original words requires a new "I," I presume that there is only the original. I assume this because I am not aware that there has been a "reply" from the "me," and so instead believe that I am immediately aware of my own "I." The "comments" of the "me," which we become aware of *as if* they were taking place at the same time as the original action, actually are happening after the original action and require a new "I" to hear them. But they happen with such rapidity that they feel as if they are taking place at the same time as the original speech. I assume my "I" is transparent to itself in the immediacy of the present, when actually mediation is required for self-consciousness (or even consciousness of meaning) to arise. This clearly is a view that seeks to avoid the need for a transcendental ego. As a matter of fact, one way of approaching Mead's model of the "I" and "me" is to view it as providing a refined social interpretation of William James's stream of consciousness.

Mead does not believe that all of our actions entail a running commentary of this sort. In fact, he argues that we can be so involved in our activities in the world that no awareness of self occurs.[40] For Mead, prior to an awareness of self and prior to the mind, there is *the world that is there*; and, from this world of immediacy, all of our intellectual and conscious activities ultimately arise.

> This immediate experience which is reality, and which is the final test of the reality of scientific hypotheses as well as the test of the truth of all our ideas and suppositions, is the experience of what I have called the "biologic individual." ... I have termed it "biologic" because the term lays emphasis on the living reality which may be distinguished from reflection. ... [A]ctual experience did not take place in this form but in the form of unsophisticated reality.[41]

Mead views us as problem-solving creatures. Problems press us out of the immediacy of the *world that is there* into the realm of hypothetical behavior. Science, in this regard, is viewed by Mead as a methodical extension of the very typical human behavior of formulating alternative responses. Problems force us to reflect; and we can reflect on problems because we have learned how to become aware of our own responses, and alternatives to them, through the use of significant symbols. The ability to reflect on a problem—that is, to engage in one of the modes of thought known as reflection—owes much to the reflective ("mirroring") dimension of signficant symbols.[42] For Mead, our engagement with the world can be divided into reflective and nonreflective spheres; and the object-self appears only in the former. It is not clear that room can be found in Mead's thought for what several commentators—Sartre, for instance—have called *prereflective* (self-)*consciousness;* this (self-) consciousness would allow us to have a sense of self without invoking a Kantian or Husserlian transcendental ego, and yet would not bifurcate consciousness into nonreflective and reflective spheres, as Mead appears to do.[43]

There is an intimate connection between problem solving and the reflective character of significant symbols; and there also is an intimate connection between problem solving and novelty. Novel events can confront us with problems and novel responses can help supply solutions. It is worth noting in this context that novelty simply may be due to ignorance; that is, something appears new because we have been unaware of its existence or have not understood it. Mead, however, is convinced that there are truly novel events in the world and that our own responses are the locus of some of them.

> We distinguish that individual who is doing something from the "me" who puts the problem up to him. The response enters into his experience only when it takes place. If he says he knows what he is going to do, even there he may be mistaken. He starts out to do something and something happens to interfere. The resulting action is always a little different from anything which he could anticipate.[44]

Because of both unexpected happenings in the world at large and the "I's" own unexpected and novel responses, problems occur and solutions are found.

The uniqueness of the self can be addressed from two basic directions for Mead. We can speak of it in terms of every individual mirroring his or her social group from a slightly different angle. In this respect, each one of us is something of a Leibnizian monad mirroring not the universe, but a community, from our own specific vantage point.[45] However, Mead does not stop at this systemic notion of uniqueness, he goes on to claim that unique individuals arise because there are novel events in our world. If there were no such events, our universe would be a static Parmenidean one. "For a Parmenidean reality does not exist. Existence involves non-existence.... The world is a world of events."[46] Once again bypassing the metaphysical—in this case questions regarding the nature of events and their degrees of novelty—we can make the general claim that (novel) events transform individuals and also guarantee their uniqueness. However, before we rush off and treat Mead as something of a proto-existentialist with such remarks, we will have to investigate the manner in which the individual adjusts to novelty.

If the self is to contain a "pole" of novelty, how then are we to understand the self as a unity? One of the basic contributions of the generalized other to the existence of the object-self is that it allows us to grasp the object-self as a whole, as a unity of certain relations. With the introduction of the "I," we may wonder how the self can maintain itself as a unity in the face of the disruptive force of the novel, especially given that foundationalist claims regarding the ego would be unacceptable to Mead. At this juncture we must turn to Mead's views on sociality to see how he replaces the static notion of a unified self with that of a unifying self, a self that can transcend the discontinuity or upsurge of the novel.

Mead views his concept of sociality as a way of thinking about systems and the changes that they undergo. Suppose that we have an ecosystem before us; for example, a small pond. The pond exists in a state of homeostasis until the introduction of a new organism or a significant mutuation of one of the pond's organisms. If we assume that the new organism will be accommodated by the pond, we must also assume that there will be some modificaiton of the original ecosystem. The old system will have to give rise to a new system; but until it does, both the pond and the new organism exist in something of a state of limbo. Mead would refer to this stage in the transformation of the pond as one of sociality. He argues that such stages are a basic feature of reality, both of the human social world and of nature in general.

> When the new form has established its citizenship the botanist can exhibit the mutual adjustments that have taken place. The world has become a different world because of the advent, but to identify sociality with this result is to identify it with system merely. It is rather the stage betwixt and between the old system and the new that I am referring to. If emergence is a feature of reality this phase of adjustment, which comes between the ordered universe before the emergent has arisen and that after it has come to terms with the newcomer, must be a feature also of reality.[47]

Mead insists that not only are there genuinely novel events, but that these events can modify and become part of the fabric of the universe. In support of this claim he would look to the random mutation and the role that it plays in the process of natural selection. Given that there are systems in the limbo of transformation and that individual organisms often pass through such a stage, sociality must be a basic feature of our world. "The social character of the universe we find in the situation in which the novel event is in both the old order and the new which its advent heralds. Sociality is the capacity of being several things at once."[48] How then do these speculations regarding nature as a whole pertain to the unification of the self?

A return to some of Mead's claims regarding language acquisition should be of assistance. Let us assume for the present that we do not have to commit ourselves to Mead's metaphysical claims regarding novelty to explore how sociality and novelty play key roles in the development of the self. We learn to respond as the other has responded to vocal gestures, and this learning entails a good deal of anticipatory experience. I speak, I hear my own words, and I presume that the other will respond to them in the manner in which he or she has in the past. But the other does not always so respond; and this is a matter that is going to have to be taken into consideration by the individual. Each of us learns to accommodate this fact by learning to anticipate a multitude of responses from the other, and by learning to anticipate the unexpected, the new, the novel. (In this context the line between novelty due to ignorance and the "truly" novel can be ignored, for the impact of the novel on the development of the individual is crucial, and this can be addressed in pragmatic terms.) A novel response, which for Mead may be made by the other or by oneself, can be, and often is, integrated into the prior repertoire of signs. After the novel response is introduced, but before it is fully integrated, we can speak of a stage of sociality. Mead would have us conclude that states of sociality are basic to language acquisition. This, however, is but the beginning of sociality's impact on us; for the rest of the story we must turn to the process of integrating the novel in connection with roles and the self.

Roles and selves can be understood as systems of behaviors; although, of course, we must include here a very unique set of behaviors that transcends the merely behavioral; that is, language. My roles, and the capacity for seeing these roles as an integrated object-self, are dependent on my interactions with others. I must be able to "see" myself from the perspective of the other if I am to become cognizant of my own responses. To make the other's responses my own and to view myself from the perspective of the other, I depend on the other to respond in a *consistent* fashion to my gestures. The consistency of the other is crucial for both language and role acquisition.

One of the intriguing aspects of Mead's position raised by the issue of consistency is that it can be seen to turn on a notion of recognition, a notion that has a certain kinship with the idea of recognition so important in the Hegelian tradition.[49] To comprehend any specific response, I must be able to view it from the perspective of the other, and I must be confirmed in this view. The other provides verbal and nonverbal cues that allow me to know (or at least believe) that my responses are the proper ones, that what I think is the case, in fact is the case. If I have certain rudimentary language skills, I may be aware of my response, but I would not know if I accurately understand it until I can re-cognize it from the other's vantage point. We might regard the response of the other that makes this possible as an instance of recognition, or of proto-recognition, that is necessary for the acquisition of a language. We might then say that what is typically spoken of as recognition occurs when the other validates and confirms us in our roles. Eventually, we learn to turn from others who recognize specific roles to generalized others for confirmation of our actions and selfhood. My actions, and my self, then can be recognized by communities that transcend my immediate surroundings; for instance, the community of scientists or internationalists.[50]

The importance of recognition, seen in terms of the consistency of the other's responses, highlights the challenge we face when confronted by the novel reactions of others. I must evaluate and integrate these responses into my prior repertoire of responses. In addition, I myself may react in new ways, perhaps due to a problem that I have never before encountered. These responses must then be integrated into the object-self that I have presumed is "me." But before such an integration takes place, there will be a betwixt and between that can be described in terms of sociality. This betwixt and between increasingly will become a feature of my world as I encounter new people, as I actively search for solutions to problems, and as I become more aware of myself as a self.

> But the animal could never reach the goal of becoming an object to itself as a whole until it could enter into a larger system within which it could play various roles.... It is this development that a society whose life process is mediated by communication has made possible. It is here that mental life arises—with this continual passing from one system to another, with the occupation of both in passage and with the systematic structures that each involves. It is the realm of continual emergence.[51]

Our social interactions lead us to become increasingly aware of our sociality. In experiencing sociality we become sensitive to both the possibility and actuality of different perspectives, for sociality places us in the midst of alternative perspectives. We stand between the alternatives confronting us—perhaps, an old habit versus a new approach—and we can reflect on the alternatives. We redefine our selves in following new approaches or in modifying old ones.[52]

The "stream of consciousness" itself can be interpreted in terms of sociality, for the "I" reacts in new ways; and these new reactions may be integrated into the "me." The phase of integration is one of sociality. Here, then, is where we can locate how the introduction of novelty does not permanently disintegrate the self. The self is not a fixed unity but, to use the jargon of our times, an open system. It fluctuates between a state of unity, when the "I" is quiescent in terms of novel responses and merely allows us to view the object-self, and one of adjustment, when novel responses place the self in a state of sociality. This state either gives rise to a newly unified object-self or results in a return to the old one (barring, of course, pathological or developmental crises). The individual becomes self-creative as he or she learns to utilize the state of sociality to engage alternative courses of action. For Mead, it is unnecessary to posit a transcendental ego to account for the integration of old and new behaviors. The "me" is a system; as such it adapts to certain novel events and rejects others, in a manner analogous to the ecosystem, which supports certain new organisms but not others.

Needless to say, Mead is far from reproach. Mead's model of the self and his views on social interaction raise a considerable number of questions, one of the more obvious ones being whether Mead's functionalist social psychology, in spite of its attempts to sidestep the metaphysical, can handle the strain that Mead's metaphysics of the novel brings to bear. Following on the heels of this, we might question the status of freedom in Mead's model, as the "I" appears to respond in its novel ways from behind our backs, so to speak, and only after it responds do we really come to appreciate its actions as part of the object-self. Or, we could cast our net a bit wider and wonder how his model can deal with the sort of conflict between self and others that Freud presents us with on the micro level and that Marx and the neo-Marxists present us with in terms of class and structure. A bit further down the road, we might wonder whether Mead's perspectivalism and rationalism sans transcendence can deal with the fulminations of a Lacan or the ruminations of the deconstructionists (or even Nietzsche himself). Questions abound—with a good number to come in the pages ahead. Perhaps, Mead and his commentators will manage to supply almost as many answers.

Part 1
Context

G. H. Mead, Socialism, and the Progressive Agenda[1]

Dmitri N. Shalin

The image of Mead many sociology students form in the years of their apprenticeship is that of an armchair philosopher, dispassionately discoursing on the nature of mind, self, and society and largely removed from the practical concerns of the day. It is usually later that they learn that Mead was at the forefront of the contemporary movement for social reform and at some point seriously contemplated a career as professional reformer. The publications by Diner (1975, 1980), Deegan and Burger (1978), and, more recently, Joas (1985) alert us to this less known facet of Mead's life. The extent of Mead's involvement in the Progressive movement and, more important, the effect it had on his social theory, however, are still far from being fully appraised.

One reason Mead's political views and engagements have until recently escaped close scrutiny is that the relevant publications (some unmentioned in any standard bibliography) appeared mostly in limited-circulation magazines and local newspapers, while a portion of his political writings—notably on socialism and the human cost of industrialization—were never published and are available only in manuscript form.[2] The impression one draws from these writings, reinforced by Mead's private correspondence, is that of a man of radically democratic convictions, keenly aware of social inequality, and deeply concerned with the effect of the division of labor on the working man. Like many other progressives of his time, Mead was engaged in a lifelong polemic with socialists. He accepted without reservation their humanitarian ends but took issue with them on the question of means, fully embracing the basic progressivist tenet that the historically unique framework of American democracy provides the best available leverage for social reconstruction. Mead's life can be seen as an attempt to prove in both theory and practice that revolutionary objectives can be achieved by essentially conservative means.

This paper examines Mead's political beliefs and his theory of social reform. It also argues that Mead's substantive thought, and particularly the dialectical premises of social interactionism, reflected his ideological commitments. An auxiliary aim of this paper is to show that, even though progressive thinkers might have failed to answer the question of how to effect radical social change by working within the constitutional framework of democracy, they deserve credit for placing this question on the political agenda and stressing the public's role as an agent of social reconstruction.

I begin with the sociohistorical context of the Progressive movement. After tracing Mead's path to Progressivism, I analyze his theory of the reform process. Next, I explore the relationships between his political beliefs and substantive ideas. And finally, I discuss the contribution of Mead and the progressives to the theory and practice of American democracy.

THE SOCIOHISTORICAL CONTEXT OF PROGRESSIVISM

> We plow new fields, we open new mines, we found new cities; we drive back the Indian and exterminate the buffalo; we girdle the land with iron roads and lace the air with telegraph wires; we add knowledge to knowledge, and utilize invention after invention; we build schools and endow colleges; yet it becomes no easier for the masses of our people to make a living. On the contrary, it becomes harder. The wealthy class is becoming more wealthy; but the poor class is becoming more dependent. The gulf between the employed and the unemployed is growing wider; social contrasts are becoming sharper; as liveried carriages appear, so are barefooted children.

These words were written in 1879 by Henry George ([1879] 1926, pp. 390-91), the prophet of American reform, and are excerpted from his book *Progress and Poverty*. Serialized in the United States, translated into the major European languages, and selling some two million copies in the next two decades, this book left an indelible impression on the generation of progressive thinkers in America. In retrospect, the enthusiastic response the book elicited from clergy, businessmen, academics, professionals, and philanthropists seems all the more startling in view of the author's expressed commitment to socialism: "The ideal of socialism is grand and noble; and it is, I am convinced, possible of realization" (George 1926, p. 319). That was written at a time when the spirit of laissez-faire reigned supreme and the principle of "the survival of the fittest" enjoyed the status of unassailable truth. The book's phenomenal success is testimony to the sweeping change in popular mood that the country underwent within two decades and that marked the transition to the Age of Reform in American politics (Aaron 1951, p. 67; Hofstadter 1955; Goldmand 1956, p. 76; Resek 1967, p. xxi).

The best indicator of the new mood in the land was the change in mainstream Protestantism. Toward the end of the 19th century, the predominantly individualistic Evangelicalism of the pre-Civil War era noticeably yielded to socially conscious and reform-oriented forms of Christianity. Throughout the country, evangelical establishments, such as Mead's alma mater, Oberlin College, were spreading the word that shaping man in the image of God meant not only purifying his soul through the gospel of Jesus but also changing the environment that corrupted his spirit and bred social ills. Henry King's *Theology and the Social Consciousness* and John Common's *Social Reform and the Church* are just two examples of the voluminous literature of the 1890s that spurred municipal reforms, the survey of immigrants, and the formation of settlements, and that helped to shape the idea of Christian social work as a practical way of improving society (Smith 1957; Barnard 1969). The Christian socialism of this period was but a radical expression of the Social Gospel movement that challenged the Christian establishment in the last decade of the 19th century. Indeed, when the Rev. W. D. P. Bliss ([1890] 1970, pp. 352-53) demanded "the ownership, or at least, the control of, city railways; the immediate cessation of giving away or selling valuable street franchises to private monopolists" and insisted that "Christian socialists should teach by fact and not by sentiment; by fact about city gas works, not by mere talk about city brotherhood," he simply was following to the end the logic of new Evangelicalism.

The reformers of the Progressive Era owed much of their inspiration to the critical ferment stirred by the Social Gospel. Their arguments against old-school liberals, for whom government interference in the free-market economy was a crime against nature, bore a particularly strong resemblance to the rhetoric of Christian socialists. Along with the latter, the progressives cast aside still-potent social Darwinism and embraced George's argument that, unless ways were found to check the relentless drive toward monopoly and the growing polarization of wealth and poverty, America would soon find itself in the same sorry state as the injustice-ridden regimes of the Old World. The most important progressive reforms—the establishment of the Interstate Commerce Commission, the Conservation Act, the Federal Reserve Act, the food and drug law, the federal workmen's compensation program, the Adamson Act mandating an eight-hour working day on interstate railroads, the electoral reforms, including the initiative, the referendum, the direct election of U.S. senators, and women's suffrage—demonstrate the extent of the break with the old liberalism that occurred in the Progressive Era. To be sure, the reforms in question fell short of the social legislation adopted around the same time in Europe, notably in England (Orloff and Skocpol 1984), but they were precipitous enough to provoke the charges—from both the political Right and Left—that Progressivism is the first step toward socialism.

If the critics on the Right saw progressive reforms as a dangerous interference with natural market forces, for the critics on the Left these were but half measures. For the very success of progressive reform, socialists charged, furnished proof that state control does work, that equalizing opportunity is indeed the government's business. That is what the socialist critics of laissez-faire capitalism had been saying all along. The progressive reforms, according to them, were palliatives designed to stem the irreversible movement toward a social and industrial democracy, half-hearted attempts to refurbish the capitalist system that needed to be revamped on a fundamentally new—socialist—basis. The appeal of this argument was considerably enhanced by moderation within the socialist movement. Emboldened by their electoral successes and the growing interest from respectable middle-class audiences, socialists all over the world were eager to assure the public that they had "no intention of appealing to force," that the time had come "to free Socialism from the Marxian system," which in the long run turned out to be "more of a hindrance than a help" (Sombart [1909] 1968, pp. 225, 90). "I am opposed to any tactics which involve stealth, secrecy, intrigue, and necessitate acts of industrial violence for their execution," delcared Eugene Debs (1912, p. 483), the pragmatic leader of the Socialist party of America. No wonder that by 1912 he could claim the support of five daily papers, 250 weeklies, 50 mayors, and one congressman and was polling close to a million votes in the presidential election—not sufficient for the party to become a mainstream one but enough to make opponents worry (Pease 1962, p. 216; Fried 1970, pp. 377-90).

There is a long-standing debate about the causes of the failure of socialism in America. According to one school of thought, socialism never had a chance in this country because it is incompatible with the individualistic American creed. Others argue that socialism did strike roots in America and that its effect on the political scene here is vastly underestimated (for an overview of this debate, see Laslett and Lipset 1974). There is also a third opinion, expressed most cogently by Albert Fried: "Socialism was not an alien but an integral part of the American past. Here, in fact, lay the root of its 'failure,' of its inability to develop into an independent sturdy movement. In Europe, Socialism, with its radically egalitarian ethic, stood in militant opposition to, or at war with, established authority.... But the ideals of American Socialism were embodied, implicitly at least, in the creation of America itself" (1970, p. 2). Although this statement cannot be accepted without serious qualifications, it does contain a kernel of truth, and it certainly helps us understand the progressive thinkers' well-known ambivalence toward socialism (Goldman 1956), p. vii; McNaught 1974, p. 415). Indeed, Woodrow Wilson was not simply using scare tactics when he reminded his audience during this first presidential campaign, "I need not tell you how many men were flocking over to the standard of the Socialists, saying neither party any longer bears aloft an ancient torch of liberty"([1912] 1962, p. 375). Nor did Theodore Roosevelt exaggerate much when he said, "I am well aware that every upholder of privilege, every hired agent or beneficiary of the special interests, including many well-meaning parlor reformers, will denounce this [Progressive platform] as 'Socialism'" ([1912] 1962, p. 318).

Herbert Croly, the first editor of *The New Republic* and a staunch supporter of the Bull Moose party, was even bolder in his recognition of the affinity between the socialist and progressivist programs: "The majority of good Americans will doubtless consider that the reconstructive policy, already indicated, is flagrantly socialistic both in its method and its objects; and if any critic likes to fasten the stigma of socialism upon the foregoing conception of democracy, I am not concerned with dodging the odium of the term" (1909, p. 209). One can also detect the unmistakable imprint of socialist ideas in Jane Addams's resolute denunciation of "the overaccumulation at one end of society and the destitution at the other" and in her keen awareness of the paradox of a "large and highly developed factory [that] presents a sharp contrast between its socialized form and its individualistic aim" (1910, p. 126; 1902,

p. 139). Socialism was very much on the minds of the progressives. The latter often sounded defensive in front of their socialists opponents (e.g., Roosevelt 1909), but they also shared with them humanitarian objectives. Progressive reforms reflected their desire to socialize American democracy, their "passion for the equalization of human joys and opportunities" (Addams 1910, p. 184). Much as they wished for the socialism of opportunity, however, progressives were leery of the socialism of property, endorsing it chiefly in such areas as municipal services and public transportation. The massive nationalization advocated by orthodox socialists, according to progressives, was a false solution, for it would only dampen the entrepreneurial spirit so essential to American life, undermine its basic freedoms, and eventually stifle the opportunity it aimed to promote. The solution to the problem was reform not revolution, a program of reconstruction that would build on the strengths of the American democratic tradition yet would not hesitate to dispense with the old institutions that stood in the way of socializing opportunity.

To sum up, the progressive agenda was shaped in the course of the polemics with the proponents of unrestrained capitalism and with the adherents of social teaching. It also reflected the considerable influence of social Christianity. Progressivism represented an attempt to come to grips with "some of the more glaring failures of capitalism" (White 1957, p. 46). It was "plainly influenced by socialism" (Goldman 1956, p. vii), which served the progressives as both a negative and positive frame of reference. In substance, Progressivism represented "a dual agenda of economic remedies designed to minimize the dangers from the extreme left and right" (Hofstadter 1955, p. 236). This dual agenda called for a new outlook, a philosophy of a different kind. It was to be both conservative and radical, pragmatic and principled, faithful to the nation's democratic heritage yet critical of its political and economic practices. This dual agenda of American Progressivism found expression in the life and work of George Herbert Mead.

THE MAKING OF A REFORMER: MEAD'S PATH FROM EVANGELICALISM TO PROGRESSIVISM

Few American reformers on the path to Progressivism escaped the influence of liberal Christian theology, and Mead in this respect was no exception. His father, Hiram Mead, a minister in the Congregational church and a prominent educator, taught homiletics at Oberlin Theological Seminary. Mead's mother, Elizabeth Storrs Billings, was a strong-willed, dignified, very religious woman; for a number of years, she served as president of Mount Holyoke College and later taught at Oberlin College. With a background like this it was logical to expect that Mead—a rather shy, serious, well-behaved boy—would take up the ministry. Oberlin College, where Mead matriculated in 1879, was a perfect place to start such a career. Founded by clergy and renowned for its piety and abolitionist sentiments, Oberlin was a stronghold of the spirit of old New England Puritanism, which for decades filled its students with "a zeal for bettering the life of mankind as the highest expression of religious duty" (Barnard 1969, p. 126). Yet just around the time when Mead was ready to enter college, the winds of change began to blow through American institutions of higher learning. Darwin's theory of evolution, reinforced by German historical criticism of the Bible, was winning numerous converts among the public, making a revision of Christian dogma a necessity. The Social Gospel movement burst onto the scene, propelled by its proponents' ardent belief in the power of Christian social work to cure society's ills. About this time, various reform schemes started attracting followers among students and faculty in colleges and universities all over the country. Oberlin College was at the center of the new currents of theological, political, and social thought. In the 1880s and 1890s, it was the site of several conferences in which the Rev. Washington Gladden, Walter Rauschenbusch, Lyman Abbot, Richard T. Ely, Carroll D. Wright, and scores of other liberal theologians and reformers debated topics ranging from Darwinism and Scripture, to intemperance and crime, to immigration and poverty. In later years, an array of progressive and socialist thinkers were invited to speak directly to student audiences, including such luminaries as Robert M. La Follette, Jane Addams, Lincoln Steffens, Jack London, and John Spargo. Among the people most talked about at Oberlin during this period was Henry George. In 1887, he visited the campus and spoke on the issues of reform to an enthusiastic audience of faculty and students (Barnard 1969, p. 62).

Mead's early correspondence amply documents the depth of his religious feelings, the earnest commitment to spreading the word of God inculcated in him during the college years. "I believe Christianity is the only power capable of grappling with evil as it exists now," wrote Mead to his college friend Henry Castle (MP April 23 and March 16, 1884, b1, f1);[3] "There can be no doubt of the efficacy of Christ as a remedial agent and so I can speak of him as such.... The moral realities of the world are powerful enough to stimulate me and Christianity lays the strongest hold upon me." There were also some indications that Mead was affected by the

critical currents of the day. These indications are not to be found in
the four signed articles that Mead (1881, 1882a, 1882b, 1882c)
published in the *Oberlin Review* and that deal with conventional
literary and philosophical subjects, but rather in the unsigned
editorials that he and his coeditor, Henry Castle, wrote during their
last year in college and that point to the influence of liberal theology
on Mead's thinking.[4] Noting with satisfaction that "the religious
craze against evolutionary theories is dying out," the editors urged a
rapprochement between church dogma and the theory of evolution
(Editorial 1882). A long editorial (1883) drew attention to the growing number of students passing up the ministry as a vocation because of their doubts about the veracity of church doctrine and
insisted that "this doubt is, as an almost universal rule, honest
doubt." At Oberlin, Mead also acquired his political allegiance. As
his letter to the editor of *The Nation* (Mead 1884) suggests, his
political views in the college years followed middle-class Republican-
ism, which was then prevalent at Oberlin and which Mead was
ready to defend against the attacks of its critics. Despite his later
ambivalence about Roosevelt and admiration for Wilson, Mead
would remain loyal to the Republican party throughout his life.

After college, Mead confronted a difficult career choice. Two
possibilities appealed to him—Christian social work and teaching
philosophy. What he liked most about the former was the chance to
work for people and somehow to make the world a better place. The
latter career attracted Mead because of the secure academic environment and an opportunity to continue his philosophical speculations,
which he had grown increasingly fond of in his last year of college.
There were problems with both lines of work. A career in Christianity required belief in God, which over the years Mead found difficult
to sustain. To follow this path, wrote Mead in a letter to Henry
Castle (MP March 16, 1884, b1, f1), "I shall have to let persons
understand that I have some belief in Christianity and my praying
be interpreted as a belief in God, whereas I have no doubt that now
the most reasonable system of the universe can be formed to myself
without a God. But notwithstanding all this I cannot go out with
the world and not work for men. The spirit of a minister is strong
with me and I come fairly by it." The alternative career had problems of its own. "There is a great deal of good work that needs to be
done in popularizing metaphysics among common people," wrote
Mead in the same letter, but this option did not appear to satisfy his
passion for commitment: "I want to give myself to that which I can
give my whole self to...." For several years, Mead remained trou-
bled by this choice. Again and again, he would weigh the

arguments, assess his chances, extol the virtues of the Christian faith, and then confess his inability to follow suit. "I need the strength of religion in my work," confided Mead to his friend (MP February 23, 1884, b1, f1); "Nothing could meet the wants of mankind as Christianity, and why not have a little deception if need be?....And yet as I look at it now, there is hardly any position I would not rather occupy than that of a dogmatic theologian. I would rather be a school teacher than a Joseph Cook dabbling in metaphysics."

No one knows how long this torturous quest would have continued had it not been for Henry Castle,[5] who finally convinced Mead to join him in Cambridge, Massachusetts, where he had settled earlier to study law. Once his mind was made up, Mead threw himself into the study of philosophy. Of all possible specializations available to him when he enrolled in the Department of Philosophy at Harvard, he selected the one most peripheral to the discipline's traditional concerns—physiological psychology. The reason for this choice, according to Castle ([1889] 1902, p. 579), was Mead's belief that he had found "a harmless territory in which he [could] work quietly without drawing down upon himself the anathema and excommunication of all-potent Evangelicism." The spirit of a minister, however, was too strong in Mead, and it was not long before the need to serve people reasserted itself in him.

In the fall of 1888, after successfully completing a year at Harvard, Mead won a scholarship and went to Germany, ostensibly to continue his studies toward a doctoral degree. Yet his mind would soon turn to politics, stimulated by the burgeoning reform movement in Germany. The extent of government involvement in the issues of social security, the popularity of the Social Democratic party, and particularly the respect socialism commanded in academic circles deeply impressed Mead, who found the situation in Germany to be in sharp contrast to the one back home, where the idea of state involvement in labor-management relations was still suspect and the term "socialism" had a somewhat odious connotation. A few months after settling in Germany, Mead experienced something akin to conversion. His letters of this period are brimming with enthusiam for social reforms and the prospect of transplanting them to the States. He talks about "opening toward everything that is uplifting and satisfying in socialism" (MP August 1890, b1, f3), urges Henry "to get a hold upon the socialistic literature—and the position of socialism here in Europe" (MP October 21, 1890, b1, f3), and deplores in the most sweeping terms American politics: "American political life is horribly idealess....

Our government in ideas and methods belongs so to the past.... We had never had a national legislature in which corrupt motives in the most pecuniary form could be more shamelessly used than in the present" (MP October 21 and 19, 1890, b1, f3).[6]

Somewhere along the way doubts about his career choice came to haunt Mead again. Invoking his abiding need for commitment, he declared a readiness to go into politics, at least on a trial basis: "Life looks like such an insignificant affair that two or three or more years of utterly unsuccessful work would not seem to me in the slightest dampening, and the subjective satisfaction of actually doing what my nature asked for of infinitely more importance than anything else.... I mean that I am willing to go into a reform movement which to my eyes may be a failure after all; simply for the sake of the work" (MP October 19, 1890, b1, f3). Soon a plan was formed in Mead's head, in which he envisioned himself and his friend, Henry Castle, after a thorough study of the German scene, coming back to the States, securing control of a newspaper, and lauching a crusade for social reform:

> The immediate necessity is that we should have a clear conception of what forms socialism is taking in [the] life of European lands, especially of the organisms of municipal life—how cities sweep their streets, manage their gas works and street cars, their *Turnvereins,* their homes of prostitution, their poor, their minor criminals, their police, etc., etc., that one may come with ideas to the American work. Now Henry you must come and at least get such a share in these subjects and hold of the social political literature that you can go right on when we are back. I must teach at first for I must earn money, but I shan't keep it long. I want more active life....My vague plan now is that I go to the university of Minnesota as a teacher—and you to Minneapolis as lawyer and that we finally get control of the Minneapolis Tribune. This is of course hazy but Minneapolis has very large attractions for this work—it is young, not sunk into the meshes of any traditional machine, and yet beyond the boom period. But this is entirely superfluous castle building but to go to some city we must and to go to work and fail if need be, but work in any case and work satisfactorily. [MP August 1890, b1, f3]

What is particularly impressive in Mead's thinking of those years is his clear understanding that the city is bound to play a special role in future reforms. City Hall, insisted Mead in a manner reminiscent of Christian socialists, is the true locus of the reform movement, and city politics is the place were the reconstruction of America should start:

> We must get into politics of course—city politics above all things, because there we can begin to work at once in whatever city we settle, because city politics need men more than any other branch, and chiefly because, according to my opinion, the immediate application of principles of corporate life—of socialism in America must start from the city.... If we can purify there, we can throughout, if we could not there, we could not anywhere. If we can give American institutions the new blood of the social ideal, it can come in only at this unit of our political life and from this starting point it will naturally spread. [MP October 21 and 19, 1890, b1, f3]

Unlike Mead, Castle was a man of more practical bent. He shared many of Mead's ideals and was strongly affected by the reform currents in Germany, where he traveled extensively,[7] yet he thought Mead's plans of going into politics and reforming America via city hall somewhat utopian and did not hesitate to impress this on Mead. Without Castle's financial backing and his editorial skills, Mead had to put his plans on the back burner. Meanwhile, his life took a decidedly new turn. In 1891, Mead was appointed an instructor at the University of Michigan, where he met his future colleague and friend, John Dewey. An academic of no small renown even in those days, Dewey shared Mead's passion for social democracy and philosophical disquisition. As early as 1888, Dewey ([1888] 1969, p. 246) speculated about the "tendency of democracy toward socialism, if not communism" and claimed that "there is no need to beat about the bush in saying that democracy is not in reality what it is in name until it is industrial, as well as civil and political ... a democracy of wealth is a necessity." The two pursuits that Mead was trying to reconcile were united in the life of this remarkable man. Indeed, Dewey was the foremost example of an American academic successfully combining research and political engagement, and, as such, he was bound to become a role model for Mead.

Not much is known about Mead's stay at Ann Arbor. He still seems to have harbored some hopes for direct political engagement, as indicated, for instance, by his enthusiastic response to the idea of a socialist weekly, which Dewey, Mead, and Park were contemplating for a while (MP February 28, 1892, b1, f3; see also Raushenbush 1979, pp. 18-21; Joas 1985, p. 21). What is clear is that Dewey and Mead formed a friendship that each of them would later claim was his most precious possession. When Dewey was offered the chairmanship at the University of Chicago, he made his acceptance contingent on the appointment of Mead (who never completed his doctoral thesis) as an assistant professor in his department. It was at the University of Chicago that Mead's career as a reformer began to flourish. In the years following his move to Chicago, Mead joined the City Club, an organization of reform-minded professionals and businessmen, of which he became president in 1918. Mead worked in close association with such people as Graham Taylor and Jane Addams, and for more than a decade he served as treasurer of the University of Chicago settlement.[8] Along with Dewey, Mead was keenly interested in reform of the Chicago school system and at some point headed the Chicago Educational Association and the Vocational Guidance League. He was vice-president of the Immigrants Protective League of Chicago. On several occasions, he served as a member of the strike settlement committees. By 1910, Mead was generally recognized as one of the leaders of the Progressive movement in the city of Chicago.

The first expressly political publication of Mead—a review of Le Bon's *Psychology of Socialism* and an article "The Working Hypothesis in Social Reform"—testify to Mead's continued preoccupation with socialism. In his words, "Socialism, in one form or another, lies back of the thought directing and inspiring reform" (Mead 1899*a*, p. 367). But one can also detect a new critical note in Mead's treatment of socialism, or rather a "doctrinaire" and "utopian" version of it, to which Mead juxtaposes the "pragmatic" and "opportunist" approach of progressive reformers. Indicative in this respect is Mead's review of Le Bon's book. He agrees with the author that socialist teaching has a tendency to become dogmatic insofar as it lays claim to a priori validity. He also renounces all versions of socialism that sanction violent means, and he expresses skepticism about Marx's economic analysis, which he finds at odds with modern economic and political realities. Nevertheless, he resolutely parts company with Le Bon and other critics of socialism who confuse its doctrinaire form with its humanistic content. The programmatic and apocalyptic aspects of socialist teaching may be obsolete, Mead argues, but its quest for justice is not; this quest is now taken over by social democrats who have denounced revolutionary violence and turned into reformers:

> The socialists are becoming opportunists. They are losing confidence in any delineation of the future conditions of society—any "vision given on the mount." ... Socialistic thinking may be different in France and England, but it is the same

great force and cannot be studied in the camp of the pro-grammist alone. It is coming to represent, not a theory, but standpoint and attitude.... We have, in general, given up being programmists and become opportunists. We do not build any more Utopias, but we do control our immediate conduct by the assurance that we have the proper point of attack, and that we are losing nothing in the process. We are getting a stronger grip on the method of social reform every year, and are becoming proportionately careless about our ability to predict the detailed result. [Mead 1899*b*, pp. 405-6, 409]

Mead's political beliefs at this point, and specifically his emphasis on pragmatism and opportunism, are reminiscent of Eduard Bernstein's brand of social democracy, with its motto, "The movement is everything, the goal is nothing." That is to say, Mead is cognizant of socialism's historical import and sympathetic to its humanitarian objectives: "Socialism presented at least for some decades the goal that society must comtemplate, whether it will or not [be] a democratic society in which the means of social expres-sions and satisfactions are placed at the disposal of the members of the whole community" (MP b2 addenda, f27). Nonetheless, Mead grows increasingly skeptical about socialist means. He continues to stress socialism's historical importance but mostly in the past tense, viewing it as a movement that shook the world from its dogmatic slumber but that had now outlived its usefulness, at least in the United States. By the early 1900s, Mead fully identified himself with the Progressive creed, to which he remained faithful the rest of his life.[9]

It would not be appropriate to speak about Mead's movement away from socialism, for there is not enough evidence to assert that he ever was a card-carrying Socialist to begin with. The question that one may pose is, Why did Mead not embrace more openly socialist premises? Part of the answer to this query, I believe, can be gleaned from the status of politically engaged scholarship in this period. The marriage of scholarship and advocacy in American academia at the time was far from peaceful and harmonious (Furner 1975). The professor's right to speak on controversial issues was acknowledged, albeit within clear limits. An outright endorsement of socialism was pretty much out of the question.[10] Instructors willing to take a political stance had to make sure that their views bore the imprimatur of science and dovetailed with the American democratic creed. Bemis, Ross, and some other instruc-tors who lost their jobs in the late 19th century because of their political engagements did, in one way or another, overstep the boundaries of what most in academia then thought were the standards of objectivity and disinterestedness. Others, such as Richard T. Ely, Charles Zueblin, and Thorstein Veblen, had to go through endless explanations and humiliating denials concerning their alleged prosocialist sentiments.[11] Still, quite a few academics with various degrees of commitment to the ideals of social democracy, such as Seligman, Commons, Bird, and Dewey, found a formula that seemingly reconciled scholarship and advocacy. The common denominator that united these otherwise disparate characters was an unswerving commitment to reform, combined with a vigorous renunciation of violence as the means of social reconstruction. That, of course, was the basic creed of Progressivism, which had just started coming into its own. It is this rising current in American politics that provided legitimation for the incipient fusion of scholarship and advocacy and that helped to secure a niche for all those who sought to partake in the reform of American society without jeopardizing their academic positions. Mead's political views, or at any rate his public stance, showed that he understood the limits of the possible for an academic in the Progressive Era.

Still, we need to bear in mind that Mead's high regard for socialism remained unchanged throughout his life. He greeted with enthusiasm the democratic February Revolution in Russia (Mead 1917d), and he supported the program of the British Labour party (Mead 1918). "What has been said [about socialism]," wrote Mead in a characteristic passage, "has been said with a profound realization of the past and future import of its economic gospel, even if it has been a gospel only according to Marx" (MP b3 addenda, f7). Mead's highest praise, however, was reserved not for socialists but for people like Jane Addams and R. F. Hoxie, radical democrats thoroughly committed to the struggle for the rights of the underprivileged (Mead 1907; 1916-17). What attracted Mead to these people was that, without wrapping themselves in the revolutionary flag, they were searching for ways of realizing the revolutionary ideals that inspired socialist critics of society. This quest for peaceful revolution provides a key to Mead's own theory of the reform process.

To sum up, Mead's intellectual and political growth was marked from the beginning by the tension between his evangelical desire to serve people and his predilection for an academic career. This tension was resolved when the emerging movement for social reform legitimized the fusion of scholarship and advocacy in the academic setting. Along with some other social scientists of his day, Mead was influenced by socialism, or rather a social democratic version of it that renounced all forms of revolutionary violence and endorsed strictly democratic and political means of effecting social change. After establishing himself in academia, Mead embraced the Progressivist creed, yet even then he did not cease to see the historical importance of socialism or to acknowledge his debt to it. By the end of the 19th century, Mead emerged as a "radically democratic intellectual" (Joas 1985, p. 10), a reformer deeply involved in progressive causes, and a budding academic searching for a theoretical rationale for a far-reaching yet peaceful reconstruction of American society.

INSTITUTIONALIZING REVOLUTION: MEAD'S THEORY OF THE REFORM PROCESS

Progressive reformers differed among themselves on the etiology of current problems, the ultimate objectives of reform, and the best strategies for social reconstruction, but they all agreed that the gap between democratic ideals and American reality had grown intolerably wide. The founding fathers envisioned the United States as a community of civil-minded and well-informed citizens consciously shaping their destiny under the protection of constitutionally guaranteed freedoms. The reality, with its predominance of poorly educated workers and illiterate immigrants, made a mockery of this Jeffersonian ideal of popular democracy. Like all progressives, Mead was very much aware of "the chasm that separates the theory and practice of our democracy," yet he went farther than most in delineating "the tragedy of industrial society" with its "routine and drudgery of countless uninterested hands" and "the blind production of goods, cut off from all the interpretation and inspiration of their common enjoyment" ([1923] 1964, p. 263; [1925-26] 1964, pp. 295-96). The plight of workers caught in the meshes of the modern factory system attracted his special attention.

The Industrial Revolution, according to Mead, makes the worker's participation in the democratic process problematic, because it minimizes his educational needs, cheapens his labor, and dehumanizes his life. The modern worker is in some sense worse than his medieval counterpart, whose skills, slowly acquired and hard to replace,

> made of him an admirable member of the older community.... It is the machine that has taken possession of the trades, has displaced the artisan, and has substituted for the artisan, who makes an entire article, a group of laborers who tend the

machine. The effect of this upon the training of the laborers
has been most deplorable. The more the machine accomplishes
the less the workman is called upon to use his brain, the less
skill he is called upon to acquire.... The man who tends one of
these machiens becomes a part of the machine, and when the
machine is thrown away the man is thrown away, for he has
fitted himself into the machine until he has become nothing
but a cog. [1908-9a, pp. 370-71; 1908, p. 20]

The machine is a product of the social forces over which no individual has control, yet its devastating effects have been multiplied
by the callous attitude of its owners:

Thus the machine is a social product for which no individual
can claim complete responsibility. Its economic efficiency is as
dependent on the presence of the laborer and the market for its
products as mechanical structure is dependent upon the inven-
tor, and its exploitation upon the capitalist. But the group morality under which the community suffers, recognizes no respon-
sibilty of the exploiter to the laborer, but leaves him free to
exhaust and even maim the operator, as if the community
had placed a sword in his hand with which to subjugate.
[1907, p. 127]

The situation is further exacerbated by the current education
system, which perpetuates the division between the two kinds of
skills—one for laborers and the other for higher orders of society. An
investment into the future worker's education beyond what is
necessary to fulfill his role as a laborer is considered a luxury, and so
he rarely moves beyond elementary school and is often compelled to
start work even earlier. The wealth of cultural goods that belongs
to everyone in the community remains closed to him: "Cultured
classes in some sense have an access to this wealth, which is denied
to masses in the community.... We are encouraging a class distinction which must be destructive of American democracy if it per-
sists..." ([1930] 1964, p. 403; 1908-9b, p. 157). Bad as the position
of the American-born worker is, it is worse for the immigrant. He is
brought to the United States as a source of cheap labor and, lacking
English and education, becomes easy prey for employers. The latter,
Mead concluded from his many encounters with Chicago businessmen,

had absolutely no feeling of responsibility to the immigrant, or
the sense of debt which Chicago owes to the immigrant.... He

[the immigrant] comes ignorant and helpless before the system of exploitation which enwraps him before he leaves the old country and may last for two generations after he enters our gates. Our government has nothing to offer him by way of protection but the doctrine of the abstract human rights of man, a vote he cannot intelligently exercise, and the police to hold him in his place. [1909, pp. 222-23; 1907, p. 123]

Whatever American democracy has to offer the well-to-do, Mead concludes, falls far short of its promise when it comes to the millions of working-class people effectively excluded from meaningful participation in the life of the community. If modern America is to fulfill the democratic aspirations of its founding fathers, it has to "eliminate the evils to which economic inferiority exposes great masses of man," it has to provide equal access to cultural goods for all members of the community, and it must imbue the laborer's work with meaning: "In the bill of rights which a modern man may draw up and present to the society which has produced and controls him, should appear the right to work both with intelligent comprehension of what he does, and with interest. For the latter one must see the product as a whole..." (1908-9a, pp. 381, 378).

Many of the above themes, as one can readily see, run parallel to the familiar socialist critique of capitalist society. The likeness is particularly striking if we think about the young Marx's philippics against the effects of the division of labor on the working man. Indeed, both Marx and Mead deplored the dehumanizing consequences of the factory system, both sought to restore the producer's sense of the product as a whole, and both resisted a wholesale renunciation of modernity and invested much hope in the future of science and technology. Beyond these parallels, however, one finds differences that set Marx's socialism sharply apart from Mead's progressivism. For Marx, the real culprit is capitalism, with its private ownership of the means of production, inherently unstable economy, and that perennial scourge—alienated labor. Capitalism must be abolished, if necessary by revolutionary force, and, if the dictatorship of the proletariat means curtailing individual freedoms, that is no great loss, since the civil liberties guaranteed by bourgeois society are a sham anyhow. When the considerations of justice and equality collide with those of freedom and democracy, the former are to be given higher priority in Marx's system. Not so in Mead's book. Democracy gets the top billing there. To be sure, justice is important for Mead, as it is for any progressive—it is a vital condition of genuine democracy—yet, if pursued for its own sake, radical equality is bound to impinge on civil liberties and undermine democratic institutions. Justice must be pursued as far, and only as far, as necessary for securing for every member of society an opportunity to participate in the democratic process. This last point needs further elaboration.

Underlying the Progressive movement was the realization that economically unregulated and socially unconstrained democracy flourishing under laissez-faire capitalism creates an underclass that is, de jure, free yet, de facto, excluded from meaningful participation in the democratic process. The United States, a country that prided itself on its commitment to democracy, was willing to tolerate utterly degrading human conditions, including the most shameful exploitation of woman and child labor. In the name of freedom of contract, freedom of trade, and so on, employers were able to impose on workers the terms of contract they wished to, even when this meant paying starvation wages. Clearly, progressives concluded, civil rights alone could not guarantee personal dignity and ensure the realization of human potential to which every member of society is entitled. A measure of economic well-being and educational opportunity is imperative for a democratic society. This is what Mead had in mind when he declared that "abstract human rights" offer little protection to immigrant workers, and what Dewey meant when he said that "actual and concrete liberty of opportunity and action is dependent upon equalization of the political and economic conditions under which individuals are alone free *in fact,* not *in some metaphysical way*" (1946, p. 116). This progressive stance had far-reaching implications. It implied that "poverty is a result of a faulty organization of society, and the organization of society can be changed" (MP b2 addenda, f26). It led to the conclusion that "community has a right to exert control over corporation" (MP b7, f8). And, by bringing to light "singular evils which have resulted from corporate property" (MP b7, f8), it hastened the end of laissez-faire capitalism in the United States.

As one could imagine, this attack on 19th-century capitalism met stiff resistance from die-hard defenders of the old ways, who decried the progressive program as an unconstitutional abridgment of democratic liberties. Yet most progressives stood firm and did not waver in their conviction that society's interference in the market process is both justifiable and necessary, that is, insofar as this interference makes democracy more equitable and to the extent that it leaves the core of civil liberties intact. The last point is particularly important, for it underscores the fact that progressives had more faith in bourgeois democracy than Marxists did. They thought that civil liberties, constitutionally guaranteed and when necessary expanded, could provide a firm foundation for social reconstruction. Radical and revolutionary as this reconstruction might be, it had to be carried out by constitutional means, and its success had to be judged by the degree to which democratic values were preserved.

There is a phrase that crops up in Mead's writings—institutionalizing of revolution. Says Mead: "Revolutions might be carried out by methods which would be strictly constitutional and legal"; "Government by the will of the people means that orderly revolution is a part of the institution of government itself"; "When you set up a constitution and one of the articles in it is that the constitution may be changed, then you have, in a certain sense, incorporated the very process of revolution into the order of society" ([1915] 1964, pp. 150-51; MP b3 addenda, f29; 1936, p. 361). These statements, so emblematic of Mead's political thought, illuminate the widely held progressivist belief that radical change can be accomplished, without recourse to violence, by legitimate constitutional means. Revolution is not in itself a bad thing, according to Mead; it is "a summary reconstruction" that takes place when "a whole population is able to assume, for a time, the larger or more universal attitude" (MP Mead to Irene Tufts Mead, September 16, 1916, b1a, f13). As such, it represents a constructive force that must be harnessed by progressive legislation and directed by enlightened public opinion. This peaceful democratic revolution naturally presupposes that the democratic machinery is already in place, as, for instance, in the United States. The democratic alternative is very much in doubt where bourgeois democracy has not yet been established, which, Mead pointed out, was the case in most of Europe at the time. The appeal of socialism is strongest precisely in those countries where the struggle for bourgeois democracy is still going on: "Socialism abroad has been the outcome of popular struggle against governments which have been in the hands of privileged classes. . . . It has been democracy's fighting formation when opposed to a modern feudalism" (Mead 1917d). Once democratic institutions are secured, socialism has done its job and must merge with other reform currents.

And what about capitalism? It certainly must be transformed but not necessarily into socialism. The future social order will be a radically democratic society that encourages personal initiative, equalizes opportunity in every sphere of life, and makes social reconstruction an ongoing concern. If capitalism is a thesis, then socialism is more in the nature of an antithesis—not a synthesis, as socialists would have it. If such a synthesis is possible at all, it is likely to be provided by progressivism. Here is how Mead laid out this idea in his course on the logic of the social sciences that he gave at the apex of the Progressive Era in the academic year 1911-12, as jotted down by one of his students:

> Take case of Socialism vs. Individualism. Individualism owns capital, and Socialism asks that community shall own property—here [is] a clash. Solution involves say this form: individual initiative, individual control must be preserved and on the other hand public control must be preserved to protect the individual. How [can we] deal practically with this? Any number of schemes now appearing—interstate commerce, control of wages, control of conditions of labor, pensions, old age, out of work, sickness [benefits]. These statements are present solutions so that the clash is done away with. [MP b8, f8]

It would be a mistake to infer from this that Mead conceived the institutionalizing of revolution as a legalistic affiar, some sort of neverending legislative process supervised by politicians and professional reformers. The legislative measures introduced by the progressive administrations were unquestionably valuable, and Mead was very enthusiastic about them (particularly about the platform of the Wilson administration),[12] yet these legislative initiatives, he thought, were not in themselves sufficient to bring about a radical democracy, nor did they go to the heart of the reform movement. The ongoing reconstruction, as Mead envisioned it, was a multifaceted process designed to further the common interests of all groups and individual members of society and required the mobilization of public opinion, persistent attention of the press, cooperation of labor and business organizations, reorganization of the school, and direct participation of members of the scientific community.

It was an article of faith with Mead, and a starting point in his theory of the reform process, that underneath the conflicting interests of groups, classes, and nations lies a public good, waiting to be discovered and realized. "The real assumption of democracy inside the society of a nation and within the society of different nations," wrote Mead in an article from his little-known series of essays on democracy and war, "is that there is always to be discovered a common social interest in which can be found a solution of social strifes.... Democratic advance, therefore, has always been in the direction of breaking down the social barriers and vested interests which have kept men from finding the common denominators of conflicting interests" (1917d; see also 1917a, 1917b, 1917c, 1917e). Mead did not specify what the public good is or how it is to be determined. Nor was he ready to identify it with majority vote.[13]

Yet he was convinced that some notion of public good must be a guiding force in the reform movement, and he vested the responsibility for its articulation in the general public. No government, elected body of representatives, or group of professional reformers in a democratic society could successfully complete its task without ordinary citizens, organized into voluntary associations. "The whole work of legislation," asserted Mead (1899a, p. 368), "is not only dependent upon public sentiment, at least in democratic countries, but it is finding constantly fuller expressions in other channels of publicity.... If only it becomes possible to focus public sentiment upon an issue in the delicate organism of the modern community, it is as effective as if the mandate came from legislative halls, and frequently more so." The public, as Mead, following Dewey, understood it, is a body of citizenry, well informed, conscious of its interests, and ready to take the problems of society as their own. This body is distinguished by its members' willingness to consider the interests of all groups and individuals from the standpoint of what is good for the community as a whole. The success of the reform process ultimately depends on how thoroughly the public is mobilized and how long it can sustain interest in the critical issues of the day.

A vital role in mobilizing public opinion belongs to the press, which has the power to focus attention on the ills of society and to keep them in the news until a consensus is reached regarding ways of dealing with the problem: "The newspaper, in its various forms of journal and magazine, is effecting changes that are assumed to be those which follow governmental action" (1899a, p. 368). So far, however, the overall performance of the press had been less than satisfactory. One serious problem, according to Mead, was that "our newspapers represent frequently, or generally, political parties, instead of bringing together the common interests of all of us—that they represent only single parts" (1912, p. 215). Another scourge, especially characteristic of the progressive press, was its pervasive "sensationalism [which] is the expression of a fundamental social conflict which the community feels but is not willing to come to terms with" (MP b4 addenda, f1). To fulfill its mission, the press would have to overcome its partisan bias and serve as a unifying force.

Mead had similar advice for the leaders of labor and business organizations. He gave his full support to labor unions, whose combative spirit "is amply explained by the simple American demand for what one has confessedly earned, and the American determination to fight, if necessary, to get one's fair rights" (1907-8, p. 133). He urged business leaders to do their share in improving the conditions of labor and to get directly involved in the issues of minimum wage, working hours, workmen's compensation, and so on. Yet, he did not hesitate to chastise both labor and capital when he thought that intransigence on either side prevented a fair resolution of labor-management disputes (see MP Mead to Irene Tufts Mead, July 16 and 20, 1919, b1, f17; see also Diner 1980, pp. 148-51). The solution to labor strife that Mead personally favored was arbitration, to be conducted with expert mediators and under the eye of the public. The important thing was to keep searching for common ground, which, Mead was convinced, could always be found if only businessmen assumed their full responsibility as members of the community and workers aimed at "immediately possible achievements, with a vivid sense of the present reality of the means used and their necessary parity with the methods of the employers. Gradually the sense of community of interest between both arises, and with it growing interest in the actual struggle and a feeling of intense meaning that does not have to be projected into the future to get reality" (1899b, p. 411).

Schools have a vital part to play in humanizing American society. Progressive education, mandatory and free for all children, could at least partially offset "social restrictions which limit the development of children of poorer classes," and it could aid the progressive cause by bringing cultural goods to the poor and thereby "freeing... culture of its class connotation" ([1930] 1964, pp. 405-6). Progressive education could also help to counteract the negative effects of the division of labor by furnishing the worker with knowledge of the industrial process as a whole. That, in turn, would require the elimination of the two-tier system of education that gives liberal education to some and industrial training to others.

> Industrial training in this century should aim to give to the laborer not only professional efficiency but the meaning of his vocation, its historical import, and some comprehension of his position in the democratic society.... Out of this will arise an interest in the whole product which may lay the foundation for that intelligence which can in some measure resist the narrowing influence of the specialized labor in the factory.... American industrial education must be a liberal education. [1908-9b, p. 157; 1908-9c, p. 213]

And last, but not least, the success of reform depends on tapping the vast resources of science. The traditional reliance on charity and philanthropy is no longer adequate to the task in hand. A path to contemporary reform is a "path from impulsive charity to social reconstruction"; to be successful, it has to lead "not only to efforts of amelioration but also to judgments of value and plans for social reforms" ([1930] 1964, p. 399). Members of the academic community can make a large contribution to charting the reform program and formulating the means of social reconstruction. This is not simply because university professors possess specialized knowledge but also because they combine scientifically trained intelligence with the knowledge of the problems of the community at large. "The university is not an office of experts to which the problems of the community are sent to be solved; it is a part of the community within which the community problems appear as its own" (1915, p. 351). What sets scientific intelligence apart and makes its contribution to the reform process so signally important is its impartial character, its "disinterestedness in existing structures, social and intellectual, and willingness to continually reconstruct these substituting for them other structures at any point and to any extent" (MP b3 addenda, f16). A scientifically trained mind can rise above conflicting values and find a solution that reconciles disparate claims in the best interests of the community as a whole. In the search for a solution to the problem, scientific intelligence is likely to be guided not by a ready-made blueprint of a future society, "a vision given on the mount," but by the sense of the possible, a realistic account of available means, and a habit of dealing methodically and rationally with the problem at hand. This habit of impartiality does not mean that progressive scholars have no interest in the outcome, no values of their own; they are after all on the side of progress, and so, when their job is done, the old social order will be replaced with a new one that is more universal, rational, and humane: "The rational solution of the conflicts, however, calls for the reconstruction of both habits and values, and this involves transcending the order of the community. A hypothetically different order suggests itself and becomes the end in conduct.... It is a social order that includes any rational being who is or may be implicated in the situation with which thought deals. It sets up an ideal world, not of substantive things but of proper method" ([1930] 1964, p. 404).

In summary, Mead's theory of the reform process stems from his belief, widely shared by the progressive reformers of his time, that a terrible gap separates contemporary American society from the Jeffersonian ideal of popular democracy, that capitalism and democracy are currently working at cross purposes, and that, unless a way is found to humanize laissez-faire capitalism, the future of democracy in America will be imperiled. One road to a more humane and equitable society lies in the institutionalization of revolution—the term by which Mead meant that radical reforms can be carried out within the constitutional framework of democracy and that social reconstruction must be an ongoing concern rather than an all-out, one-time effort to set up a perfect society. Mead refused to spell out the exact nature of the future social order aside from general statements that it should be based on public good, take account of the interests of all social groups, and broaden the scope of economic and social opportunity for disadvantaged members of the community. He focused, instead, on methods and means of social reconstruction, the most salient of which are the mobilization of the general public, continued attention of the press, arbitration of labor-management disputes, the fusion of academic and vocational education, and the participation of members of the academic community. There was no gap between Mead's rhetoric and practical action. Whether he was marching with Jane Addams on the streets of Chicago in support of women's suffrage, surveying the homes of immigrants from eastern Europe, writing editorials on the dispute between the Board of Education and the Chicago Teacher's Federation, giving public support to the beleaguered reformers at the University of Wisconsin, or serving on the citizens' committee investigating labor grievances in the Chicago garment workers' strike—he was doing exactly what he thought a member of the public should do to stay politically engaged and to further the cause of reform. The interplay between Mead's political beliefs and his other intellectual pursuits was great indeed, and it comes into clear relief in his philosophical and social theory.

SOCIALIZING HUMAN INTELLIGENCE: MEAD'S THEORY OF THE SOCIAL PROCESS

The parallels between pragmatist and progressivist thought have been frequently noted (White 1957; Featherstone 1972; Levine 1969; Cremin 1969, Shalin 1986a), yet their implications have not been fully spelled out. My argument in the present section is that there is a far-reaching elective affinity between Progressivism and pragmatism, particularly the social pragmatism of Dewey and Mead. Indeed, the pragmatist vision of the world-in-the-making— the world that is perennially indeterminate, continuously emergent, and wonderfully malleable—is a metaphysics tailor-made for the age of reform. The traditional world of rationalist thought, the world of natural law and order, left little room for conscious efforts to make it more rational and humane. In contrast, the world confronting pragmatists was crying out for reform; it had to be transformed, and not just by the impersonal forces of evolution but by human intelligence. The latter, according to pragmatist philosophers, was not a mirror faithfully reflecting natural laws but an active force capable of transforming matter according to a logic of its own. Nowhere is the transformative, constitutive power of reason more evident or urgently needed than in the social domain:

> In the physical world we regard ourselves as standing in some degree outside the forces at work, and thus avoid the difficulty of harmonizing the feeling of human initiative with the recognition of series which are necessarily determined. In society we are the forces that are being investigated, and if we advance beyond the mere description of the phenomena of the social world to the attempt at reform, we seem to involve the possibility of changing what at the same time we assume to be necessarily fixed. [Mead 1899a, pp. 370-71]

It seems logical, therefore, that, to make room for reform, pragmatists would postulate a measure of indeterminacy, that they would proclaim that "uncertainty does not belong simply to the values, it belongs to the facts as well" (MP b8, f1), that they would urge that "the individual and environment—the situation—mutually determine each other" (Mead [1908] 1964, p. 86). If one were to assert the possibility of reform, one had to decry the morality that pictured the existing order of things as inherently rational and to replace it with a new ethics, according to which "moral advance consists not in adapting individual natures to the fixed realities of a moral universe, but in constantly reconstructing and recreating the world as the individuals evolve" (Mead [1908] 1964, p. 90). These philosophical tenets found their expression in the pragmatism-inspired (interactionist) theory of society.

In one of the posthumously published volumes of Mead's works appears a telling passage in which he formulates the central problem of modern society: "How can you present order and structure in society and bring about the changes that need to take place, are taking place? How can you bring those changes about in orderly fashion and yet preserve order? To bring about change is seemingly to destroy the given order, and yet society does and must change. That is the problem, to incorporate the methods of change into the order of society itself" (1936, pp. 361-62). This question is paradigmatic to the conception of sociology as the science of social reconstruction or the science of social control that gained wide currency among American sociologists in the Progressive Era (Faris 1970;

Fisher and Strauss 1978; Janowitz 1978; Shalin 1986a). It was commonly held at the time that sociology dealt with the problems of society undergoing social transformation, that the "process of reconstructing social conditions is the process with which the social sciences deal" (MP b7, f8). It was also widely assumed that sociology could aid in efforts to minimize the more disruptive consequences of social change. Indicative of the community of assumptions underlying sociological thinking of this period was the concept of social control. This was more than a technical term; it can also be seem as a theoretical expression of progressive ideology. How can we exercise intelligent control over social processes? was the burning question of the Progressive Era, and it was in response to this query that sociologists came up with an ingenuous answer: Intelligent control over human society requires social control over human intelligence. What this meant was that the fortunes of society did not have to be decided on the barricades and in the flames of revolutions, for the real battle was for people's minds. To influence the direction in which society grows, one had to reform or, what is the same, to inform the consciousnesses of its members. That is to say, the answer to the modern predicament was not coercion and violence but social control. This answer, along with other precepts of social interactionism, was consistent with the political climate of the age of reform. Once again, Mead's writings offer us insight into the interplay between ideological beliefs and substantive theorizing in the Progressive Era.

As we have seen before, Mead fully acknowledged the socialists' role in exposing capitalism's seedier sides and raising the workers' awareness of the need to fight for their rights. There was one more, and not so obvious, thing for which Mead was ready to credit socialism—its role in striking down the then prevalent concept of man as an asocial being. In addition to exposing the economic institutions of laissez-faire capitalism, the socialist critique exposed its ideological fallacies, including the utilitarian idea of mind as biological endowment and of action as an instrument for maximizing personal pleasure. Socialist thinkers resolutely rejected this utilitarian view, substituting for it the idea of the inescapably social nature of man: "But the essence of man is no abstraction inherent in each separate individual. In its reality it is the *ensemble* (aggregate) of social relations" (Marx [1846] 1963, p. 198). Now Mead was not familiar with all the sociologically relevant works of Marx, certainly not with the writings of the young Marx, which appeared in print for the first time after Mead's death, yet he had an acute sense of socialism's sociological import. Socialist teaching is ultimately concerned with socializing man's action and thought, argued Mead: "Its reality lies in the essentially social character of all conduct, and the gospel, according to socialism, is the recognition that all self-seeking has and must have a social end, if it belongs inside a social organism. What society is struggling to accomplish is to bring this social side of our conduct out so that it may, in some conscious way, become the element of control" (1899*b*, p. 406). This insight, maintained Mead, is socialism's most useful contribution to the diagnosis of modern conditions.

Indeed, as long as our motives remain private and we act without regard for other members of society, democracy will continue to breed injustice and human misery. It is only when the individual takes into account the larger social context, when he "takes the role of the other," that social control becomes a guiding force in society and democracy realizes its true potential as a political system: "Social control depends, then, upon the degree to which the individuals in society are able to assume the attitudes of the others who are involved with them in common endeavor" (Mead [1924-25] 1964, p. 291). This, according to Mead, is the sociological essence of socialism, and this, I should add, is where his own sociological ideas intersect with those of the young Marx. Mead's premise that "the whole nature of our intelligence is social to the very core" (1934, p. 141) is consistent with Marx's view that "activity and mind, both in their content and in their *mode of existence*, are social, *social* activity and *social* mind" ([1844] 1964, p. 138). The same is true of Mead's (1935-36, p. 70) contention that "the individual is no thrall to society. He constitutes society as genuinely as society constitutes the individual," which reminds us of Marx's (1964, p. 137) motto, "*Just* as society produces *man as man,* so is society *produced* by him." There is a family resemblance between Mead's assertion that "the unity and structure of the complete self reflects the unity and structure of the social process as a whole" (1934, p. 144) and Marx's thesis that "man, much as he may therefore be a *particular* individual,... is just as much a *totality*—the ideal society—the subjective existence of thought and experienced society for itself" ([1844] 1964, p. 138). And, finally, Mead's (1934, p. 309) insight that the "relations between social reconstruction and self or personality reconstruction are reciprocal and internal" reflects the same dialectical pattern that is embedded in Marx 's idea of revolutionary practice as "the coincidence of changing of circumstances and of human activity or self-changing" ([1846] 1963, p. 198).

It would be a mistake to push the parallels between Mead and Marx too far. It would be equally mistaken to ignore them. These parallels are not spurious; they reflect the same determination to overcome the opposition between public and private, social and individual, society and man, the determination to bring into one continuum mind, self, and society that marked the thought of the young Marx and Mead. I wish to stress that Mead's interactionism is closest to Marx's romanticism, that is, to that early period in Marx's intellectual career when he was close to the idealism of Hegel and Fichte, when he did not yet break with bourgeois democratism and still had high regard for the curative powers of self-conscious reason (Gouldner 1973, pp. 337-40; Shalin 1986b, pp. 112-13). As Marx became increasingly disillusioned with the prospects for the peaceful transformation of society, the romantic-idealist themes gave way in his writings to a new emphasis on economic factors and revolutionary force. Mead, on the other hand, like most progressive thinkers, retained his youthful idealism as well as his romantic organicism with its root metaphor of man-the-microcosm (Shalin 1984, pp. 55-58). The most remarkable thing about romantic organicism is that it compels one to see man and society not as opposed entities but as aspects of the same process of the production of social reality as objective and meaningful. The individual appears here not just as one organ or part of the social whole but as a social self, or, to use the language of romantic organicism, a "species being" reflecting in unique fashion the totality of social relations. By the same token, society loses in this scheme its externality and thinglike character; it is dissolved into a series of interactions in the course of which it is continuously regenerated as a social universe, or universe of discourse. It is very important from the interactionist standpoint that the individual embraces within his self the whole of society, that he "takes the attitude of the generalized other." It is equally important that the individual does not become a passive receptacle of social norms and values but develops a critical attitude toward his social self and the society that provided him with this self.[14] The individual is both "Me" and "I"—a responsible member of various social groups and a unique personality capable of transcending a given order, a law-abiding citizen and a critic of society.

Insofar as the individual successfully integrates these two aspects of his social existence, the relationship between the individual and society can be judged organic, which is exactly what progressives wished it to be. Here is a sample of statements expressing this romantic theme, as formulated by different progressive thinkers:

> The organization and unification of a social group is identical with the organization and unification of any one of the selves arising within the social process.... Each individual self within this process, while it reflects in its organized structure the

behavior pattern of that process as a whole, does so from its
own particular or unique standpoint.... [Mead 1934, pp. 144,
201]

But human society represents a more perfect organism. The
whole lives truly in every member, and there is no longer the
appearance of physical aggregation, or continuity. The organism manifests itself as what it truly is, an ideal or spirtual life,
a unity of *will*. If then, society and the individual are really
organic to each other, then the individual is society concen-
trated. He is not merely its image or mirror. He is the localized
manifestation of its life. [Dewey 1969, p. 237]

A national structure which encourages individuality as opposed to mere particularity is one which creates innumerable
special niches, adapted to all degrees and kinds of individual
development. The individual becomes a nation in miniature,
but devoted to loyal realization of a purpose peculiar to himself. The nation become an enlarged individual whose special
purpose is that of human amelioration, and in whose life every
individual should find some particular but essential functions.
[Croly 1909, p. 414]

These utterances should not be taken to mean that progressives saw contemporary American society as an actual embodiment
of organic interaction. A contemporary industrial society, as Mead
(1934, p. 307) and other progressives repeatedly stated, is ridden
with contradictions: "Within such a society, conflicts arise between
different aspects or phases of the same individual self...as well as
between individual selves [that must be] settled or terminated by
reconstructions of particular social situations, or modifications of
the given framework of social relations, wherein they arise or
occur." Rather, the above statements should be seen as an attempt to
lay down a standard for judging contemporary reality, an ideal and
a theory that indicated the direction of social reconstruction and the
method of social control. As an ideal, the future society envisioned
by the progressive imagination was somewhat akin to the romantic
notion of gemeinschaft, in that it accentuated the virtues of the
"Great Community," "free and enriching communion," or free
intercourse, whose participants are "the constant makers of a
continuously new society" (Dewey [1927] 1954, p. 115-17; [1929]
1962, p. 143). A formal model of this future society was "the universe of discourse, a community based simply on the ability of all
individuals to converse with each other through use of the same
significant symbols"; its actualization requires an understanding
that "the brotherhood of men ... is the basis for a universal society"

(Mead 1934, pp. 282-83). As a method, interactionist theory extolled the advantages of intelligent social control over violent means of effecting social change. Its preference for peaceful, noncoercive forms of social reconstruction was already implied in its basic premises: If mind, self, and society belong to one continuum and are indeed aspects of the same social intercourse, then the reconstruction of society is largely a matter of reconstructing the human mind. "An institution is, after all, nothing but an organization of attitudes which we all carry in us" (Mead 1934, p. 211), and so, abolishing obsolete institutions means reforming our attitudes, our ways of thinking. That is, to change society, we have to change ourselves: "Thus the relation between social reconstruction and self or personality reconstruction by the individual members of any organized human society entails self or personality reconstruction in some degree or other by each of these individuals.... In both types of reconstruction the same fundamental material of organized social relations among human individuals is involved, and is simply treated in different ways, or from different angles or points of view, in the two cases respectively; or in short, social reconstruction and self or personality reconstruction are the two sides of a single process—the process of human social evolution" (Mead 1934, p. 309).

To sum up, there is an elective affinity between Mead's social philosophy and his political beliefs. Along with other pragmatists, Mead abandoned the rationalist universe of natural order, replacing it with a world brimming with possibilities and open to social reform. Translated into the language of sociological theory, this world-in-the-making yielded a peculiar version of "sociological progressivism" (Fisher and Strauss 1978, p. 488), with its dynamic picture of society as ongoing social interaction. Every individual appears in this picture as simultaneously a product and producer of society, whereas society transpires as both an antecedent and outcome of social interaction. Mind, self, and society are bound together here as parts of one continuum, or aspects of the same process of production, of social reality as objective and meaningful, which makes it imperative that each be understood in terms of the other. The circle involved in the interactionist mode of reasoning is not unintentional; it is the dialectical or hermeneutical circle that requires that the part be explained through the whole and the whole in terms of its parts. This dialectical approach, characteristic of 19-century romanticism and 20th-century Progressivism, accentuates the possibility of peaceful social transformation and predicates the reconstruction of society on the reconstruction of human mind.

The ultimate goal of social reconstruction, as envisioned in social interactionism, is a democratic community based on the ideal of free discourse or organic interaction (Habermas 1981, pp. 11-68). When the self-consciousness of all individuals is so altered that each can rejoice with the successes, empathize with the miseries, and help meet the needs of others, that is, when everyone assumes the attitude of the whole society, then the latter is transformed into a truly universal and democratic community.

CONCLUSION: MEAD AND THE PROGRESSIVE LEGACY

Many observers have commented on the contradictions inherent in the Progressive movement, on its "profound internal dialectic" (Conn 1983, p. 1; see also Hofstadter 1955, pp. 5, 236; White 1957, p. 46; Noble 1958). There is indeed a great deal of tension in progressive ideology. Its adherents extolled the virtues of entrepreneurial individualism and at the same time stressed the need for public control; they longed for a socialism of opportunity yet defended the capitalism of property; they urged a radical break with the present and reached deep into the past for an ideal of the future; above all, they were determined to escape the twin dangers of radicalism and conservatism. "There is the conflict between the old and the new, between the radical and the conservative," wrote Mead about the dominant mood of this time, "but... we may not wish to be either radical or conservative. We may wish to comprehend and to do justice to the changing valuations" (1938, p. 480). It is this desire to rise above the political extremes of the Right and the Left that brought on the scorn for the progressives from some contemporary and modern critics. Those on the Right have charged that Progressivism ultimately leads to socialism. For critics on the Left, Progressivism has been little more than an episode in the ongoing effort to stem the inexorable decline of corporate capitalism. Yet historical Progressivism defies all attempts to subsume it under a neat ideological label.

Progressive reformers were democrats of a new breed. These were "men and women longing to socialize their democracy" (Addams 1910, p. 116), working for "a more balanced, a more equal, even, and equitable system of human liberties" (Dewey 1946, p. 113) and determined "to limit and control private economic power as the Founders had limited political power" (Graham 1967, p. 5). It is arguable whether, as Scott (1959, pp. 697, 690) claims, "the Progressive Era was more original than the New Deal and more daring as well," but he is right when he stresses its historical importance, and he is justified in his critique of persistent attempts in modern historiography "to conservative Progressivism." Kolko's thesis (1963) that progressive reforms constituted "the triumph of conservatism" flies in the face of the progressives' democratic aspirations. The very term "social reconstruction" adopted by progressives was indicative of their values. It harked back to the Civil War era, when Lincoln first invoked it to describe the need to break cleanly with the past and to start the country on a radically new path. With an equal sense of urgency, progressives faced up to the task of social reconstruction, which on the eve of the 20th century meant bringing government into the marketplace, broadening the scope of economic opportunity, democratizing education, and transforming the public into an agent of social control. Although far from a monolithic movement, Progressivism was championed by the people who, regardless of their many differences, shared the belief that the key to the transformation of society is to be found in public discourse rather than in the skills of professional politicians. In their fight against laissez-faire capitalism, progressives borrowed many an insight from socialism; some claimed that "we are in for some kind of socialism, call it by whatever name we please" (Dewey [1929] 1962, p. 119). Nevertheless, there were important points of theory and method on which progressives and socialists parted company. Progressives endorsed socialism's emancipatory goals but rejected its revolutionary means. Their attempt, unsuccessful as it might have been, to work out a scheme for securing these goals without breaking the constitutional framework of democracy—an attempt that is at the core of the progressive agenda—is the most enduring legacy of the Progressive movement. It is also a source of perennial tension and contradiction in Progressivism as well as in the kindred pragmatist and interactionist movements.

Progressives recognized that democracy would self-destruct unless it provided room for justice, that society must secure minimum economic and social standards for every one of its members. But how much democracy? How much justice? Does it include socialized medicine, guaranteed employment, free college education? Both Mead and Dewey were likely to include these among the standards of social decency necessary for the development of each individual's creative potential, but there is nothing in progressive ideology that would help to resolve this matter in principle. More important, one has to wonder whether full equality of opportunity can be accomplished under private ownership of the means of production. The critics on the Left had good reason to doubt that the efforts of the progressives to socialize opportunity would ever bring about the socialism of opportunity in a capitalist America. The socialists' wholesale dismissal of Progressivism, however, was far too hasty. They did not understand the progressives' preoccupation with the means of social reconstruction and specifically with their concern for the fate of democracy in a society where economic power was radically centralized. The highest value for socialists was economic equality; once it was achieved, Marx thought, human rights would take care of themselves, and universal democracy would naturally ensue. But more recent socialist thinkers have become increasingly aware (Lynd 1974, pp. 713-39; Giddens 1981, pp. 172-73; Lukes 1985) that this outcome is far from assured. All radical attempts to nationalize the means of production in this century have resulted in the breakdown of democratic institutions: the more radical the scope of nationalization, the more deleterious effect it seems to have on human rights; the more successful the efforts to do away with bourgeois democracy, the less room left for radical social criticism. This is not to say that capitalism guarantees human rights (think of Chile or South Africa), only that human rights have invariably been a casualty of attempts to substitute a socialist (in Marx's sense of the word) for a capitalist society. In light of this historical experience, progressives' concern for democracy and the means-ends relationship in social reconstruction seems far from irrelevant. There is a dialectical tension between justice and democracy, equality and freedom, that is inherent in Western liberalism (Lasch 1983; Gutmann 1983) and that the progressives were nowhere close to resolving, but this is a creative tension, and progressives were correct in bringing it to light and stressing the need to balance the considerations of justice with those of democracy.

The amorphous notion of public good is another source of difficulty and confusion in progressive theory. Mead consistently refused to enunciate what he meant by "public good" or to spell out the values that would help one judge a policy or a program as being in the "interests of the community as a whole." Like other reformers of his time, he was confident that each contentious issue lends itself to public adjudication and that every social conflict could be amicably resolved. Critics have been attacking the excessive optimism, deliberate ambiguity, and opportunistic tendencies in pragmatist and progressive thought for a long time (Bourne 1915; Smith 1931; Niebuhr [1932] 1960; Novack 1975). What they are less likely to see is that these tendencies are not without a rationale. Pragmatists and progressives refused to specify the exact nature of a future democratic society because they believed that "every generation has to accomplish democracy over and over again," that "the very idea of democracy...has to be constantly discovered, and rediscovered, remade and reorganized" (Dewey 1946, pp. 31, 47). Any overarching scheme, "a vision given on the mount," is likely to turn into a straitjacket if followed rigidly and unswervingly, as numerous attempts in recent decades to impose a shining revolutionary ideal on an unyielding reality readily testify. It is not true that progressives had no vision of the future or that all their values were ad hoc. The failure of the progressives to endorse the comprehensive social security program, caused by their fear—again not entirely misplaced, as seen from the vantage point of the present—of irresponsible patronage politics and unwieldy federal bureaucracy, does not undermine their commitment to spreading social justice. Their emphasis on regulatory reforms and public control instead of state-run government-supervised programs, although unquestionably too limiting even for their time, was also far from disingenuous and class-motivated, as it is sometimes portrayed. Progressives were essentially right in leaving it to the public to define and redefine continuously what shape their ideal of a more democratic and humane society should assume in a given historical setting. There will always be much bickering and plenty of mistakes made, but in the long run a public forum is the best one for articulating the public good. The idea of a democratic public, as Janowitz (1952; 1978) rightly points out, that is, the idea of "the passing of functions which are supposed to inhere in the government into activities that belong to the community" (Mead 1899a, p. 369), is an enduring contribution of pragmatism and interactionism to contemporary social thought.

Another facet of philosophical and sociological progressivism that has drawn criticism is tied to the belief in scientific method as an instrument of social reform. Mead's insistence that "scientific method...is nothing but a highly developed form of impartial intelligence," that "science has become the method of social progress, and social progress itself has become a religion" ([1923] 1964, p. 256; 1918, p. 639) is bound to raise a number of critical questions. Charges of scientism and positivism are frequently leveled against pragmatism in this connection (Selsam 1950). Much of this criticism, in my view, stems from a misconception of the pragmatist idea of science. It is not true that pragmatists saw scientific knowledge as being value neutral and scientists as standing above society. "Knowing, including most emphatically scientific knowledge," stressed Dewey (1946, p. 17), "is not outside social activity, but is itself a form of social behavior, as much as agriculture or transportation." Moreover, as Mead ([1930] 1964, p. 406) indicated, "it is not until science has become a discipline to which the research ability of any mind from any class in society can be attracted that it can become rigorously scientific." Pragmatists did not seek value neutrality, nor did they espouse value partisanship. Their position is best described as value tolerance, in that it advocates "taking the value perspective of the other" and seeks truth at "the intersection of conflicting values" (Shalin 1979; 1980).[15] Mead and the pragmatists did not trust the magic powers of scientific intelligence to resolve the burning issues of the day. Rather, they valued science as a form of rational discourse in which every participant has a say, all claims are subject to testing, and each solution undergoes continuous revision. It is certainly not a perfect institution, but, warts and all, science offers the best available model of democracy in action, and we should credit pragmatists for focusing attention on the operations of value-tolerant science and the contribution it could make to rational discourse in society at large.

One final issue that needs to be addressed here concerns the progressives' boundless trust in democratic institutions and peaceful revolution in America. As many critics (Bates 1933; Selsam 1950; Purcell 1973; Schwedinger and Schwedinger 1974; Karier 1975; Novack 1975) have argued—correctly—pragmatists tended to exaggerate both the potential for and the actual extent of social change in America. They tended to confuse the normative and the descriptive in their accounts by, on the one hand, criticizing contemporary democracy and, on the other, insisting that the institutional framework of democracy necessary for social reconstruction was already in place. This confusion is clearly visible in the almost total blindness of Mead and most of the progressives to the plight of blacks. They spoke eloquently on behalf of immigrants, women, and children, but the institutionalized exclusion of blacks from American democracy did not seem to bother progressive reformers much. It should be also emphasized that Mead, along with other progressives, held a rather naive view of business leaders' readiness to heed the voice of reason and jump on the bandwagon of reform. "While a good part of the program of socialism is being put into practice," wrote Mead (MP b2 addenda, f27), "the striking difference lies in the fact that it [is] being undertaken not by the proletariat but by the whole community under the eager guidance of captains of industry, community generals, research scientists and conservative statesmen." This statement flies in the face of the long war with trade unions and dogged opposition to labor reforms that "captains of industry" waged (as they still do), using more or less preposterous excuses. It took a large-scale rebellion at Homestead and elsewhere to convince big business that reforms were unavoidable and useful after all. And we may add that it took a massive campaign of civil disobedience in the 1960s to bring blacks into American democracy. All of which suggests that American society, certainly in the Progressive Era, was far from the institutional democracy in which revolution could have been carried out by legal means alone. Having said this, I take issue with those critics who see pragmatists and progressives as dreamy idealists at best and apologists for corporate capitalism at worst. "These men were progressives and meliorists of their day, but they were realists and skeptics as well" (Janowitz 1970, p. xii). They fought hard battles in Congress for progressive legislation, they were doing tangible things to improve the lot of immigrants and the poor, and they were prepared to change the very system if necessary to make room for meaningful reform: "In order to endure under present conditions, liberalism must become radical in the sense that, instead of using social power to ameliorate the evil consequences of the existing system, it shall use social power to change the system" (Dewey 1946, p., 132). There is every reason to believe that Mead would have endorsed this statement.

Mead's Position in Intellectual History and His Early Philosophical Writings

Hans Joas

There is no doubt that Mead understood and referred to himself as a pragmatist toward the end of his life. Yet this label does not immediately help a great deal in understanding his fundamental approach, since pragmatism was by no means a clearly delimited school or a distinctly differentiated paradigm. Rather, it was the name of a programme, which had still to be elaborated and required clarification in many respects. Mead's increasing use of this description for himself is, therefore, not due to a change in his views, but merely to the growing currency of the term 'pragmatism'. Since Mead's classification as a pragmatist might conceal, rather than elucidate individual particularities of his approach, I shall, as a first step, summarize the basic concerns of his thought, as these are revealed by his biography, and generally relate them to the approaches of other pragmatists as well as to the central features of his contemporary intellectual situation. This first step will show the possible significance of Mead's work for German social theories. The second step will be to draw upon the writings on the history of philosophy and science that Mead himself submitted in order to deepen our understanding of Mead's position in intellectual history. The third step will take us to Mead's early philosophical writings and to his intellectual evolution.

The fundamental themes that can be extracted from Mead's biography can be subsumed under three headings: confidence in the emancipatory prospects of scientific rationality; a striving to root 'mind' or 'spirit' in the organism; and the attempt to elaborate a theory of intersubjectivity that would conceive of the self as socially originated. Mead's confidence in the prospects of technical and scientific progress is neither naive nor apologetic. He does not

identify technical with social progress, nor does he call for the
extension of technical rationality to the guidance of social processes.
His categorical notion of science assumes, rather, that the freedom
of scientific communication underlying scientific progress is made
the model for the reform of social decision-making processes. Thus,
the frequently proclaimed endeavour to transform social reform
into a science, and to overcome the relative falling behind of the
social sciences does not conceal the germ of positivist or technocratic
ideals. And yet Mead's concept of rationality also does not take on
that peculiar ambivalence, which—as in the case of Max Weber, for
example—interprets rationalization as a historical process occurring supra-personally and compelling the individual's adaptation, a
process for which nevertheless the name of reason is used. From this
ambivalence to resignation and the abandonment of all optimism
about civilization is indeed only a single step.

In contrast, for Mead, and his circle rationality is the remedy
for social problems. He can hold this opinion only because for him
the gap between 'higher', 'spiritual', 'cultural' attainments and
capacities and the 'material', 'technical', 'civilizing' dimension of
society had been philosophically overcome in a fundamental way.
The attempt to elaborate a 'functionalist' psychology, based on the
work of Darwin, is founded on the insight that all mental operations
can be embedded in the functions of the organism in a non-
reductionist manner. This is important both for philosophy's
founding of itself and because of individual psychological and
pedagogical consequences of this insight. With regard to the founding of philosophy, the model, first proposed by Darwin, of the organism actively safeguarding its life in a given environment made it
possible easily to go beyond the view advanced by transcendental
philosophy, which requires the antecedent reflective certainty of the
thinking ego. Thus, by means of the Darwinian model, the difficult
path followed by Feuerbach, and the Young Hegelians in general,
in their attempts to free themselves from transcendental philosophy,
is traversed with a single bound. With regard to psychology, the
acceptance of the Darwinian model resulted in a 'rehabilitation' of
organismic impulses, while with respect to educational theory it led
to the attaching of greater importance to physical activity, sensory-
motor learning, the immediate interests of the learner, and the
organically conditioned stages of maturation.

This third of the aforementioned general concerns is perhaps
the most characteristic for Mead. Through the theory of the social
formation of the self, one of the cornerstones of bourgeois ideology in
the strict sense is eliminated, namely possessive individualism. For

Mead the individual and his property is no longer a presupposition of the formation of a society, but rather individualization is a consequence of the structure of socially organized life-processes. It thereby becomes possible, despite rejection of traditional individualism, particularly that of Anglo-Saxon thought, to retain the ideal of the individual's autonomy. However, this autonomy is now no longer an original given that is to be opposed to society. Instead, it requires for its emergence a re-shaping of social life, which must be so organized that free self-determination of all is both possible and necessary. From his earliest publications on,[1] this theme can be followed in Mead's writings, even though the scientific means for carrying out the programme were only gradually elaborated, and the ethical aspects of the concept of the self only gradually freed from their close ties to religion.[a]

Now, if we ask about the relationship of these fundamental concerns to pragmatism in general, then it quickly becomes clear that the first two are, to a large extent, shared by all pragmatists, whereas the third is peculiar to Mead. This is the reason why the designation of Mead as a 'consequentialist intersubjective pragmatist' seems to me a perhaps clumsy but precise description of his position. The roots of pragmatism are to be found in the attempt, as Mead put it, to 'logically generalize' the procedures of the experimental natural sciences,[2] and in the train of Darwinism to relate all human cognitive processes to life-processes. To be sure, both of these endeavours, impressive and humanistic as they are, do not appear at all in the widespread picture of pragmatism. Rather, pragmatism is thought to be a cynical justification for acting without ultimate goals and firm principles, according to the precept that what is true is what is useful. This distorted picture of pragmatism has often occasioned imputations about its connection with the American national character, or criticism of it as an ideology. From this perspective pragmatism appears as the ideology of the adaptation of intellectuals to the formation of monopoly capitalism or as the expression of the American fetishism of success and money.[3] Even during his lifetime, Mead had to oppose these distortions; he did so ironically:

> Now this assumption of the pragmatist that the individual only thinks in order that he may continue an interrupted action, that the criterion of the correctness of his thinking is found in his ability to carry on, and that the significant goal of his thinking or research is found not in the ordered presentation of the subject matter of his research but in the uses to

which it may be put, is very offensive to many people, and, I am afraid, particularly so to the historian. Pragmatism is regarded as a pseudo-philosophic formulation of that most obnoxious American trait, the worship of success; as the endowment of the four-flusher with a faked philosophic passport; the contemputuous swagger of a glib and restless upstart in the company of the mighty but reverent spirits worshipping at the shrine of subsistent entities and timeless truth; a blackleg pacemaker introduced into the leisurely workshop of the spirit to speed up the processes of thinking *sub specie aeternitatis*; a Ford efficiency engineer bent on the mass production of philosophical tin lizzies. These disparagements are all boomerangs, but I will not constitute this a clinic in which to demonstrate the contusions which those who have hurled them have suffered, but will address myself to the single charge that this philosophy would dispossess men of the leisured contemplation and enjoyment of the past.[4].

Such misrepresentations concealed even from Marxists the extraordinary proximity between Marx's philosophy of praxis and the fundamental principle of pragmatism. And this, although the relationship of the terms 'praxis' and 'pragmatism'—extending even to their common linguistic root—was not accidental. For Peirce, the founder of pragmatism, had justified the choice of this name precisely as an attempt to overcome the Kantian distinction between 'practical' and 'pragmatic':

But for one who had learned philosophy out of Kant..., 'practical' and 'pragmatical' were as far apart as the two poles, the former belonging in a region of thought where no mind of the experimentalist type can ever make sure of solid ground under his feet, the latter expressing relation to some definite human purpose. Now quite the most striking feature of the new theory was its recognition of an inseparable connection between rational cognition and rational purposes; and that consideration it was which determined the preference for the name 'pragmatism'.[5]

Overcoming the separation between practical and theoretical reason and the primacy of praxis are, however, very much fundamental principles of historical materialism, even if they have not been elaborated in much detail by the adherents of this theory.

The superficial misunderstandings of pragmatism are only gradually being dissipated by the general renaissance of pragmatism in the USA, and in the Federal Republic of Germany through the reception of Peirce's work initiated by Apel and Habermas. Concomitant to this better understanding is an increasingly clear awareness that in pragmatism at least two different large strands must be distinguished; one of them aims at objective cognitive truth and correctness of behaviour, while the other is subjectivist in character. The latter strand of pragmatist thought is represented by William James, who, to be sure, also did not reduce truth to usefulness, but did consider it—taking the individualistic point of view—merely as an instrument at the service of the individual's existence and spiritual welfare. Mead distanced himself as unequivocally from James's theory of truth as from his psychological notions.[6] Mead did in some instances employ the same terms as James, for example, 'I', 'me', and 'self', but for Mead these expressions denoted concepts that were quite different from those of James. For Mead, James's psychology only demarcated the terrain on which he made his attempt to recover objectivity and universality.

Although there is, then, objective agreement of Mead's intentions with those of Peirce, it would be erroneous to conclude from this fact that there was a direct influence by Peirce on Mead. Such an influence simply cannot be documented. In an article written in the last year of his life Mead mentions Peirce only briefly, without discussing his work even cursorily.[7] At the present time the only other instance of a greater contact by Mead with Peirce's thought is to be found in a fragment written during Mead's early years,[8] in which he drew upon Peirce's critique of 'necessitarian', that is deterministic, metaphysics in an attempt to develop various sociological trains of thought. The influence unquestionably exercised by Peirce's theory of signs on Mead's conception of the significant symbol was indirect, and came to Mead via Royce's late writings.[9] Even taking into consideration the generally small degree to which Peirce's work was known prior to the publication of his *Collected Papers* (beginning in 1928), the extent to which Mead ignored this thinker, with whom he shared so many intellectual concerns, is still really surprising.

The reasons for this probably lie in Mead's slight interest in problems of scientific logic in the narrower sense, and especially in Peirce's rejection of attempts to apply scientific procedures to social processes and of the practical utilization of 'pure' science in general. If Mead's dominant interest can be described as *a refounding of*

pragmatism as a theory based on the biological and social sciences,
then Peirce's confidence in the salutary effects of the natural human
instincts, his optimistic anthropology, necessarily remained alien to
Mead and seemed superficial to him. Apparently for that reason he
did not see how extensively the basic model of cognition as the
solution of problems arising from action, as the way of making
possible the continuation of action—a model that he traced back to
Dewey's paradigmatic essay 'The Reflex Arc Concept in Psychology'—had already been implicity elaborated, even from a psychological point of view, in the writings of Pierce. As is well known, the
latter had attempted to criticize Cartesianism also from a psychological perspective and had adapted for this purpose the 'belief-
doubt' theory of Alexander Bain. Apel summarizes this theory as
follows:

> 'Doubt' as the irritation of a secure form of behaviour, and
> 'belief' as the reinstitution of security in behaviour constitute a
> *terminus post quem* and a *terminus ante quem* of the cognition
> process in time; in a way they stake out in each case a finite
> functional unity in the infinite process of cognition.[10]

Although it cannot by any means be maintained that Peirce really
drew all the psychological conclusions implicit in this view, or that
he developed a comprehensive concept of action,[11] it is nevertheless
very clear that Peirce and Mead were in the same tradition. For
Dewey communicated with Peirce and had been directly influenced
by him.

 Although these connections have shed some light on Mead's
relationship to James and Peirce as eminent representatives of the
aforementioned strands of pragmatism, it is still nececesary to make
a few remarks about Mead's relationship to the third famous representative of pragmatism, John Dewey. This relationship is often
presented as one-sided, with Mead in the role of student or collab-
orator. Yet it can be shown—and was stressed by Dewey's daughter
in a biographical recollection—that both the central theoretical
elements used by Mead in his definition of the 'psychical' and in his
explanation of the social formation of the self originate with him
and were only taken over by Dewey and employed in the latter's
writings often in a rather superficial manner.[12] With regard to
ethics and the theory of science, the two philosophers also differ
from one another, with Mead generally taking the more strongly
'objective' position.

 The superficial, popular misunderstandings about pragmatism unquestionably have their analogues in serious philosophical

thought. Thus the critique of pragmatism using as a criterion the ideal of pure theory, such as Max Scheler undertook, as well as the subsumption of neopositivism and pragmatism under the rubric of 'instrumental reason', which we find in Max Horkheimer's critique of this kind of thinking, are characterized by a superficial and biased interpretation of pragmatism and by counter-notions of dubious merit.[13] The most interesting phenomenon in European thought in this connection, and the one that testifies most strongly to Mead's importance for German intellectual history, is the fact that when the insights of American pragmatism were arrived at independently by European philosophers, as in Nietzsche's or Bergson's *Lebensphilosophie*, they occur with a characteristic modification. Alongside the pragmatist notion of the cognition of reality there was maintained a contemplative notion of cognition, and this was done in such a manner that the world constituted in the action of human actors appears to be deficient in comparison with the world that is accessible only through abstinence from action. The logical impossibility of this 'fictionalist' pragmatism has been rightly demonstrated many times, especially in more recent Nietzsche scholarship.[14] For Mead, Nietzsche was without significance; the position described was familiar to him, however, and thoroughly discussed by him with Bergson as the example.[15]

In his critical examination of Le Bon's crowd psychology, Mead had already posed the question: from which perspective is the thesis of the necessary distortion of reality by all perception advanced?[16] This question then becomes more precise in Mead's reflections on Bergson. In significant psychological analyses Bergson had attempted to show that all conceptual cognition arises from problems posed by action and forces the world into a framework that causes all freedom and spontaneity to disappear. Bergson's primary example was his analysis of the 'spatialization of time', that is his proof that our thinking can grasp the internal experiencing of time only in categories of the external, physical world, but thereby obliterates its specific features. To the mechanistic image of the world characterized by restriction and coercion, Bergson emphatically opposed a world of change and freedom. This world is accessible through intuition—a counter-notion to conceptual cognition —which alone opens the portal leading to creative evolution.

Mead saw in Bergson's influential analyses a justified, but irrationalist critique of scientism. In his earliest discussion of Bergson's work he asked how it was possible that Bergson attributed a creative character only to intuition and to the unplanned becoming of 'life', but not to science. He saw in Bergson's position the reverse of the positivist misunderstanding of science, according to which science consists merely of interrelated propositions about facts, not the process of discovering these facts.[17] In Bergson's view, freedom derived from the essential impossibility of exhaustively predicting the future, from which fact he concluded the superfluity of the intellect. To Bergson's position Mead opposed scientific procedure understood as a readiness continually to revise hypotheses and to make the map of the future progressively more precise. In Mead's opinion, Bergson's irrationalist tendencies were rooted in his inadequate understanding of the scientific method. The appropriate remedy for this irrationalism was, Mead believed, to work out correctly the implications of the insight into the construct-character of scientific objects, to analyse the way in which scientific knowledge is constituted. What had been only suggestively associated in Bergson's writings and in the largest part of *Lebensphilosophie*—the implications of the notion of life with regard to the natural sciences on the one hand and the critique of culture on the other hand, the directing of attention to the biological foundations of the mind, and the protest against reification and rigidification of culture—these and their interrelationships had to be developed with extreme clarity in order to oppose irrationalism. But to do so, a non-irrationalist notion of life was required. By 'life' Mead does not understand the organism's creative and complete self-regulation as a counter-notion to the intellect, but rather the continual solving of problems. Reflective experience is for him both a product and a functional necessity of human life; science is the opportunity for humanity to replace the blind rule of evolutionary laws with the self-reflective shaping of its own conditions of life. Thus the notion of life held by Mead, and other pragmatists, allows them to appropriate the achievements of *Lebensphilosohie* rather than dismissing them together with its undeniable irrationalism. By contrasting Mead with Bergson, the thesis can perhaps be made more plausible that in many respects Mead's thought offers an alternative to the course taken by German and European intellectual history since the late 19th century, inasmuch as it permits one to link together, in a synthesis, moments which seem to be mutually exclusive in the German tradition. I myself see in Mead's work a possibility of escaping aporiae which occurred in the development of German philosophy from Dilthey and Husserl to Heidegger and Philosophical Anthropology, and which are important for the grounding of the social sciences. However, I will confine myself here to pointing out this possibility rather than presenting it in detail, as that would require close discussion of the aforementioned thinkers.

The fact that Mead studied with Dilthey and was familiar with the latter's intellectual aims is not an inconsequential aspect of Mead's biography, since both had certain concerns in common. For example, they both attempted to make possible a grounding of the human or social sciences by revealing how the objects of these sciences are constituted in the communicative life-praxis of human beings. This undertaking was in contrast to materialist or idealist reductionism and stood at a critical distance from the mere resuscitation of Kant in neo-Kantianism. Also common to both— contrary to misjudgements which are widespread in the history of Dilthey scholarship—was the intention of establishing a basis for objective knowledge and an openmindedness towards the natural sciences.[18] The immediate difference between them in this regard is only a matter of accentuation, in so far as Mead was certainly more sympathetic to the natural sciences than was Dilthey. Experimental psychology, and not, as for Dilthey, historical-philological research, typified for Mead the field of non-natural-scientific investigation.

Thus, in Dilthey's eyes the approaches used by experimental psychology were all suspected of being reductionist, and he was compelled to set against 'explanatory' psychology, which he rejected, the 'descriptive' psychology that he himself had founded. The latter was directed towards answering the question of the nature of the constitutive achievements of the mind that made possible the products of the 'objective spirit'. Mead shared this concern, and, like Dilthey, held unwaveringly to the singularity of historical existence in opposition to the absolutist claims of the idealist philosophy of history, as his early writings show. The crucial difference, and the cause of the development of Mead's thought in another direction, lay in the fact that at the very beginning of his work Mead overcame the obstacle on which Dilthey's enterprise came to grief: unlike Dilthey, Mead does not maintain that the self or the structure of the psyche is in itself originally given to the actor. Despite the many fundamental premises he held in common with the pragmatists, Dilthey did not attain the same degree of philosophical radicalism and start to conceive of the self as the product of a complex of social relationships.[19] In his *Ideas Concerning a Descriptive and Analytical Psychology (Ideen über eine beschreibende und zergliedernde Psychologie)*, he clearly fails to recongize that inner experience, too, is socially mediated; it is only this failure that allows him to oppose the absolute certainty of 'inner experience' to the merely hypothetical character of 'external experience'. In *Toward a Solution of the Question Concerning the Origin of our Belief in the Reality of the*

*External World (Beiträge zur Lösung der Frage vom Ursprung
unseres Glaubens an die Realität der Aussenwelt)*, Dilthey certainly made significant steps in the direction of a theory of the
'practical constitution' of the world; however, he treated the problem of the reality of other persons only in a way parallel to the
problem of the constitution of physical objects, and did not go
beyond the assumption that the other is inferred analogically on the
basis of the self's interior experience of itself. Thus the solution
offered by Dilthey surmounted Cartesianism only through its inclusion of 'life', not, however, through its inclusion of an intersubjectivity that would ground the reality and the constitution of others.

Since this deficiency is to be found also, and to an even greater
degree, in Husserl's thought, Dilthey was unable to solve this problem by drawing on Husserl, who became very important for Dilthey's later work. Although Dilthey was led to Husserl because the
latter's concept of 'meaning' *(Bedeutung)* seemed to provide a
safeguard against the relativist dangers of a purely psychological
foundation of the human sciences and to open the way to their
'hermeneutic' grounding, which Dilthey subsequently sketched out
with his theory of expression,[20] there was nevertheless an aporia
implicit in this progress. Despite a common interest in a theory of
the constitution of scientific knowledge, Husserl's approach was
radically different from pragmatism and also from the pragmatist
features of Dilthey's thought:

> on the one hand, there is an appeal to intuitive evidence, an
> eidetic theory of meaning, the seeing of essences [*Wesens-
> schau*], and a radical absence of presuppositions; on the other
> hand, there is an appeal to the ability to make or to do
> something, an operational theory of meaning, Construction-
> ism, and the recognition of the presuppositions in the language
> and situational context of the praxis of life.[21]

Since Husserl's concept of meaning did not stem from
linguistic theory or—taking a broader view—from a theory of
intersubjectivity, Dilthey was not able to attain, by means of this
concept, a theory that preserved the range of problems posed by the
question of the truth and validity of assertions, and that belonged as
well to the realm of social psychology.[22] And conversely, Husserl's
idealism and transcendentalism grew out of his belief that they
offered the only escape from the dissolution of all values in
historicism and naturalism.[23] Husserl's later transcendentalism
seems to me to be the other side of Dilthey's inability to solve the

problem of relativism. The concept of meaning, arrived at by way of the phenomenology of essences, blocked precisely those possibilities of elucidating the anthropological presuppositions of communicatively mediated human life-praxis that were implicit in Dilthey's theories.

What was thereby left undone was also not accomplished in subsequent attempts. The most important attempt to escape from the framework of transcendental philosophy and to find a point of departure other than the self-certainty of the experiencing ego was the ontological turn which Heidegger gave to phenomenology. Admittedly, his modification of phenomenology introduced into it intersubjectivity in the form of 'being-with' (*Mit-Sein*), praxis in the form of 'care' (*Sorge*), and the structure of the relation between the organism and its environment in the form of 'being-in-the-world' (*In-der-Welt-Sein*). But this was done at the price of the possibility of posing the question of the validity of the notions of the true and the good, and by means of the philosophically arrogant claim to provide a basis for the sciences, rather than giving an elucidation of what the sciences are and how they proceed. Existential hermeneutics enunciates in philosophical language insights that, according to their entire content and for their real implementation, require the integration of philosophy and the sciences. For Heidegger, surmounting Husserl's transcendentalism is synonymous with renunciation of the critical claims of subjectivity.[24] Although in Heidegger's ontological phenomenology the proximity of philosophy and empirical science achieved by Dilthey is lost, it is restored in the various attempts to devleop a Philosophical Anthropology. But these attempts, too, flounder on the problem under discussion.

Let us consider only the two most highly elaborated and most significant variants of Philosophical Anthropology, namely those developed by Arnold Gehlen and Helmuth Plessner. It can be shown that Gehlen's anthropology suffers generally from an inadequate notion of intersubjectivity and that the substantial deficiencies of his theory of language, conceptions of perception, ethics, and theory of institutions can be accounted for by the politically motivated rejection of democratic intersubjectivity.[25] Plessner's theory, on the other hand, correctly focuses on human expressivity as an area of essential importance and performs significant preparatory work for an anthropological founding of hermeneutics. He restrics hermeneutics, however, through the connection of his theory with the framework of transcendental phenomenology, inasmuch as he grounds intersubjectivity in the

fundamental organic structure of the human being, conceived of as
'excentric positionality' rather than arriving at an understanding of
human self-reflectivity—which is to be found, Plessner shows, even
in 'sensuousness' itself—from the structures of intersubjectivity.[26]
What was thereby not achieved in the German tradition is a theory
of the fundamental structure of human sociality that is based in a
thoroughgoing way on intersubjectivity and is not apriorist and
transcendentalist,[27] that is non-relativist, and draws upon and is
consistent with the findings of natural and social science. To such a
theory, I believe, Mead made a signficiant contribution.

Neither German sociology[28] nor historical materialism can
offer an alternative to Mead's contribution to a theory of human
sociality. It is impossible to discuss here Max Weber's critical
deficiencies with regard to the theory of action or the failure of
perhaps the only Marxist who reached the level of this complex of
problems, Georg Lukács.[29] As for the development of Mead's theory,
in my opinion it was made possible by the positive relationship of
the American pragmatists to the ethical implications of a categorical
notion of democracy and to the emancipatory prospects of progress
in technology and the natural sciences.[30] In Mead's and Dewey's
hands this notion of democracy did not become a formalist ideology
legitimating certain institutions and election procedures; nor was it
undermined by the insight that the democratic ideal is often used
for the purposes of such a legitimating ideology. For them, the ideal
of democracy is not replaced by an opposing notion of the
dictatorship of the proletariat, for which it is no longer possible to
conceive of criteria for assessing its inherently democratic character.
The conception of democracy as the only value that is self-
legitimated and as the path followed by historical progress allows
one to eliminate the fictions of transcendental philosophy, without
falling into a relativism of values or taking the position that it is
necessary to simply accept one's fate. The notion of the democratically structured community of experimentation and communication
as the quintessence of the scientific method makes it possible to
abandon the separation between a philosophy that conserves values
and an instrumentally curtailed science. The insight into the effects
on personality structure of the democratic organization of interpersonal relations makes it possible radically to conceive of the self as
socially constituted. It is my impression that access to Mead's
thought is best obtained through an understanding of his relationship to the 'categorical' notion of democracy.

These assertions can be developed further through examination of
Mead's own views on the history of philosophy and science. In doing

this I make use exclusively of his statements about philosophical and scientific developments since the Enlightenment, although a wide range of material on ancient, mediaeval, and early modern philosophy is also available, the last period being represented mainly by Galileo, Descartes and Leibniz.[31] Mead's frequent study of Aristotle appears to have been carried out chiefly for propaedeutic reasons; in Aristotle's writings he found a theory of nature that was free of assumptions considered self-evidently valid by modern thinkers, and that threw precisely these assumptions into clearer relief. Mead's attention was frequently directed to Galileo because he saw in the latter's theories and work some of the sources of the mechanistic view of the world and the subjectification of the question of the meaning of reality which is linked with that world view. Mead's project was to undo this subjectification of meaning. His posthumously published book on the intellectual history of the 19th century does not contain these parts of his work nor his original reconstruction of the controversy between rationalism and empiricism. In this reconstruction he criticized both schools of thought from the standpoint of 'experimentalism', finding fault with them for an insufficient mediation of the particular and the universal, and for a false generalization in each case of a certain phase of experience, of the acquisition of data in the case of empiricism, or of interpretation of data in the case of rationalism.[32] Mead's views on rationalism and empiricism also make it clear that, unlike James, he did not at all consider himself a defender of empiricism, but rather that for him the synthesis of these two philosophical theories by Kant and post-Kantian idealism was of decisive importance.

Although the published material presents, then, only part of Mead's interests and research, it nevertheless illustrates both of the methodological characteristics of his historiography of philosophy. These are, first, strong emphasis on the social-historical contexts to which philosophical and scientific thought is related, and second, constant consideration of the development of the empirical sciences. These are viewed in their connnection with the development of social production and as both an object and problem for global philosophical interpretations. The execution of this undertaking, or more exactly the record we have of it—since this consists entirely of students' lecture notes—is admittedly of quite varying quality. That is the reason why this material is used here only to aid in interpreting Mead's position in intellectual history, and not regarded as an area of Mead's research in its own right. In his history of 19th century philosophy, one finds historical mistakes, the assignment of Hegel to Romanticism, which in all likelihood stems from Royce, on whose book on modern philosophy Mead obviously drew,[33] and a superficial discussion of Marx, standing in contrast to thoroughgoing and inspired interpretations like those of Fichte and of Bergson and French philosophy of the 19th century.

In Mead's history of philosophy, Rousseau and Smith appear as the two most important thinkers of the latter part of the 18th century. Rousseau was the first philosopher to escape from the dilemma of having to choose between the unsatisfactory alternatives of pessimistic anthropology, with its tendency toward justifying the 'strong state' and optimistic anthropology with its tendency to naive confidence in the creation of general benefits from the action of numerous separate individuals. He accomplished this by thinking out to its conclusion the possibility of reasonable agreement among human beings. For Rousseau democracy was collective self-determination, the dissolution of dominance, rendered possible by individuals' mutual recognition of one another's rights and by universally binding laws. Again and again Mead has recourse to this rudimentary intersubjectivist notion of right implicit in Rousseau's concept of property. As for Adam Smith, in Mead's opinion he was the first thinker to work out the cooperative association of members of society as the real foundation for their making decisions in common. Despite his criticism of the individualist features of Smith's ideas and of the hedonist psychology to which they gave rise, Mead called the Scottish philosopher's oeuvre 'the source of social psychology'.[34] Mead's critical but openminded consideration of the British utilitarians continued this line of reflection.

Kant, however, whom he held to be the pivotal thinker who alone could make the philosophical problematic of the 19th century comprehensible, was treated by Mead in a manner not at all taken for granted by contemporary American intellectuals. He stressed the roots of Kant's thought in that of Rousseau and candidly bestowed on him the title 'the philosopher of the revolution'. Rousseau's insight into the possibility of rational institutions was transformed by Kant into the question of the conditions for the possibility of universally valid knowledge and the moral orientation of human individuals. Kant finds this universality in the conditions of all cognition, which are inherent in the cognizing subject prior to all experience, and in a pure postulate of free and responsible action, oriented in accordance with generally binding legislation and not directed by the individual's own inclination.

Mead shared unqualifiedly the universalist orientation of the question Kant posed, but he finds his predecessor's answer to the question unsatisfactory. If the conditions of objective knowledge are to be found in the knowing subject prior to all experience, then they stand outside all communality and precede all development of the human subject. If the basis for the possibility of responsible action cannot be found in reality, and if that possibility remains a pure postulate, then we are in danger of abandoning ourselves permanently to a self-deception. Mead opposed to Kant's transcendental subject the community of acting and communicating human beings. According to Mead's view, knowledge arises from the practical engagement of members of society with an environment that they must reshape, and from their communicative collaboration and exchange of opinions. Knowledge undergoes development in the process of reaching agreement carried out by those collaboratively striving after knowledge, in the process of the individual's education and experience, and in the formation of the foundations of knowledge in the human subjects in the course of natural history. Should it not also be possible to divest the possibility of free action of its character of a mere postulate by abandoning as one's point of departure the solitary subject, considered in isolation from all human community and in abstraction from its interaction with a natural environment?

It is from this perspective that Mead regards the development of German idealism beyond Kant's philosophy by Fichte, Schelling and Hegel. Common to all three, according to Mead, is that they make the self an object of possible knowledge, of possible experience, and of genetic development. They thereby go beyond Descartes' self-experience, which merely gives evidence of the subject's own existence, and pose the problem of joining Kant's two notions of the self, the one linked with the structuring of the world in pure reason, the other with moral action in practical reason:

> What took place in the Romantic period along a philosophical line was to take this transcendental unity of apperception, which was for Kant a bare logical function, together with the postulation of the self which we could not possibly know but which Kant said we could not help assuming, and compose them into the new romantic self.[35]

Fichte, says Mead, does this by taking recourse to moral action and to the development of the self through the internalization of duties. Schelling, in contrast, shows through examination of aesthetic activity that the artist does not bring an idea to the material from without, but instead finds it in the material and in so doing

unfolds himself. Lastly, according to Mead, the theme of Hegel's philosophy is the reflective overcoming of contradictions in experience
and their final resolution in absolute knowledge. The interpretations of these three philosophers differ greatly in their fullness and
thoroughness. The best lecture, in my opinion, is the one on Fichte.[36]

Mead argues that Fichte's central concern is to demonstrate
analytically that the constitution of the world is founded in moral
praxis, and that the main problem for Fichte is the question of how
the world, which is independent of the self, can enter into immediate self-experience. From his discussion of Fichte it becomes clear
that Mead's conception of the situation in which action occurs can
in large measure be elucidated by the German philosopher's theories. Of critical significance, however, are two theses of Mead's
interpretation of Fichte, to which he attaches special importance.
The first is that Fichte shows that the formation of the self—to use a
contemporary phrase—is dependent on the objectifications of our
praxis, and cannot be achieved through mere introspection that
does not lead the subject's attention to the external world.

> One does not get at himself simply by turning upon himself the
> eye of introspection. One realizes himself in what he does, in
> the ends which he sets up, and in the means he takes to
> accomplish those ends. He gets the rational organization out of
> it, sees a relationship between means and ends, puts it all
> together as a plan; and then he realizes that the plan of action
> presented in this situation is an expression of his own reason,
> of himself. And it is not until one has such a field of action that
> he does secure himself. This process, according to Fichte, is
> what is continually taking place. The self throws up the world
> as a field within which action must take place; and, in setting
> up the world as a field of action, it realizes itself.[37]

The second thesis is that there is a dialectical relationship
between the delimitation of the self and its embeddedness. Fichte
develops this dialectic by demonstrating that the constitution of a
finite self is possible only within the framework of an overarching
unity which has the character of a self; he thereby arrives at his
notion of the absolute self. For Mead, this absolute self is analogous
to, or is an idealist anticipation of, his own concept of society.

> Now what the philosophical imagination of Fichte did was to
> go beyond this conception which united man with society, and
> to conceive of the man as an integral part of the universal Self,
> that Self which created the universe ... Now, what Fichte did

was to conceive of an Absolute Self which is just such an organization of all selves; an infinite Self which is the organization of all finite selves. Then, just as society sets its tasks in terms of the act of all its members, so this infinite and Absolute Self sets the task for itself in terms of all the functions of all the finite selves that go to make it up. The universe as such is, then, the creation of this Absolute Self in the same sense as cultivated areas and great metropolitan areas are created by the society that lives in them ... In this view we are all parts of God. We each have a finite part in an infinite creative power. Organized in the one Self we, together with an infinite number of other selves, create the universe. And for Fichte this creation is moral, for he conceives of the world as an obligation, as a task which the Absolute Self has to carry out, has to fulfil.[38]

In Mead's view, Fichte's limitation as an idealist could be seen in his attempt to interpret the evolution of the world as a phase of human moral experience; he failed at the task of conceiving of the evolutionary emergence of human beings from a pre-human age of the world's development.[39] However, his insight into the constructional character of the self, his conception of the moral problems confronting the self, which served as a paradigm for the theory of action, his thesis that self-reflectivity is related to action, the dialectic of individual and collective self contained in his notion of the absolute self, and the relationship of this dialectic to the collective transformation of the world—all of these features of Fichte's philosophy make him an important precursor of a concept of 'practical intersubjectivity', or of a philosophy of praxis that theoretically accounts for intersubjectivity.[40]

The philosophical dignity which Mead accords to the approaches to a theory of evolution in the 19th century, especially to that of Darwin, but the Lamarck's as well, is implied by his criticism of Fichte. The chapter on Schelling is disappointing, as Mead's interpretation of this philosopher focuses on the aesthetic aspect of his thought to the exclusion of all others, and does not develop the significance, for the problems addressed by Mead, of Schelling's attempt to found the concept of self-consciousness in a speculative philosophy of nature. The chapter on Hegel, too, is completely insufficient. The most striking thing about it is the contrast with the subtle understanding of Hegel to be found in Mead's early philosophical writings, to which we will turn our attention shortly. In *Movements of Thought* Hegel is presented as a speculative precursor of evolutionism, inasmuch as he tried to conceive of the categories as developing in the history of the individual human and of humanity. This interpretation of Hegel's thought could have very explosive implications, but appears in a quite clumsy form in this transcription of Mead's lectures. Considering the quality of this text, there would be no point in discussing it in detail. Nevertheless, leaving aside the question of the significance of Mead's presentation of Hegel, the arguments which are central to Mead's critique of Hegel are of interest.

Above all, Mead finds fault with Hegel for not having formulated adequate concepts of the individual and of the future. Hegel's philosophy is thus incapable of grasping individuality in its concreteness, which cannot be decomposed into the relationships dealt with by the philosophy of history. That is exactly the argument which Dilthey, too, benefiting from the empirical historical science of the 19th century, brings into play against the system-building of German idealism. But neither for Dilthey nor for Mead does this criticism of idealism give rise to a sort of existentialist protest. Rather, it led them to undertake investigation of the constitutive role of the individual's experiences and creative accomplishments for society, history and 'objective spirit'.

Mead saw a link between this deficiency in Hegel's philosophy and the latter's inadequate understanding of a history that is open to the future and that is still to be given shape. The American philosopher emphatically refused to accept the notion of absolute knowledge or of an end of history that had been reached, or even one that could only be definitely anticipated. This is an argument that has played an important role from the Left Hegelian critique of Hegel's philosophical system—especially that of Moses Hess— onward to the attempts to formulate a non-scientistic conception of historical materialism,[41] of which Merleau-Ponty's work is an example. However, Mead develops both arguments, not primarily by drawing them from political and social relationships, but rather from his conception of the procedure used by the experimental sciences:

> The grandiose undertaking of Absolute Idealism to bring the whole of reality within experience failed. It failed because it left the perspective of the finite ego hopelessly infected with subjectivity, and consequently unreal. From its point of view, the theoretical and practical life of the individual had no part in the creative advance of nature. It failed also because scientific method, with its achievements of discovery and invention,

could find no adequate statement in its dialectic. It recognized the two dominant forces of modern life, the creative individual and creative science, only to abrogate them as falsifications of the experience of the absolute ego. The task remained unfulfilled, the task of restoring to nature the characters and qualities which a metaphysics of mind and a science of matter and motion had concurred in relegating to consciousness, and of finding such a place for mind in nature that nature could appear in experience.[42]

Thus, in the philosophies of the three chief representatives of post-Kantian German idealism, the realization of the self by means of the non-self and the problem of the self-reflectivity of the actor were given central importance, while Schelling and Hegel, in addition, put the transcendental problematic of consciousness back into the world that is to be known. All this was done, however, by clinging ultimately to a process of consciousness conceived of in the manner of transcendental philosophy, and not by actually abandoning the use of the consciousness of the solitary subject as the final basis for their lines of argument.[43] As a consequence of this approach, it became impossible for these philosophers to answer certain central questions. The question of how individual perspectives could be combined into a common one was supplanted by the fiction of a divinely absolute self that occupied completely the place in these philosophers' systems that otherwise would have been given over to the decision-making of communities. The question of the historical conditions of cognition which are independent of cognition was not posed, since history and even natural history had now to be interpreted using the categories of aesthetic creation or reflection, or the categories applicable to matters of obligation. The question of the openness and plasticity of the future was eliminated, since now absolute knowledge and the supposition of an end of history would clear away uncertainty and empirical science would become a subordinate component of knowledge.

In order to overcome these aporiae Mead does not turn for help to the Left Hegelians, who seem to have been completely unknown to him, and hence also not to Marx. The presentation of the latter's thought, which obviously has only a narrow textual basis, in particular the *Communist Manifesto*, is a delineation of the Kautskyian 'Marxism' of the period of the Second International, rather than of the analyses and theories of Marx himself. Mead's emphasis on Marx's promixity to Hegel signifies that he imputes to both of them a quasi-religious philosophy of history that is deterministic in its certainty of history's goal, and a repressive tendency to subordinate the individual to the claims of the collective body. What Mead opposes to these positions can be described approximately as an anti-bureaucratic and impassioned argument for the possibility of self-determination by the producers in a society, and is indeed much closer to authentic Marxism than Mead knew. This is certainly due to the state of knowledge of Marx's works at that time: aside from Lukács's brilliant anticipation, in *History and Class Consciousness*, of a new view on Marx, Marx's philosophical relevance became apparent only with the publication of Marx's principal early writings towards the end of the twenties. Be that as it may, Mead had complete sympathy with the universalist features of a class-conscious movement of the international proletariat as a class.[44] He held Marxism to be one of the fundamental elements of truly modern thought, along with German and British neo-Hegelianism, that of T. H. Green, for example, or of F. H. Bradley, with its stress on the individual, and along with the scientific turn given to the questions of mind in physiological psychology.[45]

For Mead, though, the key figure for a new beginning in philosophy was Darwin. Darwin's model of an organism in an environment, to which it must adapt in order to survive, provides the means for founding all knowledge in behaviour and all behaviour in the necessary conditions set by nature on the organism's reproduction of itself and its kind, in contrast to the attempt to deduce the subject's behaviour and the external world from a self that is preordinate to them. Darwin's theory about the origin of species offered an escape from the dilemma of the alternative mechanistic and teleological explanations of evolution, since his theory emphasizes, anti-mechanistically, the possibility of qualitatively new forms of organisms, without having to take recourse to an immutable teleological principle that precedes and governs all history.

For Mead, and for pragmatism in its entirety, Darwin's theory was not at all decisive proof of a deterministic view of evolution and adaptation, in the manner either of a psychology of instincts or of Social Darwinism. Instead, the pragmatists undertook to conceive of the basic structure of animals' adaptive accomplishments as a primitive analogue to the intelligent behaviour of human beings and to the procedure of the experimental sciences, and to take care in doing so that they did not efface the differences between them. In the pragmatists' opinion, these differences lay in the structure of human material reproduction, which is based on a system of impulses different from that of other kinds of organism, and which becomes, by means of the active reshaping of the environment, the self-reflective control of the principles of organic evolution and liberation from their dominion.

In the synthesis that Mead sought to achieve there can be seen the outlines of a theory of society which takes into account both the natural basis of human sociality as well as the concrete forms that human societies have historically taken and the role of the unique individual. In Mead's later writings, all of these various efforts fall under the hegemony of his concern not to allow stress on the particular individual to result in the elimination of objectivity and universality, but rather to arrive at an understanding of it as the true precondition of the latter. In Mead's thought this enterprise primarily assumed the forms of a philosophy of nature and of a theory of science. It was because of their relevance to this undertaking that Whitehead's work and the discussion of the theory of relativity became important for Mead. He formulated this task in the following words:

> Stating it in as broad a form as I can, this is the philosophical problem that faces the community at the present time: how are we to get the universality involved, the general statement which must go with any interpretation of the world, and still make use of the differences which belong to the individual as an individual?[46]

Mead's early philosophical writings, that is the texts prior to 'The Definition of the Psychical', published in 1903, have a strongly programmatic character and are linked to their quite accidental provenance: most of them are book reviews. The single exception is perhaps 'Suggestions Toward a Theory of the Philosophical Disciplines', which appeared in 1900. Thus, they are chiefly useful here because they reveal the circumstances in which Mead's later ideas had their origin. In addition, in my examination of Mead's intellectual development, they also serve to document my thesis that Mead went through a Hegelian phase before he founded his intersubjectivist pragmatism.

When I say that Mead went through a Hegelian phase, I do not mean that he specialized in philosophical studies about Hegel, or that he elaborated a position with regard to Hegel's work which was carefully considered in all its details. Rather, my statement repeats a self-characterization by Mead, the meaning of which must be correctly understood if we are to appreciate its significance. The claim that Hegel was important for Mead of course appears incredible and absurd to those who are accustomed to regard Mead as a social behaviourist.[47] But for Mead's students this was by no means the case; Sidney Hook, for example, in a review of *Movements of Thought,* bluntly stated that Mead was 'out of the school of Hegel'.[48] Mead's retrospective remarks on Royce and Dewey show how strongly the liberation from the dualism of subject and object, of matter and mind, of the divine and the human, which Hegel offered, and which Royce and Dewey had stressed, had also influenced him.[49] The form taken by this influence is shown by Mead's early writings.

Admittedly, the first two do not contribute much in this respect. They are short articles on the attempt by Kurt Lasswitz, a German neo-Kantian theoretician of the natural sciences and historian of natural philosophy, to draw the epistemological implications from the theory of energy proposed by the physics of the latter half of the 19th century.[50] The first of Mead's articles is more of a summary of Lasswitz's book; the second develops its psychological implications. From these articles it becomes clear why Mead was interested in Lasswitz's undertaking. According to Lasswitz, the theory of energy put forward by contemporary physics advanced beyond the model of the earlier physics, for which mechanics was the ultimate basis of explanation, and thus presented a 'critical theory of experience'—the expression is Lasswitz's—with new opportunities and new problems. Lasswitz is referring to the question of the constitution of science in immediate experience, and the question of the relationship between qualitative sensory experience and the quantifying treatment of this experience by physics.

In his articles on this book, Mead does not develop positions of his own, but he does announce themes and points of view that run through his own work. One example is the question of an adequate understanding of the unifying function of the self, the question of a psychological reformulation of Kant's transcendental unity of apperception. Other examples are the attempt to define, for the first time, the concept of the object in categories of action, and to this end to investigate the coordination of the contact senses and those which perceive objects at a distance, and Mead's insistence that qualities are not merely subjective in character, in contrast to the ostensibly objective character of quantities. However, perhaps most important is the passage in which Mead clearly states that the absurdity of a psychology modelled on physics can be demonstrated with the aid of a theory of the constitution of science.

> In a word, the physicist has abstracted the entire mathematically statable content of the sensation—and only this; and for the psychophysicist to strive to use that which is left for the

same purpose is to make it evident that he does not comprehend the relations of the two fields. We trust with Herr Lasswitz that the substition of energy for mass in the physicist's
statement will carry home the nature of the scientist's abstraction.[51]

Thus reductionist psychology and natural sciences that have for-
gotten how they are constituted are considered as two sides of a
single development, the development that Husserl would later call
the 'crisis of the European sciences'. Mead's articles on Lasswitz
show how inconceivable it would be to classify him as the pro-
ponent of a reductionist psychology.[52]

    The next article by Mead is a discussion of a book by the
German neo-idealist Gustav Class that appeared in 1896, entitled
*Toward a Phenomenology and Ontology of the Human Mind (Unter-
suchungen zur Phänomenologie und Ontologie des menschlichen
Geistes)*. Class programmatically undertook to achieve a synthesis
of Hegel's notion of the 'objective spirit' and Schleiermacher's concept of 'personal individuality' *(persönliche Eigentümlichkeit)*.
Hegel's 'objective spirit' represents recognition of the dependence of
the mental life of human individuals on cultural formations, on the
objectifications of their activity. Schleiermacher's concept, however,
demands that the human individual be understood not only as an
example of the species, but rather that 'every man shall present
humanity in his own peculiar manner'.[53] Schleiermacher's concept
thus contains a claim to the right of individuation that was far in
advance of his time, and that, in Mead's view, had to be matched by
a theory of the social formation of the self. The conceptual means for
elaborating this theory, wrote Mead, have been provided by Hegel,
whose 'method' could be fully restated and applied to the entire content of life only upon the basis of the revelation of processes of
development that had been made by the modern physical, biological, and social sciences. Only when every substance-centred
metaphysics had been rejected, and one has attained the notion of
'organic activity', is it possible to form a conception of how 'the
individual can be completely individualized and yet present simply
the whole'.[54]

    It is very characteristic of Mead that he links here the specu-
lative notion of life, which underlies Hegel's statements, with the
biological concept of life. In his review of Class's book, Mead places
the problem of a social conception of the self, formulated in philosophical terms, in the context of the religious and political problematic of his era. He regards the notion of the soul, or personality, as an

unchanging substantial entity to be a serious obstacle to solving this problem, since this notion is drawn from the assumption of an exclusive relationship of the individual to the Deity, beyond the individual's fellow human beings and his natural environment.

> To such an individual all the social relationships here can be only of a purely superficial character except in so far as they react upon a nature [i.e. the God-given nature of the individual, (H. J.)] that is independent of them. It would be impossible to regard such a nature as the expression of the social relationships within which it finds itself. There would be no meaning in arousing a consciousness of these relations as the essence of the self. The most that could take place would be a judgement from without as to our duty with reference to them. But if I am not mistaken the tendency not only of our social sciences but also of the forces of society itself is to substitute in the individual a vivid immediate consciousness of himself as a nodal point in the operation of these social forces, for the conception of an individual who stands outside of the processes and enters in or strays out as his conscience dictates or his desires demand.[55]

As a political example of the point he is arguing in the passage quoted, Mead gives the right of the workers to form labour unions, a hotly debated topic in the USA in that period. He sees no merit in the objection that unions destroy the worker's independence; rather, he regards them as a means to a new and more profound individuality. The development of the individual personality is only possible through extension and intensification of social relations; 'personality is an *achievement* rather than a given fact'.[56] Mead criticizes Class for merely postulating individualities and the formation of the self and not being able to ground them scientifically. Class's inability to do so, says Mead, making an implicit reference to his own philosophical programme, lies in the fact that he incorrectly distinguished between a realm of mere facts (*das Tatsächliche*) and a realm of the spiritual, or that which expressed the meaning of the world (*das Sachliche*). To be sure, Class conceives of the spiritual itself as pragmatic, that is in its function as the universalization of the particular, but he forcibly separates this universalization from all that is material or belongs to nature. This means that there is a gaping chasm between material civilization and the cultural conditions of individuation, as though the two had nothing in common, instead of individuation being firmly attached to and having its roots in the social structure of human beings' material reproduction. From his discussion of Class's book it becomes clear that Mead hoped that non-reductionist psychology, based on physiology, would provide just this theoretical mooring for his conception of the formation of the self.

The programmatic joining of Hegel's thought with that of Schleiermacher, which is suggestive of Dilthey's philosophical enterprise, anticipates in some respects Mead's theory of the social formation of the self. However, Mead's detailed discussion of the interpretation and critique of Hegel given by the British theologian Charles F. D'Arcy in his book, *Idealism and Theology,* provides a still deeper insight into the roots of Mead's social psychology. D'Arcy's book is a strange attempt to combine the philosophies of Hegel and Berkeley: he conceives of a Hegelian subject-object-world that is itself held together in a higher subjectivity; as this subjectivity he posits the triune God who can be reached through an act of faith. This book appears to have been not only a provocation to Mead's secularized Hegelianism, but also to have raised the question of the point in Hegel's philosophy, or in the interpretation of that philosophy, which would provide the starting point for D'Arcy's theory. At first it seems that D'Arcy's concerns are identical with those of British neo-Hegelians, inasmuch as these, too, were always talking about the irreducibility of the individual. Mead, however, quickly shows that, in the case of D'Arcy's, this irreducibility of the individual is limited to the postulation of the individual personality as the source of the contingent, the arbitrary, the bad. To Mead's way of thinking though, this is not enough to keep the concept of personality from being an Hegelian abstraction. Underlying D'Arcy's notion of the individual personality is, says Mead, more the 18th century's individualist concept of the person, which isolated the individual from society, than Hegel's. And if D'Arcy's book has not even reached the conceptual level of Hegel's thought, then it can hardly go beyond it. The question is, rather, how that which is individual can be 'saved' by demonstrating its positive functions, its necessity for the community.

> The problem, then, comes to this: Is it possible to express the positive element in personality in terms of rationality, law, and goodness? I think the author is right in identifying the problem with the question of chasm between individuals. The freedom of the will is not a problem of the spiritual economy of an isolated individual, it is the problem of fixing responsibility within a community of individuals who isolate themselves in

certain phases of their conduct. It is a social, not an individual, problem...It is the working together of individuals, the mutual dependence which is involved in the social ends and means, that presents the something which always resists the complete necessary formulation of our world. Finally, the problem of evil is not one of its existence or its reality, but of its social significance, and the possibility and duty of overcoming it. If the self is in its reflective processes isolated, there is no solution of these problems possible. No such individual can fix responsibility upon another or accept it when fixed by another. If the means and ends are not identical, there can be no community in meeting the problems of social existence. If the suffering of another is not a reality in my own world and is not identified with myself, there is no possibility of giving to the instinctive reaction against it the large social meaning and value which we feel it should have. The chasms between individuals in a social consciousness represent, not insoluble epistemological problems, but points at which reorganization needs to take place.[57]

In what respects then does D'Arcy fail to understand Hegel? First, by maintaining that individuality manifests itself in an impassable chasm and irreducible alienness between individuals. D'Arcy tries to admit the possibility of objective knowledge of nature, but to deny that knowledge of other persons, and hence the social sciences, can be rational to the same degree. Mead argues against any possibility of making this distinction, since the claim that there can be objectively valid knowledge originally has nothing at all to do with the kind of object which is to be known. A more serious objection, though, is that D'Arcy's thesis flagrantly contradicts our immediate experience, in which other persons are more certain than physical things are.

There is nothing more immediate than the personalities of our fellows. There is nothing so clearly conceived, so distinctly thought out, as those elements of our world. We depend as surely upon the rational organization of the social world as upon that of the material, and there is the same source for this rational organization as subsists for the world of the physical sciences.[58]

Mead's insistence on a unitary and uncurtailed notion of rationality, his acknowledgement of a chasm between individuals as a social fact and as a practical task, and his refusal to accept this chasm as humanity's ineluctable metaphysical fate—these all show

how well pondered the foundations of his social psychology are. However, the manner of his critique of the English theologian's work makes it clear that he is still far from carrying out the project of a theory of the social formation of the self and from demonstrating the primacy of the constitution of social objects over that of physical objects.

For Mead, the way to the realization of this programme seems to be offered by the Hegelian 'method', and his second principal criticism of D'Arcy is that the latter has completely failed to comprehend the character of this method. D'Arcy understands Hegel's philosophy as a metaphysical system that substitutes the category of the subject for that of substance. What D'Arcy does not grasp is that this transformation precludes a metaphysics of fundamental entities and makes philosophy a method of thought. Mead shows his understanding of Hegel's procedure in his interpretation of the situation in which a moral decision is made and that in which a new thought is developed. In both cases the problem is solved by a synthesis, which the individual must constructively and creatively effect, and which philosophy must reconstructively match in an analogous act. Entities are formulations of certain stages of this process; they must not be considered separately from the process of reflection that constitutes them. To Mead, Hegel's dialectical method was a discovery, the significance of which Hegel himself did not fully understand, and one which reveals that the procedure of the experimental sciences, correctly understood, is the fundamental structure of human reflection in its highest form. For Mead, therefore, the pragmatist interpretation of the situation of action and Hegel's dialectic of reflection converge. Philosophy, then, is

> not a formulation of entities ... not in search of being, but is a statement of the method by which the self in its full cognitive and social content meets and solves its difficulties.[59]

The most ambitious and most systematic of Mead's early writings is his attempt to establish a classification of the philosophical disciplines, published in 1900. In this article Mead undertakes nothing less than laying the groundwork for a new logic in the sense in which Hegel used this term, that is, a theory encompassing all of the fundamental determinations of thought. Going beyond Hegel, Mead projects this new logic as a general theory of intelligent action. He bases his undertaking on Dewey's essay about the reflex-arc concept, in which the latter construes all thought as an attempt to solve problems in immediate experience, and more specifically in situations of action. It would be inappropriate to discuss this thesis here in detail, since Mead does not defend it, but only presupposes it in this text. The comprehensive 'logic' is, then, the theory of the reconstruction of objects, the validity of which has been made uncertain, and Mead seeks to assign to each of the philosophical disciplines its own particular origin in the action-situation. Metaphysics is not rejected as meaningless, in the manner of positivism, but instead has the role of the keeper of problems which cannot be solved at the present time.

> Metaphysics I wish to identify with the statement of the problem. It may take psychological form or not. If the result of the recognition of the problem is only to bring to consciousness the meaning of the object in terms of past experience, we get the universal—the ideal—and the use of the object thus defined can be systematized in a manner which is described in deductive logic. If, on the contrary, we abandon the old universals—the interpretations involved in the objects as we have constructed them—and frankly look forward to a new meaning, the immediate experience can claim only subjective validity, and we have the subject matter with which psychology deals. The use of this material to reach the new universal is evidently the procedure of inductive logic. The application of either of these methods to conduct as a whole, in their relation to the ideal or to the larger self to be attained, fulfils the function of ethics, while aesthetics deals with the artistic representations of the object either as ideal or as a phase in the process of development. Finally, the general theory of the intelligent act as a whole would fall within that of logic as treated in works such as that of Hegel.[60]

What this formulation contains in condensed form is developed in the course of the article. Mead's interpretation of deduction and induction from the perspective of the theory of action—reminiscent of Piaget's interpretation of deduction as a correlate of accommodation and of induction as correlative of assimilation[61]—or his interpretation of aesthetics as the field of activity in which unresolvable contradictions or unattained goals are expressed in given objects—these must be particularly stressed as original and as indicating fruitful lines of reflection. However, one can sense that, in addition to the principle of his general theory of intelligent action, Mead is primarily concerned in this article with one phase of the act and with one of the philosophical disciplines: with the psychical and with psychology, which he still understands as a philosophical discipline here. These he treats at remarkable length. By the psychical Mead means that phase of the act in which hypotheses are formed, in which the old validities of objects have become uncertain and new ones have not yet established themselves; in which a free play of subjectivity is necessary for the origination of new hypotheses. What Peirce discussed as 'abduction' in his logic of scientific research and placed alongside deduction and induction, becomes the 'psychical' in Mead's refounding of pragmatism as a theory based on the biological and social sciences. Mead does not draw here upon Peirce, though, but only Dewey's psychology, and, with respect to the logic of scientific research, also on Whewell, whom Peirce, too, held in high esteem.[62]

In opposition to a simplifying interpretation of the psychical as merely intensified attentiveness, Mead stresses that the critical characteristic of this phase of the act consists in the fact that here attention is not directed to objects whose validity is recognized, but instead to the generating of such validity. From this sketchily presented notion of the psychical Mead develops a critique of the received form of the elementarist and associationalist pscyhology, derived from empiricism. This critique leads him to a train of thought, already implicit in the articles on Lasswitz, and its conclusion that a physicalist reduction of human perception does not solve the real problem of comprehending the givenness of the world for perceiving subjects, but rather bars the way to its solution.

> Parallelism is pure epistemology, and does not get within the realm of the psychical. The distinction between the immediate content of the world of perception, and the physical theory of these perceptions, does not touch that distinction which lies between the world of unquestioned validity, and the state of consciousness which supervenes when it has lost that validity and there is nothing left but the subjectivity out of which a new world may arise.[63]

Psychology is thus divided into two fields, each with a different task: into the theory of the constitution of experience, which Mead understands in the sense of the analyses undertaken by Kant and continued by Hegel in his *Phenomenology of Mind*; and into the analysis of the psychical situation which is prototypically represented by William James's examination of the stream of consciousness.

The significance of Mead's internally consistent attempt to elaborate a pragmatist classification of the philosophical disciplines has to date remained completely unrecognized, especially as it contrasts with Peirce's efforts late in his philosophical career to establish a hierarchy of the philosophical disciplines, and with the danger that these efforts might require for their basis a 'phenomenology' that Peirce's initial premises make wholly impossible. It appears that Mead did not pursue this project further in this form. His interest turned to the notion of the psychical and to the grounding of psychology in a comprehensive theory of action. What he developed in a rudimentary fashion in 'Suggestions Toward a Theory of the Philosophical Disciplines' in 1900, Mead soon dealt with again more thoroughly and comprehensively in 'The Definition of the Psychical'. With this paper Mead's mature work begins.

Part 2
Functionalism and
Social Behaviorism

The Development of G. H. Mead's Social Psychology

Gary A. Cook

The least neglected facet of George Herbert Mead's much neglected contribution to American thought has clearly been his social psychology. Yet even here, as Anselm Strauss noted some years ago,[1] interest has generally been restricted to certain portions of the posthumously published *Mind, Self and Society*. This volume, which is based primarily upon a stenographic copy of Mead's 1927 course in social psychology at the University of Chicago, provides a readable account of the conclusions at which Mead had arrived in this field near the end of his career. But there is little in it that would help the reader to trace the roots of Mead's social psychological work in the functionalism of the early Chicago School or to locate this work in the larger framework of his thought as a whole. For a fuller appreciation of Mead's contributions to the study of man as a social being we must look beyond *Mind, Self and Society* to selected portions of his other writings, particularly—as I hope to show in the present essay—to the best of those periodical articles written during the first half of his career at Chicago.

A careful examination of selected essays published by Mead during the period from 1900 to 1913 tends to confirm an observation made by John Dewey in his prefatory remarks for the 1932 publication of Mead's *The Philosophy of the Present:*

> When I first came to know Mr. Mead, well over forty years ago, the dominant problem in his mind concerned the nature of consciousness as personal and private. . . . I fancy that if one had a sufficiently consecutive knowledge of Mr. Mead's intellectual biography during the intervening years, one could discover how practically all his inquiries and problems developed out of his original haunting question.[2]

Mead's sustained struggle with this "original haunting question," I shall suggest, led him to a growing emphasis upon the social dimensions of human conduct. And his consequent analysis of sociality as a dominant feature of conduct greatly enriched the organic model of action initially set forth by Dewey, thus providing the conceptual framework in terms of which Mead's mature social psychology was to develop.

I. MEAD'S EARLY FUNCTIONALISM

As Darnell Rucker has recently pointed out in his admirable study, *The Chicago Pragmatists,* it was Dewey and Mead who were primarily responsible for the creation of that functionalist approach to psychology which was to constitute the basis for much that was distinctive in the philosophy of the so-called Chicago School.[3] At the heart of their funcationalism was a new organic concept of action, a concept whose most celebrated articulation is to be found in Dewey's 1896 essay "The Reflex Arc Concept in Psychology."[4] Since Mead's earliest published attempts to deal with the nature of human consciousness "as personal and private" involve extensive references to Dewey's essay it will be worthwhile to begin here by summarizing briefly some of its central points.

In this essay Mead's more famous colleague strongly criticized the stimulus-response model of action (the "reflext arc concept") as being based upon a serious conceptual confusion. The advocates of this model had failed to see that "stimulus and response are not distinctions of existence, but teleological distinctions, that is, distinctions of function, or part played, with reference to reaching or maintaining an end."[5] Dewey argued persuasively that stimulus and response were to be understood as functional moments within an ongoing process of coordination, a process which "is more truly termed organic than reflex, because the motor response determines the stimulus just as truly as sensory stimulus determines movement."[6] Dewey's analysis of the kind of mutual adjustment involved in concrete action is well illustrated by the example of a child reaching for a flickering candle: In this reaching the act of vision must not only stimulate but continue to control the movement of the child's arm. "The eye must be kept upon the candle if the arm is to do its work; let it wander and the arm takes up another task."[7] The movement of the arm must in turn control the act of seeing; if it does not, the eye will wander and the reaching will be without guidance. What most requires emphasis here is that the coordinated acts of seeing and reaching continually exchange functional roles within the complex act of which they are phases. What is at one moment a guided response may at the next moment become a guiding stimulus. Furthermore, not only does the stimulus guide the response, but the response shapes the quality of what is experienced. As Dewey put it, the response is not simply *to* the stimulus; it is *into* it. The response does not merely replace the sensory content of the stimulus with another sort of experience; rather it mediates, transforms, enlarges, or interprets that initial content in terms of its significance for ongoing conduct. When a child responds to the act of seeing a flickering candle the mere seeing is transformed into (say) a seeing-of-a-light-that-means-pain-when-contact-occurs.[8]

Now as long as such conduct proceeds smoothly, Dewey contended, it involves no conscious distinction of stimulus and response. But suppose that the child of our example is torn between a tendency to grasp the candle and a tendency to avoid it as a possible source of pain. In this type of situation doubt as to the proper completion of the act gives rise to an analysis whose purpose is to resolve the inihibiting conflict.

> [T]he initiated activities of reaching,... inhibited by the conflict in the co-ordination, turn round, as it were, upon the seeing, and hold it from passing over into further act until its quality is determined. Just here the act as objective stimulus becomes transformed into sensation as possible, as conscious, stimulus. Just here also, motion as conscious response emerges.[9]

Thus we see that the reflective isolation of stimulus and response as components of action has a particular genesis and function. It is the failure to take note of this genesis and function, Dewey held, which lies behind the mechanical conjunction of stimulus and response characterisic of the reflex arc model of action.[10]

Dewey concluded this now classical statement of functionalism with the observation that the real significance of the organic conception of action would be seen only in its application to fundamental problems of psychology and philosophy. And it was just such application that Mead undertook in two essays published in 1900 and 1903.[11] The first of these essays, "Suggestions Toward a Theory of the Philosophical Disciplines," was an ambitious neo-Hegelian attempt to characterize the respective provinces of metaphysics, psychology, deductive and inductive logics, ethics, aesthetics, and the general theory of logic in terms of the "dialectic within the act" as organically understood. The second essay, entitled "The

Definition of the Psychical," is less ambitious in scope although unfortunately more obscure in development; here Mead narrowed his focus to the discipline of psychology, seeking to delineate more fully its distinctive subject matter as a phase of "psychical consciousness" or "subjectivity" within conduct. It is the considerable space both essays devote to this latter topic which makes them important for our present purpose.

In "Suggestions Toward a Theory of the Philosophical Disciplines," Mead presented his discussion of subjectivity as an extension of Dewey's remarks concerning the genesis and function of our awareness of sensation as a distinct element in experience:

> Professor Dewey maintains in his discussion of the Reflex Arc that the sensation appears always in consciousness as a problem; that attention could not be centered upon a so-called element of consciousness unless the individual were abstracting from the former meaning of the object, and in his effort to reach a new meaning had fixed this feature of the former object as a problem to be solved (SW 6).

Holding with Dewey and William James that the content or meaning of the objects we experience is derived from their roles in our conduct, Mead pointed out that so long as action with respect to objects proceeds without a hitch their meanings typically remain unquestioned. But when an object tends to call out conflicting reactions, its content is to that extent ambiguous and in need of examination. In situations of this sort "our conscious activity finds itself unable to pass into an objective world on account of the clash between different tendencies to action" and "we are thrown back upon an analysis of these spontaneous acts and therefore upon the objects which get their content from them" (SW 8). Our experience takes a subjective turn, Mead suggested, when such conflict or ambiguity cannot be adequately resolved by a simple reshuffling of already existent meanings. For in these cases the conscious solution of our problem requires an abandonment of old universals and a quest for new meanings or objects to which we can more successfully relate. During the period when this quest is underway, our attention must turn from the temporarily impoverished world of objects to the flux of immediate and personal consciousness. Subjectivity thus enters conduct as "a position midway between the old universals, whose validity is abandoned, and the new universal, which has not yet appeared" (SW 12).

Subjective or psychical consciousness takes as its starting point whatever unproblematic meanings can be abstracted from the conflicting elements of the problem to be solved. For instance, the child who hesitates when faced by the flickering candle has before him "Neither the object which burned nor yet the plaything," for both of these meanings are in question. But he does have "something behind each and true of each—a bright moving object we will say" (SW 13). This latter meaning is objective (i.e. it is part of the world of unproblematic objects) but not sufficient by itself to give direction to the conduct which has been inhibited. The task of subjectivity or the psychical phase of experience is to take conduct beyond this stage of abstraction to a stage of synthesis in which the abstracted meanings find their places in a reconstructed world of objects. This is accomplished by giving free play to conflicting tendencies to respond, tendencies which must for the time being be regarded merely as elements peculiar to the immediate consciousness of the individual attempting to solve the problem at hand. It is this "constructive power proportional to the freedom with which the forces abstracted from their customary objects can be combined with each other into a new whole... that comes nearer answering to what we term genius than anything else" (SW 20). The problem is solved to the extent that these tendencies find a harmonious expression in terms of new objective meanings. When a solution is found the subjective phase of conduct has done its work and attention is once again focused on a realm of unproblematic objects.

Mead thus proposed that we construe the distinction between subjective and objective elements of experience as a functional, rather than a metaphysical, one. The marks of the subjective or psychical state are to be understood in terms of "their position in the act, the when and the how of their appearance" rather than as characteristics of some entity that exists independently of conduct (SW 16). Failure to appreciate the functional nature of subjectivity, Mead maintained, has characteristically led either to an untenable psycho-physical parallelism or to a kind of idealism in which all experience is reduced to states of individual consciousness. In either case, the mistake lies in the attempt to "objectify the psychical state, and deprive it of the very elements that have rendered it psychical" (SW 16).

Mead continued his attack on traditional conceptions of subjectivity and also further articulated his own view in "The Definition of the Psychical." In the constructive portion of this essay which must concern us here, he again took as his point of departure a suggestion attributable to Dewey: that when an object loses its validity because of a conflict in our activity, it also loses its form and organization. According to this view, the meanings abandoned in such cases are not simply transferred intact to the subjective realm. Rather the psychical character of the situation is due precisely to the fact that the problematic objects have disintegrated and the whole effort of the individual is toward a reconstruction of them (SW 40-42). In what form then, Mead asked, do the meanings or objects which have become problematic enter into psychical consciousness? He found the clue to his answer in the same source which had provided Dewey with much of his inspiration, William James's *Principles of Psychology*. No better description of psychical consciousness can be found, Mead suggeted, than that supplied by James in his famous chapter on "The Stream of Consciousness." For all the characteristics James attributes to the stream of consciousness are unmistakably present in the psychical phase of problemsolving.

> The kaleidoscopic flash of suggestion, and intrusion of the inapt, the unceasing flow of odds and ends of possible objects that will not fit, together with the continuous collision with the hard, unshakable objective conditions of the problem, the transitive feelings of effort and anticipation when we feel that we are on the right track and substantive points of rest, as the idea becomes definite, the welcoming and rejecting, especially the identification of the meaning of the whole idea with the different steps in its coming to consciousness—there are none of these that are not almost oppressively present on the surface of consciousness during just the periods which Dewey describes as those of disintegration and reconstitution of the stimulus—the object (SW 42-43).

Psychical consciousness as here described is clearly concerned with the immediate, with that which is peculiar to the individual and a moment of his existence. And it is just these characteristics, Mead maintained, that enable it to perform its functional role in the reconstruction of conduct (SW 36). For the task of subjective consciousness, as we have seen, is to introduce novelty into a situation in which the old has broken down, and this can be accomplished only by a consciousness which is not essentially tied to the world of accepted meanings and objects. Inspection of the old world can supply us with data, with conditions for the solution of the problem that has arisen, but it cannot be expected to supply us with the new meanings required for the reconstruction of that world. New meanings must arise from the reflecting individual's immediate awareness of his own activities and shifting attention as he seeks to harmonize the habitual tendencies which have come into conflict within his own conduct (SW 52, 45). It is here "in the construction of the hypotheses of the new world, that the individual qua individual has his functional expression or rather is that function" (SW 52).

II. INTRODUCTION OF THE TERMS "I" AND "ME"

Mead thus argued in "The Definition of the Psychical" not only for the functional importance of personal and private consciousness as the locus of cognitive reconstruction; he went beyond this to suggest that the human individual qua individual could be defined in terms of this reconstructive function. But herein lies a problem that Mead himself was quick to see. The human individual or self as ordinarily construed is an object, and as such it belongs to the world which it is the task of subjectivity to reconstruct. To the extent that the self as object is not infected with the problem at hand it may, of course, enter into the statement of the conditions to be met by any possible solution of that problem, but it cannot be expected to provide that solution (SW 53). How then can it be said that the task of reconstruction is performed by the human individual?

It was in his attempt to deal with this problem that Mead first employed the terms "I" and "me" to refer to the self functioning as subject and the self functioning as object, respectively. These terms had been given popular currency by William James in the chapter of his *Principles of Psychology* which dealt with "The Self," and now Mead borrowed them for his own purposes. In speaking of an "I" and a "me" Mead sought to make the point that, according to the functionalist view, the human individual or self may enter into conduct in two distinguishable senses. On the one hand, the self may enter into conduct as a meaningful stimulus for the intelligent control of action. In this case the self functions as an object; this is what Mead had in mind when he spoke of the "me." The "me" is thus a *presentation* that performs a mediating role within an ongoing process of experience or action (SW 53-54). On the other hand, as Mead's discussion of subjectivity makes clear, the human individual may also enter into conduct as an agent of reconstruction. Here the immediate and direct experience of the individual qua individual functions as a source from which spring suggestions for new ways of ordering the process of conduct when habitual actions and meanings have become problematic. The self functioning in this latter sense is what Mead meant by the "I"; it is "the self in the disintegration and reconstruction of its universe, the self functioning, the point of immediacy that must exist within a mediate process" (SW 53-54).

This distinction does not, however, appear to provide a wholly adequate solution to the problem which was its occasion. For if the objective status of the "me" renders it an unacceptabale candidate for the functional role of reconstructor, then a similar reservation must apply to the qualifications of the "human individual" with whom Mead wished to link psychical consciousness. More generally, it would seem that any attempt to identify psychical consciousness as belonging to a finite self must inevitably tie that consciousness to an item in the world of experienced objects. Thus Mead's introduction of the term "I" in this context appears to be either a misleading use of the personal pronoun to refer to immediately felt action (as opposed to objects which may arise within it), or a device for bringing in through the back door an implicit reference to the same object self he has thrown out through the front. The former interpretation seems most consistent with Mead's descriptions of subjectivity and with his reference to the subject self as "the act that makes use of all the data that reflection can present, but uses them merely as the conditions of a new world that cannot possibly be foretold from them" (SW 54). Unhappily, "The Definition of the Psychical" leaves much room for doubt concerning Mead's precise view on this matter. Perhaps this is one of the reasons he was to refer to this essay some years later as one in which his position had been developed "somewhat obscurely and ineffectually, I am afraid" (SW 106).

III. PERCEPTUAL OBJECTS AND THE SOCIAL GENESIS OF CONSCIOUSNESS

While the two essays we have considered emphasize the self functioning as subject, Mead's subsequent early publications show a dominant concern with the self as object. His initial inquiries into the reconstructive role of subjectivity seem to have led to a greater interest in the functional nature of those objects to which subjectivity stands in contrast. And this latter interest came, in turn, to be focused in his social psychological work upon questions concerning the social and functional nature of the object self.

The first step in this line of development is to be seen in Mead's contributions to the functionalist view of perceptual objects in his 1907 essay "Concerning Animal Perception." Here, as in his earlier articles, he carried on the articulation of the organic model of action advocated by Dewey in 1896. But now Mead turned his constructive efforts to the task of locating human perceptual consciousness of physical objects within conduct and distinguishing it from so-called animal perception. Two of the basic ingredients of perceptual consciousness, he pointed out, are readily found in animal conduct. These are the two classes of sensory experiences involving respectively the "distance" sense organs (e.g. the visual, olfactory, and auditory organs) and those of "contact" (e.g. touch, taste). But although animal behavior contains a coordination of these two types of experience, Mead was inclined to doubt that it involved any perceptual consciounsness of physcial things as these are encountered in human experience. The grounds for this doubt are revealed in his examination of the prerequisites for the appearance of physical objects within the act.

Physical objects are to be understood as presentations arising through a particular kind of mediation within conduct. More specifically, they take shape within conduct only insofar as the contact experience that is likely to be encountered in responding to a particular distance stimulus is presented along with that stimulus (SW 79). Mead expressed this point best when he said several years later (in the introductory paragraphs of "The Mechanism of Social Consciousness") that the physical object is "a collapsed act" in which immediate sensuous content is merged with imagery drawn from previous responses to similar stimuli (SW 134). Now the presentation of such objects can take place only if the appropriate elements within experience are consciously isolated and the relational connections between them attended to. But Mead found no convincing evidence that non-human animals possess the capacities required to accomplish these tasks. Consequently, he believed it likely that animal conduct proceeds without any awareness of perceptual relations; its modification presumably takes place in the unconscious manner typical of certain kinds of human learning— for instance, the development of finer sensory discrimination and related muscular adjustments involved in improving one's tennis game through practice (SW 74).

Furthermore, Mead held that if physical objects are to appear within the field of stimulation then that field must be organized around enduring substrates with which varying sensory qualities can be associated. The experiential basis for such substrates, he suggested, had been correctly located by G. F. Stout in what the latter termed "manipulation," the actual contact experience or handling to which distance experience characteristically leads (SW 77). "[O]ur perception of physical objects always refers color, sound, odor, to a possibly handled substrate," a fact that is reflected in the familiar philosophical distinction between primary and secondary qualities (SW 78). Here again the human individual has a clear advantage over non-human animals in that his hands provide him with a wealth of manipulatory contents which can be isolated from the culminations of his activities. In non-human animals, however,

> the organs of manipulation are not as well adapted in form and function for manipulation itself, and, in the second place, the contact experiences of lower animals are, to a large extent determined, not by the process of manipulation, but are so immediately a part of eating, fighting, repose, etc., that it is hard to believe that a consciousness of a "thing" can be segragated from these instinctive activities (SW 79).

These early suggestions outlining a functional view of perceptual objects were to be greatly elaborated in Mead's later philosophical writings. Indeed, well over 150 pages of the posthumously published volume *The Philosophy of the Act* and almost half of *The Philosophy of the Present* are devoted to the further working out of this view, especially with reference to the nest of epistemological and ontological problems raised by the impact upon philosophy of the twentieth century revolution in physics. But of more immediate interest for our present purpose is Mead's extension of his earlier discussion, in a series of articles published between 1909 and 1913, to include the *social* dimension of perceptual consciousness. An examination of these articles discloses the sources of several of his most important social-psychological ideas and reveals the manner in which he employed these to greatly enrich the functionalist understanding of human conduct and consciousness.

Beginning with his article "Social Psychology as a Counterpart to Physiological Psychology" (1909), Mead's thought is less dependent upon Dewey's work than had previously been the case. Mead continued to maintain the functionalist orientation of Dewey's paper on the reflex arc concept but he now came to believe that an adequate functionalism had to emphasize not only the organic nature of human conduct but its fundamentally social character as well. Whereas his earlier discussions had sought to clarify the manner in which perceptual objects and subjective consciousness function in the control and reconstruction of conduct, his emphasis now fell upon the objective social conditions which make these developments within conduct possible. He moved, in short, toward a genetic and increasingly social functionalism.

Following the lead of such thinkers as William McDougall, Josiah Royce, James Mark Baldwin, and Charles Horton Cooley, he began to maintain that human conduct was shaped from the outset by social instincts—where by the term "social instinct" is meant "a well defined tendency to act under the stimulation of another individual of the same species" (SW 98).[12] Mead found in this idea, first of all, an important suggestion bearing upon his discussion of perceptual objects. An adequate recognition of the social dimension of human action, he now realized, would allow one to enlarge that discussion by pointing out how social objects, particularly human selves, arise within the process of conduct. If objects are to be functionally understood as meaningful presentations which guide action, and if human action is characteristically social, then clearly it becomes reasonable to speak of selves as social objects. The content of such objects is implicit in those social instincts that sensitize us to social stimuli; their structure and meaning is implicit in the organized responses we make to these social stimuli. "The implication of an organized group of social instincts is the implicit presence in undeveloped human consciousness of both the matter and form of a social object" (SW 98).

But how do the social objects which are "implicit" in our organized social instincts become explicit elements of consciousness? The problem here, as Mead saw it, was to explain in terms of a functional conception of the social act how the individual might come to analyze the relations within his social experience and thereby grasp the meaning of what he and others were doing. Baldwin and Royce had earlier suggested that the solution to this problem was to be found in instinctive human tendencies to imitate and then oppose the responses of others. Through such imitation and opposition, it was supposed, the individual comes to differentiate between self and other, thus making it possible for him to grasp the social meaning of his own conduct. Mead, however, found this theory to be quite implausible. The idea of an imitative instinct, he pointed out, does not fit well with the observed nature of social conduct:

> The important character of social organization of conduct or behavior through instincts is not that one form in a social group does what the others do, but that the conduct of one form is a stimulus to another to a certain act, and that this act again becomes a stimulus at first to a certain reaction, and so on in ceaseless interaction (SW 101).

Moreover, if we mean by "imitation" what is usually meant by that term, then this theory puts the cart before the horse. It attempts to account for the rise of human consciousness by means of a mechanism which itself presupposes such consciousness. "Imitation becomes comprehensible when there is a consciousness of other selves, and not before" (SW 100). The notion of imitation as it has been employed in social psychology, Mead concluded, must be replaced by a fully developed "theory of social stimulation and response and of the social situations which these stimulations and responses create" (SW 101). Baldwin and Royce were correct in arguing that mature human consciousness is of social origin, but they erred in giving undue emphasis to those social situations in which one individual does what others are doing. The social foundations of consciousness are rather to be found in conduct where the action of one individual calls out an appropriate (and usually dissimilar) response in another individual, and where this response becomes in turn a social stimulus to the other individual.

Mead's own social-psychological theory concerning the genesis of consciousness was only briefly sketched in his 1909 article, but he sought to supply the needed details almost immediately in three subsequent essays: "What Social Objects Must Psychology Presuppose?" (1910), "Social Consciousness and the Consciousness of Meaning" (1910), and "The Mechanism of Social Consciousness" (1912). The central concept of the theory developed in these essays was that of "gesture," a notion which had first been spelled out in Wilhelm Wundt's *Völkerpsychologie.* The gesture, as Mead understood it, is a preparatory stage of social response—a bracing for movement, or an overflowing of nervous excitement which might reinforce the agent and indirectly prepare him for action. Examples include changes of posture and facial expression, flushing of the skin, audible changes in the rhythm of breathing, and certain vocal outbursts (SW 110, 123). These early indications of incipient conduct acquire their status as gestures through their functional role in social interaction, for they quite naturally come to serve as stimuli calling out anticipatory responses from the other individuals involved in the social act. The initial phases of these latter responses in turn serve as gestures which may call out a modified social response from the first individual, and so on. In this manner there is set up a "conversation of gesture," a "field of palaver" consisting of "truncated acts" (SW 109,124). Unlike the imitative conduct emphasized by Baldwin and Royce, such conversations of gesture presuppose no consciousness of meaning or of social objects. Consider, for instance, the familiar preliminaries of a dog fight. Here we have a palaver of mutual bristling, growling, pacing, and maneuvering for position. The two animals appear to communicate quite effectively, yet it is highly doubtful that either has any consciousness of self or is able to assess the significance of its own actions.

The importance Mead attributed to the conversation of gesture as a social condition for the emergence of human consciousness derives from his Jamesian view regarding the behavioral basis of meaning, a view he shared with such thinkers as Royce, Dewey, and James Roland Angell (SW 111). The meaning contents in our consciousness of objects, he held, are supplied by our consciousness of our own "generalized habitual responses." These contents are the consciousness of attitudes, of muscular tensions and the feels of readiness to act in the presence of certain stimulations" (SW 129). But if we are to appropriate these contents in a genuine consciousness of meaning we must isolate them from the stimuli which call them forth and then grasp the relation between these two elements of our experience. Only in this manner is it possible to understand the one as meaning the other. The importance of the conversation of gesture, Mead argued, lies in the fact that apart from this type of conduct there is no functional basis for such an analysis within the act:

There is nothing in the economy of the act itself which tends to bring these contents above the threshold, nor distinguishes them as separable elements in a process of relation, such as is implied in the consciousness of meaning (SW 129).

Only in the conversation of gesture do we find a situation in which the attention of the individual is naturally directed toward his own attitudes; here alone do we find conduct in which "the very attention given to stimulation, may throw one's attention back upon the attitude he will assume toward the challenging attitude of another, since this attitude will change the stimulation" (SW 131). Moreover, the conflicting acts and consequent inhibitions inherent in the conversation of gesture are ideally suited to bring about within the act the continual analysis of stimuli from which consciousness of relation may eventually arise (Ibid.).

The apparent failure of the conversation of gesture to produce consciousness in non-human animals, Mead suggested, can be traced in part to the relatively low level of inhibition to be found in their behavior. The higher level of inhibition present in human conduct is "an essential phase of voluntary attention" and leads to an abundance of gesture not found in other animals (SW 110). Furthermore, the non-human conversation of gesture lacks the diversity of *vocal* gesture to be found in even the most primitive human social interaction. Such vocal gestures, which may have originated in the sudden changes of breathing and circulation rhythms associated with preparation for violent action, have come to "elaborate and immensely complicate" the human conversation of gesture (SW 136). The vocal gesture, moreover, is of particular importance in the development of consciousness because it, more than any other kind of gesture, presents to its author the same stimulus content as it presents to the other individuals involved in the social act. It thus provides an ideal mechanism through which the individual can become conscious of his own tendencies to respond (SW 137).

It should be noted here that Mead had little to say concerning the physical basis of the consciousness whose development he sought to describe. The determination of the physiological conditions necessary for the rise of consciousness, he held, is a task for physiological psychology. As the title of his earlier essay ("Social Psychology as a Counterpart to Physiological Psychology") suggests, he viewed his own social-psychological work as complementing the physiological approach by providing an account of the equally important social conditions for the genesis of consciousness. It was a cause of considerable dismay to Mead that many psychologists of his day acknowledged the physical foundation of consciousness but were apparently oblivious to its social basis. They spoke of introspective self-consciousness as if it were the source of all experience and they maintained that one could only hypothesize concerning the existence of selves other than the one present to introspection. A proper understanding of the role played by the conversation of gesture in the genesis of consciousness, Mead argued, reveals how profoundly mistaken this kind of psychology is. For from the social-psychological standpoint introspective consciousness is a relative latecomer to the field of experience. It is a subjective phase of human conduct ("subjective" in the functional sense explained previously) which is preceded and continually conditioned by experience in an objective world of social objects (SW 112).

The first steps in the child's development of introspective self-consciousness, Mead pointed out, are to be found in his instinctive social responses to the gestures of those about him. Gradually through the conversation of gesture the child comes to attend to his own responses and begins to merge the imagery of past responses with the stimulus content provided by the gestures of others. It is through the merging of these two components that the child "builds up the social objects that form the most important part of his environment" (SW 137). The social consciousness of other selves achieved in this manner precedes the consciousness of self which is analyzed in introspection. The self of introspective consciousness, the "me," is constituted by the merging of imagery drawn from the remembered responses of others with the gestures by which the child stimulates himself. But this merging takes place only after other selves have arisen as social objects in the child's environment. The child acquires his consciousness of himself as object by transferring the form of these earlier social objects to his inner experience (SW 139). The "me" of introspection is thus

> an importation from the field of social objects into an amorphous, unorganized field of what we call inner experience. Through the organization of this object, the self, this material is itself organized and brought under the control of the individual in the form of so-called consciousness (SW 140).

The child's social consciousness of other selves antedates even his consciousness of physical objects. Or, more accurately, his experience becomes reflective—becomes perceptual in the fullest sense— in the recognition of selves, and only gradually does he arrive at a reflective experience of things which are purely physical (SW 112-113). The physical form of the "me," like its social structure, is an importation from the child's environment. The form of the physical object is given first in things other than his physical self. "When he has synthesized his various bodily parts with the organic sensations and affective experiences, it will be upon the model of objects about him" (SW 138).

IV. THE SOCIAL SELF

Having thus traced the social genesis of introspective self-consciousness, Mead returned in the concluding paragraphs of "The Mechanism of Social Consciousness" and in the final essay to be discussed in the present study, "The Social Self" (1913), to a topic he had briefly discussed ten years earlier: his functional understanding of the sense in which the self is both subject and object. A comparison of these two discussions is worthwhile not only for what it reveals about the development of Mead's thought but also for the light it throws on his subsequent employment of the terms "I" and "me."

Let us recall that Mead's initial emphasis upon the distinction between a subject and object self was dictated by his functionalist treatment of psychical consciousness. In the context of that early discussion the "me" was taken to be a meaningful object serving to guide ongoing conduct, while the "I" was identified with the immediate flow of experience as distinguished from the objects that ordinarily control it. The "I" becomes available to introspective consciousness, Mead held, only in the presence of a situation in which old objects have broken down and new ones adequate to guide conduct have not yet appeared; here the "I" takes the form of an immediatley experienced interplay of conflicting suggestions, an interplay from which arise novel meanings allowing for the reconstruction of problematic elements in the world of objects.

Such, in outline, was Mead's position in 1903. When we turn to the essays of 1912 and 1913 we find his approach to these matters modified in accordance with the genetic and social orientation he had increasingly adopted in the intervening years. There is no indication here that he had changed his earlier view of the reconstructive function of psychical consciousness, but his emphasis now fell primarily upon its social origin and structure. Instead of involving merely an interplay of conflicting suggestions, inner consciousness is said to possess a dramatic or dialogic structure imported from the individual's social experience. The "I" and the "me" are understood in terms of their functional roles within this process.

The "me," as has been remarked previously, becomes an object of consciousness through a development of the conversation of gestures. The crucial mechanism here is the human individual's capacity to respond to his own gestures. In thus responding the individual tends to bring to bear upon his own conduct memory images of responses made by others to similar gestures. These images are merged with the stimulus content of the gesture to constitute the "me" as a social object (SW 140, 146). This object self remains, as in Mead's earliest essays, a presentation within conduct; but its functional role is now understood in terms of the thorough-going sociality of human conduct. The "I," on the other hand, is the response the individual makes to the "me." Or, better, it is the immediate act within which the "me" functions as a meaningful presentation. This identification of the "I" is the same as that somewhat dimly articulated in Mead's 1903 essay "The Definition of the Psychical," but now Mead avoided any suggestion that the "I" could appear in immediate awareness. Rather, he held that the "I" always remains "behind the scenes" (SW 141); it is "a presupposi-tion, but never a presentation of conscious experience" (SW 142). The elusiveness of the "I" is to be explained by the fact that "we can be conscious of our acts only through the sensory processes set up after the act has begun" (SW 143). Our acts or responses can, of course, become presentations within a subsequent act, but they are then parts of a "me" and no longer an "I."

This last point is amplified by Mead's attempt, in "The Social Self," to do justice to the full complexity of the self as presented in introspective consciousness. Analysis of such consciousness, he pointed out, does reveal moments in which we are aware of the self as both subject and object. "To be concrete, one remembers asking how he could undertake to do this, that, or the other, chiding himself for his shortcomings or pluming himself upon his achievements" (SW 142). But the subject self thus presented is not the "I." It is rather another "me" standing alongside of, evaluating or making suggestions to, the first "me." Just as one can respond to his own actions with respect to another self and thereby be presented with a "me" standing over against that self, so one can respond to his action with respect to the "me" and thereby be presented with a second "me" standing over against the first. Confusion of this second "me" or reflective self with the "I" is what leads to the mistaken assumption that one can be directly conscious of himself as acting and acted upon (SW 145).

Since one tends to respond to himself in the roles of others in the social environment, sometimes even assuming their characteristic intonations and facial expressions, both the structure of inner consciousness and the content of the "me's" there presented are largely importations from objective social experience. In the young child such inner consciousness is loosely organized and quite personal; it involves an obviously social interplay between the remembered "me" who acts and the response of an "accompanying chorus" of others who figure prominently in his social experience. Later this drama becomes more abstract and we have in its place an inner process of symbolic thought. "The features and intonations of the *dramatis personae* fade out and the emphasis falls upon the meaning of inner speech, the imagery becomes merely the barely necessary cues" (SW 147).

We may note in this connection that Mead's view concerning the relation of this dialogic structure of inner consciousness to the "I" and "me" is easily misunderstood. Consider, for instance, the problems of interpretation posed by the following typical passage:

> The self-conscious, actual self in social intercourse is the objective "me" or "me's" with the process of response continually going on and implying a fictitious "I" always out of sight of himself (SW 141).[13]

Now it is natural, I suppose, to think of this as meaning that the "I" first responds to the "me," then the "me" responds to the "I," and so on. But this line of interpretation must surely be incorrect. For Mead's functional definitions of the "I" and "me" rule out this kind of interaction by placing the two on different ontological levels. We may, consistently with Mead's view, speak of the "me" as an agent in relation to other *objects*; but in relation to the "I" it can be no more than a presentation. This being the case, the correct interpretation of Mead's meaning here must be as follows: The "I" of one moment functions as a gesture calling out the "I" of the next moment, which in turn functions as a gesture for the "I" of a succeeding moment, and so on. Any or all of these "I's" may carry memory images of previous social responses, these images merging with the immediate stimulus content of the gesture to yield a corresponding presentation of a "me." And since the memory images involved in different acts may be as various as the social roles we play (SW 146), we may have a plurality of "me's."

Because Mead was primarily concerned with the social character of inner consciousness in his essays of 1912-13, he did not emphasize the factor of novelty as he had done in "The Definition of the Psychical." But this omission was not indicative of any loss of interest in that topic, for the claim that novel elements are continually emerging within conduct is one which appears again and again in his later works. Moreover, in the lectures of *Mind, Self and Society* he attributes the introduction of novelty in human conduct to the "I," just as he had done in 1903. This attribution is, I think, perfectly consistent with the interpretation of the "I" and "me" sketched above. To say, as Mead does in his 1927 lectures, that the "I" is responsible for the fact that "we are never fully aware of what we are,... we surprise ourselves by our own action,"[14] is simply another way of making the point that the living act is always something more than the presentations which arise within it.[15]

Unfortunately, the lectures recorded in *Mind, Self and Society* do not provide any clear discussion of the functionalist conception of conduct which underlies the whole of Mead's thought. And, consequently, his treatment of the "I" in this context seems unduly arbitrary and mysterious. Indeed, at least one able critic has gone so far as to argue that in these lectures Mead employed the "I" primarily as a residual category for a group of "heterogeneous phenomena" which could not conveniently be explained in terms of the social structure attributed to the "me."[16] But if my reading of Mead's early essays is correct, his later use of the terms "I" and "me" is a consistent outgrowth of his early functionalism and, viewed in this light, the phenomena he identifies with the "I" are not at all "heterogeneous."

V. CONCLUSION

By the time he published "The Social Self" in 1913, Mead's struggles with that "original haunting question" of which Dewey spoke had led him to almost all the major ideas of his mature social psychology.[17] His later essays and lectures extend and refine these ideas in important ways but they involve no significant departure from the genetic and social functionalism developed in the essays we have examined. That this continuity of Mead's social psychological work has been so often overlooked is due in part to his tendency in later years to refer to his position as a "social behaviorism." Mead's thought was indeed always concerned with conduct or "behavior," but never in quite the sense now suggested by the term "behaviorism."[18] Rather his work remained rooted to the last in that organic model of conduct he had embraced in the early years of the Chicago School. It is their testimony to this fact which makes his publications of 1900-1913 valuable documents for any student of Mead's social psychology.

A Social Behaviorist Interpretation of the Meadian "I"[1]

J. David Lewis

Communication is essential for establishing and maintaining any form of social organization, but it is equally true that the communicative act itself is supported by an even more fundamental level of social organization. Garfinkel (1967) and other ethnomethodologists justifiably charge that this level is frequently neglected in sociological inquiries. As a result, these inquiries are weakened theoretically and methodologically by taking for granted what should be treated as problematic in its own right. We begin to appreciate this problem when we ask such basic questions as, How is symbolic communication possible? or, stated slightly differently, What are the fundamental mechanisms of signification?

The social behaviorism of George H. Mead provides valuable insights regarding these questions by recognizing that the communicative act cannot be analyzed adequately at the level of the individual organism, inasmuch as overt verbal behavior by one organism affects both speaker and hearer in qualitatively similar ways. Accordingly, the generalized effect of a significant symbol is not subjective but intersubjective; however, this intersubjectivity is not usually recognizable if we attend merely to the overt responses made to the invocation of the symbol. From Mead's perspective, we cannot explain the occurrence and sequence of overt social behaviors without tracing their histories back to the covert behaviors of the organisms.[a] It is through the calling out in ourselves of the covert response which the other makes to our gesture that a consciousness of the meaning of the gesture can arise, and it is by virtue of this consciousness that the social self emerges from interaction.

For Mead, the fact that these covert physiological processes are so intimately implicated in the social act means that social psychology and physiological psychology are complements of each other (Mead 1964, pp. 94-104). Research in psychophysiology of direct relevance to Meadian social behaviorism has been progressing steadily. O'Toole, Smith, and Cottrell (1978) have surveyed parts of this literature, which can be summarized briefly here. The Meadian process of taking the physiological attitude of the other while engaging in various forms of mental activity has been investigated in a variety of contexts. A large number of experiments have documented Mead's claim that linguistic activities involve covert oral responses. The early work of Berger (1929), Jacobson (1931, 1932), and Wyczoikowska (1913) has been expanded more recently by a series of related studies with the further aid of electromyography (EMG) and electroencephalography (EEG) (see Jacobsen 1973).

As can be predicted from Mead's theory, covert oral behavior (tongue or lip EMG) has been shown to attend mathematical and verbal problem solving (Bassin and Bein 1961). Similarly, Max (1937) was able to demonstrate the presence of activity in the linguistic mechanism of the fingers of deaf subjects while they were solving cognitive problems (see also Novikova 1961; McGuigan 1971). A number of studies which have investigated subvocal speech during silent reading offer additional support for the Meadian contention that mental activity is internal conversation (McGuigan, Keller, and Staton 1964; McGuigan and Rodier 1968; McGuigan and Bailey 1969; McGuigan 1967, 1970). When hearing something read aloud to them, listeners exhibit a significant increase in EMG activity in their dominant arms "as if the subjects were making covert linguistic writing responses" (McGuigan and Schoonover 1973, p. 356).

These studies generally focus on the more universalizable aspects of the phenomenon and therefore do not take into account variations in covert response resulting from the social characteristics of the subjects or the situation (see Davis 1966, p. 286). Consequently, researchers have shown that the covert behaviors Mead postulated do, in fact, occur, but they have not fully grapsed their sociological significance. This work generally shows the same limitations as biologically oriented ethologies do (Reynolds 1976, p. 19).

The psychophysiologists will begin to explain the relationships their instruments reveal when they explicitly recognize that these covert behaviors are, at bottom, being caused by social processes. This admission will call for the incorporation of sociological variables into their research designs, and, eventually, a new interdisciplinary field may emerge (which might be called "sociophysiology") to address problems lying in the interface between social psychology and psychophysiology.

Mead should be identified as an early pioneer in this field who established its basic theoretical and philosophical principles but lacked the sophisticated instrumentation required to pursue it in depth as a scientific research program. Nevertheless, his social behaviorism provides the vital theoretical linkages between physiological psychology and social psychology necessary to get such a research program started. The few sociologists who have followed the social behaviorist interpretation of Mead's theory have devised credible experimental designs and generated supporting evidence (see O'Toole and Dubin 1968; Smith 1971; Cottrell 1971), but, with the notable exception of Cottrell and his students, (Cottrell 1942a, 1942b, 1971, 1978; Foote and Cottrell 1955; Varela 1973), this research program has remained nearly dormant in sociology in the decades since Mead's death.

This situation is certainly regrettable. Mead's discussion of the social self deserves a central place in social psychology, but sociologists' misreadings of Mead's writings have diverted researchers from much of its potential usefulness. In particular, sociologists' interpretations of the "I" and "me" components of self have become a stumbling block to an adequate understanding of Mead's perspective.

The defense of these claims requires two separate lines of argumentation. First, in Sections I-IV below, I will defend the social behaviorist interpretation of Mead's concept of the "I" against the more popular interpretations. Of the various concepts in Mead's theory, the "I" is selected as a focal point because it is the Meadian concept most generally regarded as forbidding a social behaviorist interpretation. Moreover, the alternative interpretations of the "I" have been used as a defense in classifying Mead as a phenomenologist or symbolic interactionist rather than as a social behaviorist. Although there may be no substantial intellectual payoff in debating what Mead "really meant" by these concepts, some reexamination of his intentions seems appropriate when interpretations of the "I" are offered which are incommensurable with his basic ontological and epistemological tenets, but which are, nevertheless, set up as targets for criticism. I will identify instances in which this has occurred.

Following this propsed social behaviorist interpretation of the Meadian "I," Section V of the paper will explore further the theoretical and methodological fruitfulness of this view of Mead. Meadian social behaviorism will be theoretically extended and elaborated and additional research implications suggested. Thus, the overall aim is to show that (1) the social behaviorist interpretation of Mead's theory of the social self (and, more specifically, the "I" concept) is more consistent with textual evidence than are the alternative interpretations and (2) this interpretation opens up lines of theorizing and research which are promising, though still underdeveloped.

I. THE "I" AS A REMEDIAL AND RESIDUAL COMPONENT OF MEAD'S THEORY

To date, most proposed interpretations of the "I" fall into two general categories. First, there are scholars, such as Meltzer (1978, p. 25), who see the "I" as a *remedy* introduced into the theory in order to evade "a complete collective, or sociological, determinism of human conduct." Morris (1934, p. xxv), Strauss (1964, pp. xxiii-xxiv), and Thayer (1968, pp. 236-44) also argue that the "I" represents unsocialized, animal impulses intruding into and disrupting what would otherwise be a stable social process. In a leading symbolic interactionist social psychology text, Lindesmith, Strauss, and Denzin (1977, p. 326) portray the "I" as "impulses which, in a sense, are supervised by the 'me,' either being squashed as they get underway or afterward, or diverted into acceptable channels." Rose (1962, p. 12), in an earlier popular symbolic interactionist reader, equated the "I" with one's "self-conception" which "acquires a purely personal aspect once the individual establishes a relationship to himself." Despite the obvious differences between these conceptions, they are both remedialist since they view the "I" as something which may counteract or oppose the socially constraining force of the "me." In general, the remedialists offer either a biological ("impulses") or a vaguely existentialist ("personal self") interpretation of the "I." Thus, they conceive of the "I" as having a definite function in Mead's theory; namely, that of avoiding the social determination implied by the "me."

The second popular account of the "I," represented by Kolb (1978) and Gillin (1975), regards the "I" as a *residual* component of the theory. Kolb contends that Mead erred by positing the "I" as a way of explaining behavioral phenomena not predictable from the operations of the "me" upon the individual. Mead's mistake, according to this interpretation, was in attempting to enclose heterogeneous behaviors within the same theoretical framework instead of forthrightly admitting the inherent limitations of the explanatory scope of his perspective. Gillin (1975, pp. 35-37) has pushed this residual interpretation to even further extremes by suggesting that the "I" is essentially superfluous. There is no inner dialogue between the "I" and "me" because there is no duality, only the "me." In contrast to the remedial theory, the residual interpretation accords no legitimate purpose to the "I" and thus holds that Mead's theory would be more cogent if all references to it were omitted.

To summarize, proponents of the residual interpretation see Mead as advocating an essentially social deterministic conception of behavior and argue that the "I" is irrelevant to the core explanatory theory. Supporters of the remedial interpretation view Mead as struggling to preserve an indeterministic, if not voluntaristic, theory through the introduction of the "I." Thus, both interpretations conceive of the "I" and its theoretical implications in similar terms but differ regarding the question of the degree of fit between the "I" and the other elements of Mead's theory. Specifically, the residual interpreation argues that the "I" is logically precluded by the "me" and generalized other in the sense that if, as the "me" and generalized other suggest, behavior is always dictated by a fixed social attitude, there is no room left for creativity or impulsive action. Hence, the "I" must be seen as a clumsy non sequitur in relation to the rest of Mead's theory. But from the standpoint of the remedial interpretation, the "I" is seen as complementary to the "me" in that behavior is partly socially influenced but sometimes impulsive and nonsocial in origin.

II. COPING WITH TEXTUAL AMBIGUITIES

Both the remedial and residual interpretations of the "I" misrepresent Mead's views in some fundamental ways. Basically, the misinterpretations arise from a failure to take seriously Mead's thoroughgoing commitment to social behaviorism. The interpretations virtually begin with the assumption that the "I" is alien to the social behaviorist perspective and then proceed to explain why it must be seen as a remedial/residual appendage to the core theory. It would be more charitable to Mead if analysts began with the opposite assumption. A reader who is disposed to see inconsistencies surely will see them by the score, but when the reader can see consistency, it is more likely that the interpretation is within the author's perspective. Just as it is easier to misintepret than to interpret, it is easier to see inconsistency than consistency; therefore, as a rule of hermeneutic methodology, we should presume that a writer's concepts are logically consistent with each other until rigorous analysis forces a contrary conclusion. By this rule, we should resist jumping to the conclusion that the "I" introduces a view of human nature or freedom contrary to that implied by the "me." Few, if any, of Mead's interpreters and critics have been faithful to this rule; consequently, none has proposed a strict social behaviorist interpretation of the "I."

Lest it be inferred that Mead's interpreters are entirely to blame for the current state of ambiguity and confusion regarding the "I," it should be pointed out that part of the problem stems from ambiguities in Mead's writings themselves. These inconsistencies in the usage of the term "I" occur almost exclusively in *Mind, Self, and Society* (1934) (hereafter, *Mind*)—a book compiled from Mead's lectures instead of written by his own hand. Unfortunately, most of Mead's interpreters rely on this source rather than on his published essays, although the latter are far more cogent. The term "I" is used equivocally in *Mind*. In some passages, the "I" is identified as a response, while on other occasions it is defined as ego or that which is responsible for the response. To illustrate this difficulty, we can group a few representative phrases which depict the "I" in each of these ways. In cateogry A below the "I" is the response, and in category B it is that which responds. All page references are to Mead (1934):

Type A Characterizations:
1. "The response...constitutes the 'I'" (p. 175).
2. "The 'I' is the response..." (p. 175).
3. "...his response is the 'I'" (p. 176).
4. ". . . there would not be a 'me' without a response in the form of the 'I'" (p. 182).
5. "The 'I' is the response..." (p. 196).

Type B Characterizations:
1. "The 'I' reacts to the self..."(p. 174).
2. ". . . we react to it as an 'I'" (p. 174).
3. "Now it is the presence of those organized sets of attitudes...to which he as an 'I' is responding" (p. 175).
4. "...this response of the 'I'" (p. 176).
5. "The 'I'...is something that is, so to speak, responding..." (p. 177).
6. "The response of the ego or 'I'..." (p. 199).
7. "...the individual responds as an 'I'" (p. 186).

If one substitutes the word "response" for the word "I" in type B characterizations, a ludicrous statement results. Thus, whatever the "I" is intended to mean in type B phrases, it cannot be taken intelligibly to mean response. Yet it is equally clear that in type A phrases the "I" is equated with response. One must conclude that there is a genuine inconsistency between type A and type B characterizations of the "I" in *Mind*.

III. THE "I" AS AN ELEMENT OF MEAD'S SOCIAL BEHAVIORISM

Although the type B characterizations lend support to the remedial and residual interpretations by implying that the "I" is some type of entity which is separable from the social behaviorist physiological attitude-response process, it is actually the type A characterization which is most consistently (though not universally) advanced in Mead's published articles and which conforms to the position of social behaviorism. For this reason, as I shall argue below, the interpretational problems offered by *Mind* ought to be resolved in favor of type A statements.

Let us begin to substantiate this claim by sketching some of the outlines of the social behaviorist position and then show how the "I," when interpreted as a response (type A), fits neatly into such a scheme, wherein it has neither a remedial nor residual status. Mead (1964, p. 310) wrote that "it is only insofar as the individual acts not only in his own perspective but also in the perspective of others, especially in the common perspective of a group, that a society arises and its affairs become the object of scientific inquiry." And further, "thus, in the study of the experience and behavior of the individual organism or self in its dependence upon the social group to which it belongs, we find a definition of the field of social psychology" (Mead 1934, p. 1). He (1964, p. 244) posed the question: "In what does this significance consist in terms of a behavioristic psychology?" The significant symbol calls out an attitude in the individual. This attitude consists in an emotional state and/or physiological preparedness to perform a specific physical action. In Mead's words: "Insofar then as the individual takes the attitude of another toward himself, and in some sense arouses in himself the tendency to action, which his conduct calls out in the other individual, he will have indicated to himself the meaning of the gesture. This implies a definition of meaning—that is an indicated reaction which the object may call out. When we find that we have adjusted ourselves to a comprehensive set of reactions toward an object we feel that the meaning of the object is ours" (1964, p. 244). When the significant symbol is invoked by another organism, it is represented by some objective manifestation (sound, visual phenomenon, etc.) which causes both organisms to adopt the same attitude —or "readiness to respond in certain ways to the object" (Mead 1964, p. 244). When the significant symbol is initiated by the

organism and directed toward itself (i.e., thinking), the organism
still takes the attitude of the generalized member of the community
for which the symbol is significant. In the limiting case, this community may be only two persons.

The process of conversing with oneself (i.e., thinking) involves
symbols, attitudes, and responses in the same structural relations to
each other as is required in talking to another person. That is, the
necessary conditions for meaningful conversation (complexes of
symbols, attitudes, and responses) hold with equal force for inner
conversation and for outer conversation. However, there are some
obvious differences in the manner in which symbols are represented
and responses occur. In outer conversations, the symbol must be
represented through an overt gesture, but in inner conversation we
learn to truncate the act (thus, adults usually do not talk "out loud"
to themselves as does a child who is first learning to think and
speak).[2] If the inner representation of the symbol is some self-
instruction for behavior, such as "move the pawn," the response to it
may terminate in some physical movement of the hand. However,
in addition to the stimulation of the neuromuscular "pawn-moving"
attitude in the organism, the self-conscious individual is aware of
this attitude and is capable, through self-interaction, of evaluating
and modifying it. In this case, a covert response intervenes between
the original attitude and the subsequent one. This response may
occur on an emotional or on a cognitive level, but frequently it also
takes the form of an image of the consequences of carrying through
the overt response which the attitude prepares. For example, the
chess player images the position which would be created by moving
the pawn and may thereby discover a better move.

The relations among these three concepts—significant symbol,
attitude, and response—form the substructure of Mead's social
behaviorist theory of social action. The theory is more fully detailed
in Mead's essay "A Behaviorist Account of the Significant Symbol"
(1964, pp. 240-47). It is to be especially noted that Mead made a
clear distinction between the organism's attitude and its response.
The attitude, insofar as we are referring to social behavior, is always
deterministically[3] produced within the organism by the significant
symbol, and it is always a social attitude in the sense that it can be
created in any member of the community by any other member
while simultaneously calling it out in itself. The attitude is the
covert phase of the act, while the response may culminate in some
overt, physical activity. Although the attitude prepares a certain
response, under certain conditions that response may not be exe-
cuted because of the inhibiting effects of feedback mechanisms

intervening between the attitude and the response, as in the example of the chess move (these mechanisms are further explored in a later section). Moreover, even in cases where the preparatory (attitude) phase of the act flows smoothly toward the response intended by the significant symbol, it must be recognized that no two such responses are ever exactly alike. Since we do not always succeed in doing what we intend to do, mechanical imperfections of the human organism must be taken into account in explaining the precise nature of the organism's response. Consider Mead's (1934, p. 175) illustration of the baseball player. By practicing regularly, the player can enhance the likelihood that he will throw accurately on any given occasion, but, when the crucial moment arises, the outcome is always in doubt.

Where do the "I" and "me" fit into this scheme? If we assume that Mead was still operating within the social behaviorist perspective, as outlined above, when he referred to the "I" and "me," the "me" can be interpreted as the social *attitude* and the "I" as the *response*. Mead (1934, p. 355) put it thus: "Thinking is simply the reasoning of the individual, the carrying-on of a conversation between what I have termed the 'I' and 'me.' In taking the attitude of the group, one has stimulated himself to respond in a certain fashion. His response, the 'I,' is the way in which he acts." This interpretation is also in accord with Mead's published writings concerning the "I" and "me." In his most thorough explication, namely, the essay entitled "The Social Self," Mead (1964, p. 145) clearly stated that the response ("I") generates observable activity which is attended to by both self and other: "At the back of our head we are a large part of the time more or less clearly conscious of our own replies to the remarks made to others, of innervations which would lead to attitudes and gestures answering our gestures and attitudes toward others." Since our remarks, or "I," thus stimulate the formation of the next "me" (our reply to our own remark), it is clear why Mead held the "I" to be a logical presupposition of the "me."

For example, if the "me" hears, it follows that the "I" (speech act) must have occurred in the previous instant. "The past is what must have been before it is present in experience as a past" (Mead 1964, p. 249). We infer its occurrence, but we are never directly conscious of it. At most, we are conscious only of the meaning (attitude) stimulated in both organisms by the air vibrations. The varying level of consciousness with respect to the attitude can be understood in terms of the complexity of neurological classificatory processes operating upon the original sensory nerve impulse. When the activity is highly habituated, we are often unconscious of our attitudinal dispositions (see Bateson 1972, p. 138). For instance, if I am accustomed to driving a car with the gearshift on the floor and then drive one with the shift on the steering column, I may be surprised to see my hand reaching to the floor to shift gears. The gear-shifting response has become unconscious; it is blocked from the higher centers of the brain. "In fact it is essential to the economy of our conduct that the connection between stimulation and response should sink below the threshold of consciousness" (Mead 1964, p. 127). When the activity is less habituated, more dangerous, important, and so on, we monitor our attitudinal dispositions closely in order to reduce undesirable responses.

Understood in this way, the "I" is indispensable to Mead's theory of social self in that it is the material from which successive "me's" are constructed. As Mead (1964, p. 140) explained, "It is a commonplace of psychology that it is only the 'me'—the empirical self—that can be brought into the focus of attention—that can be perceived. The 'I' lies beyond range of immediate experience. In terms of social conduct this is tantamount to saying that we can perceive our responses only as they appear as images from past experiences, merging with the sensuous stimulation. We cannot present the response while we are responding."

As a further clarification, it may be helpful to indicate briefly a major point of difference between Mead's social behaviorism and the psychological behavorism of Watson (1930) and Skinner (1957). The contrasts are clearly evident from Mead's writings, especially his comparisons between the processes involved in animal interaction and human interaction. For Watson and Skinner, human verbal behavior is fully explicable in terms of conditioned stimulus and conditioned response. Any appeal to consciousness as a process sometimes intervening between stimulus and response is strictly denied. In particular, psychological behaviorism cannot account for (and refuses to acknowledge) the social self. Recall that Mead suggested that the significant symbol has the same meaning for both speaker and listener only because speakers take the attitude of the other toward their own vocal gestures. By imaging the effects one's own gesture will have upon the other, one can consciously control the response of both self and other. Consequently, language and self operate over behavior as a social control mechanism (cf. Shibutani 1961, p. 277). The psychological behaviorist, on the other hand, construes meanings as personal, since the meaning of any event, such as vocal gesture, will vary from one individual to the next according to each person's prior conditioning and present biological state.

To take an example from Skinner (1974, pp. 100-103), individual A asks individual B what time it is, and B responds, "It's three o'clock." According to Skinner, the meaning of this response for person B is the "stimulus which controls it" (e.g., the position of the hands on his watch), but the meaning of the response for person A includes all of the idiosyncratic contingencies relevant to his situation (e.g., he is nearly late for an appointment).[4] It follows that vocal gestures cannot have the same meaning for both persons, and so Skinner (1974, pp. 102-3) understandably concludes, "One of the unfortunate implications of communication theory is that the meanings for speaker and listener are the same...." Skinner's formulation obviously precludes Mead's social behaviorism as well as all other theories of language which treat symbols as universals. It does so by ignoring the crucial role of Meadian attitudes which intervene between stimulus and response. For the social behaviorist, it is the social (shared) attitude rather than some external object or behavior which constitutes the meaning of the symbol.

Besides being faithful to Mead's writings, the social behaviorist interpretation of the "I" and "me" has the further advantage of suggesting some rejoinders which Mead could offer to the interpreters and critics of this theory. The following section aims to address both the remedial and residual interpretations from the point of view of social behaviorism as presented thus far.

IV. HOW MEAD MIGHT HAVE ANSWERED HIS INTERPRETERS AND CRITICS

Kolb (1978, pp. 192-93) interprets the "I" as an attitude or impulse which is prevented from fruition in overt action by the intervention of another attitude, namely, the "me." By making the "I" into an attitude, Kolb has entirely eliminated the response as its defining characteristic. Therefore, the "I" and "Me" relation is seen as an interplay between attitudes rather than between attitude and response. Kolb is correct in his assertion that the "I" is meaningless in Mead's illustration of the baseball player if it is understood as an attitude or impulse, but, as I have argued above, the "I" is not an attitude—it is a response. Kolb has demolished a straw man. When Mead (1964, p. 142) called the "I" a presupposition, but not a presentation, of conscious experience, he simply meant to point out that conduct must occur before it is possible for the organism to reflect backward and assume some attitude toward it. Attitudes do not arise out of other attitudes unless one postulates some form of telepathy—which Mead certainly did not. Rather, the possibility of social attitudes arises from organisms' common access to each other's overt gestures. Of course, once the self is established, we can take a social attitude toward our covert responses, but note that this remains an attitude-response linkage rather than the attitude-attitude connection presented by Kolb.

When the "I" is viewed simply as the organism's response, it is understandable why Mead said that it is unpredictable and not present in consciousness. Normally we can predict what the baseball player will try to do because we know his "me," but we cannot predict what has actual response will be. Also, the "I" is out of consciousness because, at that instant during which the attitude is generating the response (in conjunction with a multitude of unique factors such as the banana peel which Kolb's player slipped upon), the organism is not reflecting. It is merely functioning physiologically during the unconscious moment. If the shortstop tried consciously to think about every movement involved in throwing a baseball while at the same time trying to throw it, the runner would have reached first base before he released the ball. As Polanyi (1958) has observed, all such motor skills are performed best by concentrating on the overall task rather than on the individual movements.

Since the response is not known during the social act, it is clear that the shortstop, like the other observers, must wait for auditory and visual cues which signal to him what his response was. For example, say that he throws the ball 10 feet over the first baseman's head. Perception of the flight of the ball is available to all observers. Yet the shortstop takes a somewhat different attitude toward the percept because he is the only observer who, in effect, says to himself "that was *my* throw." Although the flight of the ball is, in one sense, "out there" in the public arena as a social object constituted within the game of baseball, perception of it also enters into another social process, namely, the shortstop's inner dialogue as he heaps reproach upon himself for allowing the winning run to score. When after repeated errors he and others begin to define him as a poor player, his baseball "me" undergoes a significant transformation. Thus, for socially integrated individuals, these internal and external social processes are closely interconnected. That is, covert behavior is, nonetheless, behavior and must be understood as such if the social psychologist is to grasp the relationships between these internal and external social processes. "The process of identifying the object and correcting our attitudes in the presence of unsuccessful conduct through the use of significant symbols (social in origin) in inner conversation is itself only a form of conduct, and as conduct is as immediate as any other type" (Mead 1938, p. 17).

The organism's response ("I"), defined in strictly physiological terms, is of no immediate sociological interest precisely because it is not directly observed, but the "I" which the organism reconstructs by inference form available evidence—a process Mead (1964, pp. 142 ff.) called "redintegration"—is infused with social significance. Depending upon such factors as the availability of relatively objective evaluative criteria, there will be some degree of correspondence between the behavioral "I" and the redintegrated "I." For instance, it is generally unlikely that a shortstop who consistently makes inaccurate throws will continue indefinitely to be defined by self and others as an accurate thrower. Accounting for inconsistencies between the behavioral and redintegrated "I's" in various situations is itself an interesting sociological problem.

Clearly, this view of the "I" contrasts sharply with the "remedial theory." Recall that the remedial theory interprets the "I" as something inserted into an otherwise overly deterministic theory as a way of accounting for the unpredictability of responses. This is Meltzer's (1978, pp. 19, 25) understanding. His position can be contrasted with Morris's (1934, pp. xxv) and Lauer and Handel's (1977, p. 67) claim that the "I" represents impulsive animal drives or the Freudian id. Although Mead (1934, p. 210) did on at least one occasion discuss the "I" and "me" in a Freudian context, it would be grossly incorrect to hold that Mead's theory of social self is essentially a neo-Freudian formulation. Consequently, to define the "I" and "me" in Freudian rather than in social behaviorist terms is an extremely misleading representation of Mead's thought. Thus Meltzer is justified in his rejection of the Freudian interpretation, but his own version of the remedial interpretation is unclear. Perhaps he prefers to think of the "I" as the transcendental ego of the idealist philosophers, but he offers no clue to its nature, except such vague phrases as "impulsive tendency" and "initial, spontaneous, unorganized aspect of human experience." Such a conception of the "I" does not provide an adequate definition of the term; still less is it usable in experimental inquiry.[5]

That Mead's philosophy of science demands a far more rigorous, objective elaboration of concepts is revealed, for example, by his (1964, p. 34) assertion that "...scientific method can only assume psychical elements that correspond to definite conditions of objective experience....Even the most abstract speculation must have some point of sensuous contact with the world to render it real." Ironically, Meltzer (1978, p. 25) has criticized Mead for being vague in describing the "I," although much of the confusion has been generated by Mead's interpreters, including Meltzer himself, and by equivocations in *Mind*.

Meltzer and Petras (1972, pp. 49-50), in effect, distinguish the Iowa and Chicago schools of symbolic interactionism according to what I have called the residual (Kuhnian) and remedial (Blumerian) interpretations of the "I." Between these interpretational disputes, Mead—the social behaviorist—has somehow been almost lost.[6] If all this mystification of the "I" were discarded and the concept interpreted as meaning simply the organism's response, we would not only be closer to Mead's intention, but we would also have a theory of the social self which is far more open to empirical interpretation.

Thus, much more is at stake here than the rescue of Mead from his critics and interpreters. Social behaviorism, unlike the remedial and residual formulas, offers a number of potentially fruitful hypotheses for empirical research. It is a testimony to Mead's prescience that his thought anticipated some recent developments in linguistics, cybernetics, and cognitive anthropology. Rather than end this discussion on the purely interpretive level of the preceding sections (which might satisfy a few historians and Meadian scholars but not many others), I shall in the following section try to indicate briefly some promising lines of research and theorizing which could be built upon Mead's social behaviorist theory of self. Merton (1968, pp. 331-32) has commented that sociologists should honor their forefathers by extending and elaborating their formulations rather than by merely repeating "definitive" passages from their works. The remainder of this essay is dedicated to this principle.

V. FURTHER EXTENSIONS OF SOCIAL BEHAVIORISM

Most commentators on Mead's theory of social self have provided little more than a brief exposition of the "I" and "me" concepts. Relatively little attention has been given to Mead's use of Whitehead's philosophy of time or to the central role of imagery in Mead's theory of the act. Clearly, Mead's aim was to integrate these components of his perspective, and therefore one risks distortion if any of them are analyzed in isolation. In this section, I will examine some of these less heralded corollaries and implications of Mead's theory. Although a good deal of this discussion is at least implicit in Mead's works, the orientation of this section, unlike the previous sections, is one of free exploration rather than strict interpretation. The purpose is to uncover some interesting issues surrounding Mead's perspective and to indicate possibly productive lines of further theoretical development.

For simplification, I will break the social behaviorist theory of social action into several interrelated analytical units, but this strategy can be misleading. As a preliminary caution, it must be recognized that the same element of behavior can be the final phase of one act as well as the first phase of the act that follows. If one were to think in purely linear terms, this assertion would seem inconsistent in its specification of causal relations. On one hand, the attitude ("me") prepares the way for the response ("I"), but it is also claimed that the response leads to, or makes possible, modification of the attitude. The linear theorist would not be satisfied by this formulation and would demand to be told (once and for all) whether the attitude determines the response or the response determines the attitude, since we obviously cannot have it both ways. He would also demand to know whether the attitude is temporally prior to the response or vice versa, since the theory seems equivocal on this point as well. These questions presuppose a framework which is alien to social behaviorism and, therefore, cannot be given a simple answer without compromising the theory. For the social behaviorist, the act is not a discrete, unitary phenomenon but extends both backward and forward in a temporal stream. There is no danger in talking of *the* act, provided it is understood that we are referring to a cross-section of a temporal sequence complete with its history and future; the first phase of one act might just as well be thought of as a residue of the previous act.

The same problem arises if, using an alternative Meadian terminology, we describe the social act as beginning with an impulse and moving toward a goal through self-interaction. Mead (1964, pp. 358, 392 ff.) viewed impulses as biological instincts for sex, hostility, cooperativeness, and the like. Within the broader theory, these impulses are a subcategory of attitudes which sensory stimulation calls out in the organism. Indeed, Mead's (1938, pp. 3-8) discussion under "The Stage of Impulse" in *The Philosophy of the Act* describes the impulse stage of the act in terms of his general categories of attitude and response. For instance, erotic art may stimulate the sex impulse, possibly leading to an image of a statue as if it were a living person. As such, the fantasied person becomes a "goal" (or "distant object") toward which one assumes a sexual attitude. This attitude may be followed by self-consciousness that one is daydreaming in front of the statue while the rest of the party is leaving the art museum. This example illustrates that symbol-attitude-response complexes occur in interlocking series (A-R-A-R, etc.) or in spiral rather than linear segments (A-R, A-R, etc.). Consequently, except

for special analytical purposes, it is a moot point whether the atti-
ude precedes and causes the response, or vice versa.

   With this caveat in mind, if we arbitrarily take the invocation
of a significant symbol as the beginning of an action sequence and
the receiver's response to it as the end, a theory of social action is
required to supply analysis of the factors and processes which connect the significant symbol and the response. Mead, as a philosopher, was more interested in developing a general theory of meaning than a completely detailed account of factors which facilitate,
block, or otherwise mediate between symbol and response. Although
Mead (1938) described four phases of the act (impulse, perception,
manipulation, and consumption), his discussions are incomplete in
some critical respects (List 1973, pp. 127-30). In the following subsections, I will indicate four aspects of his theory of action which can
be extended further and thereby merged with related theories and
research in sociology and psychology.

A.   From Symbol to Attitude

What conditions determine the attitude that the organism takes
toward the sensory stimulation? Mead generally discussed this
question in relation to his object-medium-organism triad, pointing
out that the attitude taken is the result of the combined characteristics of all three elements (Mead 1938, pp. 11, 125-39). This seems
plausible as a generalization but leaves much unexplained. For any
given social situation, each of these components will have a certain
range of tolerance within which the sensory stimulation can vary
while stimulating the same attitude. But outside this range, miscom-
muncation will occur (i.e., both organisms do not take the same
attitude toward the gesture). It seems that, in this regard, the
principal relevant aspects of the object are mode of presentation
(i.e., word selection, vocal intonations, body language, etc.) and the
environment in which it is presented (including both physical and
social environmental features).

   Among the important aspects of the medium are the degree of
"noise" (i.e., disruptions, distractions, competing messages, etc.) and
the perceived legitimacy of the medium: is this channel an appropriate medium for this transmitter to send this message to this
receiver? McLuhan (1964, pp. 7-21) has argued that in many cases
"the medium is the message"; that is, because we associate certain
types of messages with certain media, we respond to any medium
according to the message we expect it to carry. Furthermore, in
many organizations, messages sent through "unauthorized" channels are frequently blocked or distorted. Finally, the organism itself

will vary in its sensitivity to, receptivity to, and prior experience with the sensory material. Presumably, the variability of each of the three components of the object-medium-organism triad depends not only upon features of the other two components, but also upon structural parameters of the larger social system within which the social action is embedded.

For example, experiments could be done across a variety of organizational structures in order to determine how, for specific types of communications systems, controlled variations in organism, object, and medium affect the speed and effectiveness of communications. Depending upon the organizational structure, variations in one element of the triad may have a more disruptive effect on communications than would variations in either of the other two. Hypothetically, Meadian theory would predict that the organism element is most critical in organizations in which relations are highly personalized, that the medium is most critical in highly stratified organizations, and that the object is most critical when the "perspective" (Mead 1964, pp. 306-19) is not well established. Obviously, there are numerous other variables of interest, but this should suggest the general direction in which inquiry into the symbol-attitude relation could be developed.

B.   The First Feedback Phase

Once the organism is affected by the external stimulus and the attitude is engendered, the response does not follow immediately and automatically. The "delayed response" is the advantage which language-bearing organisms have over lower animals which act according to the dyadic stimulus-response principle. "The attitude which we, and all forms called intelligent, take toward things is that of overt or delayed response" (Mead 1938, p. 7). In Mead's philosophy of science, for example, great emphasis is placed on the pragmatic value of "mental experiments" in which the scientist can eliminate hypotheses without having to resort to trial-and-error physical experiments. Similarly, in ordinary experience we often rehearse our responses before making them. This takes place through covert communication with oneself in which the attitude is assessed as to its cognitive, cathectic, or evaluative adequacy, to borrow part of Parson's (1951, pp. 45-51) scheme.

Maines (1977, pp. 240-43) has discussed some theoretical parallels between the place of role taking in Mead's social psychology and that of feedback in cybernetics and information theory (e.g., Buckley 1967, 1968). I shall limit the present discussion of feedback mechanisms to three problems: (1) feedback and habituated conduct, (2) feedback closure, and (3) feedback through imagery. I intend this analysis of feedback mechanisms to be simply an explication and unpacking of Mead's phrases "inner conversation," "communication with oneself," and the like. All three areas pose intriguing theoretical and methodological problems for social behaviorism.

As to the question of exactly what it is that is fed back during this mediate phase of the act, the following subsections will make it clear that feedback inputs may take the form of subvocal speech, images (word images, creative images, memory images), emotions, or muscular sensations. Potentially, all of these modes of human experience may supply feedback data to which the organism covertly or overtly responds.

1. Feedback and habituated conduct. Is feedback always present? Phenomenological evidence suggests that it is not. Recall, for example, the gear-shifting experience mentioned above. Even the slightest reflection would have been sufficient to prevent the habituated response from occurring. Are we left with the conclusion that habituated activities take place according to a simple stimulus-response model? For Mead (1938, p. 657), habituated actions are performed unconsciously, since consciousness arises only when "one is deliberately adjusting one's self to the world, trying to get out of difficulty or pain...." Consciousness enters at the point where one's hand reaches down for the gearshift and contacts nothing but air. However, Mead seems wrong in his assertion that consciousness or "inner conversation" arises only in cases where one's habitual mode of conduct has been blocked. A good example is the activity of cutting diamonds. For the expert diamond cutter, this is an activity which has been done many times before. There is nothing "problematic" about it in the sense intended by Mead or Dewey; on the contrary, the diamond cutter knows precisely how to proceed. Nevertheless, presumably there is a great deal of inner conversation taking place as every move is checked and double-checked before it is made. If this activity is "unconscious" at all, it certainly is not unconscious in the sense in which it can be said that gear shifting is unconscious. It therefore appears that even some habituated activities are attended to consciously if they are vital to the interests of the organism and involve avoidable risks.

2. Feedback closure. Once feedback begins, what prevents it from continuing indefinitely and preventing the response which the original attitude prepared? Apparently, the pattern of feedback closure can take several forms. In some cases, it may simply stop or else become so minute that it escapes the organism's attention, and the response ensues. At other times, the organism may override the feedback by assuming what might be called the "feedback-ignoring" attitude which permits it to push on with the response despite all doubts, fears, and other feedback. Alternatively, the feedback may indeed continue far beyond what is functional for the organism, leading to psychological disorders such as chronic worry or insomnia.[7] The explanation of these various patterns of feedback closure is of both theoretical and clinical significance.

3. *Feedback through imagery.* Further refinements of Meadian social behaviorism could make valuable contributions to our understanding of the role of imagery in conduct. Imagery is not a popular notion in modern psychological theory, probably because it connotes mentalistic phenomena all of which conflict with the physicalism of behaviorist psychology. Mead (1934, pp. 9-13) contended that mind cannot be reduced to physical relations but can be explained behaviorally. Moreover, he argued that images are not mental or spiritual stuff (1964, p. 242). What, then, are they? Although Mead gave an enormous amount of attention to the role of imagery in the social act, I know of no concise definition of the term anywhere in his writings. When he refers to imagery, his general approach is to assume that we all know what it is and, therefore, the only problem is that of explaining its function in perception. For example, he (1964, p. 134) wrote, "A percept is a collapsed act in which the result of the act to which the stimulus incites is represented by imagery of the experience of past acts of like nature." This assumption is justified on the level of unreflective experience in that we all have experienced both memory imagery and creative imagery many times, but the definition of imagery nevertheless poses difficulties for any behaviorism, including Mead's. Yet, as William James would remind us, the reality of imagery is undeniable and must not be dismissed, as Watson (1930, p. 266) did, simply because it is theoretically embarrassing to behaviorism.

The centrality of imagery in Mead's theory is evidenced by his analysis of the so-called distant object (1938, pp. 108-9), in which the influence of Whitehead's objective relativism is apparent. The future is real only because there are sentient, intelligent organisms into whose experience enter images of physical contact experiences that are stimulated by the attitude represented as the distant object (1938, p. 265). For example, one is hungry and sees a banana. The perception constitutes the distant object while stimulating pleasant memory images of the feel, smell, and taste of bananas. This orients the organism toward bringing the distant object within its manipulatory field, at which point it manipulates and consumes the object.

Although Mead's four stages of impulse, perception, manipulation, and consumption seem ideally suited to analyzing banana eating, the "distant object" would be a more useful concept if Mead had broadened his analytical categories. Clearly, we orient ourselves toward distant objects which we do not see and which may not exist (e.g., the dream house on the hill). Another example would be the image or "mental template" (Deetz 1967, pp. 45-46) artists maintain of their finished object which serves as a guide for their activity. Moreover, the contact image is frequently far less salient than the emotive or cognitive image attached to the distant object. Perhaps it was Mead's determination to remain within a clearly behavioristic framework which usually kept his discussion closely tied to actually perceived objects and physical contact experiences (see, e.g., Mead 1938, pp. 108-9, 122, 174-77, 211, 241, 281-83). The life of a rational being is ordered through fantasied futures which are much richer in content and experiential texture than Mead's general paradigm allows; nevertheless, his model offers a valuable starting point for constructing a more complete phenomenological analysis of imagery.

Mead's view of imagery can be seen as a corrective to that of the associationalist psychology of Bristish empiricism. For Hume and other associationlists, a memory image is a discrete "idea" which can be juxtaposed with sense impressions through association processes. Mead (1964, p. 134), on the other hand, argued that imagery and sensations are merged to form a simple construct. It is through conjunction with images that sense impressions contribute to meaning. Following Kantian princples, Mead held that raw sensory impulses per se carry no intrinsic meaning. The organism's response is not to the sensation, to the image, or to their "association," but to the neurological condition which both set up in a nonadditive manner (i.e., their merged effect). That is, it is not the case that we experience first the brute sensation, then the image, and finally their association. Instead, all we are conscious of is the experience of a unit, not an association.

The critical role of imagery in Mead's theory is further illustrated by the following passage: "As long as one individual responds to the gesture of another by the appropriate response, there is no necessary consciousness of meaning. The situation is still on a level of that of two growlings dogs walking around each other, with tense limbs, bristly hair, and uncovered teeth. It is not until an image arises of the response, which the gesture of one form will bring out in another, that a consciousness of meaning can attach to his own gesture. The meaning can appear only in imaging the consequence of the gesture" (1964, p. 111). This bringing into consciousness of the content of the response (i.e., the meaning) requires awareness of our habitual modes of response to the object: "The general habit of reacting to objects of a certain class, such as a book, must be got before the mind's eye before a recognition of the meaning of a book can appear. No amount of enrichment of the sensuous content of the book through the eye, hand, or memory image will bring this habitual generalized attitude into consciousness" (1964, p. 128). Mead's phrase "must be got before the mind's eye" implies that imagery is involved not only in the execution of responses to symbols but also in attaining consciousness of what those generalized habitual responses are (1964, p. 129). Hebb (1969, 1972) offers a similar account of consciousness.

In addition to the external-internal causal relation between stimulus (significant symbol)-sensation-image-attitude, there is also an internal-internal causation between images and other images (cf. Horowitz 1970). For example, in trying to remember where we put an object, one memory image often leads to another. In these types of behavior patterns, most of the feedback between attitude and response consists in what Mead might have called a "conversation of images."

C. From Attitude to Response

This would appear to be the least sociologically interesting phase of the act. Following the feedback phase of an unblocked act, the attitude is "released" and a response occurs. For Mead, the intervening processes are purely physical; no consciousness is present. It could be argued convincingly that Mead overlooked cases in which the response involves a sustained effort of some kind, allowing the organism to monitor its response while maintaining it.[8] However, this is a special class of responses; in general, Mead's view of the "I" as an unconscious response seems correct. Weigert (1975, p. 49) argues against this position by suggesting that consciousness of meaning is concomitant with the response; otherwise, there is no basis for the experience of self-continuity.

In Mead's defense, it can be argued that self-continuity is more a product of experiential coherence than of concomitant awareness. By this, I mean that our sense of the unity of a core self across time (i.e., my self of today is continuous with my self of 10 years ago) is produced by our memories of our past experiences which form a coherent spatiotemporal order and continuity. Hence even admitting that we have an experience of self-continuity, it is unnecessary to postulate an ego which is concomitantly aware of itself in order to account for such experience. On the other hand, proponents of the reality of concomitant awareness of self during action can retort that without concomitant awareness we would be unable to ascribe memories and past experiences to ourselves. We could not recall the past experience as being our own if we had not experienced concomitant awareness while it was occurring. One example of the significance of this issue is that Mead's theory and Weigert's entail radically different explanations of (and therapies for) the loss of self-continuity and self-identity involved in schizophrenia.

D. The Final Feedback Phase

Following the organism's response to the significant symbol, the response is defined and evaluated by the actor and others. Feedback data are provided by three principal sources: (1) the organism's perception of physical events, (2) the response by others present to ego's response (call them "immediate others"), and (3) ego's conception of how the "generalized other" would interpret the response (Mead 1964, pp. 284-85). These inputs may, and frequently do, interact with each other. Lehman (1974, p. xiii) suggests: "...perceptual strategies must exist by which we monitor behavior as we generate performance, so that behavioral sequences necessarily abort as earlier subsequences are found to have no plausible interpretation or categorical characterization." Through the process of self-conscious reflection, the whole experience is redintegrated into the self.

But the self should not be understood as a type of mental entity constituted by a set of adjectives and identities (e.g., strong, friendly, female, student, etc.). This is the theoretical orientation almost always taken by those who have done research on the self by the Twenty Statements Test (TST) (Kuhn and McPartland 1954) and other self-rating devices. Although much of this research has been done in the name of Mead, the results are more easily assimilated into labeling theory or attribution theory than into social behaviorism. For the social behaviorist, the self is simply the whole structure of social attitudes which the organism acquires through life in the community.

It is a structure of attitudes, then, which goes to make up a self, as distinct from a group of habits...We cannot be ourselves unless we are also members in whom there is a community of attitudes which control the attitudes of all...The individual possesses a self only in relation to the selves of the other members of his social group; and the structure of his self expresses or reflects the general behavior pattern of this social group to which he belongs, just as does the structure of the self of every other individual belonging to this social group. [Mead 1934, pp. 163-64]

In what I have termed the final feedback phase, the organism brings its perceived response into relation with this antecedent attitudinal complex or, more precisely, with what is taken as the relevant parts of it, given the existence of many subcomplexes or selves within the larger self (Mead 1934, p. 142). There are several types of possible outcomes. Where there is a perceived correspondence between attitude and response, the original symbol-attitude connection may be strengthened, or, if the anticipated response apparently fails to occur, the connection may be weakened or extinguished (e.g., "I will no longer believe his promises"). Also, a new attitude may have been created and either supported or rejected in the process of the act (further evidencing the existence of acts within acts). Another possibility is that the organism finds itself unable to fit the response into its perspective and thus remains in a state of "subjectivity" (Mead's classic example is the scientist whose perspective has been upset by an unaccountable experimental result). But these outcomes depend as much upon the perceived conditions surrounding the act as the latter does upon the perceived attitude-response relationship itself. This is reflected in legal codes which take into account all three components:

1. Did the accused commit the act? (response)
2. What were his/her antecedent intentions? (attitude)
3. Were there extenuating circumstances? (conditions)

During the process of "selfing," individuals put these questions and others to themselves, and their range of responses encompasses the whole spectrum of defense mechanisms. Indeed, selfing is very much akin to a legal inquiry. Although we have defined self as a structure of attitudes, it is a structure continuously subject to transformation by its participation in the selfing process. The production, maintenance, and transformation of the structure can be understood only when placed within the context of the process in which it enters, registers its effects, and is reciprocally affected. Consequently, those who wish to study the self as conceived by Mead should study selfing as an ongoing process rather than only treating the self as a bundle of self-ascribed attributes waiting to be tapped by the right diagnostic device. These static approaches ignore the whole physical and social "situational field" (Cottrell 1942b, p. 381) impinging upon the organism in the concrete situation. Study of the dynamics of selfing could focus on the three evaluative components described above in their relations to the three principal sources of feedback input (perceived physical conditions, immediate others' responses, and the generalized other). Concerning the feedback input sources, Mead's thinking was largely confined to the effects of the generalized other. This leaves open a wide area for theoretical and empirical inquiry into the other two sources, particularly into those cases in which the organism must resolve conflicing inputs from the three sources. Experiments such as the famous Asch (1955) study mark a step in that direction, but much work remains. I know of no experiment, for instance, in which generalized societal expectations, specific group expectations, and sensory data all provide different feedback to the subject in a complex factorial design, although I see no technical reason why such a design is not feasible.

While Mead's own statements about the generalized other are not theoretically sophisticated enough to account for the complex interactions among the three sources of feedback input, we can add further theoretical assumptions which allow us to study these more subtle aspects of the final feedback phase of the act without moving outside the social behaviorist paradigm. This requires relativising the generalized other in two ways; we assume (1) that the clarity and strength of the generalized other is variable across and within different social groups in a manner closely analogous to Durkheim's concept of the volume of the collective conscience, and (2) that, with respect to any specified social situation, individuals will have their generalized others ordered into a hierarchy of relevancies and that this ordering is also variable across and within different social groups.

In experiments, the first of these variables can be controlled by restricting the availability of information to groups and individuals and the second by setting up and manipulating reward structures within and between groups. With these factors under experimental control, one could begin to establish how these factors affect the organization and processing of the feedback inputs. The interesting research problems concern interactions between the clarity and strength of a generalized other and its position in the hierarchy of relevancies. These types of experiments should suggest some general principles of selfing which can then be explored in more naturalistic settings. For example, this research program is obviously relevant to the study of social discrimination, prejudice, and social perception in general.

VI. CONCLUSION

Keeping in mind Mead's (1934, pp. 168-69) distinction between consciousness and self-consciousness, the theme of the preceding section is that the social act is a series of four (alternating) unconscious and self-conscious moments. Both the symbol-to-attitude phase and the attitude-to-response phase are essentially mechanical, involuntary processes of which the organism lacks self-conscious awareness. At most, the organism grasps their occurrence by post hoc inference. In contrast, after each of these first and third phases may occur moments of self-conscious reflexivity during which the organism may process feedback inputs regarding, first, its attitude aroused by the significant symbol and, later, its ultimate response. I suggested a few of the many interesting topics for further research and theoretical extension associated with each of these four phases.

If it is asked why so much of the potential of Meadian social behaviorism still remains unrealized after more than 40 years and the emergence of two "schools" of Meadian scholars, I must reply that the answer lies, to a considerable extent, in the profound misunderstandings arrived at by some of Mead's interpreters who have tried to squeeze his theory into paradigms that it does not fit. Perhaps it is time to suspend the disputes between "remedialists" and residualists" long enough to give Mead's social behaviorism the fair trial it deserves.

Part 3
Language

The Paradigm Shift in Mead

Jürgen Habermas

THE FOUNDATIONS OF SOCIAL SCIENCE IN THE THEORY OF COMMUNICATION

Early in the twentieth century, the subject-object model of the philosophy of consciousness was attacked on two fronts—by the analytic philosophy of language and by the psychological theory of behavior. Both renounced direct access to the phenomena of consciousness and replaced intuitive self-knowledge, reflection, or introspection with procedures that did not appeal to intuition. They proposed analyses that started from linguistic expressions or observed behavior and were open to intersubjective testing. Language analysis adopted procedures for rationally reconstructing our knowledge of rules that were familiar from logic and linguistics; behavioral psychology took over the methods of observation and strategies of interpretation established in studies of animal behavior.[1]

Despite their common origins in the pragmatism of Charles Sanders Peirce, these two approaches to the critique of consciousness have gone their separate ways and have, in their radical forms, developed independent of one another. Moreover, logical positivism and behaviorism purchased their release from the paradigm of the philosophy of consciousness by reducing the traditional roster of problems with a single coup de main—in one case through withdrawing to the analysis of languages constructed for scientific purposes, in the other by restricting itself to the model of the individual organism's stimulus-induced behavior. The analysis of language has, of course, freed itself from the constrictions of its dogmatic beginnings. The complexity of the problematic developed by Peirce has been regained along two paths—one running from

Carnap and Reichenbach through Popper to postempiricist philosophy of science, the other from the early Wittgenstein through the late Wittgenstein and Austin to the theory of speech acts. By contrast the psychological theory of behavior has, notwithstanding occasional moves for liberalization, developed within the bounds of an objectivistic methodology. If we want to release the revolutionary power of the basic concepts of behavior theory, the potential in this approach to burst the bounds of its own paradigm, we shall have to go *back* to Mead's social psychology.

Mead's theory of communication also recommends itself as a point of intersection of the two critical traditions stemming from Peirce.[2] Although Mead took no notice of the linguistic turn in philosophy, looking back today one finds astonishing convergences between his social psychology and the analysis of language and theory of science developed in formal-pragmatic terms. Mead analyzed phenomena of consciousness from the standpoint of how they are formed within the structures of linguistically or symbolically mediated interaction. In his view, language has constitutive significance for the sociocultural form of life: "In man the functional difffferentiation through language gives an entirely different principle of organization which produces not only a different type of individual but also a different society."[3]

Mead presented his theory under the rubric of "social behaviorism" because he wanted to stress the note of criticism of consciousness. Social interactions form symbolic structures out of sentences and actions, and analyses can deal with them as with something objective. There are however two methodological differences separating Mead's approach from behaviorism. The model from which he starts is not the behavior of an individual organism reacting to stimuli from an environment, but an interaction in which at least two organisms react to one another and behave in relation to one another: "We are not, in social psychology, building up the behavior of the social group in terms of the behavior of the separate individuals composing it; rather, we are starting out with a given social whole of complex activities, into which we analyze (as elements) the behavior of each of the separate individuals composing it."[4] Mead rejects not only the methodological individualism of behavior theory but its objectivism as well. He does not want to restrict the concept of "behavior" to observable behavioral reactions; it is to include symbolically oriented behavior as well, and to allow for the reconstruction of general structures of linguistically mediated interactions: "Social psychology is behavioristic in the sense of starting off with an observable activity—the dynamic, ongoing social process, and the social acts which are its component elements—to be studied and analyzed scientifically. But it is not behavioristic in the sense of ignoring the experience of the individual—the inner phase of that process or activity."[5] In comparison with the aspect of behavior, the meaning embodied in social action is something non-external; at the same time, as something objectivated in symbolic expressions, it is publicly accessible and not, like phenomena of consciousness, merely internal: "There is a field within the act itself which is not external, but which belongs to the act, and there are characteristics of that inner organic conduct which do reveal themselves in their own attitudes, especially those connected with speech."[6]

Because Mead incorporated a nonreductionist concept of language into behaviorism, we find combined in him the two approaches critical of consciousness that otherwise went their separate ways after Peirce: the theory of behavior and the analysis of language. His communication theory is not restricted to acts of reaching understanding; it deals with communicative *action*. Linguistic symbols and languagelike symbols interest him only insofar as they mediate interactions, modes of behavior, and actions of more than one individual. In communicative action, beyond the function of achieving understanding, language plays the role of coordinating the goal-directed activities of different subjects, as well as the role of a medium in the socialization of these very subjects. Mead views linguistic communication almost exclusively under these last two aspects: the social integration of goal-directed actors, and the socialization of subjects capable of acting. He neglects the achievement of mutual understanding and the internal structures of language. In this respect, his communication theory stands in need of supplementary analyses of the sort carried out since in semantics and speech-act theory.[7]

The paradigm shift prepared by Mead's social psychology interests us here because it clears the way for a communication concept of rationality.[a] ... In this section I want (A) to characterize the problem that serves as the point of departure for Mead's theory of communication, in order (B) to show how he explains the transition from subhuman interaction mediated by gestures to symbolically mediated interaction. (C) The results of Mead's theory of meaning can be rendered more precise by drawing upon Wittgenstein's investigations of the concept of rule. (D) I would like then to show how language is differentiated in respect to the functions of mutual understanding, social integration, and socialization, and how this makes possible a transition from symbolically mediated to normatively guided interaction. (*E*) A desocialized perception of things, a norming of behavioral expectations, and a development of the identity of acting subjects serve as the basis for a complementary construction of the social and subjective worlds.[b] Mead did not develop the basic concepts of objects, norms, and subjects from a phylogenetic perspective—as he did the basic categories of the theory of meaning—but only from an ontogenetic perspective. This gap can be closed by drawing upon Durkheim's theory of the origins of religions and ritual.

A. Mead sets himself the task of capturing the structural features of symbolically mediated interaction. What interests him here is that symbols that can be used with the same meaning make possible an evolutionarily new form of communication. He views the *conversation of gestures* found in developed vertebrate societies as the evolutionary starting point for a development of language that leads first to the *signal-language* stage of symbolically mediated interaction and then to *propositionally differentiated speech.* Mead uses the term 'significant gesture' for simple, syntactically unarticulated symbols that have the same meaning for at least two participants in the same (i.e., sufficiently similar) contexts, for he regards such symbols as having developed from gestures. Examples would be vocal gestures that have taken on the character of languagelike signals, or the one-word utterances with which the child's acquisition of language begins, but which are usual among adult speakers as well, albeit only as elliptical forms of linguistically explicit utterances.

Calls such as "Dinner!" or "Fire!" or "Attack!" are context-dependent, propositionally nondifferentiated, and yet complete speech acts, which can be used only quasi-imperatively, quasi-expressively. One-word utterances are employed with communicative intent, but as syntactically unarticulated expressions they do not yet permit grammatical distinctions among different modes. Thus "Attack!" is a warning when, for example, the context is such that enemies have turned up suddenly and unexpectedly; the same call can be a command to confront an enemy that has suddenly appeared in this way; it can also be an expression of alarm at the fact that the unexpected enemy is threatening one's own life or the lives of close relations, and so on. In a way, the exclamation signifies all of these at once; in cases such as this we speak of a "signal."

Signals or one-word utterances can be used only situation-dependently, for singular terms by means of which objects could be identified relative to a situation and yet context-independent are lacking.[8] Signals are embedded in interaction contexts in such a way that they always serve to coordinate the actions of different participants—the quasi-indicative meaning and the quasi-expressive meaning of the utterance form a unity with the quasi-imperative meaning. Both the warning statement of the fact that enemies have suddenly and unexpectedly turned up and the expression of alarm at the threat posed by their sudden appearance point to the *same* expectation of behavior—and this is given direct expression in the command to offer resistance to the unexpected enemy. For this reason there is an unmistakable relation between the meaning of a signal—in all its modal components of significa-tion—and the sort of behavior that the sender expects from the addressee as an appropriate response.

Linguistic signals can be replaced by manufactured symbols (such as drumming or the tolling of a bell) that are languagelike without being linguistic. Likewise, the beginning of a significant action can take on signal functions (as when a leader demonstra-tively reaches or his weapon). In such cases we are, however, al-ready dealing with signs that have a conventional meaning; their meaning no longer derives from a naturelike context. It is character-istic of the stage of symbolically mediated interaction that the language community in question has at its disposition only signals —primitive systems of calls and signs. For analytical purposes, Mead simplifies the situation by disregarding the fact that the meaning of a symbol holds for all the members of a language community. He starts from the situation in which two independent participants can employ and understand the same symbol with the same meaning in sufficiently similar circumstances. To be sure, the condition that meaning conventions be fixed in the same way for a plurality of participants holds only for genuine signal languages not for the gesture languages that are found at the subhuman level.

Mead illustrates the latter with examples of gesture-mediated interactions between animals belonging to the same species, such as a fight between two dogs. The interaction is set up in such a way that the beginnings of movement on the part of one organism are the gestures that serve as the stimulus eliciting a response on the part of the other; the beginnings of this latter movement become in turn a gesture that calls forth an adaptive response on the part of the first organism: "I have given the illustration of the dog-fight as a method of presenting the gesture. The act of each dog becomes the stimulus to the other dog for his response. There is then a relationship between these two; and as the act is responded to by the other dog, it, in turn, undergoes changes. The very fact that the dog is ready to attack another becomes a stimulus to the other dog to change his own position or his own attitude. He has no sooner done this than the change of attitude in the second dog in turn causes the first dog to change his attitude. We have here a conversation of gestures."[9]

Interaction between animals that is mediated through gestures is of central importance in genetic considerations if one starts, as Mead does, with the concept of objective or natural meaning. He borrows this concept of meaning from the practice of research into animal behavior. Ethologists ascribe a meaning to a certain pattern of behavior that they observe from a third-person perspective, without supposing that the observed behavior has this meaning (or indeed any meaning) for the reacting organism itself. They get at the meaning of behavior through the functional role that it plays in a system of modes of behavior. The familiar functional circuits of animal behavior serve as a foundation for these ascriptions of meaning: search for food, mating, attack and defense, care of the young, play, and so on. Meaning is a systemic property. In the language of the older ethnology: meanings are constituted in species-specific environments (von Uexküll), they are not at the disposition of the individual exemplar as such.

Mead traces the emergence of linguistic forms of communication using as his guideline the step-by-step transformation of objective or natural meanings of systemically ordered mean-ends relations between observed behavioral responses into the meanings that these modes of behavior take on for the participating organisms themselves. Symbolic meanings arise from a subjectivizing or internalizing of objective structures of meaning. As these structures are mainly found in the social behavior of animals, Mead tries to explain the emergence of language through the fact that the semantic potential residing in gesture-mediated interaction becomes symbolically available to participants through an internalization of the language of gestures.

Mead distinguishes two steps in this process. At the first stage, a *signal language* emerges that converts the objective meanings of typical behavior patterns into symbolic meanings and opens them up to processes of reaching understanding among participants in interaction. This is the transition from *gesture-mediated* to *symbolically mediated* interaction, and Mead studies it from the standpoint of meaning theory as a semanticization of natural meanings. At the second stage, social roles make the natural meaning of functionally specified systems of behavior—such as hunting, sexual reproduction, care of the young, defense of territory, status rivalry, and the like—not only semantically accessible to participants but normatively binding on them. For the time being I shall leave this stage of *normatively regulated action* to one side and concentrate on the stage of symbolically mediated interaction. I want to elucidate how Mead understands his task of "explaining," by way of reconstructing the emergence of this early stage of languagelike communication.

He begins with an analysis of gesture-mediated interaction because he finds there the beginnings of a process of semanticization. A certain segment of the meaning structure embedded in the functional circuit of animal behavior is already made thematic in the language of gestures: "Meaning is thus a development of something objectively there as a relation between certain phases of the social act; it is not a psychical addition to that act and it is not an 'idea' as traditionally conceived. A gesture by one organism, the resultant of the social act in which the gesture is an early phase, and the response of another organism to the gesture, are the relata in a triple or three-fold relationship of gesture to first organism, of gesture to second organism, and of gesture to subsequent phases of the given social act; and this three-fold relationship constitutes the matrix within which meaning arises, or which develops into the field of meaning."[10] Thus in the language of gestures the relations obtaining between the gesture of the first organism and the action that follows upon it, on the one side, and the response it stimulates in the second organism, on the other, form the objective basis of the meaning that the gesture of one participant assumes *for the other*. Because the gesture of the first organism is embodied in the beginnings of a repeatedly occurring movement, and is in that respect an indication of the state in which the completed movement will result, the second organism can respond as if the gesture were an expression of the intention to bring about this result. It thereby gives to the gesture a meaning—which, to begin with, it has only for the second organism.

If we assume that the first organism undertakes a similar ascription, the situation looks as follows. Inasmuch as the second organism responds to the gesture of the first with a certain behavior, and the first organism responds in turn to the beginning of this behavioral response, each organism expresses how it interprets the gesture of the other, that is, how it understands it. In this way, each participant in the interaction connects with the gestures of the other a typical meaning—which obtains only for that participant.

When this is clear, we can specify the transformations that have to take place along the way from gesture-mediated to symbolically mediated interaction. First, gestures are transformed into symbols through replacing meanings that exist for individual organisms with the meanings that are the same for both participants. Second, the behavior of participants changes in such a way that an interpersonal relation between speaker and addressee replaces the causal relation between stimulus-responses-stimulus—in interacting with one another, participants now have communicative intent. Finally, there is a transformation of the structure of interaction, in that the participants learn to distinguish between acts of reaching understanding and actions oriented to success. The problem of the transition from the stage of gesture-mediated interaction to the stage of symbolically mediated interaction is resolved in these three steps.

Mead tries to explain this transition by means of a mechanism he calls "taking the attitude of the other." Piaget and Freud also introduced learning mechanisms of internalization—one in the sense of "interiorizing" action schemata, the other in the sense of "internalizing" relations to social objects, that is, to given reference persons. Similarly, Mead conceives of internalization as making objective structures of meaning internal [*Verinnerlichung*]. Unlike the case of the reflective relations that come about when a subject turns back upon itself in order to make itself an object for itself, the model of internalization says that the subject finds itself again in something external, inasmuch as it takes into itself and makes its own something that it encounters as an object. The structure of assimilation [*Aneignung*] differs from the structure of reflection [*Spiegelung*] by virtue of its opposite direction: the self relates itself to itself not by making itself an object but by recognizing in an external object, in an action schema or in a schema of relations, something subjective that has been externalized.

To be sure, these elucidations remain tied to the model of the philosophy of consciousness. Mead takes his orientation from an older model, which was already employed by Augustine—the model of thought as an inner dialogue, a dialogue made internal: "Only in terms of gestures and significant symbols is the existence of mind or intelligence possible; for only in terms of gestures that are significant symbols can thinking—which is simply an internalized or implicit conversation of the individual with himself by means of such gestures—take place."[11]

This model illuminates the mechanism of "taking the attitude of the other" from one side only. It makes clear that the intersubjective relation between participants in interaction, who adjust to one another and reciprocally take positions on one another's utterances, is reflected in the structure of the relation-to-self.[12] However, a higher-level subjectivity of this type, distinguished by the fact that it can turn back upon itself only mediately—via complex relations to others—alters the structure of interaction as a whole. The more complex the attitudes of the other are, which participants "internalize in their own experience," the more there is a shift in what connects the participants (to start with, organisms) beforehand, in virtue of systemic features—from the level of innate, species-specific, instinctual regulations to the level of intersubjectivity that is communicatively generated, consolidated in the medium of linguistic symbols, and secured finally through cultural tradition.

In his chapters on the social constitution of the self, Mead gives the mistaken impression that taking the attitude of the other and the corresponding internalization of objective meaning structures are to be understood primarily as a mechanism for generating higher-level subjectivity. But this mechanism has consequences for an entire system; its operations bear on all the components of the interaction system—on the *participants* engaging in interaction, on their *expressions*, and on the *regulations* that secure the continued existence of the interaction system through coordinating actions to a sufficient degree. If Mead wants to use the mechanism of taking the attitude of the other to explain how symbolically mediated interaction arises from gesture-mediated interaction, he has to show how the regulative accomplishments of gestures, which function as economical release mechanisms for instinctually anchored discharges of movement, devolve upon communication in signal language; he has to show how an organism responding to stimuli grows into the roles of speaker and addressee, and how communicative acts differ from noncommunicative actions, that is, how processes of reaching understanding *with* one another differ from exerting influence *upon* one another with a view to consequences. This is not merely a question of the emergence of the relation-to-self that is reflected in itself, or of a higher-level subjectivity; these ideas are still tied to the subject-object model Mead is trying to overcome. It is a question of the emergence of a higher-level form of life characterized by a linguistically constituted form of intersubjectivity that makes communicative action possible. There are, however, problems with the way Mead carries out his analysis, for he does not adequately distinguish the stage of symbolically mediated interaction from the stage of linguistically mediated and normatively guided interaction. I shall begin by sketching the way in which Mead develops his theory from the three viewpoints mentioned above.

B. Mead's basic idea is simple. In gesture-mediated interaction, the gesture of the first organism takes on a meaning for the second organism that responds to it. This response expresses how the latter interprets the gesture of the former. If, now, the first organism "takes the attitude of the other," and in carrying out its gesture already anticipates the response of the second organism, and thus its interpretation, its own gesture takes on *for it* a meaning that is like, but not yet the same as, the meaning it has *for the other.* "When, in any given social act or situation, one individual indicates by a gesture to another individual what this other individual is to do, the first individual is conscious of the meaning of his own gesture—or the meaning of his gesture appears in his own experience—in so far as he takes the attitude of the second individual toward that gesture, and tends to respond to it implicitly in the same way that the second individual responds to it explicitly. Gestures become significant symbols when they implicitly arouse in an individual making them the same responses which they explicitly arouse, or are supposed to arouse, in other individuals, the individuals to whom they are addressed."[13] Mead thinks he can explain the genesis of meanings that are the same for at least two participants by one organism internalizing the relation between its own gesture and the response of the other; the internalization comes about through one organism taking up the attitude in which the other responds to its gesture. If this were the case, it would remain only to specify the conditions under which taking the attitude of the other—that is, the process of internalizing objective meaning structures—can get under way.

On this point Mead vacillates between two lines of thought. The first rests on the thesis of inhibited or delayed reactions.[14] By virtue of a break in the direct connection between stimulus and response, intelligent conduct arises, characterized by "the ability to solve the problems of present behavior in terms of its possible future consequence."[15] The organism pauses and becomes aware of what it is doing when it arouses certain responses to its own gestures in another party. Mead does not notice that this explanation of taking the attitude of the other already draws upon a mode of reflection that will itself have to be explained in terms of an orientation to the meaning that one's own actions have for other participants—unless Mead wants to slide back into the philosophy of consciousness.

For this reason, his other line of thought—Darwinian in inspiration—is more consistent: the pressure to adapt that participants in complex interactions exert upon one another—whether from the need to cooperate or, even more so, in situations of conflict —puts a premium on the speed of reaction. An advantage accrues to participants who learn not only to interpret the gestures of others in light of their own instinctually anchored reactions, but even to understand the meaning of their own gestures in light of the expected responses of others.[16]

Furthermore, Mead stresses that acoustically perceptible gestures are especially suited for this. With vocal gestures it is easier for the organism that makes the sounds to take the attitude of the other, because the sender can hear acoustic signals as well as the receiver.[17] Thus Mead sees in the fact that phonemes, vocal gestures, are the sign-substratum of linguistic communication confirmation of his assumption that taking the attitude of the other is an important mechanism in the emergence of language.[18]

I will not go into these empirical questions here, but will restrict myself to the conceptual question of whether it is possible for Mead to reconstruct the emergence of signal language from the language of gestures by appealing to one participant's taking the attitude of another. Insofar as nothing more is meant by this than that one participant takes in advance the attitude with which the other will respond to its vocal gesture, it is not at all clear how languagelike symbols, vocal gestures with the *same* meanings, are supposed to arise from this. Mead could only explain by this the emergence of a structure with the characteristic that the first organism is stimulated by its own sounds in a way *similar* to the second. If the same gesture arouses in both a disposition to *like* (sufficiently similar) behavior, an observer can notice a concurrence in the way they interpret the stimulus, but this does not yet imply the formation of a meaning that is the same for the participants themselves. "It does not follow from the fact that the one is disposed to do the same as that to which the other is stimulated that there is something identical in relation to which both are behaving."[19] That both concur in the interpretation of the same stimulus is a state of affairs that exists in itself but *not for them.*

In many passages Mead understands the mechanism of "taking the attitude of the other" as "calling out the response in himself he calls out in another." If we understand "response" not in behaviorist terms as the reaction to a stimulus, but in the full dialogical sense as an "answer," we can give "taking the attitude of the other" the more exacting sense of internalizing yes/no responses to statements or imperatives. Tugendhat suggests this interpretation: "The reaction of the hearer which the speaker implicitly anticipates is the former's response with 'yes' or 'no'... when one deliberates, one speaks with oneself in yes/no responses in the way that one would speak with others with whom one was discussing what should be done."[20] Apart from the fact that this way of reading Mead's text does violence to it,[21] it would rob the mechanism of taking the attitude of the other of the explanatory power that it is meant to have. Internalized dialogue cannot be constitutive for achieving understanding via identical meanings because participation in real or external dialogues already requires the use of linguistic symbols. What is more, if speakers and hearers are to be able to respond to statements and imperatives with a "yes" or a "no," they must be equipped with a propositionally differentiated language. Mead, however, locates languagelike communication one stage deeper, in the modally undifferentiated expressions of signal language.

Nevertheless, we have to look for the solution to the problem in the direction marked out by Tugendhat. Taking the attitude of the other is a mechanism that bears first on the response of the other to one's own gesture, but it gets extended to additional components of interaction. Once the first organism has learned to interpret its own gesture in the same way as the other organism, it cannot avoid making the gesture *in the expectation* that it will have a certain meaning for the second organism. This consciousness means a change in the attitude of the one organism toward the other. The first organism encounters the second as a *social* object that no longer merely reacts adaptively to the first's gesture; with its response it expresses an interpretation of that gesture. The second organism appears to the first as an interpreter of the first's own behavior; this means a change in the attitude of the latter to the former as well. The first organism behaves toward the second as toward an addressee who interprets the coming gesture in a certain way, but this means that the first produces its gesture with communicative intent. If we further assume that this holds for the other organism as well, we have a situation in which the mechanism of internalization can be applied once again: to the attitude in which the two organisms no longer simply express their gestures straightaway as adaptive behavior, but address them to one another. When they can take this "attitude of addressing the other" toward themselves as well, they learn the communication roles of hearer and speaker; each behaves toward the other as an ego that gives an alter ego something to understand.

Mead does not distinguish adequately between two categories of attitudes that one organism takes over from the other: on the one hand, reacting to its own gesture; on the other hand, addressing a gesture to an interpreter. However there are numerous passages that show he has both in mind: "The process of addressing another person is a process of addressing himself as well, and of calling out the response he calls out in the other."[22] The expression "response" changes its meaning unawares when what is presupposed is not merely the simple operation of taking the attitude of the other, but the expanded one—for then the stimulated response does indeed become an "answer." We have a situation "where one does *respond* to that which he *addresses* to another and where that response of his own becomes a part of his conduct, where he not only *hears* himself but *responds* [i.e., answers—J.H.] to himself, *talks* and *replies* to himself as truly as the other person replies to him."[23]

With the first taking of the attitude of the other, participants learn to internalize a segment of the objective meaning structure to such an extent that the interpretations they connect with the same symbol are in agreement, in the sense that each of them implicitly or explicitly responds to it in the same way. With the second taking of the attitude of the other, they learn what it means to employ a gesture with communicative intent and to enter into a reciprocal relation between speaker and hearer. Now the participants can differentiate between the social object in the role of speaker or hearer and the other as an object of external influence, between communicative acts addressed to one's counterpart and consequence-oriented actions that bring something about. And this is in turn the presupposition for a *third* way of taking the attitude of the other, which is constitutive for participants ascribing to the same gesture an *identical* meaning rather than merely undertaking interpretations that are objectively in agreement.

There is an identical meaning when ego knows how alter *should* respond to a significant gesture; it is not sufficient to expect that alter *will* respond in a certain way. According to the first two ways of taking the attitude of the other, ego can only predict—that is, expect in the sense of prognosis—how alter will act if he understands the signal. As we have seen, ego does already distinguish two aspects under which alter can respond to his gesture: (*a*) alter's response is a directed action oriented to consequences; (*b*) at the same time it expresses how alter interprets ego's gesture. Since ego has already interpreted his own gesture by way of anticipating alter's response, there is on his part a prognostic expectation in regard to (*b*), an expectation that can be disappointed. Let us suppose that ego, surprised in this regard by an unexpected response from alter, expresses his disappointment. His reaction reveals disappointment regarding a failed communication and not regarding, say, the undesirable consequences of alter's actual course of action. If we further suppose that this also holds true of alter, we have a situation in which the mechanism of internalization can be applied for a third time—now to the responses through which ego and alter mutually express disappointment at misunderstandings. In adopting toward themselves the critical attitude of others when the interpretation of communicative acts goes wrong, they develop *rules for the use of symbols*. They can now consider in advance whether in a given situation they are using a significant gesture in such a way as to give the other no grounds for a critical response. In this manner, *meaning conventions* and symbols that can be employed with the same meaning take shape.

Mead does not work out this third category of taking the attitude of the other in any precise way; he does touch upon it when explaining the emergence of meaning conventions in connection with the creative accomplishments of the lyric poet: "It is the task not only of the actor but of the artist as well to find the sort of expression that will arouse in others what is going on in himself. The lyric poet has an experience of beauty with an emotional thrill to it, and as an artist using words he is seeking for those words which will answer to his emotional attitude, and will call out in others the attitude he himself has ... What is essential to communication is that the symbol should arouse in oneself what it arouses in the other individual. It must have that sort of universality to any person who finds himself in the same situation."[24]

The creative introduction of new, evaluative, meaning conventions into an existing, already propositionally differentiated, language system is far from the emergence of a signal language. Yet it is instructive on just the point that interests us here. A poet searching for new formulations creates his innovations from the material of existing meaning conventions. He has to make intuitively present to himself the probable responses of competent speakers so that his innovations will not be rejected as mere violations of conventional usage. It remains, nonetheless, that Mead never did become sufficiently clear about the important step of internalizing the other's response to a mistaken use of symbols. This gap can be filled with Wittgenstein's analysis of the concept of a rule.

C. The system of basic concepts that permits us to demarcate 'behavior' from observable events or states,[25] and that includes concepts such as 'disposition', 'response', 'stimulus', was made fruitful for general semiotics in the wake of Mead and Morris, and later in the framework of language theory. Morris drew upon the basic concepts of behaviorism to develop the basic semiotic concepts of sign, sign interpreter, sign meaning, and the like. He did this in such a way that the structural relation of intention and meaning could be described objectivistically, without anticipating the understanding of rule-governed behavior.[26] In laying the foundations of semiotics in behavior theory, Morris appealed to his teacher George Herbert Mead; but he missed the real point of Mead's approach.[27] Mead understood the meaning structures built into the functional circuit of animal behavior as a feature of interaction systems that guarantees a prior, instinctually based commonality between participating organisms. The idea is that internalization of this objectively regulated pattern of behavior gradually replaces instinctual regulation with a cultural tradition transmitted via communication in language. Mead has to attach importance to reconstructing the linguistically sublimated commonality of intersubjective relations between participants in symbolically mediated interactions *from the perspective of the participants themselves*. He can not content himself, as does Morris, with ascribing to individual organisms concurring interpretations of the same stimulus, that is, a *constancy* of meaning as viewed from the perspective of the observer. He has to demand *sameness* of meaning. The use of the same symbols with a constant meaning has to be not only given *as such*; it has to be knowable for the symbol users themselves. And this sameness of meaning can be secured only by the intersubjective validity of a rule that "conventionally" fixes the meaning of a symbol.

In this respect the transition from gesture-mediated to symbolically mediated interaction also means the constitution of rule-governed behavior, of behavior that can be explained in terms of an orientation to meaning conventions. I would like to recall here Wittgenstein's analysis of the concept of a rule, in order, first, to elucidate the connection between identical meanings and intersubjective validity—that is, between following a rule and taking a critical yes/no position on rule violations—and second, to capture more precisely Mead's proposal regarding the logical genesis of meaning conventions. In the concept of a rule, the two moments characteristic of the use of simple symbols are combined: identical meaning and intersubjective validity. The generality that constitutes the meaning of a rule can be represented in any number of exemplary actions. Rules lay down how someone produces something: material objects, or symbolic formations such as numbers, figures, and words (and we shall be dealing only with such formations). Thus one can explain the meaning of a (constructive) rule through examples. This is not done by teaching someone how to generalize inductively from a finite number of cases. Rather, one has grasped the meaning of a rule when one has learned to understand the exhibited formations as examples of something that can be seen *in* them. In certain situations a single example can suffice for this: "It is then the rules which hold true of the example that make it an example."[28] The objects or actions that serve as examples are not examples of a rule in and of themselves, so to speak; only the application of a rule makes the universal in the particular apparent to us.

Not only can the meaning of a rule be elucidated in connection with examples of it; the rule can, inversely, serve to explain the meaning of examples. One understands the meaning of a particular symbolic action—a move in a chess game, say—when one has mastered the rules governing the use of the chess pieces. Understanding a symbolic action is linked with the competence to follow a rule. Wittgenstein stresses that a pupil learning a series of numbers through examples understands the underlying rule when he can go on by himself. The "and so on" with which the teacher breaks off a series of numbers—for example, one exemplifying a geometric progression—stands for the possibility of generating an indefinite number of further instances that satisfy the rule. A pupil who has learned the rule is, by virtue of his generative ability to invent new examples, potentially a teacher himself.

The concept of rule competence refers not only to the ability to produce symbolic expressions with communicative intent and to understand them; nevertheless it is a key to our problem because we can explain what we mean by the *sameness* of meaning in connection with the ability to follow a rule.[29]

The "identity" of a meaning cannot be the same as the identity of an object that can be identified by different observers as the same object under different descriptions. This act of identifying an object about which the speakers are making certain statements already presupposes the understanding of singular terms. Symbolic meanings constitute or establish identity in a way similar to rules that establish unity in the mulitplicity of their exemplary embodiments, of their differnt realizations or fulfillments. It is owing to conventional regulations that meanings count as identical. In this connection, it is important to recall Wittgenstein's remark that the concept of rule is interwoven with the use of the word 'same'. A subject *S* can follow a rule only by following the *same* rule under changing conditions of application—otherwise he is not following a rule. The meaning of 'rule' analytically entails that what *S* takes as a basis for his action orientation remains the same. This remaining-the-same is not the result of regularities in *S's* observable behavior. Not every irregularity indicates a rule violation. One has to know the rule if one wishes to determine whether someone is deviating from it. Irregular behavior can be characterized as a mistake, as the violation of a rule, only in the knowledge of the rule that has been taken as a basis for action. Consequently, the identity of a rule cannot be reduced to empirical regularities. It depends rather on intersubjective validity, that is, on the circumstances that (*a*) subjects who orient their behavior to rules deviate from them, and (*b*) they can criticize their deviant behavior as a violation of rules.

Wittgenstein's famous argument against the possibility of subjects following rules for themselves alone, so to speak, has its place here: "And to *think* one is obeying a rule is not to obey a rule. Hence it is not possible to obey a rule 'privately': otherwise thinking one was obeying a rule would be the same thing as obeying it."[30] The point of this consideration is that *S* cannot be sure whether he is following a rule at all if there is no situation in which his behavior is exposed to critique by *T*—a critique that is in principle open to consensus. Wittgenstein wants to show that the identity and the validity of rules are systematically interconnected. To follow a rule means to follow the *same* rule in *every* single case. The identity of the rule in the mulitplicity of its realizations does not rest on observable invariants but on the intersubjectivity of its validity. Since rules hold counterfactually, it is possible to criticize rule-governed behavior and to evaluate it as successful or incorrect. Thus two different roles are presupposed for the participants *S* and *T*. *S* has the competence to follow a rule in that he avoids systematic mistakes. *T* has the competence to judge the rule-governed behavior of *S*. *T's* competence to judge presupposes in turn rule competence, for *T* can undertake the required check only if he can point out to *S* his mistake and, if necessary, bring about an agreement concerning the correct application of the rule. *T* then takes over *S'*s role and shows him what he did wrong. Now *S* takes over the role of a judge and has in turn the possibility of justifying his original behavior by showing *T* that *he* has applied the rule incorrectly. Without this possibility of reciprocal criticism and mutual instruction leading to agreement, the identity of rules could not be secured. A rule has to possess validity intersubjectively for at least two subjects if one subject is to be able to follow the rule—that is, the *same* rule.

With this analysis of the concept of 'following a rule', Wittgenstein demonstrates that sameness of meaning is based on the ability to follow intersubjectively valid rules together with at least one other subject; both subjects must have a competence for rule-governed behavior as well as for critically judging such behavior. A single isolated subject, who in addition possessed only one of these competences, could no more form the concept of a rule than he could use symbols with identically the same meaning. If we analyze the intersubjective validity of a rule in this way, we come across two different types of expectations: (*a*) *T*'s expectation that it is *S*'s intention to carry out an action in applying a rule, and (*b*) *S*'s expectation that *T* will recognize or admit his action as satisfying a rule.

Let *S* and *T* stand for a student and a teacher with the competence to follow rules and to judge rule-governed behavior. Let *R* be a rule, and *m, n, q* . . . be symbolic expressions that can count as instances of *R* in a given context. Let *BE* stand for the teacher's expectation of behavior, which is based on *R* in such a way that $q(_R)$, for instance, represents a fulfillment of *BE*. Finally *J* is a judgment concerning whether a certain action can be identified as $q(_R)$ that is, recognized as a fulfillment of *BE*; *JE* is the corresponding expectation of this [judgment of] recognition, so that *S*, when he expresses *q* in the expectation *JE*, raises a claim that *T* can recognize through *J*. *BE* and *JE* symbolize the two types of expectations—of behavior and of recognition—that I am concerned to distinguish. We can now state the conditions that must be satisfied if *R* is to be intersubjectively valid for *S* and *T*, that is, to have the same meaning for them; we shall presuppose that *S* and *T* possess the competence both to follow rules and to judge rule-following behavior. Then, to say that *S* is applying a rule *R* in a given context means

1. *S* produces the symbolic expression $q(_R)$,
2. with the intention of fulfilling *T*'s expectation of behavior *BE* in a given context,
3. while expecting in turn $JEq(_R)$ that in the given context *T* will recognize *q* as a fulfillment of his expectation of behavior.
4. *S* thereby presupposes that (1') *T* is in a position to produce $q^1(_R)$ himself, if necessary,
5. by fulfilling (2') in a given context *BEq'*;
6. *S* further presupposes that (3') in this case *T* would have the expectation $JEq'(_R)$ that *q'* will be recognized by *S* as fulfilling his expectation of behavior *BEq'*.

S has to satisfy these conditions if he wants to produce an expression that can be understood as $q(_R)$. Correspondingly, *T* has to satisfy *S*'s presuppositions (4)-(6), and has either to fulfill or fail to fulfill the expectation $JEq(_R)$, that is, to give either a "yes" or "no" response. Should *T* disappoint *S*'s expectation of recognition, he takes over in turn the role of *S* and has to satisfy conditions analogous to (1)-(3), whereas *S* then has to satisfy the corresponding presuppositions of *T* and either fulfill or fail to fulfill the expectation $JEq(_{R'})$, that is, to say "yes" or "no." The sequence can be repeated until one of the participants fulfills the other's expectation of recognition, the two arrive at a consensus grounded on critical positions, and are certain that R is intersubjectively valid for them—which is to say, that it has the same meaning for them.

In our reconstruction we have assumed that S and T believe they know the meaning of R. Student and teacher already know what it means to follow a rule; they want only to be certain whether they know what it means to follow the specific rule R. We can distinguish from this the case in which someone is teaching some-one else the *concept of a rule*. I shall not go into that here but shall proceed directly to the extreme case of the genesis of rule-consciousness on *both* sides—for this is the case that interests me.

I have recaptiulated Wittgenstein's analysis of the concept of following a rule so as to be in a position to apply the results to the employment of communicative symbols. To this point 'q' has stood for any symbolic object produced according to a rule. In what follows I shall restrict myself to the class of symbolic objects we have called significant gestures, or signals, which coordinate the goal-directed behavior of participants in interaction.

To return to our example of a simple symbol: if a member of the tribe, S, shouts "Attack!" in an appropriate context, he expects those fellow members $T, U, V...$ within hearing distance to help be-cause they understand his modally undifferentiated expression q_1 as a request for help in a situation in which he sees enemies appear unexpectedly, is alarmed by the sudden danger, and wants to set up a defense against the attackers. We shall assume that such a sit-uation meets the conditions under which q_1 can be used as a request for assistance. A corresponding rule fixes the meaning of q_1 in such a way that addressees can judge whether "Attack!" is used correctly in a given context, or whether the one shouting has allowed himself a joke in making a systematic mistake—trying, for example, to frighten his comrades upon the arrival of a neighbor by letting out a battle cry—or whether perhaps S does not know how this symbolic expression is used in the language community, whether he has not yet learned the meaning conventions of the word. This example is in some respects more complex and more difficult to get hold of than that of the teacher who wants to check whether a student has learned the rule for constructing a certain number series. However, this complexity proves helpful when we turn to a genetically interesting case, namely, the situation in which S uses the same symbolic expression without being able to rely upon a conventional determination of its meaning, that is, in which 'q_0' does not yet have an identical meaning for the participants. On the other hand, the structure of interaction is assumed already to exhibit all the features that Mead introduces when, on the basis of a *double* taking-the-attitude-of-the-other, he equips participants with the ability to agree in their interpretations of a gesture and to use vocal gestures with communicative intent.

On our presupposition, S produces q_0 *not* with the intention of following a rule, and *not* in the expectation that his hearers T, U, V... will recognize "q_0" as an utterance conforming to a rule. S can certainly *address* q_0 to his hearers in the expectation that (a) they will respond to it with the intention of lending assistance, and that (b) in so responding, they will give expression to the fact that they are interpreting "q_0" as a call for help in a situation in which S sees enemies appear unexpectedly, is alarmed by the sudden threat, and wants help. However, the expectations that S connects with q_0 have only the prognostic sense that T, U, V... *will* behave in a certain way; they differ from BEq and JEq_R in that the conventional elements of meaning are still missing. S's expectations can be disappointed by the nonappearance of the *predicted* behavior, but not by incorrect behavior.

Let us recall how Mead reconstructed these nonconventional expectations of behavior: (a) S anticipates the behavior of T (lending assistance) when he has learned to take the attitude in which T responds to S's gestures; (b) S anticipates the interpretation that T expresses with his response to S's gesture (a call for help in a situation in which...) when he has learned to take the attitude with which T, on his side, addresses gestures to him as something open to interpretation. Now what is the nature of the attitude of T which S has to take over if he is to acquire a rule-consciousness and be in a position henceforth to produce "q" *according to a rule.*

Let us assume that S's utterance "q_0" falls on deaf ears, that T, U, V... do not rush to his aid. The failure to lend assistance is a circumstance that directly disappoints S's expectation (a). There can be trivial reasons for this: his comrades are not within hearing distance, his shouts reach only young and infirm members of the tribe, the men went to get their weapons and thereby fell into a trap, and so forth. If there are no circumstances of this sort, it is not a question of assistance *failing to appear,* but of T, U, V... *refusing* to lend assistance. Of course, Mead's construction rules out already understanding this refusal as the voluntary rejection of an imperative; what is happening is still at the presymbolic level of interaction based on a species-specific repertoire of behavior and proceeding according to the schema of stimulus and response. Thus a refusal to lend assistance can be understood only in the sense of the situation that obtains when S's expectation (b) is disappointed: T, U, V... did not interpret "q_0" in the expected way. Again, there can be trivial reasons for this—but they lie at a different level than in the first case. S may have been mistaken about the relevant circumstances of the situation that form the context in which q_0 is regularly (*regelmässig*) understood as a call for help; for example, he may not have recognized the strangers as members of a friendly tribe, he may have taken their gestures of greeting as gestures of attack, and so on. The fact that T, U, V... have disappointed S's expectation (b) shows a failure of communication for which S is responsible. Those hearing the call react to this failure dismissively by refusing their assistance. The decisive step consists now in the fact that S *internalizes this dismissive reaction by* T, U, V... *as a use of* q_0 *that is out of place.*

If S learns to adopt toward himself the negative positions that T, U, V... take toward him when he goes wrong "semantically" (and if T, U, V..., for their part, deal with similar disappointments in like manner), the members of this tribe learn to address calls to one another in such a way that they *anticipate critical responses* in cases where q_0 is used inappropriately to the context. And on the basis of this anticipation, expectations of a new type can take shape, behavioral expectations (c) based on the convention that a vocal gesture is to be understood as "q" only if it is uttered under specific contextual conditions. With this we have reached the state of symbolically mediated interaction in which the employment of symbols is fixed by meaning conventions. Participants in interaction produce symbolic expressions guided by rules, that is, with the implicit expectation that they can be recognized by others as expressions conforming to a rule.

Wittgenstein emphasized the internal connection that holds between the competence to follow rules and the ability to respond with a "yes" or "no" to the question whether a symbol has been used correctly, that is, according to the rules. The two competences are equally constitutive for rule-consciousness; they are equiprimordial in regard to logical genesis. If we explicate Mead's thesis in the way I have suggested, it can be understood as a genetic explanation of Wittgenstein's concept of rules—in the first instance, of rules, governing the use of symbols, that determine meanings convention-ally and thereby secure the sameness of meaning.[31]

D. Mead offers only a vague description of the evolutionary point at which symbolically mediated interaction appears; the transition from gesture-mediated to symbolically mediated interaction is said to mark the threshold of anthropogenesis. In all likelihood primitive call systems developed already in the phase of hominization, that is, before the appearance of Homo sapiens. There are also indications that significant gestures, in Mead's sense—that is to say, expressions of a signal language—were used spontaneously in primate societies. When interaction became guided by symbols employed with identical meanings, the status systems typically found in vertebrate societies had to change. I cannot go into such empirical questions here.[32] What is important for our conceptual considerations is that with the concept of symbolically mediated interaction, Mead only explains how mutual understanding through use of identical meanings is possible—he does not explain how a differentiated system of language could replace the older, species-specific innate regulation of behavior.

We have followed Mead to the point where he has outfitted participants in interaction with the ability to exchange signals with communicative intent. Signal language also changes the mechanism for coordinating behavior. Signals can no longer function in the same way as gestures—as release mechanisms that "trigger" dispositionally based behavior schemes in organisms. One can imagine that the communicative employment of signs with identical meanings reacts back upon the organism's structure of drives and modes of behavior. However, with the new medium of communication—to which Mead restricts his reflections on the theory of meaning—not all the elements of the structure of interaction have been brought to the level of language. Signal languages do not yet reach into the impulses and behavioral repertoire of participants. As long as the motivational bases and the repertoire of modes of behavior are not symbolically restructured, the symbolic coordination of action remains embedded in a regulation of behavior that functions prelinguistically and rests finally on residues of instinct.

Up to this point we have looked at one-word expressions as examples of symbolically mediated interaction. This description implicitly presupposes the standpoint of a differentiated system of language. But symbolically mediated interactions require neither a *developed* syntactic organization nor a *complete* conventionalization of signs. Full-fledged language systems, by contrast, are characterized by a grammar that permits complex combinations of symbols; semantic contents have been cut loose from the substratum of natural meanings to such a degree that sounds and signs vary independent of semantic properties. Mead did not himself clearly set the stage of symbolically mediated interaction off from this higher stage of *communication* characterized by grammatical language, but he did distinguish it from a more highly organized stage of *interaction* characterized by role behavior. He goes abruptly from symbolically mediated to normatively regulated action. His interest is in the complementary construction of subjective and social worlds, the genesis of self and society from contents of interaction that is both linguistically mediated and normatively guided. He traces the development that starts from symbolically mediated interaction only along the path that leads to normatively regulated *action*, and neglects the path that leads to propositionally differentiated *communication* in language.

This problem can be dealt with if we distinguish, more clearly than did Mead himself, between language as a medium for reaching understanding and language as a medium for coordinating action and socializing individuals. As we have seen, Mead viewed the transition for gesture-mediated to symbolically mediated interaction exclusively under the aspect of communication; he shows how symbols arise from gestures and how symbolic—intersubjectively valid—meaning conventions arise from natural meanings. This entails a conceptual restructuring of relations between participants in interaction; they encounter one another as social objects in the communicative roles of speakers and hearers, and they learn to distinguish acts of reaching understanding from actions oriented to consequences. This new structure of sociation is still coincident with the new structure of reaching understanding made possible through symbols. This is not the case with regard to further development, but Mead does not take that into his account. After he has constituted signal language, he restricts himself to aspects of action coordination and of socialization, that is, to the formative process that takes place in the medium of grammatical language and from which both social institutions and the social identity of socialized organisms proceed with equal originality.

> A person is a personality because he belongs to a community, because he takes over the instititions of that community into his own conduct. He takes its language as a medium by which he gets his personality, and then through a process of taking the different roles that all the others furnish he comes to get the attitude of the members of the community. Such, in a certain sense, is the structure of a man's personality. There are certain common responses which each individual has toward certain common things, and insofar as those common responses are awakened in the individual when he is affecting other persons he arouses his own self. The structure, then, on which the self is built is this response which is common to all, for one has to be a member of a community to be a self.[33]

Mead is here viewing socialization from an ontogenetic perspective, as a constitution of the self mediated by grammatical language; he explains this construction of an inner world once again by means of the mechanism of taking the attitude of the other. But now ego takes over not the behavioral reactions of alter but alter's already normed expectations of behavior.

The formation of identity and the emergence of institutions can now be approached along the following lines: the extralinguistic context of behavioral dispositions and schemes is in a certain sense permeated by language, that is to say, symbolically restructured. Previously, only the instruments for reaching understanding were transformed into signals, into signs with conventionally fixed meanings; at the stage of normatively guided action, however, the symbolism penetrates even into motivation and the behavioral repertoire. It creates both subjective orientations and suprasubjective orientation systems, socialized individuals, and social institutions. In this process language functions as a medium not only of reaching understanding and transmitting cultural knowledge, but of socialization and of social integration as well. These latter do, of course, take place in and through acts of reaching understanding; unlike processes of reaching understanding, however, they are not sedimented in cultural knowledge, but in symbolic structures of self and society—in competences and behavior patterns.

Self and *society* are the titles under which Mead treats the complementary construction of the subjective and social worlds. He is right to start from the assumption that these processes can get underway only when the stage of symbolically mediated interaction has been attained and it has become possible to use symbols with identical meanings. However, he does not take into consideration the fact that the instruments for reaching understanding cannot remain unaffected by this process. Signal language develops into *grammatical speech* when the medium of reaching understanding detaches itself simultaneously from the symbolically structured selves of participants in interaction and from a society that has condensed into a normative reality.

To illustrate this I shall take up once again our example of a call for help, but with two modifications: this time those involved have mastered a common, propositionally differentiated language; moreover, there is a difference in status between S and the other members of the tribe T, U, V..., a difference that arises from S's social role as the chief of the tribe. When S shouts "Attack!", this symbolic expression "q" counts as a communicative act with which S is moving within the scope of his social role. By uttering q, S actualizes the normative expectation that tribal members within hearing distance will obey his request for assistance by performing certain socially established actions. Together, the role-conforming utterance of the chief and the role-conforming actions of tribal members make up a nexus of interaction regulated by norms. Now that the participants can perform explicit speech acts, they will understand "q" as an elliptical utterance that could be expanded so that the hearers understand it, alternatively

1. as a report that enemies have appeared unexpectedly; or
2. as an expression of the speaker's fear in the face of imminent danger; or
3. as the speaker's command to his hearers that they lend assistance.

Those involved know that

4. *S's* status authorizes him to make this request, that is, that he is *entitled* to make it, and
5. *T, U, V...* are *obligated* to lend assistance.

The utterance "q" can be understood in the sense of (1) because, as we have assumed, those involved know what it means to make a statement. Further, "q" can be understood in the sense (3) on the strength of (4) and (5), that is, when those involved know what it is to follow a norm of action. Finally, as we shall see, "q" can be understood in the sense of (2) only if, once again, (4) and (5) obtain—because a subjective world to which a speaker relates with an expressive utterance gets constituted only to the extent that his identity is formed in relation to a world of legitimately regulated interpersonal relations.

If we submit the case of communicative action embedded in a normative context to the same sort of analysis we applied to symbolically mediated interaction—in which participants are not yet in a position to resolve the meaning of the symbols exchanged into its modal components—clear differences emerge not only as regards the degree of complexity but as regards the setting of the problem. We have occupied ourselves with the conversion of communication from gestures over to language, and we have dealt with the question of the conditions for using symbols with identical meanings; now we have to trace the conversion of interaction from a prelinguistic, instinctually bound mode of steering over to a language-dependent, culturally bound mode of steering, so as to throw light on the new medium for coordinating action. This question can in turn be approached from two sides: in terms of communication theory—for in communicative action, reaching understanding in language becomes the mechanism for coordination—or, and this is the way Mead chooses, in terms of social theory and psychology.

From the point of view of communication theory, the problem looks as follows: how can ego bind alter by a speech act in such a way that alter's actions can be linked, without conflict, to ego's so as to constitute a cooperative interrelation? Returning to our example of a call for help, we can see that the actions of S, T, U... are coordinated via the addressees' positive or negative responses, however implicit, to the speaker's utterance. This utterance has an illocutionary *binding effect* only when it permits responses that are not simply arbitrary reactions to expressions of the speaker's will. The term 'arbitrary' is used here to characterize, for example, responses to demands or imperatives that are not normed. In our example, however, the call for help "q" allows for positive or negative repsonses to criticizable validity claims. Hearers can contest this utterance in three respects: depending on whether it is expanded to a statement of fact, an expression of feeling, or a command, they can call into question its truth, its sincerity, or its legitimacy.... [T]hese are precisely the three basic modes available in communicative action. It is easy to see in the case of the assertoric mode that the offer contained in the speech act owes its binding power to the internal relation of the validity claim to reasons; the same holds for the other two modes as well.ᶜ Because, under the presuppositions of communicative action oriented to reaching understanding, validity claims cannot be rejected or accepted without reason, there is in alter's response to ego a basic *moment of insight,* and this takes the response out of the sphere of mere caprice, sheer conditioning, or adjustment—at least that is how participants themselves see it. So long as in their speech acts they raise claims to the validity of what is being uttered, they are proceeding in the expectation that they can achieve a rationally motivated agreement and can coordinate their plans and actions on this basis—without having to influence the empirical motives of the others through force or the prospect of reward, as is the case with simple impositions and the threat of consequences. With the differentiation of the basic modes, the linguistic medium of reaching understanding gains the power to *bind* the will of responsible actors. Ego can exercise this illocutionary power on alter when both are in a position to orient their actions to validity claims.

With the validity claims of subjective truthfulness and normative rightness, which are *analogous to the truth claim,* the binding/bonding effect of speech acts is expanded beyond the range of convictions with descriptive content that is marked out by utterances admitting of truth. When participants in communication utter or understand experiential sentences or normative sentences, they have to be able to relate to something in a subjective world or in their common social world in a way similar to that in which they relate to something in the objective world with their constative speech acts. Only when these worlds have been constituted, or at least have begun to be differentiated, does language function as a mechanism of coordination. This may have been a reason for Mead's interest in the genesis of those worlds. He analyzes the constitution of a world of perceptible and manipulable objects, on the one hand, and the emergence of norms and identities, on the other. In doing so he focuses on language as a medium for action coordination and for socialization, while leaving it largely unanalyzed as a medium for reaching understanding. Furthermore, he replaces the phylogenetic viewpoint with the ontogenetic; he simplifies the task of reconstructing the transition from symbolically mediated to normatively guided interaction by presupposing that the conditions for socializing interaction between parents and children are satisfied.[d]

MEAD'S GROUNDING OF A DISCOURSE ETHICS[e]

Durkheim...credited only universalistic morality with the power to hold together a secularized society and to replace the basic, ritually secured, normative agreement on a highly abstract level. But only Mead grounded universalistic morality in such a way that it can be conceived as the result of a communicative rationalization, an unfettering of the rationality potential inherent in communicative action. In his rough sketch of a critique of Kantian ethics, he attempted to justify such a discourse ethic genetically.[34]

Mead starts from an intuition common to all universalistic moral theories: the standpoint we adopt in judging morally relevant questions has to allow for the impartial consideration of the known interests of *everyone* involved, because moral norms, rightly understood, bring a *general* interest into play.[35] The utilitarians are in agreement with Kant in requiring universality of basic norms: "The utilitarian says it must be the greatest good of the greatest number; Kant says that the attitude of the act must be one which takes on the form of a universal law. I want to point out this common attitude of these two schools which are so opposed to each other in other ways: they both feel that an act which is moral must have in some way a universal character. If you state morality in terms of the result of the act, then you state the result in terms of the whole community; if in the attitude of the act, it must be in the respect for law, and the attitude must take on the form of a universal law, a universal rule. Both recognized that morality involves universality, that the moral act is not simply a private affair. A thing that is good from a moral standpoint must be a good for everyone under the same conditions."[36]

This intuition, which has been given expression in the dogmatics of world religions no less than in the topoi of common sense, is better analyzed by Kant than by the utilitarians. Whereas the latter, with their idea of the general welfare, the greatest happiness for the greatest number, are specifying a point of view from which to test the universalizability of interests, Kant proposes a principle of legislation that all moral norms have to be able to satisfy. From a generalizing compromise among fundamentally particular interests we do not get an interest outfitted with the authority of a general interest, that is, with the claim to be recognized by everyone involved as a shared interest. Thus, the utilitarian is unable to explain that moment of uncoerced, well-considered, rationally motivated consent that valid norms demand of everyone involved. Kant explains the validity of moral norms by reference to the meaning of the universality of laws of practical reason. He presents the categorical imperative as a maxim by which each individual can test whether a given or recommended norm deserves general assent, that is, counts as a law.

Mead picks up this line of thought: "We are what we are through our relationship to others. Inevitably, then, our end must be a social end, both from the standpoint of its content . . . and also from the point of view of form. Sociality gives the universality of ethical judgments and lies back of the popular statement that the voice of all is the universal voice; that is, everyone who can rationally appreciate the situation agrees."[37] Mead gives a characteristic twist to the Kantian argument by responding in social-theoretical terms to the question of why moral norms may claim social validity on the basis of their universality. The authority of moral norms rests on the fact that they embody a general interest, and the unity of the collective is at stake in protecting this interest. "It is this feel for social structure which is implicit in what is present that haunts the generous nature and causes a sense of obligation which transcends any claim that his actual social order fastens upon him."[38] On this point Mead is in accord with Durkheim. The "ought" quality of moral norms implicitly invokes the danger that any harm to the social bond means for all the members of a collectivity—the danger of anomie, of group identity breaking down, of the members common life-contexts disintegrating.

To the extent that language becomes established as the principle of sociation, the conditions of socialization converge with the conditions of communicatively produced intersubjectivity. At the same time, the authority of the sacred is converted over to the binding force of normative validity claims that can be redeemed only in discourse.[f] The concept of normative validity is cleansed in this way of empirical admixtures; the validity of any norm means in the end only that it *could* be accepted with good reasons by *everyone* involved. In this way of viewing the matter, Mead agrees with Kant that "the 'ought' does involve universality ... Wherever the element of the 'ought' comes in, wherever one's conscience speaks, it always takes on this universal form."[39]

The universality of a moral norm can be criterion of its validity only if by this is meant that universal norms express in a reasonable way the common will of all involved. This condition is not met merely by norms taking on *the grammatical form* of universal ought-sentences; immoral maxims, or maxims without any moral content, can also be formulated in this way. Mead puts the point as follows: "Kant said we could only universalize the form. However, we do universalize the end itself."[40] At the same time, he does not want to surrender the advantage that comes from the formalism of Kant's ethics. He poses the problem in the following terms: "But when the immediate interests come in conflict with others we had not recognized, we tend to ignore the others and take into account only those which are immediate. The difficulty is to make ourselves recognize the other and wider interests, and then to bring them into some sort of rational relationship with the more immediate one."[41] Faced with moral-practical questions, we are so caught up in our own interests that *the impartial consideration of all interests affected* already presupposes a moral standpoint on the part of anyone who wants to arrive at an unbiased judgment. "I think all of us feel that one must be ready to recognize the interests of others even when they run counter to our own, but that the person who does that does not really sacrifice himself, but becomes a larger self."[42] Mead makes methodological use of this insight to replace the categorical imperative with a procedure of discursive will-formation.

In judging a morally relevant conflict of action, we have to consider what general interest all those involved would agree upon if they were to adopt the moral standpoint of impartially taking into account all the interests affected. Mead then specifies this condition by way of projecting an ideal communication community:

> In logical terms there is established a *universe of discourse which transcends the specific order* within which the members of the community, in a specific conflict, place themselves outside of the community order as it exists, and agree upon changed habits of action and a restatement of values. *Rational procedure*, therefore, sets up an order within which thought operates; that abstracts in varying degrees from the actual structure of society... It is a *social order that includes any rational being who is or may be in any way implicated in the situation with which thought deals.* It sets up an ideal world, not of substantive things, but of proper method. Its claim is that all the conditions of conduct and all the values which are involved in the conflict must be taken into account in abstraction from the fixed forms of habits and goods which have clashed with each other. It is evident that a man cannot act as a rational member of society, except as he constitutes himself as a member of this wider common world of rational beings.[43]

What was intended by the categorical imperative can be made good by projecting a will-formation under the idealized conditions of universal discourse. Subjects capable of moral judgment cannot test each for himself alone whether an established or recommended norm is in the general interest and ought to have social force; this can only be done in common with everyone else involved. The mechanisms of taking the attitude of the other and of internalizing reach their definitive limit here. Ego can, to be sure, anticipate the attitude that alter will adopt toward him in the role of a participant in argumentation; by this means the communicative actor gains a reflective relation to himself, as we have seen. Ego can even try to *imagine* to himself the course of a moral argument in the circle of those involved; but he cannot *predict* its results with any certainty. Thus the projection of an ideal communication community serves as a guiding thread for *setting up* discourses that have to be carried through *in fact* and cannot be replaced by monological mock dialogue. Mead does not work out this consequence sharply enough because it seems trivially true to him. Its triviality is already attested to by the psychological argument to the effect that we are always tempted "to ignore certain interests that run contrary to our own interests, and to emphasize those with which we have been identified."[44] Mead does, however, also deploy an argument-in-principle. It holds only on the assumption that the justification of hypothetical norms cannot, finally, be isolated from the constructive task of forming hypotheses.

Kant and the utilitarians operated with concepts from the philosophy of consciousness. Thus they reduced the motives and aims of action, as well as the interests and value orientations on which they depended, to inner states or private episodes. They assumed that "our inclinations are toward our own subjective states—the pleasure that comes from satisfaction. If that is the end, then of course our motives are all subjective affairs."[45] In fact, however, motives and ends have something intersubjective about them; they are always interpreted in the light of a cultural tradition. Interests are directed to what is worthwhile, and "all the things worthwhile are shared experiences... Even when a person seems to retire into himself to live among his own ideas, he is living really with the others who have thought what he is thinking. He is reading books, recalling the experiences which he has had, projecting conditions under which he might live. The content is always of a social character."[46] But if motives and ends are accessible only under interpretations dependent upon traditions, the individual actor cannot himself be the *final* instance in developing and revising his interpretations of needs. Rather, his interpretations change in the context of the lifeworld of the social group to which he belongs; little by little, practical discourses can also gear into this quasi-natural process. The individual is not master of the cultural interpretations in light of which he understands his motives and aims, his interests and value orientations, no more than he disposes over the tradition in which he has grown up. Like every monological procedure, the monological principle of Kantian ethics fails in the face of this: "From Kant's standpoint, you assume that the standard is there... but where you have no standard, it does not help you to decide. Where you have to get a restatement, a readjustment, you get a new situation in which to act; the simple generalizing of the principle of your act does not help. It is at that point that Kant's principle breaks down."[47]

Mead develops the basic assumptions of a communicative ethics with both a systematic and an evolutionary intent. Systematically he wants to show that a universalist morality can best be grounded in this way. But he wants to explain this very fact in terms of an evolutionary theory. The basic theoretical concept of the ethics of communication is "universal discourse," the formal ideal of mutual understanding in language. Because the idea of coming to a rationally motivated, mutual understanding is to be found in the very structure of language, it is no mere demand of practical reason but is built into the reproduction of social life. The more communicative action takes over from religion the burdens of social integration, the more the ideal of an unlimited and undistorted communication community gains empirical influence in the real communication community. Mead supports this contention, as did Durkheim, by pointing to the spread of democratic ideas, the transformation of the foundations of legitimation in the modern state. To the extent that normative validity claims become dependent on confirmation through communicatively achieved consensus, principles of democratic will-formation and universalistic principles of law are established in the modern state.[48]

Mead: Symbolic Interaction and the Self

Ernst Tugendhat

SYMBOLIC INTERACTION

Aside from Heidegger, George Herbert Mead is the only philosopher I know of who has attempted to free the relation of oneself to oneself from the conception of a reflexive relation. He thereby sought to extricate it from the traditional subject-object model, and to reconceptualize it in a structurally new way. Perhaps Gilbert Ryle should also be mentioned in addition to Mead; I will return to his work later in this lecture. According to Mead, the relation of oneself to oneself must be understood as talking to oneself, and this in turn is to be understood as the internalization of communicative talking to others. Therefore, the relation of oneself to oneself is essentially both linguistically and socially conditioned. But for Mead the reverse of this conditional relation is equally operative: Only beings that can relate themselves to themselves by virtue of their capacity to talk to themselves can speak the specifically human form of language and can have the specifically human (i.e., normative) form of sociality. The thesis of the connection of language and normative sociality is old—going back to Aristotle[1]— but the addition of the relation of oneself to oneself to this complex of conditions is new.

Thus we are confronted with two conceptions: (a) the Heideggerean acount, which insists that the relation of oneself to oneself is to be understood as a relation to one's own to-be, and (b) Mead's conception, which claims that it is to be understood as a form of talking to oneself.[a] If Mead's conception should prove (when properly interpreted) to be as valid as Heidegger's, we will have to assume that the two conceptions do not represent alternatives, but supplement one another; for there is surely only one truth regarding these matters.

[There are] weak points in Heidegger's conception that demand supplementation.[b] ... Heidegger cannot grasp that eminent form of the relation of oneself to oneself which is termed self-determination as a reflective self-relation because he abandons the standpoint of reason. Deliberation and justification, however, are precisely modes of talking to oneself, and they represent a form of talking to oneself in which the deliberating agent counsels himself from an objective perspective, that is, from the perspective of any given partner. [In *Self-Consciousness and Self-Determination*] we encountered the question of whether the projection of one's own being in terms of a meaning is not essentially dependent upon the social dimension. And this question can easily lead to the assumption that there cannot even be something like a relation to one's own being outside an intersubjective context.

On the other hand, Mead's structural approach contains a clear possibility of connection with Heidegger's structural approach, especially if the latter is understood in light of my interpretation (which deviates a little from Heidegger's own).... Heidegger himself emphasizes the linguisticality of the understanding of being, although he shrinks back from the necessary conclusion that the understanding of being, and particularly the relation of oneself to one's own to-be, is expressed in sentences. Now the yes/no polarity [is] a fundamental aspect of the understanding of being—and, on my interpretation, of the understanding of sentences. This yes/no-polarity contains a reference of all speech to a possible reply. And conversely we will see that Mead's unelaborated conception of the semantics of human language as essentially anticipating the reaction of a partner only attains a clear meaning through recourse to the yes/no-structure. Furthermore, ... Mead is mistaken when he claims that a relation of oneself to oneself is contained in talking to oneself as such. This relation to oneself is given only if the act of talking to oneself concerns one's own to-be; thus, Mead's conception is itself tenable only when it is linked with Heidegger's framework.

These preliminary remarks are intended both to provide an orientation and to justify myself, since such an attempt to connect Heidegger and Mead may appear somewhat peculiar from an external point of view.

Mead did not systematically present his conception of the "self" in a published work but elaborated it in a continually revised course on social psychology that he gave at the University of Chicago during the first third of this century. The relevant source for us is the book *Mind, Self and Society*, which was edited by Charles Morris on the basis of two sets of lecture notes from the years 1927 and 1930. The German translation that appeared in

1968 is entitled *Geist, Identität und Gesellschaft.* Thus, the translator rendered "self" as "identity"—not only in the title, but throughout the text—although in German there is a word *"Selbst"* that corresponds precisely to the English term "self." The term "identity" in the sense that is relevant here came into use in the school of social psychology that originated with Mead, but it was not used by Mead himself; and I must say that this was fortunate because the term is quite unclear. Since it plays such an important role in the contemporary discussion, I will return to it after the interpretation of Mead.[c] Such an overly interpretive translation would be unacceptable even if there were substantive grounds for it, because it denies the reader the chance to be able to evaluate the term for himself. Still, I would like to show you an example of the grotesque consequences to which it leads in the case under consideration. In his concluding reflections on the concept of the self Mead explains: "It is the characteristic of the self as an object to itself that I want to bring out. This characteristic is represented in the word 'self', which is a reflexive, and indicates that which can be both subject and object" (pp. 136ff.). I was curious to see what the translator would make of this, since here Mead explicitly uses the word *self.* He translates the second sentence in the following way: "In the case of identity a subject as well as an object can be involved" (p. 178). This sentence not only fails to render what Mead says but is also unintelligible. The example may suffice to indicate that the translation not only contains a faulty choice of terminology but also is so unreliable that it should not be used. For this reason I will always refer only to the page numbers of the English edition in what follows.

The book is divided into four sections. The first is entitled "The Standpoint of Social Behaviorism," and it serves as a general characterization of Mead's position in contrast to other contemporary schools of psychology. The second section is entitled "Mind," and in contrast to *self* this term is really quite difficult to translate; in the context of Mead's usage it signifies the form of intelligence that is specifically human. In this section Mead develops his conception of human speech as a special kind of interaction, and he characterizes human intelligence as a capacity essentially characterized by the ability to speak. The third section is entitled "Self," and the fourth is entitled "Society." In our context, of course, the third section is the most important. I will begin with a consideration of it, and will subsequently have to return to the second section.

The substantival expression *the self* might lead us to expect the worst.... Isn't a nucleus within the person ... postulated here just as ... in talking about 'the I'? In fact Mead will later discuss "the

I" as a particular aspect of the self that is distinguished from another aspect that he calls "the me." But... it is not the substantival mode of speaking in itself that is bad, since nothing rests upon the expression as such; rather, the question is how the expression is explained. The issue is whether one allows oneself to be misled by the expression into claiming that it involves a something, or whether the explanation discloses that the expression only indicates a mode of behavior of the person. Since Mead understands himself as a kind of behaviorist, he considers only the latter possibility. In contrast to vulgar behaviorism, which disregards the so-called inner sphere, Mead's program (as sketched in the first part of the book) is precisely to show how an inner sphere is constituted on the basis of a specific form of external behavior, namely, communicative behavior. This means that a very specific type of inner sphere is envisioned. It is not the inner sphere that the tradition concerned with the problem of epistemic self-consciousness had in view, but an inner sphere in the sense of the relation of oneself to oneself; and the word *relation* is now meant in the sense of "behavior." Mead is also familiar with the topic of the epistemic self-consciousness of "ϕ" states to which (as he says) only the person himself has access (166).[d] But in contrast to Wittgenstein he did not make it his task to elucidate this sphere of the (in his words) "subjective" in behavioral terms. For him it is a sphere of mere consciousness and not self-consciousness. He says that this subjective sphere is not "reflexive" (ibid.), and we can acknowledge that he was correct in this regard in view of... Wittgenstein. On the other hand, the term *self* is supposed to signify a reflexive mode of relation, and we therefore will have to see how he explains these concepts of self and reflection in behavioral terms.

At the outset Mead introduces the term in an entirely traditional way. I have already cited the following remark: "It is characteristic of the self that it is an object for itself." Thus Mead begins with the traditional subject-object model. The self is basically characterized as that which is "both subject and object"; and Mead also subsequently uses the term *self-consciousness* synonymously (138). At first glance this seems just like the conception... found in the Fichtean tradition. But Mead only uses this conception as a formal indication of the phenomenon that he is seeking. In the tradition this relation of reflection was conceived as an immediate inner relation. But in Mead's view the point is to find criteria for it in behavior.

The following reflection represents a first step for Mead. From a behavioral standpoint, it seems relatively intelligible that a person relates to other people as objects. The question then arises:

"How can an individual get outside himself (experientially) in such a way as to become an object to himself?" The answer reads: "The individual experiences himself as such, not directly, but only indirectly...he becomes an object to himself only by taking the attitudes of other individuals toward himself" (138).

Now, this thesis is so general that it is not tied to the specific subject-object model. It can also be formulated with the aid of the expression *relation of oneself to oneself*, which does not prejudge the structural question. It then reads: Something like a relation of oneself to oneself cannot be conceived as something immediate; a person can only relate himself to himself by relating himself to others and adopting the relation of others to himself. In this formulation the thesis also acquires relevance against Heidegger. But admittedly it is still only a thesis. It is not only not yet justified but also completely unclear with regard to the structure that it postulates. It is unclear how the relation of others to me is to be understood, and which 'attitudes' are involved; and in particular it is unclear what my capacity to take on the attitude of the other toward me is supposed to mean. And above all we must not forget that according to Mead's own methodological claim this entire complex structure is supposed to be explicable in behavioral terms. But from a behavioral standpoint we are not allowed to talk about 'attitudes' at the outset, and we are also not permitted to speak of a relationship to another person as object or of relating oneself to him; rather, we are to speak only of the responses of two or more organisms to mutual stimuli. Hence Mead must confront the task of specifying those stimuli and responses on whose basis something like an attitude toward the behavior of another is constituted; for this is in turn supposed to be the condition for the possibility of constituting a relation to oneself.

Such modes of behavior or action of an organism whose function is to serve as stimuli for actions of members of the same species have a communicative function. If an action Z of organism A functions as a stimulus for an action of organism B, then it serves B as a signal that a state of affairs S that is relevant for B is present. This state of affairs can involve either the organism A itself (e.g., one dog indicates to the other by his aggressive bearing that he is about to attack him) or another state of affairs in the environment that is relevant for B (e.g., the existence of food or the proximity of an enemy). The signaling character of Z can also be understood quasi-prescriptively instead of quasi-indicatively, so that Z has the function of evoking a response from B that is appropriate in the social context of cooperation among organisms. In the normal case of animal communication as exhibited in any of the ways indicated,

B obviously does not grasp the stimulus originating from A *as a signal*; indeed, B does not 'relate' to Z at all, but simply responds to it.

If the 'attitudes' the two organisms that we can call persons are to have to one another must be constituted in a specific interplay of stimuli and responses, this implies that the relation of persons to one another under consideration must consist in a special form of communication. And Mead's thesis is that the constitution of the specifically human form of communication is identical with the constitution of the relevant relation of persons to one another and to themselves. Thus the thesis is not merely that the relation of persons to one another, which itself is supposed to make the relation of oneself to oneself possible, is made possible by the structure of human communication. Rather, it is equally true in a reverse sense that communication only attains the structure that is characteristic of human language when the sending and receiving of signals proceeds in such a way that the sender not only has an effect upon the receiver but also anticipates his reaction, and the receiver does the same thing.

Mead calls the signs of the human language "significant symbols" (46) in contradistinction to the signs of the animal languages that function as signals; the former have a "meaning." What does this mean? Mead provides the following definition: "Meaning is that which can be indicated to others while it is by the same process indicated to the indicating individual" (89). Thus, the characteristic feature of human language is supposed to be that its signs mean *the same thing* for everyone, for those who employ them and for those who apprehend them, and this is the case in spite of the fact that they are responded to in a great diversity of ways (54, 56). This implies two things: The meaning is not simply contained in the response, but is detached from the latter; and in this way it becomes possible that something like an *identical meaning* for sender and receiver is constituted. The communication does not take place in a one-way direction as it does in the simple stimulus-response schema; rather, the sender also indicates the same thing to himself that he indicates to the receiver. It thereby becomes possible for sign giving to be experienced *as* sign giving—and from both sides. This stands in contrast to a situation in which the sign is merely produced or responded to. Here the thesis again reads: The two partners can only relate themselves to an identical meaning of the sign, and hence to the sign as sign, insofar as they relate themselves reciprocally to one another. But the reverse is also true: They can only relate themselves reciprocally to one another insofar as they employ significant signs, and this requires that they use signs in such a way that they have an identical meaning.

This is still merely a thesis, but we now know more precisely what is being sought. The task that emerges for Mead is to discover an interplay of stimuli and responses that fulfills the specified conditions. A preliminary presupposition appears to be that there must be a reciprocal interplay of stimuli and responses that involves more than the mere procession of stimuli from A to B and B to A; rather, it is further required that B responds to the stimulus originating from A with a stimulus that reacts back upon A, and that A itself again responds to this reactive stimulus from B, and so on. Mead locates a phenomenon of this structure in the ritual through which members of the same species adjust to one another in preparing for a social action like fighting, sexual intercourse, or feeding their young. An example is the fighting ritual between dogs (42ff.). The attacking dog does not immediately attack, but makes a gesture that gives notice of the impending attack; the dog under attack responds to this gesture by adjusting in one way or another to the indicated attack, namely, by assuming a specific position; and this position functions once again as a stimulus for the first dog to change his position, and so on. Thus a "conversation of gestures" (43) emerges. As Mead emphasizes, however, these gestures are "not gestures in the sense that they are significant" (43). Mead also wants to avoid as far as possible the connotation of the word *gesture*, which implies that gestures are signs of inner states. *Gestures* are to signify merely "that part of the act" which "is responsible for its influence upon other organisms. The gesture in some sense stands for the act as far as it affects the other organism" (53). Thus the word hardly implies more than the word *stimulus* in this context.

It is clear that the 'dialogue of gestures' described above still does not fulfill the condition that was stipulated by the concept of meaning, since nothing is constituted as identical here and a "separation of the stimulus and the response" (121) also does not yet take place. The two dogs merely respond alternately to the behavior of the other, and they do so in respectively different ways; one still cannot speak of an adoption of the attitude of the other. But it might be argued that this would be attained as soon as each of the two not only responded to the stimulus of the other but also responded to his own stimulus in the same way that his partner does. For under these circumstances it might seem as if each one takes on the attitude of the other, and each also indicates to himself what he indicates to the other. At the beginning of his exposition Mead in fact asserts: "The vocal gesture becomes a significant symbol...

when it has the same effect on the individual making it that it has on the individual to whom it is addressed" (46).

It is possible that a mistake in the lecture notes is involved here, because in the first place it is easy to see that such a simultaneous self-stimulation by itself in no way fulfills the specified condition. If each member responds in the *same* way as the other, this still does not mean that he takes on the attitude *of* the other; and nothing is constituted as identical for both of them as long as they only behave in the same way. Second, Mead himself subsequently points out that there is a form of behavior that possesses this characteristic of simultaneous self-stimulation, but is precisely not symbolic—namely, the vocal behavior of birds and small children, which (as he says) is mistakenly designated as imitation.[2] In the case of birds he states that if the gestures that serve for the reciprocal accommodation to a social action are (a) largely the same for both partners and (b) perceived by the creature itself that expresses them (as is the case for vocal gestures), then the reciprocal stimulation functions at the same time as self-stimulation (361ff.). In addition, a sound that originates from A can be imitated by B in order to stimulate himself to respond appropriately. Mead interprets the behavior of the small child in this way when it alternates between crying and imitating the calming voice of the parent (364). At this point Mead adds: "This childish type of conduct runs out later into the countless forms of play in which the child assumes the roles of the adults about him." This connection appears quite dubious. An understanding of norms is a necessary part of role playing in the strict sense, and hence role playing is linguistically founded; it certainly cannot be linked up so immediately with the vocal interplay of the small child described above. To be sure, Mead also does not want to claim that this interplay already represents a symbolic form of behavior. According to Mead, gestures that are perceived by the being itself that performs them (such as the vocal type) are a necessary presupposition for symbolic behavior. In order for a sign to have the same meaning for communication partners, they both must be able to perceive the same sign; sameness here is to be understood on a phonetic level, although the medium can be a different one. But this sameness, of course, still does not provide the constitution of identity on the crucial semantic level.

What is still missing? Let's grant that one could characterize the child's behavior described above by noting that the child alternates between the adoption of its own attitude and that of the mother; in contrast, the characteristic feature of symbolic communication would be that the speaker anticipates the response of the hearer while performing his speech act. In an essay written in 1922, Mead formulates this point with idealistic exaggeration in the following way: "It is through the ability to be the other *at the same time* that he is himself that the symbol becomes significant."[3] Mead indicates what this is supposed to mean concretely on page 47: "When, in any given social act or situation, one individual indicates by a gesture to another individual what this other individual is to do, the first individual is conscious of the meaning of his own gesture—or the meaning of his gesture appears in his experience— insofar as he takes the attitude of the second individual toward that gesture, and tends to respond to it implicitly in the same way that the second individual responds to it explicitly. Gestures become significant symbols when they implicitly arouse in an individual making them the same response which they explicitly arouse, or are supposed to arouse, in other individuals, the individuals to whom they are addressed."

This is the most extensive account that Mead provides, and we must rely upon the wider context for a more precise understanding. Two questions immediately arise. First, it might be argued that Mead strays from the behavioristic model of explanation through his recourse to implicit responses. But this is not the case if an implicit response is understood as a disposition to the corresponding explicit response; and this is obviously how Mead meant it. Thus the second question becomes all the more pressing: How do we have to conceive of the implicit response of the speaker? That is, what is the explicit response to which it is the disposition? In the passage cited and in other, similar passages Mead has an imperative expression in mind (the gesture indicates to another individual "what he is to do"). This seems to indicate that the disposition of the speaker is the readiness to perform the action himself that is required of the other person, and Mead occasionally provides this interpretation (67) without systematically developing it.

This conception is untenable, and it also cannot be reconciled with other things that Mead says. In the first place it is obvious that if the speaker merely produced the disposition in himself to do the same thing that the hearer is supposed to do, he still would not there- by relate himself to the hearer or to the action that is demanded of him; we still would not have gone beyond the structure of a simul- taneous self-stimulation. It does not follow from the fact that one of them has a disposition to do the same thing to which the other is stimulated that there is something identical to which they both relate. Furthermore, the difficulty arises as to how such a concep- tion is to be applied to nonimperative expressions, in particular, to assertoric expressions; and in many contexts it is clear that Mead has the latter in mind as well. What could the hearer's response be here, which is implicitly produced by the speaker in himself? Perhaps the belief that something is the case? A belief, however, is not a response; it is itself a disposition. Indeed, it is correct that the speaker indicates to himself the same thing that he indicates to the hearer; if he is not lying he has the same belief. But how this takes place is what must be explained by means of the behavioristic model, and we cannot simply smuggle in the concept of belief in this context.

The solution to the problem emerges if we take note of two aspects of Mead's conception: First, the response of the hearer is supposed to be able to react back upon the action of the speaker; an *interaction* is supposed to be involved. This was already taken into account on an elementary level in the "conversation of gestures," but it has fallen out of consideration in the present interpretation of imperative expressions. The second aspect is closely connected to this: The symbolic interaction is supposed to be "internalizable," and this internalization of the relevant relation to the behavior of the other provides the basis upon which the 'self,' the relation of itself to itself, is to be constituted. Now, whenever Mead deals with this internalization, he makes it clear that it involves a form of talking to oneself: The person "talks and replies to himself as truly as the other person replies to him." For "thinking...is simply an internalized or implicit conversation of the individual with himself" (47).

Now this also means that communication, talking to others, has the character of a dialogue. The consequence for our question regarding the explicit response of the hearer and the corresponding implicit (dispositional) response of the speaker is that it must always involve a symbolic response. The response must itself be verbal. This may not appear very plausible for the example of the imperative that is favored by Mead. But the reflections that Mead himself develops in paragraphs 14-16 confirm this hypothesis. Here the understanding of the imperative is dealt with from the perspective of the hearer. "The dog cannot give to himself that stimulus which somebody else gives to him.... In significant speech the person himself understands what he is asked to do, and *consents* to carry out something.... The hearer is not simply moving at an order, but is giving to himself the same directions that the other person gives to him" (108-109, my emphasis). Thus the verbal stimulus of the speaker is not directly related to the requested action of the hearer, but is mediated through the verbal answer of the hearer.

Mead speaks merely of consent, but consent only has significance against the background of the possibility of refusal. The response of the hearer, which is implicitly anticipated by the speaker, is thus his answer of yes or no. Mead does not formulate it explicitly in this way, but the fact that he speaks of a "separation between stimulus and response" in this connection, and of a "delayed response" (98, 117), can only be understood on this basis. This hiatus between stimulus and response differentiates not only imperative communication but also all action that is motivated by symbolic thinking from "reflex" and "habitual behavior"; and this hiatus is characterized by "reflection" (98). Reflection is connected to choice for Mead as well, and is always related to "alternative possibilities of response" (98, 117). Someone who relfects or deliberates speaks to himself in adopting yes/no positions in the same way he would speak to others with whom he was consulting about what to do.... [T]his same yes/no structure is constitutive for the sentences of intention that are considered in deliberation, and also provides the foundation for the range of free possibilities that serve as the presupposition for understanding and employing an imperative as an imperative and not as a signal. Mead clearly recognizes the connection when he says that the addressee of an imperative does not immediately carry it out, but must first give himself the directions that the other gives to him.

Mead's ideas concerning symbolic communication remained in outline form, and he did not develop them into an actual theory of meaning. Thus he explicitly examined neither the special character of the yes-or-no response nor the difference between imperative and assertoric expressions. It would have been plausible within his framework to have expanded upon the characterization of symbolic language in terms of the indicated "separation between stimulus and response" by noting that symbolic language is particularly distinguished from signal language by virtue of its clear separation of practical and assertoric expressions. While the presymbolic organism responds immediately to a given fact in the environment, the symbolically thinking organism apprehends a state of affairs in assertoric sentences and then deliberates in practical sentences about how to respond. A presymbolic communication can be described in both the assertoric and the imperative mood, depending on whether one considers the outlook of the speaker or the addressee; for example, a warning cry can be viewed as information that an enemy is in the area, or as an order to run away. It is neither one thing nor the other, because it does not yet have a unitary meaning for the speaker and addressee. The question of whether the addressee understands the expression assertorically or practically is only decided when the addressee can assume such or such a position toward it; and according to Mead, this adoption of a position is anticipated by the speaker. To be sure, understanding is not exhaustively explained by the adoption of a yes/no position; but the adoption of a yes/no position of speaker *and* hearer refers to rules of action, which in one case govern the justification of what is affirmed and in the other case govern its practical execution. The concrete elaboration of the theory of meaning would consist in the systematic formulation of these rules in behavioral terms.

Of course, the adoption of a yes-or-no position is not the only possible verbal response to a practical or assertoric sentence, and Mead did not even explicitly characterize it in this way. Thus I must emphasize that this is an interpretive addition that seems to me to be indispensable; for it is solely on this basis that Mead's claim regarding the essential feature of symbolic communication— namely, that the response is anticipated by the person who expresses a sentence—can be sustained. It is part of the meaning of both assertoric and imperative sentences that the person who expresses them anticipates in uttering them a possible no from the addressee, and thereby enters into a yes/no dialogue. This yes/no dialogue is readily internalizable, and all further assumptions of a position to what is said (or in any case those that are internalizable) presuppose the adoption of a yes-or-no position. It is also on this basis that it becomes comprehensible that the speaker and hearer relate to something identical, for this is precisely what is affirmed or negated. To be sure, it cannot be argued that the identity of what is said is constituted in the adoption of a yes/no position; it is presupposed in adopting a position. Mead did not demonstrate how this identity is constituted, and this can only be demonstrated in my view by attending to those rules of action to which the yes/no structure itself refers. Mead also did not take another characteristic feature of symbolic speech into account: namely, the fact that its elementary expressions —sentences—contain component expressions that signal languages do not contain; these are the singular terms. In my view, it is in the rules of use of these sentence components that an identity is constituted that makes it possible to speak also of an identity of what is expressed by the sentence as a whole.[4]

Thus Mead did not succeed in establishing those modes of behavior that make a symbolic language possible in his sense. He merely specified criteria that a behavioristic theory of symbolic language would have to fulfill; and in this respect he still seems to me to be a reliable guide for a contemporary theory of meaning. These criteria include an identical meaning for hearer and speaker, and a separation between stimulus and response. This separation is to be understood behavioristically in the following way: A special type of response intercedes between stimulus and response, that is, a verbal response, and it arises in such a way that a dialogue results, which is itself internalizable.

The incomplete character of Mead's theory of meaning is not a problem in our context, since for us the issue is only the extent to which a relation of oneself to oneself is constituted in symbolic interaction as characterized by Mead. Mead's thesis is this: As soon as someone "talks and replies to himself as truly as the other person replies to him, we have behavior in which the individuals have become objects to themselves" (139). One can only relate oneself to oneself in talking to oneself: "I know of no other form of behavior than the linguistic in which the individual is an object to himself, and, so far as I can see, the individual is not a self in the reflexive sense unless he is an object to himself. It is this fact that gives a critical importance to communication, since this is a type of behavior in which the individual does so respond to himself" (142).

This thesis can be evaluated from various positions of proximity and distance. As long as one considers it from the remote perspective of the intuitive reader, it seems entirely plausible that we can only become objects to ourselves by somehow getting outside ourselves, and that this can happen precisely by putting ourselves in the perspective of others who make us their objects.

On the other hand, if we examine Mead's thesis through the language-analytical magnifying glass, we must conclude that the genuine insight it may contain is presented in a structurally absurd way. First, he proceeds from the untenable traditional conception of a reflexive relation in which the subject is itself turned into an object for itself; second, he makes something bad even worse by thinking that he can provide a behavioral foundation for the subject-object model through the stimulus-response model. A way of responding to objects, however complex, still remains a response; a reference to objects only arises through a special type of symbol and its rules of use, that is, the singular terms; and it is in this context that the use of the word *I* is constituted, which makes a reference of the speaker to himself possible. This reference is reflexive in the logical sense, but it does not presuppose a reflexive act.

Let us now make a third attempt by retreating one step. We shall disregard both the traditional and behavioral conceptions through which Mead presents his thesis, and focus only on the aspect of symbolic interaction. The thesis then reads in this way: A relation of oneself to oneself is contained in talking to oneself; and we can add that it is a different type of relation of oneself to oneself from the one that is involved in the mere reference to oneself by means of *I*. In examining the validity of Mead's thesis we must set aside the practical inner dialogue, since in this case one might argue that one's own being is always at issue and therefore that a relation of oneself to oneself is implied. The question is whether Mead is correct in claiming that a distinct relation of oneself to oneself is already contained in the structure of the inner dialogue as such. If the thesis is correct, it must also apply to the theoretical inner dialogue, and Mead obviously has this in mind. Let us therefore imagine that we have to solve some theoretical problem. Such a dialogue might have the following structure: "p because q, and q because r; or is it false that p, since s and t obtain; furthermore, it is surely true that u, but u and p are contradictory. Then wouldn't r have to be false? Or perhaps p doesn't follow from r after all." A relation of oneself to oneself is not contained anywhere in such an argumentation, not even in the adoption of a negative or questioning position toward a preceding simple assumption of a position. In such a train of thought I do not think of myself. Thus, the word *I* also does not even normally occur, and this would be the most minimal condition for being able to talk about a relation of oneself to oneself. And if it does occur, such as when we say "I believe that p," it does not have a meaning that extends beyond epistemic self-consciousness.

Such a meaning is present, however, as soon as the inner dialogue is a practical one, that is, a deliberation. When I deliberate about what I want to do, I relate myself reflectively *to my doing*. Now is this a relating to *oneself*? It certainly is if we grant the Heideggerean conception that in all one's relating to one's own possibilities of action one also implicitly relates oneself to one's own being. But one can also reply affirmatively to this question without recourse to Heidegger's thesis. For it can be argued that in adopting a position toward one's activity one always thereby relates oneself to oneself in just the same way that in adopting a position toward another person's activity one thereby always relates oneself to this person.

Here we encounter a structure that is also discussed by Gilbert Ryle in the *Concept of Mind* in connection with the problem of self-consciousness. Ryle does not limit himself either to the adoption of positions or to linguistic actions in general; rather, he proceeds from a general concept of higher-order actions that are defined by virtue of being related to another action in such a way that the "performance of the former involves the thought of the latter" (191).

Some of the many examples cited by Ryle are replying, retaliating, scoffing, buying, bribing, extorting, resisting, rewarding, criticizing, and approving. This concept of higher-order actions is somewhat larger than the sociological concept of interaction, because it does not presuppose that the actions are those of two individuals who are reciprocally related to one another (e.g., one can scoff at someone behind his back). To be sure, this is connected with an obscurity in Ryle's concept. He did not realize that the relatedness of one action to another cannot be generally understood by assigning the first action to a higher level than the second; for it is characteristic of some of the actions that he himself specifies that the actions to which they are related are related to them in just the same sense, such as the action of buying. The crucial point for Ryle was to make clear that there are such complex actions not only with reference to the actions of other persons; on the contrary, one also learns as a child to perform such actions with reference to one's own actions (193). Ryle certainly speaks as if such a self-reference is conceivable for all actions of this type, although it is quite evident that one cannot, for example, blackmail oneself or sell oneself something. Perhaps Ryle's primary interest in actions that are related to one's own actions also explains why he could overlook reciprocal actions. As far as I can see, actions that are related to one's own actions are always of a higher level: One cannot cooperate with oneself, make a contract with oneself, and so on. And if we say that someone talks to himself or plays with himself, this only means that he talks or plays without someone else, but not that his talking or playing is related to another instance of talking or playing. But it seems to me that still another qualification is necessary. Ryle emphasizes that it is an intellectual prejudice always to conceive of higher-order actions as linguistic (192). As far as I can see, however, all higher-order actions that are related to one's own actions are linguistic.

If this is correct, one would have to concede to Mead that a relation of oneself to oneself is involved in talking to oneself practically, but this is not (as he contended) because it is a form of talking to oneself in which one talks to oneself as one would talk to someone else. Rather, it is a function of the fact that in deliberation one relates oneself to future possibilities of action with a view toward adopting a position (and also evaluatively toward one's past actions). Mead's broader thesis that the relation of oneself to oneself has "essentially a social structure" is not particularly convincing in light of what he has argued so far about the self. It is certainly correct that talking to oneself—both theoretically and practically—is genetically a derivative of communicative speaking, and it is also correct that all talking to oneself can be extended into conversation with others at any time. But it is not clear what is supposed to be *structurally* communicative about speaking to oneself. Indeed, one is obliged to say that from a structural standpoint speaking to oneself is precisely not communicative. Although we sometimes address ourselves by *you* in talking to ourselves, there are here not two quasi-persons who communicate with one another. In a monologue nothing is communicated, and no process of understanding someone takes place; and for this reason there is also no possibility of a misunderstanding, but only one of a lack of clarity.

It is essential to realize that (a) speaking to oneself as such does not constitute a relation of oneself to oneself, and (b) even the form of speaking to oneself that can be understood in a certain sense as a relation of oneself to oneself—namely, the practical form—is still not essentially interactive. This is crucially important for recognizing the special character of the structure that Mead elaborates in the following sections, where he speaks, first, of the "genesis of the self" (sections 19-20) and then distinguishes between "the me" and "the I," which describe the two structural aspects of the self (sections 22, 25). In my view Mead succeeds here, in his theory of roles, in showing that a relation to oneself is only constituted in conjunction with a relation to another. But this relation to oneself is not just any form of talking to oneself, but an adoption of a yes/no position toward one's own being; and it is not just any adoption of a position on the part of others that is involved, but a set of normative expectations. Mead obscured both his theory of language and his theory of roles by not separating them clearly—something that many interpreters regard as his special merit. Thus in his general remarks on language, he speaks as if the anticipation of the other's assumption of a position already involves taking on his role as well. The indefinite talk of "taking the attitude of the other" had unfortunate consequences. An adoption of a position is not yet a role.

THE SELF

In section 19 in which he discusses the "genesis of the self," Mead introduces the problem in such a way that it appears as if the same self is involved that is supposedly constituted in the talking-to-oneself-and-others. But in my view it is clear, first, that a more specific structure is involved, although Mead can correctly claim that this structure is only conceivable symbolically. But the reverse is precisely not true: Talking to oneself and to others does not in itself have this structure. Second, I believe that Mead can correctly claim only that this relation of oneself to oneself is structurally and not merely genetically interactive. Finally, it is my view that a relation to oneself is implied here that can only be understood with the aid of Heidegger's concept of the relation to one's own to-be. Thus if Mead is correct, this relation would have to be understood as something that is constituted through interaction.

In the "genesis of the self" Mead distinguishes "two general stages" (158). The distinction is described differently by him in two places. In the first passage the distinction is not directly elaborated, but is specified in connection with the kinds of children's play that are typical for the respective stages (150ff.). It is characteristic for the first stage that the children play at being something, such as a mother, a teacher, or a policeman. In doing this "they take on different roles" (150). The children only learn that form of play which Mead calls games at the second stage (he mentions baseball as an example). He describes them as "organised games"; and they are essentially games for several people in which each individual performs a specific role in such a way that he must be ready to take the role of everyone else. This description is somewhat misleading. It is not essential that one must actually be ready to take the role of someone else; rather, the point is that each role can only be understood in the context of its interplay with the other roles. The characteristic feature of such games is that they are constituted through rules (152); and the rules determine the reciprocal rights and duties of the players. A child can only play such a game if he has understood what it means to join with others in a common activity that is determined by rules and to act in accordance with such rules. (One reason why Mead's successors also did not make a sharp distinction between his theory of language and his theory of roles is that speaking is also performed according to rules. But linguistic rules do not define rights and duties; linguistic rules are not norms in the narrow sense, but technical rules: Failure to comply with them does not lead to a sanction, but to a lapse in understanding.)

In the second passage in the text Mead describes the two stages directly instead of circuitously indicating the kinds of play that are characteristic for them: "At the first of these stages, the individual's self is constituted simply by an organisation of the particular attitudes of other individuals toward himself and toward one another.... But at the second stage in the full development of the individual's self that self is constituted not only by an organisation of these particular individual attitudes, but also by an organisation of the social attitudes of the generalised other or the social group as a whole to which he belongs" (158).

These descriptions give rise to many questions, and some of them can be answered on the basis of Mead's further explanations. I find it particularly difficult to bring together the accounts of the first stage that Mead provides in the two places; and it is correspondingly difficult to form a clear picture of his conception of the first stage. The first characterization suggests that at the first stage roles can only be played and not exercised, because an understanding of the rights and duties that are constitutive for roles does not yet exist. Other places suggest that Mead is also concerned with the difference (that has been extensively analyzed in subsequent role theory) between the capacity to exercise an individual role and the capacity to exercise different roles in different social contexts without (as is often said) losing one's identity. Mead sees this identity ensured in the development of what is called "character" (162ff.), and he thinks that this "organisation of the personality" arises as an "individual reflection" out of the organization of the group to which the individual relates at the second stage (158ff.). This thesis is not particularly convincing, and it would seem more plausible to regard the transition from role identity to character identity as an additional gradation within the second stage. I will return to this later.

The question of precisely how Mead wanted his first stage to be understood is not that important here, because we are mainly concerned, not with genetic, but with structural questions. And these pertain above all to the second stage; only at the second stage is "self-consciousness in the full sense of the term" supposed to be attained (152). And it is not difficult to see how the descriptions that Mead provides in both places for the second stage harmonize with one another: The structures of the games described in the first characterization correspond to the structures of real social life described in the second characterization. In both places Mead's principal term is the *generalised other*. This term signifies the "organised community or social group" (154). An organized community is a totality of individuals who stand in a relation of "cooperation" (155). Aristotle had already defined the term *koinonia* in this way, and it was subsequently translated into Latin as *societas*.[5] A *koinonia* is a free association of individuals for the reciprocal promotion of their well-being. And Aristotle calls a *koinonia politike* a community that is indispensable for the existence of its members; thus it is a community that is entered into, not for the sake of a particular end, but for the sake of existence itself. This is to be distinguished from a merely contractual community, of which the game group is also an example. The qualification "free" is employed neither by Aristotle nor by Mead, but it seems to me to be necessary in order to distinguish a human community from an animal one. And this qualification is also implied both for Aristotle and for Mead by virtue of the fact that such a community is mediated by the form of language that is specifically human. If someone is a member of an "organised community," he is free to resign his membership despite the fact that this may mean his death (as is certain in the case of the slave). Even in the fundamental community of the *koinonia politike* cooperation is based upon a yes that is at least implicit.

Upon this the special character of the regularities that govern cooperation in the context of a human community is founded: They are norms. Mead does not employ this concept, but it is implied by him. Indeed, he uses the even more general concept of rule (152) without explaining it more precisely. The meaning of rules of action, and specifically of norms,[6] can be elucidated by contrasting them from two sides; a form of rule-governed behavior is on the one hand different from a form of behavior that is merely *regular* as a result of causal factors, and on the other hand it is to be distinguished from behavior that is governed by imperatives. An "imperative" is an *individual* order to action: someone who follows a rule acts in accordance with a *general* standard for action under specified conditions. In this respect rule-governed behavior is similar to behavior that exhibits regularity, but it is different from the latter by virtue of the fact that the rule 'demands' an action just as an imperative does. This is expressed linguistically in a prescriptive sentence, and is manifested in behavior through the agent's capacity to respond by yes or no just as he does to an imperative. This implies that the agent is free to follow the rule or not; and the fact that the agent does or does not follow the rule *for reasons* (just as he does or does not follow an imperative *for reasons*) indicates that freedom is involved here in the strong sense that pertains to the sphere of the practical question and deliberation. Someone who follows a rule may merely have good reasons to adhere to it—for example, in order to avoid a greater evil (such as punishment). But he also can adhere to it of his own accord, and in this case he not only has good reasons to follow it but also considers the rule itself to be well justified. Rule-governed behavior is most often distinguished from cases of behavioral regularity by looking at the way that exceptions are handled. In the case of a behavioral regularity, an exception necessitates the admission that the assumed regularity only takes place with a certain frequency; in the case of rule-governed behavior, it is presumed that the rule is 'broken,' and the behavior can be criticized in this respect. But a critical attitude involving words of praise or blame is also possible in relation to the behavior of an animal or a small child, which is only more or less regular. The crucial aspect of rule-governed behavior is that the agent himself can criticize his behavior. This presuppoes that he *recognizes* the rule, whether he acknowledges its validity as such or relative to his other ends. Thus the criterion of criticism is founded upon the criterion according to which the rule represents a reason for action.

Norms are a type of rule. Many authors even employ the term coextensively with that of *rule.* But it seems more plausible only to designate social rules as norms. These involve rules that are followed out of regard for others, and for this reason are also ordinarily socially sanctioned in one way or another in contrast, for example, to technical rules or private maxims of action. We can now understand more fully what Mead means in talking about the "attitudes" of the social group. He is referring to the normative expectations that members of the group reciprocally have regarding their behavior. (I should note here in parentheses that it was customary for a while in sociology to define norms simply as "expectations of expectations." But this expression can only mean that the agent expects (and this means he *knows*) that the others expect (and this means they *require*) a specific action from him. Thus the expression *expectations* has a different meaning at the first point in this formula from the one it has at the second point. Since at the second point it stands for expectations that are themselves already normative, this formula does not fulfill its claim to define the concept of norm; on the contrary, it presupposes it.)

Within the domain of norms, those norms that govern cooperative practices form an essential nucleus; their eminent status derives from the fact that it is only on their basis that a community is constituted. Furthermore, it is only in the case of norms governing cooperative practices that it seems self-evident that for every obligation of one individual there are corresponding rights of other individuals. The concept of cooperation should not mislead one into thinking that cooperation must be coordinative, so that all members have equal rights; rather, it can just as well be a largely subordinative relation, the extreme case being that of the slave who has no rights and only duties. Now Mead calls the nodal points of organized social cooperation roles. Someone who occupies a specific role—for instance, a mother, teacher, or policeman (to return to the examples cited by Mead for children's role-playing)—has specific cooperative duties and rights; in other words, the role consists in a collection of cooperative rights and duties.

We can now understand what Mead means by the "generalised other" and his "attitudes." Mead speaks of the "generalised other" not just because attitudes of the "social group" are at issue but also because these attitudes are normative expectations, and this implies that they are generalized demands. These expectations do not simply arise from all the individuals of the group, but they are grounded in the organization of cooperation within the society. They are directed toward the individual, not as an individual, but as the bearer of specific roles; they are directed "toward the various phases or aspects of the common social activity" (155). In this respect the "reaction of the community" has "what we call an institutional form" (167).

The structure developed by Mead has now been sufficiently clarified so that the following question can be raised: To what extent can he claim that an individual attains what he calls self-consciousness (or what we may term self-relation "in the full sense of the word") merely on the basis of this structure (152), that is, merely by taking on roles and thus situating himself in one way or another within the totality of cooperative activities of a society? A relation of oneself to oneself is obviously implied here that does not merely consist in an assumption of a position toward one's own possibilities of action, as is the case in any practical form of talking to oneself. In the relation of oneself to oneself that is currently under consideration, the individual no longer relates himself merely to individual actions; or more precisely, since he always relates himself to individual possibilities of action, he relates himself to these in light of the extent to which they correspond to how (or as what) he wants to understand *himself.* In adopting a role I understand *myself* as a so-and-so; and since I develop a definite character in the mulitplicity of roles, the issue in a more significant sense becomes who (what kind of a person) I want to be, that is, how I understand *myself.* What is contained in this "myself" or "oneself"? Mead did not pose this question, because he thought he had already explained the meaning of this reflexivity by means of the structure of speaking to oneself. The mistaken character of this belief can also be seen from the fact that when Mead designates the second stage in the genesis of the self as the "fully developed self" and as "self-consciousness in the full sense of the term" (152), he does not want to contrast this designation with that "self" which is supposedly contained in the formal structure of talking to oneself; rather, he contrasts it with the first stage of role behavior (whose precise structure admittedly has remained unclear). But this means that the talk of a "self" and of a relation to oneself has a specific meaning in the context of role behavior, and in *this* sense a "self" and a relation to oneself still cannot be found in talking to oneself as such, even if the latter is practical.

We have [in *Self-Consciousness and Self-Determination*] encountered this structure of understanding oneself as a so-and-so in Heidegger, and it seemed clear [in that work] that this structure can only be understood in connection with the to-be. The fact that I understand myself as a so-and-so means that my to-be, my life, has this meaning for me. Must we return to this structure of the to-be for the purpose of understanding Mead's thesis that a relation to oneself is constituted in role behavior? You might say that understanding oneself as a so-and-so simply means ascertaining that such and such role predicates apply to oneself, such as being a mother or a teacher. But there are other predicates that apply to me for which it is obviously not appropriate to say "I understand myself as..."—for example, "I understand myself as having black hair or as now giving a lecture." And even role predicates can apply to someone without one being prepared to say "I understand myself as a so-and-so." For example, it is conceivable that someone could say "Indeed I am a teacher (or a mother), but I don't understand myself as a teacher (or a mother)." The implication here is that one occupies the role, but does not 'identify' oneself with it. What does this mean? It obviously means that the cooperative activities that exist through this role do not 'fulfill' me, that is, my will to live; in other words, they do not constitute or help to constitute the meaning of my life.

The following consequences can be drawn from these considerations: First, a relation to oneself (i.e., to one's to-be) is contained in the assumption of roles, because roles as cooperative activities are constitutive of meaning. Second, the role is only an offer of meaning, and whether I make it my own or not depends on me. Thus, we also encounter the phenomenon of the adoption of a yes/no position here, and we will later see that this aspect of role behavior is crucial for Mead himself. The tension between identification and distance has relevance for the aspect of the self that he designates as "I." But taking a position toward roles is a relation to oneself, not because it involves taking a position toward something, but because it is taking a position toward possibilities of understanding *myself*; and here *myself* means my life. Even if one experiences a role that one occupies as not meaningful for oneself—for one's life—one relates oneself precisely in this way to oneself, to one's life and its potential meaning.

Thus we can only understand Mead's thesis that a self-relation is contained in the performance of cooperative activities that are maintained through roles if we align it with Heidegger's concept of the relation of oneself to oneself. But Mead claims not only that a relation to oneself is contained in role behavior but also that a relation to oneself is constituted only in role behavior: "One has to be a member of a community to be a self" (162). Or if we want to formulate this point in terms of the perspective that was just outlined, he is claiming that the cooperative possibilities of action marked out by roles are not only offers of meaning but also the only possible offers of meaning. This thesis cannot simply be refuted by pointing out that to a great extent we are unable to identify ourselves with our roles, and that so many of the socially given cooperative activities can be experienced only as 'alienated labor.' Rather, the fact that given forms of cooperative activity are experienced as meaningless can equally be regarded as an indication that cooperative activities always involve the claim to provide a basis of meaning; hence, it is only for this reason that they can be experienced as meaningless. Thus a critique of socially given cooperative activities from the standpoint of their meaning would always be conceivable only on the basis of a model of a better society—or in any case this is Mead's conception. Such a critique cannot be developed from the perspective of an activity that is not socially related; the latter is not a possible source of meaning at all.

Mead merely advanced this position as a thesis, and perhaps this was a consequence of his mistaken belief that the essentially social character of the relation of oneself to oneself already is established through the supposedly communicative structure of talking to oneself. Mead seems to me to have come closest to a proper justification of his thesis in his reflections on the connection between recognition and self-respect (Sec. 26). We [can] find in Hegel this conception that self-consciousness is only constituted in the process of being recognized by others. Here we finally encounter the colloquial meaning of *self-consciousness*,[7] which implies something like the feeling of self-worth. This self-consciousness has nothing to do with theoretical self-consciousness, but is a mode of the relation of oneself to one's own to-be: It is the consciousness that one's life has value and is not worthless. And this seems to be the condition of the capacity to affirm one's life in the sense of being willing to continue to live. We must apparently experience ourselves as worthy of affirmation in order to be able to affirm ourselves. And we only experience ourselves as worthy of affirmation, at least genetically speaking, if others have affirmed us—that is, have loved and recognized us; and structurally speaking, this occurs only if we believe that others can affirm us.

Here I must again introduce a wider perspective. [According] to Aristotle . . . the characteristic feature of human volition is that it is not only indirectly related to the preservation of its own life through the feelings of pleasure and pain (as is animal volition); thus, a human being not only is directed toward the satisfaction of his needs but also, as a user of language, has a consciousness of his life. Consequently, he no longer blindly does what is good for the preservation of his life by being guided by his sensations; rather, he can himself reflect upon what is good or bad for him. And since a human being has a directly volitional relationship to his life—that is, relates himself to himself—he is dependent upon being able to affirm his life; hence he must give his life a 'meaning' and seek to live a good life.

The last-named expressions—"affirming one's life," "giving it meaning," "wanting to live a good life"—are not equivalent. It is no accident that Aristotle only focuses upon the last of these three expressions, and that in Heidegger precisely this expression or one equivalent to it is missing.

In order to see the interconnections correctly, we first have to clear up an ambiguity that can have confusing consequences for the first of these expressions. We obviously are only dealing here with practical affirmations. But these can themselves have different meanings. The yes to one's own life in the sense of a willingness to continue to live has the meaning of a sentence of intention: It expresses a volition. On the other hand, when we say that one person affirms another, *affirm* always means something like "esteem"; and *esteem* means to find something good: It involves a value judgment. And if it is correct that we can affirm our life in the sense of wanting to continue to live only if we think that our life has 'value' (i.e., that it is worthy of affirmation, which means worthy of esteem), then self-affirmation in the first sense of "affirmation" presupposes or requires self-affirmation in the second, evaluative sense. And this second sense is essentially an intersubjective one.

The requirement that life have a 'meaning' stands, so to speak, between these two meanings of affirmation. This requirement is more formal than the second meaning and merely implies that there is something in terms of which one can understand oneself in one's will to live. Now if Mead had talked to Heidegger, he would have advanced the following thesis: (a) we only find meaning in a form of life that we can regard as worthy of esteem along with others; and in connection with this, (b) the relevant activities are those that we engage in not only for ourselves but at the same time for and with others: that is, cooperative activities.

There are views in Heidegger that approach the second half of this thesis, since it is also true for him that human existence is essentially being-with (*Mitsein*), a being with and for (or against) others (BT Sec. 26). But this aspect remained peculiarly faint and undeveloped in his work. On the other hand, there is nothing in

Heidegger that corresponds to the first part of the thesis—namely, to the idea that the will can only fulfill itself in something that is 'good' in the sense that it requires intersubjective recognition. He merely touches upon this idea in discussing that inauthentic albeit widespread form which he designates as "distantiality" (BT, p. 164) and which also belongs to inauthentic existence for him. This form is characterized by "concern about one's difference from others" in which the issue is merely one's "priority over others," and one is only intent upon either "catching up" to the others or "holding them down." In contrast, Mead points out that the productive possibility of a "sense of superiority" (208) should not be overlooked simply because of this "disagreeable type of assertive character" (205); in particular, one must not overlook the fact that a structure is involved that "seems to belong essentially to self-consciousness" irrespective of all moral evaluation. I can also reformulate what Mead means here by saying that self-consciousness in the ordinary [German] sense of the word seems to belong essentially to the relation of oneself to oneself.

Heidegger's neglect of this structure in its constitutive meaning for the relation of oneself to oneself results from his lack of consideration of the concept of the good; and this in turn is connected to the fact that Heidegger eliminated the aspect of reason—of objective justification—from the relation of oneself to oneself. Something is called good—or, more precisely, better—if it is preferable on objective grounds, and accordingly I was able [in *Self-Consciousness and Self-Determination*] to interject some aspects of the good into the context of the practical question that is constitutive for authentic existence. Nonetheless, the ultimate reference point of deliberation remained one's own well-being. On the other hand, we now come across a use of the word *good* that could not even be acknowledged in a supplementary way in the interpretation of Heidegger [in the aforementioned work] because its reference point is not one's own well-being, although as soon as it does come into play it becomes relevant for the question of what is best for me.

It is generally characteristic of human abilities that they can be developed in ways that are better or worse; they stand on a scale of preferability. Whatever one 'can' do, one can do better or worse, and this also means better or worse than others, for example, singing, swimming, cooking, or repairing cars. Depending upon how important a particular ability is to us or how much we like to exercise it, we will be intent upon exercising it as well as possible. Aristotle tended to understand *good* in this sense as aptness for the production of the work to which the activity is related.[8] But this account cannot be sustained universally,[9] first, because there are activities such as swimming and singing that are not directed (like repairing a car) toward the production of something, and, second, because there are activities such as cooking that are directed toward the production of something, but the produced work does not provide a simple criterion for their good (as it does in the case of a repaired car). On the other hand, it is obvious that my formal definintion of *good* also works here. X can sing, swim, cook, repair cars, better than y if those who properly understand the activity in question prefer the performance of x to the performance of y. A subjective element thus enters in here, although the preference is not simply subjective and arbitrary but is objectively justified. The criterion for this claim to objective justification, however, is merely that those who properly understand the matter make the decision on what is to be preferred. I see the look of doubt in some of your faces, but I must let this stand as a thesis.[e] For this reason I also only want to give an equally programmatic answer to the next question that arises here—namely, the question of how it is to be decided which people understand the matter properly if there are no objective criteria. The answer runs as follows: It is those individuals who are most experienced in the affair at issue; and a person x is more experienced in something than a person y if there is a course of experience from y to x that results in y sharing the value judgments of x, but no course of experience from x to y. Thus, good or better in this sense is what would be acknowledged as such by everyone once they have had the necessary experiences: The consensus (qualified in the way just indicated) is not a consequence of objective criteria, but is itself the sole criterion. Heidegger's complete neglect of this meaning of *good* does not seem to be based merely upon the fact that like every other use of *good* this use appeals to objective justification. Rather, this form of justification contains an indissolubly social, intersubjective aspect; thus if *good* in this sense were also to be relevant for the relation of oneself to oneself in the mode of authenticity, a form of self-determination would no longer be conceivable in which one could simply choose for oneself without referring to the agreement (even if only potential) of others.

But you might raise the following question: Why must the striving for excellence in some abilities be relevant for the relation of oneself to oneself, especially if the latter is considered in the mode of authenticity? In my view we can distinguish three levels in both a structural and genetic sense, even if there are no sharp boundaries. Of course, that affirmation which we experience at the beginning of our lives and which constitutes the basis of our feeling of self-worth cannot yet be related to roles. But at a very early stage it does contain moments of esteem that refer to various kinds of ability, to the development of abilities that have a social significance in at least a broad sense.

Now Mead's thesis is that it is only when abilities are expanded into roles that a dimension is opened in which the individual relates himself to himself. This involves two aspects. First, roles are also contexts within which abilities are exercised; and this implies that the exercise of a role stands on a continuum ranging from "better" to "worse," and here these words have the same meaning that they have in relation to abilities generally. Second, it is not sufficient for the individual merely to perform particular socially recognized actions more or less well; rather, he can only develop a relation to *himself* and a feeling of self-worth in the strict sense when he attains a specific social place for himself (and this means for his life) with a long-term cooperative function.

The third level, which is only intimated by Mead through his reference to the development of a character, arises as a consequence of the fact that the exercise of roles is constitutive but not sufficient for the development of a relation of oneself to oneself. We say, for example, that "as a teacher he is excellent, but as a person I cannot approve of him"; and obviously the question "Who do I want to be?" with reference to myself is not exhausted by answers such as "a good teacher," "a good mother," but always has the more comprehensive sense of the question "What kind of a person do I want to be?" I do not have a theory of how this question is to be understood more precisely, I will therefore restrict myself to critical remarks concerning the way in which both Heidegger and Mead deal with it; and in both cases I will return to Aristotle.

As criticism of Heidegger: Aristotle bases his ethics on the idea that the same mode of use of *good* and *bad* that applies in general to human abilities and activities also applies to the activity of human life as such; thus since every person is concerned about his being, he must be concerned to carry it out in the best possible way.[10] And in this context the question of which life is a good one is again decided by those individuals who properly understand this matter, that is, those who have the greatest practical wisdom.[11] I do not think this is a theoretical trick on Aristotle's part, but rather corresponds to our ordinary understanding. This understanding is not to be found in our use of the expression *good person* (here the word *good* has assumed a more specific connotation in modern usage), but it appears in many other expressions; it is evident, for example, when we say "I admire or think highly of him as a person," "he is a wonderful or exemplary person," or "I find such a way of life right." By virtue of their form such value judgments raise the claim to be objectively justifiable statements, which present two possibilities: Either they prove to be mistaken or onesided, or we must be able to convince others of their validity. This implies neither that there is only *one* ideal possibility of human existence nor that someone could simply adopt some ideal conception as his own; furthermore, the irretrievably individualizing and volitional components in choosing oneself that we established in the interpretation of Heidegger [in *Self-Consciousness and Self-Determination*] do not have to be denied. It is certainly true that every path of self-discovery and self-determination must be an individual one; nevertheless, this does not preclude but rather accommodates the insight that a criterion of the correctness of this path is that it would have to meet with the approval of those who 'understand something of this matter.' We saw [in the aforementioned work] that one cannot speak of self-determination if either the volitional or the rational aspects are omitted. And we can now see that the rational aspects are omitted to the extent that one either dispenses with learning from others in relation to one's own decisions, or gives up being able to convince others of their merit. Heidegger made a mistake in thinking that the 'self' in the talk of "I myself" is only to be understood on the basis of the contrast with others. In reality this manner of speaking is to be understood in terms of the decision that I myself make, and in this respect it stands in contrast to a decision that is not made by me but by something in me; and this is precisely the case when the rational aspects (which involve intersubjective aspects, as we have just seen) cease to assert their role.

As criticism of Mead: It seems that the only perspective that Mead has in mind with regard to the question of transcending individual roles is that of integrating various roles. But one can readily ask whether the 'question of identity' should be so exclusively oriented toward the concept of roles, especially when the meaning of this question is what kind of a person I want to be. It might be argued that the question of what kind of a person I want to be always means the following: What kind of a person do I want to be in relationship to my fellow men? But precisely at this point one must ask whether it is warranted to understand the relationships between people exclusively as as normative relationships (as has become customary in sociology). Although the normative relationships are the ones that count from the perspective of the institutional organization of society, this does not apply from the perspective of the individual. Here affective relationships have at least as much fundamental significance, and it is worthwhile in this context to recall that for Aristotle the question of what it means to be an excellent person focused entirely on this aspect. Since in affective relationships I relate myself *to myself in* my relationships *to others*, the task in these affective relationships is to strike an optimum, that is, a proper mean;[12] and one must grant Aristotle that what is called character is the affective behavioral disposition of a person. Thus the question concerning the right way of being of a person cannot center upon the integration of various roles, because in the first place this question can be crucial in deciding which roles I select for myself to the extent that this falls within my freedom. More important, however, this question can also already be relevant within the context of exercising a *single* role; thus, for example, a postal clerk can impress us in the way he does his work, not because of the way he functions in his role (e.g., as a good postal clerk), but because of the human qualities by which he exercises it. And if he has found such a standard in himself, in his affective character, it naturally follows that he also will remain 'the same' in another role.

Does this problem concerning the question of what kind of a person one wants to be represent the same stage in Mead's work that Heidegger addresses in his account of 'authenticity'? No, this is still not the case. For even if one explicitly raises this question, it does not have to be raised from an independent standpoint; it can be exclusively oriented toward what 'one' regards as appropriate. And it is noteworthy that in his distinction between *me* and *I* (Sec. 22, 25) Mead envisages a contrast that is similar to the one made by Heidegger by means of his concepts of 'the they' and authentic existence.

Mead defines the "me" as "the organised set of attitudes of others which one himself assumes.... The taking of all of those organised sets of attitudes gives him his 'me'" (175). Thus, the me constitutes the picture of the normative expectations that others have of me. It is the projection of expectations emanating from the society onto me. Mead obviously selected this expression because he thereby wanted to refer to what I am as an object of social expectations; or, more simply, he wanted to refer to how I ought to be in my roles and in my other behavior from the standpoint of society. Mead comes very close to Heidegger's description of 'the they' when he says, "The 'me' is a conventional, habitual individual. It is always there. It has to have those habits, those responses which everybody has" (197).

In contrast, the "I" is "the answer which the individual makes to the attitude which others take toward him ... the 'I' gives the sense of freedom" (177). This concept is more extensive than that of self-determination.[f] It represents in a general sense the response of the individual to the expectations directed at him—the yes or no (accepting or declining, 194). Thus, Mead fixes the conceptual boundary at a different place from that of Heidegger, but this difference is relatively unimportant; it can be done in one way or the other. For Heidegger, the 'they' is a mode of being-oneself; hence, he speaks of the 'they-self'—that is, the self that accommodates itself to what is regarded as correct. In Mead's conceptual framework this is *one* possible response of the 'I' to the 'me.' For Mead, the entire spectrum of possible responses to social expectations pertains to the "I." The person acts in his own peculiar way no matter how he responds, no matter how he performs the role expected of him. Thus an aspect of innovation always pertains to the 'I' (177, 203). But the crucial alternative is the one between yes and no, between "devotion" and "self-assertion" (192), and this means between "adjusting one's self or fighting it out" (193).[13]

It is important to understand this concept of self-assertion correctly. First, there is no connection between this concept and that of the sense of superiority. Rather, the need to distinguish oneself from others functions within the context of what is universally acknowledged. In contrast, by means of the concept of self-assertion Mead considers the possibility of giving a negative reply to what is universally acknowledged. Second, it must be noted that for Mead such a negative reply cannot consist in a simple refusal in which the individual goes his own way; rather, it can only consist in a new universal conception that is directed toward gaining recognition against the others. For this reason, this "self-assertion" is a "fighting it out." "If one puts up his side of the case, asserts himself over against the others," this implies that he "insists that they take a different attitude toward himself." Mead continues: "Then there is something important occurring that is not previously present in experience" (196). Innovations in the real sense rest upon such acts of self-assertion, which in some instances are collective; this promotes the development of society and prevents its ossification.

We have now reached the point at which the real contrast to Heidegger's conception becomes evident, since Mead's concept of self-assertion represents his concept of self-determination. Although Mead scarcely elaborates his conception, it contains the essential characteristics of self-determination in germ: that is, that the individual himself chooses who (how) he wants to be, and does not thereby orient himself toward any accepted or conventional points of view. Mead does not describe this as self-determination but rather as self-assertion, because the individual relates himself to himself in such a way that he thereby relates himself to others who relate themselves to him; and for this reason he cannot understand himself in a new way without at the same time understanding social relations differently. Thus the individual is directed toward asserting and implementing his new view of the being of persons— of social being—against the others. If it seems in Heidegger as if authentic existence is a turning away from the 'they,' one has to ask: Where can it turn to? To be sure, a turning away from the 'they' is required, but only in the sense that the existing normative conceptions are no longer accepted simply because *one* accepts them. But this only happens to the extent that one grapples with precisely these normative conceptions; if one tries to turn one's back on them, one remains bound up with them in reality. While the 'they' in Heidegger has no positive significance aside from constituting the actual structure of our everyday existence, the 'me' for Mead has the positive connotation that normative conceptions must first be existent in conventional form in order for a society as well as a relation of oneself to oneself to be constituted. Furthermore, conventionally preexistent norms provide the only material on whose basis an autonomous self-relation can be worked out; and the result of this work can only be improved conventional conceptions.

How is the self-assertion that Mead has in mind to be understood concretely? "The demand is freedom from conventions, from given laws. Of course, such a situation is only possible where the individual appeals, so to speak, from a narrow and restricted community to a larger one, that is, larger in the logical sense of having rights that are not so restricted" (199). "A man has to keep his self-respect, and it may be that he has to fly in the face of the whole community in preserving his self-respect. But he does it from the point of view of what he considers a higher and better society than that which exists" (389). Mead conceives of such a higher society as one in which more "democracy" in the sense of more "brotherhood" is realized, that is, in which "every individual stands on the same level with every other" (286); thus the subordinating structures of social cooperation are dismantled.

"The only way in which we can react against the disapproval of the entire community is by setting up a higher sort of community which in a certain sense out-votes the one we find. A person may reach a point of going against the whole world about him.... But to do that he has to speak with the voice of reason to himself. He has to comprehend the voices of the past and of the future. That is the only way in which the self can get a voice which is more than the voice of the community," and it is the only way in which it "can change the attitude of the community" (167ff.).

Mead's conception remained a sketch. Although the irreducibly individual and volitional aspects of self-determination that we were able to extract (and want to retain) from Heidegger's conception are lacking, we now see that Mead's view corrects Heidegger's conception not only with regard to its social deficiency but also with regard to its rational deficiency. Both aspects esentially belong together for Mead. The appeal to reason in practical matters is the appeal to a consensus that would have to result if there were "universal discourse," that is, a discourse of all rational beings (157ff., 195). This appeal is necessary if an individual arrives at a conception of the good life different from that held by others. We saw earlier that "good" is something that is preferable on objective grounds, and we have no material criteria for this; rather, it is the most experienced who decide on this matter. When I advanced this position you may have suspected that the decision regarding the good is thereby surrendered to what is merely conventional. But there is a difference between those who are most experienced and those who are regarded as such. For this reason an individual can assert the correctness of a divergent view in opposition to the prevailing one, but he cannot simply appeal to his intuition or his authenticity in so doing; rather, he has to be aware that the criterion for the correctness of his view is the possibility of ultimately convincing the others.

This is a troublesome affair in any concrete case. Let us therefore find consolation in the fact that at least it sounds noble in the abstract. We now have a concept of a reflective self-relation in which a position is deliberatively taken toward the existing individual and social beliefs that are implied in one's own actions, in social actions and in institutions; and deliberating here means raising questions regarding what is actual, possible, and better. This deliberative adoption of a position pertains in particular to the beliefs implied in one's own conceptions and social conceptions of the right form of life or, more precisely, the right form of communal life. And this form of talking to oneself at the same time is implicitly a discourse with all rational beings.[g]

Part 4
The Interpersonal and Intrapersonal

The Powers and Capabilities of Selves: Social and Collective Approaches

Guy E. Swanson

PERSPECTIVE

> Luther knew that in his own eyes he would never add up. He would always be tugged apart by the antitheses which confronted him at every turn, by theology and philosophy, by spirit and letter, by gosepl and law, by faith and works. But God acts upon him with a singleness of love.... And God saw Luther as an integrated human being.
>
> What God chooses to see is, at his seeing, real. His vision is creative. He sees and makes good. It had been so from the first world: "God said let there be... and there was.... God saw... it was good.".... As at the new creation, God looks graciously upon his creatures and they are full of grace. God's seeing renders human beings just.
>
> There is nothing very odd in all this.... [I]t is a common experience that we may take on the character that another sees....
>
> (Swanston, 1982: 56-57)

INTRODUCTION

Most of the research labeled explicitly as a study of the self has to do with the rise in infancy and early childhood of people's awareness of their own minds and the minds of others (for example, research on the growth of insight, empathy, modeling, or role taking: e.g., Bandura, 1971; Berndt and Berndt, 1975; Flavell and Others, 1968j; Selman, 1980). Or it concerns people's feelings about themselves (e.g., Hales, 1980; Rosenberg, 1979; Schranger and Schoeneman, 1979; Wylie,

1974) or concerns differences between behavior "as a self" and other behaviors (e.g., Bandura, 1977a; Langer, Blank, and Chanowitz, 1978; Ofshe and Christman, 1985; Schacter and Singer, 1962).

My own recent work has had a different focus. I have looked for social, especially collective, sources distinctive to one rather than another of serveral adaptive processes (e.g., reflective intelligence, psychological defenses) that people display as selves. In this paper, I sketch some of the background from which these studies are emerging, review a sample of problems and findings, and suggest some directions for new research.

For anyone who comes from G. H. Mead (1934), it is axiomatic that selves are socially constituated and that any activity "as a self" (e.g., thinking reflectively, defending one's "ego," "savoring a joke," "going mad," "being fulfilled") will operate according to an internalized "social-logic" rather than a "psychologic." For anyone who comes from sociology, a further suggestion of Mead's is of special interest: the suggestion that many adaptive processes distinctive to action as a self operate according to criteria that are not only social in origin and relevance but are, specifically, collective: a structure through which people carry on joint activities. This is illustrated in Mead's treatment of reflective thinking as an internalized conversation conducted in terms of a division of labor. It also appears in Freud's (e.g., [1933]) and Parsons' (1955a; 1955b) analyses of much of psychodynamics as the operation of internalized familial relations (see also Bandura, Ross and Ross, 1963; Liem, 1980; Parsons and Olds, 1955; Reiss, 1981; Whiting, 1960). This way of thinking requires that one find in collective relations some principles of operation which, if acquired and used by participants, could reasonably be understood as constituting some aspect of the dynamics of personality (or cognition) "at the level of the self."[1]

Seen historically, Mead's interests and approach, and Freud's, are those of a liberalism present around the turn of the century (Lerner, 1934; Mead, 1930; Mills, 1964; Mannheim, 1929-1931; Petras, 1986; Schorske, 1980; Shibutani, 1968). There is the conviction that personal strengths and weaknesses make a difference in people's ability to get what they want, to prevail, to find happiness. There is the belief that many strengths can be cultivated and many weaknesses overcome, and by a means—education or therapy—that does not directly challenge the wider social order and that is well within its ability to provide. There is the view of personality and society as structures that arise to facilitate adaptation and the view that both are continuously modified in the course of adaptation. There is the stress on rationality as the most important personal power, not only for individuals but for social progress and for that amelioration of social conflicts that can come through people's understanding of the perspectives of others. (Freud was, of course, less sanguine than Mead about the prospects for social and personal betterment.) And there is the assumption that human life is, in important respects, life in community.

Whatever its limitations, this outlook does focus attention on forms of action distinctive to persons, and on their sources, interrelations, and vicissitudes: on people's powers (abilities to do, act, or produce) and capabilities (capacities for being used or developed as selves). As Rawls (1979: 443-444) says, these powers and capabilities take their meaning from their value for the people who "have" them and for others (severally and collectively) and are a foundation for people's self-concepts, especially their self-esteem. He writes,

> Let us distinguish between things that are good primarily for us (for the one who possesses them) and attributes of our person that are good both for us and for others as well.... Thus commodities and items of property (exclusive goods) are good mainly for those who own them and have use of them and for others only indirectly. On the other hand, imagination and wit, beauty and grace, and other natural assets and abilities of the person are goods for others too: they are enjoyed by our associates as well as ourselves.... They form the human means for complementary activities in which persons join together and take pleasure in their own and one another's realization of their nature. This class of goods constitutes the excellences: they are the characteristics and abilities of the person that it is rational for everyone (including ourselves) to want us to have.... [T]hey enable us to carry out a more satisfying plan of life enhancing our sense of mastery. At the same time these attributes are appreciated by those with whom we associate, and the pleasure they take in our person and in what we do supports our self-esteem.
>
> ...natural shame...arises...from the injury to our self-esteem owing to our not having or failing to exercise certain excellences....

My own research has focused on people's powers and capabilities as selves and especially on their social sources. Like Mead and Freud, I pay special attention to collective sources because these seem the bases for those abilities as selves that people employ across many situations and because experiences in collectivities (e.g., families, schools, businesses, social movements, societies) are usefully understood as the particular source of some of those abilities. These are points I elaborate and illustrate as I go along.

ORGANISM, EGO, SELF

I use the words self and person interchangeably, somewhat preferring "person." "Person" has several meanings, among them—across the last 1500 years (Danto, 1967)—its reference to the individual when he takes account of his own behavior—of its components, dynamics, and determinants (takes account, for example, of his own attitudes, desires, purposes, knowledge, developmental trajectory, or abilities)—and acts accordingly. That is the way "self" is used in the functionalist psychology associated with the names of Royce, Peirce, Dewey, and G. H. Mead and on which I draw (Baldwin and Stout, 1902; Dewey and Others, 1903; Heidbreder, 1933: 201-233; James, 1904; Misiak and Sexton, 1966: 320-326; White, 1943: 134-148).

In that psychology, the individual self is distinguished from, and related to, the individual as ego and as organism. (But never in just this terminology!) All of these aspects of his life are interdependent and each is, in some respects, independent of the others. A sampling of its points will recall this familiar line of argument: 1) Life as an organism precedes and is a part of the life of anyone who is an ego: of anyone, that is, who has learned to behave: has learned to relate to an environment in an instrumental way. (In this sense, all animals operate to some extent as egos.) 2) Life as an ego precedes and is a part of life as a self since selves (or persons) are egos paying attention to their own behavioral processes. 3) Organisms, egos, and selves differ in the kind of sustenance they require: for organisms, oxygen, perhaps, or protein and carbohydrates, for egos, such things as stimuli and reinforcement; for selves, love, respect, empowerment, and so on. 4) And the "health" or "vigor" of any one of these aspects of individuals has no necessary connection with that of the others: individuals who are sick or weak as organisms may be competent as egos and strong and vigorous as selves: or, as in many psychopathologies, we see healthy organisms and competent egos joined to incapacitated selves.

THE SOCIAL CONSTITUTION OF A SELF

It has been common since the 18th century to see individuals as becoming selves through experience in social relations. (The writings of the Scottish moralists [Hume, Ferguson, and others], and of

Montesquieu, provide examples). Since the early part of the 19th century—in Hegel's thought, for example, or in that of Marx—a link between development as a self and social experience has been found in the provision in social relations of points of view, individual and collective, from which people can pay attention to their own behavioral processes and take them into account. This is a key idea that Mead, Piaget, and Freud bring into modern research.

Mead argues that other people, individually and collectively, and only they, pay attention to our behavior as behavior and they use what they learn to shape, manipulate, or help us. They also teach us how to analyze behavior, theirs and our own. They give us standardized symbols that are especially important in our objectifying our inner life: its phases, processes, and contents. They hold us responsible for taking their behavior and our own into account: taking account, for example, of their and our desires, plans, knowledge, abilities, and potentialities.

Thus, for Mead, a self is socially constituted in being created through social relations: through people's being led, trained, equipped, and motivated to see their own point of view as one among many and to take simultaneous account of it and of any others that may be relevant. But it is also socially constituted in consisting of expectations, motivations, and methodologies concerning social relations.

Such arguments, in the form in which Mead offers them, are unlikely to be testable. To know whether he is right we should study people who grow up with no social contacts. Given that they are unavailable, the practical importance of Mead's argument is its suggestion that we look especially to people's relations with others to understand their functioning as selves.

To anticipate a criticism, Mead's is not another "oversocialized" (Wrong, 1961) view of people. Individuals may act as selves on behalf of their requirements as organisms or egos. They may use their abilities as selves to exploit or abuse others as well as to conform to others' wishes or to promote others' interests. And Mead's view does not preclude our seeing that each person is an individual: a separate being who must be separately nourished and gratified; who has had a particular history of experiences; who participates in several social relationships and, because these usually compete for his allegiance and resources, must find his way among them; who can anticipate the span of life and the experiences remaining to him. In short, it does not preclude our treating each individual as having, in important measure, a separate organic and psychic "economy" and as evaluating experience against the present and anticipated state of that economy.[2]

But Mead does tend to underplay the role of motivation and the need, in becoming a self, to deal with strains inherent in social relations. "There are passages in Mead which suggest a belief that the cognitive taking account of the other is a sufficient condition for the distinctively human self to emerge. It is this which the Freudian interpretation...denies..." (Selznick, 1960: 256).

Freud reminds us that we are interested in other people because they can do things to and for us. Social relations always grow and persist because they in some sense serve the personal interests of their participants as well as their shared interests (many interests, of course, are both). And personal gain is always a part of the "social contract" that is at least implicit as the ground of a social relationship: a statement of the basic terms and procedures through which people are willing to help others and do what is required to keep their relationship alive.

Freud also underscores the ambivalence involved in these contracts; the fact that individuals tend to give only what they think they must in order to get what they want from a relationship: the fact that, if they could, they would take the benefits a relationship offers without accepting the constraints or providing the service required to maintain that relationship. For Freud, individuals with the attributes of persons or selves are products of a reasonably satisfactory resolution of the Oedipal conflict: of their acquiring the proper commitments to authorities and sources of nurturance; of their discovering that, through these commitments, they will be amply fed. "The resolution of the Oedipus complex...decisively alters psychic functioning. It makes the child autonomously self-regulating. The formation of this new structure (i.e., the superego) constitutes the definitive differentiation of the ego from the id..." (Gedo and Goldberg, 1973; 78).[3]

THE COLLECTIVE CONSTITUTION OF A SELF

We may take it as a rule of thumb that any experience, orientation, ability, or skill, which is defined by an individual's paying attention to his own mind and another's has its origin and organization in social relations. It is hard to imagine the appearance of such "states" of individuals as embarrassment, submissiveness, extraversion, pride, or jealousy in the absence of social relations. The same can be said of insight, empathy, self-management, communication, person perception, "decentering" (Inhelder and Piaget, 1955; 342–350), "role-taking" (Mead, 1934) and the like.

What leads to an emphasis on collective relations? The observation that some of an individual's interests are activities as a self entail—again, by definition—his taking account of his own mind and the interests and activities of a group, especially of a group in which he participates (or wants to participate) and which he wants to support.

> Social relations are relations among people as persons: that is, relations in which people take account of whatever is on their own minds and the minds of others and seek to articulate the two ... Social relations are collective to the extent that persons are engaged, whether knowingly or not, in a common under-taking: taking account of concerns, capacities, and potential-ities for joint action: trying to make use of the common life or to promote or change it. (Swanson, 1980: 190-217)

In general, this will mean the individual's relating his interests and activities to such things as the collective purposes, systems of authority, division of labor, and bases of solidarity that make joint action possible. These, it is often suggested, are the conditions that give meaning to loyalty, judiciousness, guilt, and perfectionism; to deference, rebelliousness, objectivity, a sense of transcendence: and so on. Durkheim (1912) proposed that experiences with collective purposes and processes were a source of experiences of gods and spirits: of trancendent personalities (Swanson, 1960) and therefore of, for example, experiences of sin, perfectibility, justification, salva-tion, and inspiration. Such experiences seem also a source of beliefs in one or another form of personal immortality (Swanson, 1960: Chapters 6, 7, 8 and 9). Mead suggests that reflective thinking is grounded in collective relations because, in his view, such thinking is internalized argumentation and real argumentation assumes con-tending points of view that will be evaluated in terms of collectively-derived standards of evidence and reasoning and collectively-prescribed standards and procedures for determining whether beliefs and commitments have become sensible or obligatory. Ex-tending this line of thought, he suggests that highly formalized re-flective thinking (what Piaget would call formal operations or consolidated formal operations) entails a universality in point of view that could come only in consequence of participation in a soci-ety in which many well-established points of view contend: a highly pluralistic society or one having an elaborate division of labor. Thus, in Mead's view, reflective thinking is occasioned by the need to deal with actual or anticipated arguments and it proceeds by means of standards and methods (e.g., adjudication, setting "objec-tive" tests, negotiation, reconciliation) employed in actual argumenta-tion. In this view, the occasion for reflective thinking and the terms of resolution are given collectively: the "dynamics" of the person's action, and not just its components, are given in the processes and imperatives of collective relations, becoming intrapersonal as a result of participants' internalizing those relations through learning and commitment. It is obvious that Freud moves along similar lines in analyzing the existence and possible resolution for Oedipal conflicts.

Two additional points:

1) In analyses based on collective relations what is sometimes only implicit in those based on social relations becomes clear: individual's activities as selves are seen as arising from their involvement in a process and pattern of relating socially. By contrast, some expositors, while writing of the social or collective constitution of selves, write as though action as a self was the result of an individual's being subjected to this discipline or that (Rapaport, 1959: 15) or of learning one role or another (Brim, 1960) (or of learning about variations in the formal properties of all roles) (e.g., Newcomb, 1950; 264–334; Sarbin, 1950, 1952, 1954; Sarbin and Allen, 1968; Stryker, 1980, 1981; Turner, 1978). What becomes clearer in analyses of individuals' relations with collectivities is the sense in which people's functioning as selves turns on their learning some of the *systematics* of a social relationship and acting in terms of experiences with the relationship *as a whole*, this including the principal differentiations of role and activity that it embodies and the individual's own position and rights and obligations within the whole.

2) People's more persistent and characteristic orientations and abilities as selves, and the ones that they and other people tend to think are the most important, are likely to be grounded in collective, and not just social, relations. This is so because collective relations are more likely to endure and therefore to provide continuing conditions that effect the lives of their participants. Social relations encompass all instances of people's relating to others and themselves as persons. Taken in the aggregate, they are pervasive. But, taken individually, most are transient. Only a few are required and sustained for longer periods and this is because they are collective as well as social: social relations through which people are trying to pursue a common undertaking. And some collective relations—for example, the family, friendships, and community, the national state —tend to exist for long periods of their participants' lives and even beyond. It is, of course, of great importance that individuals' principal needs are met through such enduring collective relations and that, through them, the main course of individuals' socialization and life careers are determined. It is for these reasons that analysts who, like Mead and Freud, are interested in the structure and dynamics of "personality" or of enduring cognitive systems are more

likely to find relevant social considerations in collective than in merely social relations.

SOME STUDIES OF COLLECTIVE RELATIONS AND PERSONALITY

The usefulness of distinguishing collective from other forms of social relations has been shown in studies of the systematics of the main "traits," "dimensions," or "orientations" of personality as a self. It now seems conclusively established that the great bulk of these are constituted by main dimensions of collective relations (e.g., Bales, 1968, 1970; Conte and Plutchik, 1981; Couch, 1960; Foa and Foa, 1974, 1980; Leary, 1957; Longabaugh, 1966; Parsons, Bales, and Shils, 1953; Schaefer and Bayley, 1963; Schutz, 1960; Wiggins, 1979).

It seems, however, that people's powers and capabilities as persons (e.g., such as their adaptive processes as reflective intelligence and other procedures for analyzing problems, trying out solutions, and coping with pressures) tend to be more stable as features of their behavior than are traits or orientations (Bem and Allen, 1972; Block and Haan, 1971; Eichorn and Others, 1981; Mischel, 1968, 1973). My own recent research has focused on possible collective sources distinctive to one self process rather than another. In the section that follows, I describe research on three such processes: reflective intelligence, losing oneself in imagined worlds, and defending one's ego. (For collective sources of what Freud called "primary process," see Swanson, 1974b. For collective sources of "pregenital" styles of social behavior, see Swanson, forthcoming).

To the extent that these self processes are internalized collective processes, the systematics of each, and the relations of each with the others, should be helpfully understood as collective in character. Thus, as I shall treat them, reflective intelligence is a process of analyzing problems as would the participants in a group; losing oneself in imagined worlds involves looking at oneself and other things from the perspective of a group taken as whole; ego defenses are socially available methods for finding oneself acceptable in one's own and others' eyes despite one's deviance from commitments to joint ventures.

To me, each of these processes is an activity of an individual as a self: an individual's taking account of what is "on his mind" and acting accordingly. Each is a kind of broad adaptive process and should, therefore, be more stable as a feature of individuals' action than are most personality "traits." Each is a kind of personal power: an ability to adapt the world and one's behavior to one another for personal and/or social benefit: in reflective intelligence, the ability to dissect problems and assemble a solution; in losing oneself in imagined worlds, the ability to enter and live from the objectives of a group (the better to use or serve the group); in ego defenses, the ability to develop an account of one's conduct that will enable one to live equably with oneself and others despite one's being self-condemned and, at least implicitly, socially condemned for deviant tendencies. Each is also a capability: a way one can be used as a self or a way one may develop as a self: a special potentiality as a self.

Beyond these considerations, each of these processes has had a strategic role in past thought about our lives as persons or selves. Mead, following Kant, Hegel and the philosophers on whom they built, took reflective intelligence to be the activity that distinguished people from other animals and the precondition for any "moral" or "social" life beyond the most rudimentary. Freud pictured the ego defenses as resolutions of great inner conflicts through the exercise of what are simultaneously personal and social controls. The experience of losing oneself in an imagined world (e.g., as in hypnosis) is one of a family of activities that seem to entail a powerful social penetration of personal life, even to the extent of interfering with action as a self through the supplanting of one's own will by another's. The clarification of such processes can give us a better understanding of the constitution and vulnerabilities of selves: of the boundaries between life as a self and other states and forces.

REFLECTIVE INTELLIGENCE

Mead suggests that, to the extent a group's action embodies collective purposes and a clear division of labor through which those purposes are implemented, its members are led to see themselves, one another, and their situation in their relevance, simultaneously, for several interests, individual and collective, and to act accordingly. They may be able to articulate very little of this. The collective "purposes" or "interests" (Hirschman, 1977) exist implicitly in people's having to act together if their own interests are to be furthered and in the "terms" or basic "rules of procedure" they have discovered that must be met if joint action is to proceed. Again, and whether participants recognize it or not, a division of labor implies specialized activities that serve some over-arching collective activity and embodies in those specialized activities distinctive points of view from which the whole enterprise and each separate aspect are evaluated and guided. And the specialized activities must themselves be carried out and coordinated in such a way that the over-arching interests are advanced. Think, Mead says, of an athletic team and the way players in the several positions act in dealing with a fast-changing situation, adapting to one another and to the situation at large in making a particular play and getting in a favorable position for the next. Or think of any collectivity (because it is a part of the very definition of a collectivity as against a collection of individuals that there is some sense of who is and is not a "member"— rightful participant—and of joint activity) however simple. There, Mead says, one finds conditions that train people in the activities that comprise reflective intelligence.

There are many qualifications that should be attached to Mead's argument, but it contains a testable prediction. Other things equal, people with more experience in collectivities having the features he specifies—features that constitute "principled" collective decision-making—should be more likely to employ reflective intelligence in solving problems. I tried to test that prediction in a population of adolescents, using as an independent variable the patterns of decision-making found in their families (Swanson, 1974a).

The use of decision-making to operationalize collective organization was not arbitrary. A principal difference between a group and a collection of people who are interacting, is that a group consists of arrangements through which joint or common activities can be pursued and such arrangements necessarily entail some criteria or procedures for making collective as against individual choices: for defining common objectives and participants' shares in the work, costs, and benefits of the undertaking (Swanson, 1971a). In short, collective action requires arrangements for collective choice: collective decision-making.

In this study, I used a typology of nine patterns of decision-making (Figure 1) devised originally for use with primitive and early modern societies (Swanson, 1967, 1969) and adapted now for use with families (Swanson, 1971a). In this system, collectivities are classified as having or lacking a head (a person or sub-group that can legitimately decide for the group), as having or not having persons or sub-groups the head must consult in making decisions, and as legitimizing or not legitimizing attempts by participants to influence decisions in the service of their special and personal interests as well as collective interests.[4] Groups that have a formal system of government are easy to code on these dimensions. Groups like families or primitive societies which lack such a formal system can be coded if we have a record of collective choice made in the course of one or several years. For my study of families such a code could be based upon life-history interviews with parents and adolescent children and covering the previous five to ten years of their lives. Coders read all the interviews from a given family and derived

Figure 1
Patterns of Decision-Making in Families

Below are nine models of ways families make decisions. We would like your impression about how ... [this] family makes it decisions. Read through all nine of the models and choose the *one* that *best* describes ... [this] family. Put a *1* in the blank beside that model. Then put a *2* beside the model that is the *next best* description of the family.

Note that each model focuses on the parts the *parents* play in making family decisions. Models 1-4 describe families in which *one* parent has final decision-making responsibility, if he wants, and models 5-9 describe families in which the parents have *joint responsibility* for most decisions.

_____ 1. In this family, one parent is seen by *all* as being the "head" of the family. He makes the final decisions. However, the other parent has the right to give advice and to expect that his advice will be sought and taken into account.

_____ 2. This family is identical with the one just described except that the "head" of the family makes the final decisions on the most *important* issues the family has to decide. In less important family matters, each parent has his own areas of responsibility and competence and has considerable freedom to decide what will be done.

_____ 3. In this family, one parent is without question the head of the family. He can, if he chooses, have the final word in deciding what the group will do, and how it will do it. The other parent does not usually expect to be consulted for advice, even though he sometimes is.

_____ 4. This family is identical with the one just described except that the decisions of the head of the family usually apply to the *most important* issues the family has to decide. In less important family matters, each parent has his own areas of responsibility and competence and has considerable freedom to decide what will be done.

_____ 5. In this family, both parents discuss a problem together and agree on a solution *before* they announce their decision to the family or begin to carry it out.

_____ 6. This family is identical with the one just described, except that "decision" is too strong a word for the parents' standard way of doing business. They talk over problems, or talk around them, until a sort of *common view* emerges. This view is then the basis for action.

_____ 7. In this family, the parents often consult together about what the family will do, and agree on a solution before they announce their decision to the family. However, each parent also has the right to make decisions and act on his own. If the other parent wishes, he then can review this decision, and question and even delay the action, until both parents have consulted together and reached an agreement about the final course of action.

_____ 8. This family is identical with the one just described except that, should the parents disagree on something that is urgent and important, one in particular has the right to break the tie and make the decision.

———— 9. In this family it is difficult to identify a standard procedure of decision making. Things are often done, or not done, pretty much as the moment dictates. The parents may or may not consult together about decisions. If either dislikes what the other is doing, about all he can do is to withhold resources (like money, time, encouragement) that are necessary for his partner's activities. Similarly, he often finds that the best way to get his partner moving, is to supply some of these resources specifically for the purpose he intends.

a picture of the basic system of authority. Families were coded as meeting Mead's criteria for principled collective action if the interviews with both parents were coded by any combination of the following patterns from Figure 1: 1, 2, 4, 6, or 7.

Reflective intelligence was taken to mean what Piaget has in mind by operational intelligence. Parents and children worked on two of Piaget's cognitive tasks: pendulum and correlations. Scores for each task were available as was a composite score.

The median Piagetian scores for the children in the family prove to be significantly higher if the familily has a pattern of decision-making embodying the properties Mead specified. This relationship survives controls for the socio-economic status of the family, the Wechsler (WISC or WAIS) scores of the children and parents, and the Piagetian scores of the parents. In short, cognitive and collective complexity are associated as Mead thought.

"LOSING" ONE'S SELF IN IMAGINED WORLDS

People participating in collective action pursue interests that are peculiarly theirs and also interests they have made their own but that are also the collectivity's. Thus they, individually, support the interests of the group or the cause, seeing their situation as supporters or agents of the collective effort and acting accordingly. They can have the experience of "losing themselves" (i.e., not paying attention to other things) in collective pursuits; of "travelling in imagined worlds" (i.e., living for a time only from the perspective afforded by the collectivity).

As Theodore Sarbin (1950) and Josephine Hilgard (1970) show, there are wide individual differences in the propensity to lose oneself in imagined worlds: in a novel, perhaps, or in nature, music, religion, roles, sex, or some physical activity (e.g., in skiing or swimming). Ease and depth of hypnotizability provides only a dramatic example of these processes that are found in everyday life.

A basic distinction: in some of these examples, people lose themselves in a world already created and into which they enter (e.g., the novel, or a movie or play, or the hypnotic relationship) whereas, in others, as in skiing or seeking out new roles to play, they partially create the world—the perspective and relationship—in which they then will "travel." I will refer to losing one's self in an already created world as receptive trance; to losing oneself in a world one helps to create as active trance.

Could it be that people who are trained and encouraged to act in terms of collective interests are more likely to be ready, receptive, and skilled in entering experiences of receptive trance? A point of view—a world—that exists independently and into which they can enter and move? The typology of collective decision-making in Figure 1 distinguishes between patterns that provide legitimate place in collective action only for the pursuit of collective interests (Patterns 1, 2, 3, and 5) and patterns that provide such a place for the pursuit of special or personal interests as well (Patterns 4, 7, and 8). (Pattern 6 is an intermediate case.) Is it the case that individuals reared in families having the first sort of decision-making are more likely to have experiences of receptive trance?

I asked three samples of Berkeley students to rate themselves on the likelihood of losing themselves in already created worlds; novels, movies, nature, and so on and to indicate which patterns of decision-making in my typology were most like those operative in the families from which they came (Swanson, 1978a, 1978b). At Stanford, Ernest and Josephine Hilgard had students use that same typology as part of a questionnaire with two samples they were testing for hypnotizability. Among Berkeley students, those reared in families they describe as stressing collective interests in familial decision-making are significantly more likely to experience receptive trance in everyday life. In the Hilgards' samples, hypnotizability scores are significantly higher for students who report coming from such families.

Active trance is a different matter. Here we deal with people who do something to create social roles and relations. They like to do this, they see themselves as good at it, and they tend to "lose" themselves in their creations. These skills are useful in relatively unstructured or diffuse social relations: relations in which people are constantly adapting to one another, singly and severally, rather than relying upon formal leaders or role specialists or formal principles to formulate what must be done. In my samples, Berkeley students who say that they like to try out new roles, that they frequently do so, and that they tend to lose themselves in these or other self generated relations are more likely to come from families that are low in formal structure (e.g., small in size, egalitarian, low in use of the procedures Mead described for making principled collective decisions, having few clearly specialized roles). They tend also to come from families high in the percentage of their members that are female. (But are not more likely to be female themselves!) Perhaps families with a greater proportion of males are also more likely to give more sustained and explicit attention to task demands: to be organized for the orderly pursuit of instrumental action in the environment.

The findings on active trance can be cross-checked by using codes that Bourguignon (1976) has published for a large sample of primitive societies. I find that the societies in her sample that are the simplest in organization (e.g., are small, egalitarian, not organized for principled decision-making, depend for sustenance on hunting and fishing) are most likely to have high scores on her codes for active trance (Swanson, 1978b).

INDIVIDUAL DIFFERENCES IN STYLES OF DEFENSE

Projection, repression, and other ego defenses can be seen as justifications that people make to others and themselves. They are warrants for accepting one's self despite deviant desires or actions (Scott and Lyman, 1968). It is crucial that these warrants seem adequate to the person himself and not just to other people. They cannot, therefore, be lies or be utterly fantastic. They must seem plausible against some standards of argument and evidence.

Defenses are usually treated as differing in cognitive complexity. In looking for social sources of individual differences in type of defense, I have worked from the idea that the complexity of the social relations that seem threatened by a person's deviance will be positively associated with the cognitive complexity of the defenses he employs.

Studies of group growth and development have identified a sequence of relationships, those coming later being more differentiated and more abstractly integrated than those that went before. When a group begins to develop out of a collection of individuals, relations consist at first of interpersonal ties centered by some vague sense of people's interdependence. Later on, some leaders emerge. Any elaborate division of labor tends to wait upon the appearance of these leaders. Still later, a sharp distinction may be drawn between the "persons" of the leaders and the broad purposes of the group which all participants are supposed to serve (Swanson, 1970). Five or six such steps have frequently been identified both in studies in the laboratory and in research on large-scale instances of elementary collective behavior: crowds, social movements, and the like (reviewed in Swanson, 1970).

A new appreciation is that the forms of relationship found in the earlier stages in this sequence do not disappear when new steps are taken but come instead to be organized under the new arrangements. This is the argument of the sort we find in Piaget or Freud when they suggest that children do not stop using the skills associated with sensory-motor behavior or orality but combine these with other skills and orientations in the course of development. Of special importance is the developmentalists' proposal that the earlier skills and orientations persist and constantly interact with those that come later.

How is this idea to be applied to groups? We catch something of the continued existence, and separate organization, of several levels of relationship when we observe that interpersonal relations in a family are close and supportive but that there are grave problems of coordinating specialized roles. Or when we say that an athletic team works well as a formal organization but that, interpersonally, there is distance and distrust.

I have used these ideas in studies of defenses employed by samples of adolescents, looking to their families as one source of such defenses (Swanson, 1970; 1988). Specifically, I have tried to identify five levels of social relationship within each of these families and to determine at which, if any, of these levels, there seem to be strains in social solidarity. Let it be said at once that the presence or absence of strains in relations at any given level is related randomly to the existence of strains at other levels and the level or levels at which such strains occur is not related to the family's size, socio-economic status, percentage of members of a particular sex, or other common demographic indices or to the mental ages of the parents or children. But there is a strong association between the complexity of the level of familial relations at which strains appear and the cognitive complexity of the defenses employed by adolescent children from that family. I take this to mean that an adequate defense must take account of the nature of the social relations threatened by deviance and that the more complex such social relations the more complex must be the defense.

ANSWERS TO SOME POSSIBLE
QUESTIONS/SUGGESTIONS FOR RESEARCH

My recent studies are very much in process. I have moved from one aspect of activity as a self to another, trying in each case to find a conceptualization that would open possible connections with distinctive features of social and collective relations. It may be useful here to look at two questions about the relations between the conceptualizations I have offered and others that are commonly advanced:

1. Does my treatment of selves make them "the learned repertoire of roles" (Brim, 1960: 141)? Or "structures of positions and roles" (Stryker, 1980: 68)? Not as "role" is ordinarily defined. In the broadest sense it is the relevance people have for another's behavior, individual or collective. The more technical meaning of "role" is that of a set of rights and duties given to individuals according to their relevance for collective action. Individuals probably come to pay attention to their own behavioral processes—therefore to be selves—because others force or encourage it and therefore because they are relevant for others, but many aspects of these processes are extra-social in character and these play a part in the way individuals subsequently behave. And people certainly pay attention to characteristics of their own and others' behavior apart from the ones that are linked specifically to established rights and duties. Were this not so, it would be hard to see how unaffiliated people would come to develop rightful claims on one another and, reciprocally, duties.

2. Have I treated differences in reflective intelligence, losing one's self and ego defenses as products of role relation? In a sense, but what proves important in these analyses are not roles as such but the way people are organized to do things together. Thus reflective intelligence correlates with a family structure characterized by action through a division of labor and by its having the means for coordinating the activities of specialists. It is this system of relations, and not some other system composed equally of roles, that is important and it is the system and not just this or that role within it.

And I should like to suggest some directions for research that continues the lines of work described in this paper:

1. If we find that a certain self process, traveling in imagined worlds, for example, seems, at least in gross

terms, to embody a particular social or collective relationship (in our example, embodying processes of taking a group's point of view and anticipating what things would then be like), it becomes possible to see whether the micro-structure of that process is also helpfully understood as operating according to the principles that explain the operation of the social relationship concerned. Thus travels through inner space may conform to patterns of movement and change especially characteristic of functional social relations, the latter being an outgrowth of people's relating to one another in terms of collective purposes (Parsons and Smelser, 1956; Swanson, 1974b, 1976). The micro-structure of reflective thought may involve that of argumentation: claims and counter-claims, the negotiation of meanings, collectively authenticated procedures for determining commitment, and the like.

2. Emotions as states of persons are once again a major interest of sociologists (Hochschild, 1979; Kemper, 1978) and social psychologists (Gordon, 1981). It has been found that taxonomies of emotions can be systematized according to main dimensions or aspects of collective life (e.g., Russell, 1980). It seems an even greater challenge to develop a treatment of at least some forms of motivation and desire as states of individuals as selves—not omitting experiences of insatiable lusts and undying passions. Many leading theorists in psychoanalytic circles (e.g., Gedo, 1979; Rosenblatt and Thickstun, 1978; Schafer, 1976, 1978, 1981; Swanson, D., 1977) as well as in academic psychology (e.g., Atkinson and Birch, 1970; Weiner, 1980) have concluded that energic conceptions of motivation in persons are untenable but, except for some reformulations of motivation in cognitive terms, the phenomena seem more avoided than understood. So also are consummatory experiences: experiences of personal fulfilment, completion, and the like.

3. Existing theories tend to assume that the consequences of a social relationship for its members will be uniform. This is obviously wrong. It is a special challenge for social psychologists and sociologists

interested in the self to account on socially systematic grounds for differences in self-hood and self processes among members of a group—among siblings, for example, especially if age and sex are controlled. (Among siblings, birth order is presumably of some importance but is insufficient to handle the variance observed and no powerful alternatives have emerged [Lamb and Sutton-Smith, 1982].)

4. Selves are constituted not only in intimate social relations—family, peer groups, and the like—but in involvement in the wider community and society. A major task for the future is that of systematizing relations among these several aspects of a self (e.g., between familial and political or religious commitments).

5. The editor of this symposium suggests that the study of people as persons or selves has come to life again in the behavioral and social sciences, this following a rising public interest.[a] Selfhood or some aspect of it has repeatedly become problematic. As Bellah shows, the experience of a gulf between self and the wider society was important in the rise of the world religions (Bellah, 1964) and the experience of an unbridgeable separation between social institutions and the major cultural values basic for identity was central in the development of Protestantism and related religious movements (Swanson 1967, 1968, 1971b). The Renaissance (Greenblatt, 1980) and the waves of Romanticism (Morse, 1981; Peckham, 1962) entailed great re-evaluations of the nature and status of the self. And so have many later developments. And many of these social changes, old and new, have led to a new understanding of personhood. If we can identify the reason for our present-day interest, we will be more likely to gain what fresh understandings of self this new perspective can offer. (I have reviewed some leading interpretations and offered another in Swanson, 1980.) And, as always, this sort of development affords an opportunity to sharpen our definition of personhood which, itself, tends to be the standard by which we judge whether societies are fit for people.

Self-Consciousness and the Quasi-Epic of the Master

Mitchell Aboulafia

The life and death struggle in Hegel's dialectic of lordship and bondage is followed by the appearance of different consciousnesses, the master and the slave. While we can grasp the necessity of a turn in the dialectic of self-consciousness that brings forth unequal consciousnesses, our curiosity regarding the characteristics of those who fill these roles remains unsatisfied, a curiosity that is heightened by our knowing that at this juncture in the *Phenomenology of Spirit* Hegel is dealing with the development of individuals.[1] We can understand that some consciousness must take one role and some other the other role, but why do individuals take these different paths?

In this article I address the formation of unequal consciousnesses from the vantage point of the following question: How are we to interpret a self, the master, whose very formation in a quest for recognition leads it to scorn life? In answering this question here I am *not* concerned with the broader sociological and historical considerations that foster the development of masters in different historical settings, but with the genesis of the form of consciousness known as self-consciousness, and how, in the context of Hegel's work, this formation can lend itself to a psychology that seeks to dominate others. Although Hegel's type of analysis cannot adequately explain the appearance of the multitude of forms of domination that our planet has had the misfortune to accommodate, it does present a view of interpersonal experience that deserves continuing discussion.

For Hegel, the master's willingness to sacrifice biological life is intimately connected with the nature of self-consciousness. Yet he does not provide an acceptable account of the genesis of self-consciousness in the individual, in spite of the fact that it is the maturation of self-consciousness that sets the stage for the master and slave struggle. One cannot help but wonder whether there might not be differences in the development of self-consciousness that can account for the characteristics of master and slave as described in Hegel's text. As reported by both Kojève and Hyppolite, Hegel assumes that the master spontaneously comes into being through the courage of an individual. This seems to be a most undialectical explanation, while at the same time remaining a plausible reading of Hegel's text.[2] In my opinion, not only must self-consciousness be inherently a social consciousness, but what is viewed in terms of courage—by both Hyppolite and Kojève—must be explained as a possible non-capricious outcome of the general development of self-consciousness.

To provide a social psychological reading of Hegel's account requires that I modify his dialectic of master and slave by extracting it from the confines of the *Phenomenology of Spirit.* Hegel deals with the consciousness of adults, whereas my approach will also appeal to child development; and, in so doing, I take a turn to the empirical and non-teleological, which Hegel would, no doubt, find disturbing. The questions I pose are not questions that one might ask while absorbed in the flow of Hegel's book, but they are legitimate questions, given the historical importance of the master and slave dialectic, and the general inadequacies of Hegel's system in dealing with child development and individual agency. I do not, however, intend simply to sidestep Hegel's dialectic and insights, but to offer a plausible social psychological approach to development that can make sense of critical elements in Hegel's account, for example, negation, otherness, recognition, and independence. In other words, I will be employing several of the key elements of Hegel's master and slave dialectic to explain what is not explained by Hegel, that is, the kind of social pscyhology necessary to have individuals act in the manner he describes.

My approach will draw on the work of George Herbert Mead and Freud. Mead has a dialectical and cognitive model of the development of self-consciousness that owes much to Hegel, in spite of his ties to behaviorism. His analysis of the genesis of self-consciousness in the child is compelling and will prove valuable in the present context. Freud is of assistance because he is sensitive to the repercussions of conflict in a way Mead is not, and this sensitivity is necessary in order to make psychological sense of Hegel's model. Although I utilize Mead's and Freud's ideas, this paper should not be approached as a strict Freudian or Meadian reading of Hegel's dialectic, for in addition to merely borrowing certain ideas from them, I go on to modify their approaches. In other words, this paper is not intended as a comprehensive or historical treatment of their ideas. I begin with a brief and limited summary of Hegel's dialectic, and then turn to Mead and Freud and my modification of their work.[a]

I.

The development of self-consciousness is crucial to the project of the entire of *Phenomenology*, and crucial to the individual who can be referred to as a self-consciousness is the achievement of mutual recognition. As Hyppolite notes:

> I am a self-consciousness only if I gain for myself recognition from another self-consciousness and if I grant recognition to the other. This mutual recognition, in which individuals recognize each other as reciprocally recognizing each other, creates the element of spiritual life—the medium in which the subject is an object to itself, finding itself completely in the other yet doing so without abrogating the otherness that is essential to self-consciousness.[3]

Complete recognition of this sort is not to be found within the dynamics of the master and slave relationship. However, in the section of the *Phenomenology* that precedes the master/slave dialectic, Hegel sketches a preview of this state when he declares, "What still lies ahead for consciousness is the experience of what Spirit is... 'I' that is 'We' and 'We' that is 'I'."[4]

The dialectic that brings forth a master in need of recognition first presents nascent self-consciousness attempting to be completely for-itself. Self-consciousness is desire, and what it desires is not to be other than itself.[5] It wishes to assert that for it there is no otherness, that its "world" is in no way external, alien, to itself. Self-consciousness contests the existence of anything that may be defined as external to it, by seeking to negate what it takes to be other. Only it, self-consciousness, is entitled to independence, to a world without the challenge of otherness. In order to rid the world, its world, of objects that appear as other, it has recourse to negation through the act of consumption; for example, it eats the fruit or animals it finds or kills. But this procedure for achieving the independence of a "world" without otherness must fail. We find that self-consciousness seeks to prove its unity with itself through the negation of that which threatens it with otherness. Paradoxically, the other must exist for self-consciousness to manifest its unity and independence through the negation of otherness. Self-consciousness must negate in order to be itself, and, hence, comes to depend on the other.

Self-consciousness will only be able to gain the truth and certainty of itself by being recognized as a self-consciousness by another self-consciousness, who also has the power of negation. "*Self-consciousness achieves its satisfaction only in another self-consciousness.*"[6] However, when self-consciousness first encounters another self-consciousness it confronts it as if it were just another object. "Appearing thus immediately on the scene, they are for one another like ordinary objects, *independent* shapes, individuals submerged in the being [or immediacy] of *Life*."[7] Self-consciousness approaches all objects as other than and external to itself, and thus open to negation. Even its own biological life, the life of its body, the merely natural, is seen as external to and other than self-consciousness. Self-consciousness must prove that it is *pure* self-consciousness, unattached to objects, and "not attached to life."[8]

At first it might appear that self-consciousness would "prefer" not to treat a second self-consciousness as in any way unique, for to do so might deprive it of its own unique status. But the other confronts it as a source of negation, and, in so doing, it acts as the first does. Each challenges the other, and this engagement reveals a vital connection to the other. Self-consciousness does not simply "wish" to rid the world of otherness, but to be recognized as the one who can overcome otherness, that is, as a self-consciousness. Given that only another self-consciousness can provide this recognition, self-consciousness utilizes the opportunity afforded by its encounter with the other to force the other to recognize it, and it is willing to go to the utmost extremes in its quest. "As each stakes his own life, so each must seek the other's death, for it values the other no more than itself; its essential being is present to it in the form of an 'other,' it is outside of itself and must rid itself of its self-externality."[9]

Why is its essential being outside of it?[10] Self-consciousness cannot be complete unless it is recognized by the other. Its truth will be found through the other, but, at this juncture, its essence appears to lie out there in the other. The other has the power to make me what I believe I am by recognizing me. Self-consciousness cannot tolerate this condition of externality, so its presence in the other must be negated. Since both self-consciousnesses present themselves in this manner, the meeting of two burgeoning self-consciousnesses gives rise to a struggle to the death. Each seeks to prove that it is unconcerned with life and particularity, and each seeks to rid itself of its "alienation" in the other.

Self-consciousness, as we have noted, not only wishes to be rid of externality, it also desires to be recognized as self-consciousness, to declare its essence to be consciousness and not mere animal existence. It is willing to risk and lose biological life for the sake of asserting that consciousness is its essence. It is willing to battle to the death in order to be recognized as a self-consciousness, as a completely independent being, independent of natural, biological existence. Animals, on the other hand, act as if preservation of the body is an inviolable first law; they would never risk life to prove the uniqueness and independence of their consciousness.

Death, however, would not satisfy the desire of self-consciousness for recognition, the recognition that it needs to confirm that it actually is a unique being. "Death is the *natural* negation of consciousness, negation without independence, which thus remains without the required significance of recognition."[11] Death is but another form of the natural, for in being the simple negation of the natural, it remains itself natural. The lesson is clear, "self-consciousness learns that life is as essential to it as pure self-consciousness."[12]

If recognition is to occur the participants in the struggle to the death cannot die. It is at this juncture in the dialectic that unequal consciousnesses appear. One consciousness, the master, is prepared to meet death in the struggle so that it can rise above thinghood, above externality. Another consciousness, the slave, is not prepared to give up its biological life to prove its uniqueness, and is reduced to a thing in the eyes of the first consciousness. The master is seemingly independent because it has risen above life by risking biological life, while the slave has not been able to rise above animal existence. The turn to unequal consciousnesses is a necessary consequence of the development of Hegel's dialectic of the struggle unto death, for the only other alternative, given the manner in which the dialectic unfolds, would be the death of one or both of the protagonists, and an end to the quest for recognition. But if the turn to unequal consciousnesses is necessary, what accounts for a specific consciousness becoming a slave, and another a master?

Kojève and Hyppolite speak of fear and resoluteness in the face of death when attempting to clarify the rise of the master and fall of the slave. Kojève claims:

By irreducible, or better, by unforeseeable, or "undeducible" acts of liberty, they must constitute themselves as unequals in and by this very fight. Without being predestined to it in any way, the one must fear the other....[H]e must "recognize" the other without being "recognized" by him. Now, "to recognize" him thus is "to recognize" him as his Master and to recognize himself and to be recognized as the Master's Slave.[13]

Kojeve goes on to declare that the categories of master and slave are as old as the social reality of human beings. "In his nascent state, man...is always, necessarily, and essentially, either Master or Slave."[14]

Kojeve's argument assumes that inequality occurs in and as a result of the struggle unto death. His approach makes it impossible to examine the social and psychological genesis of the master and slave, for it is not until the struggle that the master and slave become differentiated, and then it is due to an "act of liberty," a liberty that entails the contingency and capriciousness of the individual, a capriciousness that must remain beyond the horizon of the dialectic.

Hyppolite argues that there was an original immediate unity of the moments involved in the development of self-consciousness.

> Through risking life, consciousness experiences it to be as essential to it as pure self-consciousness is. For that reason, the two moments which at first are immediately united separate. One of the self-consciousnesses rises above animal life; able to confront death and not fearing the loss of its vital substance. ...This is the noble consciousness, that of the master.[15]

> He is a slave because he has retreated in the face of death, preferring servitude to liberty in death. He is, therefore, less the slave of the master than of life.[16]

In Hyppolite's reading there was a unity, which due to the necessity of the moment of differentiation in the dialectic, developed into two different sorts of consciousness. In this manner, both of the necessary moments of the dialectic, life (slave) and being-for-itself (master), are preserved. Hyppolite suggests that a consciousness becomes the master because of courage in the face of death, while the consciousness of the slave is dominated by fear. Yet, if we were to agree with the necessity for the different moments in Hyppolite's reading, and obviously there is such a necessity in order to avoid the end of the dialectic, we might still wish to know: how and why does one consciousness give itself over to fear, while the other is able to rise above it?

II.

In the willingness to risk life the master seems to embody the ideal of independence, being-for-itself, that self-consciousness comes to believe it requires in order to be a self-consciousness. The master appears to have gained the recognition that it sought because the slave is present to recognize the master as the ideal; the slave must come to accept the master's ideology of independence. Hyppolite remarks, "In the first place, the slave regards the master outside him as his own essence, his own ideal."[17] And he also tells us that "men [Les hommes]...imperiously desire to be recognized as self-consciousnesses, as something raised above purely animal life. ... *Consciousness of life rises above life.* Idealism is not only a certainty; it also proves itself, or rather establishes itself, in the risk of animal life."[18]

There is little question that the movement of Hegel's dialectic depends on the importance of recognition in human experience, and that mutual recognition is the key to developing a fully human self-consciousness. However, if we are to achieve a more complete understanding of the actions of the participants in the master/slave dialectic, then we require an explanation for why recognition appears to become more important to some than to others, while remaining basic to all. Further, if we are to make sense of Hegel's claims, we must also grasp how the impact of ideals can lead to a willingness to forsake biological life for them. Mead's approach provides an interesting avenue for beginning to address these questions.

Mead's account of the self, which brings together the insights of behaviorism and a Hegelian dialectic of self and other, is both critical and constructive. It challenges outmoded Cartesian assumptions and provides a way of understanding how self and self-consciousness emerge together through symbolic interaction. "The essence of the self," Mead declares, "... is cognitive: it lies in the internalized conversation of gestures which constitutes thinking, or in terms of which thought or reflection proceeds. And hence the origin and foundations of the self, like those of thinking, are social."[19]

Mead's developmental approach sees the self as coming into being through the individual's capacity to take the responses, roles, of the other and to make them one's own. Because human beings use verbal gestures, words, the interplay of stimulus and response has different repercussions than among the animals.[20] When a dog bares its fangs at another dog, the second animal can respond in a given number of ways to the gesture of the first animal. For example, the second dog may snarl, attack, or run. For Mead, the meaning of a gesture is determined by the response it elicits; in this case the baring of fangs can mean: run, attack, snarl, etc. When a human being speaks, on the other hand, the other not only responds to the verbal gesture of the first, the first hears the gesture as if s/he were the other. Human beings are aware of meanings, hence their gestures are significiant symbols. I say to you: close the window, and there is a tendency in me to walk over to the window in order to close it, because I also hear the words: close the window. In hearing the gesture in this manner, I *implicitly* respond as the other actually responds. I do not close the window, but I am aware of the meaning of the words. In responding to others and being responded to by others, individuals learn to respond to their own words when the other is not present, as if they were the other.[b] "The critical importance of language in the development of human experience lies in this fact that the stimulus is one that can react upon the speaking individual as it reacts upon the other."[21] Further, not only does one learn to respond to specific verbal gestures as if one were the other, one learns to respond to complex sets of responses known as roles.

According to Mead, we acquire the social roles we must play by taking the role of the other. Although roles can be thought of as sets of responses or behaviors, the roles taken by human beings are quite different from the sets of behaviors an animal might learn in order to perform certain tricks. This is due not only to their unique complexity, but to the fact that human beings have the capacity to be aware of the roles they take and live. The process of becoming aware of a role entails learning to play both one's own role and the role of the other; that is, one learns to "see" oneself from the outside, so to speak, as if one were the other. For example, the child learns to play the role of a doctor by taking the role of patient, and vice versa. In learning a language children learn to take the responses of others, and to view their own responses as if they were these others, through a symbolic medium. Human beings learn to respond to their own responses in the absence of the other, and can play roles in the absence of the other, by alternatively taking the perspectives of subject and object.

> It is by means of reflexiveness—the turning back of the experience of the individual upon himself—that the whole social process is thus brought into the experience of the individuals involved in it; it is by such means, which enable the individual to take the attitude of the other toward himself, that the individual is able consciously to adjust himself to that process.... Reflexiveness, then, is the essential condition, within the social process, for the development of mind.[22]

The child learns to take the attitude of the other toward him/herself; in the case of the doctor and patient, s/he learns to take a number of attitudes that make up two specific roles. As one develops this capacity, the multitude of one's responses in various circumstances becomes an "object" that one identifies as one's self. I am the totality of responses given in a myriad of circumstances. But what is the source of unity for this object self? For Mead, the unity of the self reflects the unity of the social order. As one develops, the attitudes of one's social group or society are internalized and generalized. One comes to "watch" one's responses from the perspective of the *generalized other;* and what one comes to "see" is a unified social object called the self.

> The organized community or social group which gives to the individual his unity of self may be called "the generalized other." The attitude of the generalized other is the attitude of the whole community. Thus, for example, in the case of such a social group as a ball team, the team is the generalized other in so far as it enters—as an organized process or social activity— into the experience of any one of the individual members of it.[23]

We can understand the generalized other as a pattern or set of attitudes that are related to each other in a manner that forms a system. The self develops through the behavioral and symbolic interactions of human beings, and comes to mirror the whole of the generalized other from a multitude of slightly different angles, given the unique history of each individual. Properly speaking, however, the self is not simply reducible to internalized behaviors, even in the form of linguistic behaviors, because the self exists only insofar as one is self-conscious. One must be aware of the self (as an object) for the self to be, and one only becomes so aware because one can take the roles of the other and the generalized other. It is our cognition of organized behavior that allows us to have a self, and our ability to be thus aware is the result of our unique capacity to have and use language.

> So the self reaches its full development by organizing these individual attitudes of others into the organized social or group attitudes, and thus becoming an individual reflection of the general systematic pattern of social or group behavior in which it and the others are all involved—a pattern which enters as a whole into the individual's experience in terms of these organized group attitudes which, through the mechanism of his central nervous system, he takes toward himself, just as he takes the individual attitudes of others.[24]

One is a self insofar as one is aware of certain patterns of behavior that are built up through years of symbolic interaction with others. To have a self one must first be able to "see" oneself (originally one's behaviors and roles, and then the organization of these responses into a whole self), and this seeing of oneself depends on taking the responses and roles of the other. The capacity for having a self, and being self-conscious, are intimately connected. But, if the other does not respond in a consistent fashion to certain symbols, the individual cannot make them his or her own. We learn to respond through the responses of others in particular contexts, and without consistency we could not make these responses our own, and the development of language and the self would be impossible.

As we have seen, the other is crucial to the development of the self for Mead, for without the other there is no possibility of "distance" from one's behaviors that allows them to be viewed as one's own. No self without the other, a maxim Hegel would find so congenial that he might even be willing to struggle to the death to defend it. But there is a further connection between Mead and Hegel that interests us here, and this is found in the notion of recognition.

If there is no self without reflection, and if reflection develops through the other, then the knowing of oneself entails recognition. The child learns to become aware of his/her own behaviors through the other, and in so doing "sees" these behaviors as the other sees them. The other is the mirror through which I come both to have and know myself. In becoming aware of my responses, I look to the other for verbal and non-verbal confirmation of my awareness. I look to the other to reply: "yes, you are doing (saying) what you think you are doing (saying)." In other words, I look to the other for recognition in order that I might re-cognize myself in these responses. If the general drift of Mead's analysis is correct, then recognition is not only what we receive for (exceptional) achievements; it is necessary for the development of language and a coherent self.[25]

The use of the term "recognition" in the above passage is directed toward the recognition of specific behaviors, which may be seen as characteristics of the personality of a child. This recognition appears one sided, for the adult recognizes the child in order to provide consistency in the child's development. On the other hand, the child does come to recognize the adult as he or she learns to take various roles and behaviors. Each recognizes the behaviors of the other. Nevertheless, this does not seem to provide us with what Hegel calls *mutual recognition* in the fullest sense of the term. Recognition of this sort appears to entail the confirmation of the whole and unified self by the other, and the other by the self, in what might be called a mediated I and Thou relationship. Discussion of this issue is beyond the scope of this paper, although I would argue that we can arrive at a variant of mutual recognition from Mead's position, but only after a comprehensive modification of it.[26]

However, one difficulty with his model must be mentioned. Mead argues that conflict is an important feature of development. Human beings are conflict or problem solving creatures, and what he calls mind is intimately linked to the solving of problems. We solve problems by viewing them from various perspectives, and our unique capacity to see different perspectives is a result of our social existence. Mead, however, does not appear attuned to the repercussions of a form of psychological conflict that cannot be viewed solely in terms of problem solving.

For Mead, the child must internalize various prohibitions, and these prohibitions often conflict with *impulses* that could lead the child in other directions.[27] Mead tells us that if a child desires a certain object, we might find that "In the role of the parent the object is taboo....The child's capacity for being the other puts both of these characters of the object before him in their disparateness."[28] There are impulses for Mead, and although they are not as fixed as what are usually termed instincts, they can run up against internalized roles and behaviors. Now we know that for Freud such conflict is at the heart of much of our neurosis, but Mead does not see this type of conflict in this light. It is an avenue of new possibilities, of new ways for dealing with the environment.

> In a word, the sympathetic assumption of the attitude of the other brings into play varying impulses which direct the attention to features of the object which are ignored in the attitude of direct response. And the diverse attitudes assumed furnish the material for a reconstruction of the objective field in which the co-operative social act may take place, giving satisfactory expression to all the roles involved.... Time with its distinguishable moments enters, so to speak, with the intervals necessary to shift the scene and change the costumes. One cannot be another and yet himself except from the standpoint of a time which is composed of entirely independent moments.[29]

From Freud's perspective, confrontation with the other entails much pain and requires certain mechanisms for dealing with one's impulses, if one is to survive in civilization. The repercussions of conflict should not be limited to problem solving and exploration of the environment.

We have seen that recognition may very well be a fundamental feature of the self's and self-consciousness's development. Perhaps we should stop at this point and simply say that, for idiosyncratic reasons, the master has an extraordinary need to be confirmed by the other. The master's self is so fragile that it needs the continuing recognition of the other in order to exist, and is even willing to risk biological life for this confirmation. But in addition to desiring recognition, self-consciousness also feels the need to achieve self-unity, assert independence, satisfy an ideal, and negate all otherness. These features of its development must be addressed, and related to the need for recognition. Here is where Freud's sensitivity to conflict will be of some use.

III.

One of the most noteworthy features of self-consciousness is its antipathy to all otherness and its striving to negate this otherness. Self-consciousness is confronted with a world that appears different from itself. It seeks to be in unity with itself, and in order to accomplish this must negate that which confronts it as other. In so doing it reveals that it is not a static being, a mere tautological being, an abstract I = I, but a being that strives to "contain" otherness, difference. Hyppolite comments:

> The movement of self-consciousness, without which it would not exist, requires otherness, that is, the world of consciousness which in this way is preserved for self-consciousness. But it is preserved not as a being-in-itself, as an object which consciousness passively reflects, but as a negative object, as the object which must be negated in order that through this negation of the being-other self-consciousness establish its own unity with itself.... The I is the truth of being, for being exists only for the I which appropriates it and thus poses itself for itself.[30]

The other-being of self-consciousness is here the sensuous world. Self-consciousness requires difference as well as identity, for to be a self-consciousness one must have a distance or difference from self; at this juncture in the *Phenomenology*, it is the overcoming of the objects of the sensuous world that appears to supply this difference. I am aware of myself in the negation of the given as I deny its otherness. Yet we know that self-consciousness can never attain both the certainty and truth of itself in relation to this world; to achieve certainty and truth it must recognize and be recognized by the other. In other words, the negation of the objects of the sensuous world cannot produce the awareness of the self in the other (self) that a developed self-consciousness requires. "A self-consciousness exists *for a self-consciousness.* Only so is it in fact self-consciousness; for only in this way does the unity of itself in its otherness become explicit for it."[31]

The development of the *Phenomenology* makes it clear that our social being is basic to us, and that self-consciousness only becomes fully explicit in relation to others, but it does not explain how self-consciousness is generated in the child through interaction with others. This, as we have seen, is a task Mead set for himself. Nor does Hegel explain the genesis of the peculiar power of negation that is at the heart of self-consciousness. Of course, no explanation is called for from Hegel's perspective, since negation is the source of all movement and change in the universe, and the consciousness of human beings is found to be "imbued" with it. It is, for example, the power that allows the slave to transform the world. With the assistance of Mead and Freud, we can gain a better understanding of the genesis of this "power," as well as of the special role of ideals in the master and slave dialectic. Now that we have seen how Hegel and Mead can be compared, we may proceed to add Freud to the picture.

Both Freud and Hegel claim that crucial phases of the individual's development entail a denial of otherness, which ultimately cannot be denied. For Freud, there is the struggle of the instinctual "self" with the physical world, and with civilization's prohibitions and regulations. For Hegel, self-consciousness responds to the discovery of otherness by attempting to deny or negate the seeming non-identity of itself and *its* world. For Freud, when the individual's early narcissism is challenged by an external world, it reacts by attempting a return to an earlier phase of its development, an earlier phase that is characterized by unity. In *Civilization and its Discontents* he argues that originally the individual experiences a state of boundlessness in which there is no distinction between self and world. Gradually the world impinges, so that as adults we are left with "only a shrunken residue of a much more inclusive—indeed, an all embracing—feeling which corresponded to a more intimate bond between the ego and the world about it."[32] From Freud's perspective the quest of self-consciousness to achieve unity, by denying otherness, would not be a quest to assert self-consciousness, but an attempt to flee to an earlier state of boundlessness.

According to Freud, to understand what has come to be called our higher nature, our moral ideals, we must look to the formation of what he first called the *ego ideal*, and then came to call the superego. He argues that one of the ways in which the superego is formed in through the process of identification.

> By means of identification he takes the unattackable authority into himself. The authority now turns into his super-ego and enters into possession of all the aggressiveness which a child would have liked to exercise against it.... The relationship between the super-ego and the ego is a return, distorted by a wish, of the real relationships between the ego, as yet undivided, and an external object.[33]

Human beings develop their capacity for self-observation and moral conscience in confrontation with parental authority.[34] The ego, not being capable of denying external authority, due to fear of punishment (e.g., through loss of love), identifies with the authority and internalizes (introjects) it. This internalized authority becomes the superego, which is constantly on guard against conscious or unconscious violations of its standards. "That activity of the mind which took over the function of conscience has also enlisted itself in the service of introspection, which furnishes philosophy with the material for its intellectual operations."[35] The ego ideal, the superego, appears to give rise to self-consciousness, when seen in terms of its conscious, as opposed to its unconscious, functions.

Clearly there are similarities to Mead's model of the development of self-consciousness, with the superego playing a role comparable to, though not identical with, the generalized other. But what of the role of conflict in the birth of self-consciousness and the rise of the master and slave?[c]

If we assume that the birth of self-consciousness is linked to the development of the superego, we notice that the formation of self-consciousness requires an original departure from an earlier state of self-sameness or unity. The external world does not always satisfy the needs of the infant, and this leads the infant to begin to separate "self" and world for Freud. But soon the infant, and then the young child, is subjected to a much more profound assault in the form of the prohibitions and taboos of civilization. The confrontation with an external authority—in the form of parents or caretakers—that the child cannot defeat or repel, calls for some strategy to deal with this power. As mentioned earlier, the child internalizes the prohibitions of the parents and they are then converted into the superego. Through the ability to introject the external authority's prohibitions, the other is transformed into self.

Mead argues that there is no self without the taking of the role of the other. We can, however, presume that the young child must learn the verbal gesture *No*, as it learns many other gestures. In learning the word or sign for *No* the child has a tool to repel the other. It can say *No* to the other. On the other hand, even if we do not follow Freud's presumption of omnipotent instincts of love and death, and instead use Mead's more modest definition of impulse, we can still see how the impulses, desires, of the young child lend themselves to being thwarted in the socialization process.[36] The child cannot always say *No* to the other, and must often learn to say *No* to him or herself. In Mead's terms, the child takes the role of the other in relation to its own impulses, and says *No* to its old impulsive "self." Eventually the responses of the other become one's own, and one views them as aspects of the burgeoning (object) self. Prohibitions that were originally foreign, are now features of the self. Often young children tend to be excessively severe with other children or adults who break the rules that they are just learning. If we were to give a Freudian twist here to Mead, we would say that this behavior is quite intelligible because the child is attempting to see these rules as part of him/herself, and violation of the rules threatens to "remind" the child of the old "self" he or she is superseding.

The introduction of taboos and prohibitions sets up a conflict within the child. It must resolve this conflict in some fashion. Mead emphasizes the positive outcome, that is, the possibilities these responses and roles open up. Freud sees the invasion of the other as the destroyer of our boundless unity with the universe, the harbinger of neurosis, and the general unhappiness that is our lot. For Hegel, conflict in the form of contradiction is the moving principle of the dialectic. The self that is in disunity with itself is a self that contradicts itself, and this calls for the negation of the otherness responsible for the disunity, so that a higher unity might be realized. The "higher unity" will not obliterate the otherness, but will include it within itself.

A burgeoning self-consciousness, however, does not know of this higher unity, and might "prefer" to be an abstract static $I = I$; that is, self-consciousness might find itself "preferring" not to be a being that must confront otherness and contain difference, "wishing" instead to return to a unitary state. But if we assume that there is nascent self-consciousness, a split must have developed and be developing—in Freud's terms, between super-ego and ego; in

Mead's between consciousness and the object of consciousness—so that the individual has already become a being that contains otherness. Hegel begins his account with a "split" between (self-)consciousness and the sensuous world, and with self-consciousness attempting to negate objects in order to encompass the world in self-unity. This strategy must fail because there must be negation of otherness if self-consciousness is to be, and this, in turn, requires the existence of independent objects to negate. Hence, self-consciousness depends on the other in order to be.

In the social world of the rise of self-consciousness we find a situation that also reveals the virtual imposssibility of living in a unitary state without otherness and negation. The child has learned the verbal gesture *No* from the other, and has learned this *No* by being told *No*. It attempts to turn this *No* on the other in order to refuse the prohibitions of the other. But as we have seen, the other is too powerful, and the child's *No* ends up (to some degree) being turned against its own desires. No matter how the child turns, negation infiltrates its experience. In reacting against the other, it avails itself of the *No*, which it learned from the other. If it says *No* to its own impulsive "self," it also employs negation, in a manner learned from the other. It can never return to a unitary state once negation has entered its experience, with the possible exception of certain extreme psychotic states.

Nevertheless, self-consciousness may struggle to deny its own burgeoning self-consciousness and inner diremption. Perhaps it can do away with otherness by further identifying with the other. Might not a strategy of the complete denial of its own impulses in favor of the other's prohibitions achieve self-identity? The other's terrifying power and potential for generating pain leads to a situation in which self-consciousness seeks total identification with the other. It strives to become all superego. Where ego and Id is, superego shall be. Of course, we know such a strategy is doomed to failure because the other is not monolithic and itself contains otherness, and because the learning of language requires the experience of otherness.

This would rightly be regarded as a rather extreme developmental strategy. Yet there are those who are so identified with the rules and regulations of an established order, or of a leader who embodies this order, that it is not far-fetched to speak of the genesis of a superego self, a genesis that entails far more than the internalization of a punitive external authority, as we shall see below. (The issue of the origin of authority will also be addressed below.) In Freud's scheme, when confronted by a commanding authority, the impulsive child proceeds to identify with it, and the identification helps give rise to a harsh and punitive superego that insists on conformity to its authority, even in adulthood.

> To this ideal ego is now directed the self-love which the real ego enjoyed in childhood. The narcissism seems to be now displaced on to this new ideal ego, which, like the infantile ego, deems itself the possessor of all perfections.[37]

The child's *No* is not permitted to express itself against the other, but is instead turned inwards. In other words, the individual is not allowed to develop unique dispositions based on various biological and socially nurtured impulses.

Hegel claims that in the struggle unto death, we find self-consciousness with, "its essential being ... present to it in the form of an 'other,' it is outside of itself and must rid itself of this self-externality."[38] What self-consciousness wishes is not merely the death of an other individual being, but the negation of all externality, including its own. It is outside of itself here because the other possesses the power of recognizing it, and thereby "controls" its essence. The other has a power over us because we are shaped through the responses of the other, and in the case of the so called superego self the power of the other is excessive. The superego self denies all otherness, all differences from the other, in order to be just like the other. The object self is usually constituted of diverse responses and has a multitude of sides. It is "organized" in relation to a complex and multifaceted generalized other, and can even be seen in relation to several generalized others, for there can be more than one generalized other for Mead.[39] In dealing with a highly constricted individual, we may discover that not only were its impulses severely curtailed during its development, but that the number and complexity of roles it could take—and see as its own—were also limited by a restrictive superego (acting as an "undeveloped" generalized other). The power of the other to restrict the development of the individual should be seen here as a function of its punitive power *and* its power to define the burgeoning self by what it recognizes.

There is another critical point Mead might raise regarding this restricted individual; it is not living its *sociality*. Sociality is a key concept for Mead, and it denotes a prevalent feature of reality. For Mead, we live in a universe of various physical, biological, and social systems, which undergo transformations. The introduction of something novel into a system can begin a transition from an old to a new system. For example, think of a pond as a relatively stable ecosystem. Introduce a new organism or have an existing organism mutate. If the system is to go on to form a new ecosystem by including this organism, there will be a time betwixt and between the old and new. This being-between Mead refers to as sociality, and we can speak of a pond or an organism as being in a state of sociality.

The social life of human beings is one in which sociality is prevalent, and its presence has a unique importance for us.

> But the animal could never reach the goal of becoming an object to itself as a whole until it could enter into a larger system within which it could play various roles.... It is this development that a society whose life process is mediated by communication has made possible. It is here that mental life arises—with this continual passing from one system to another, with the occupation of both in passage and with the systematic structures that each involves. It is the realm of continual emergence.[40]

Human beings develop selves in interaction with others. We take on various roles and these roles are shaped into a whole in relation to the generalized other. These roles often undergo modification or transformation in interaction with others. While the self may be thought of as a system of relations that has congealed together over time, it is not a closed system. Further, unlike the system of the pond, human beings, whether in taking specific roles or in being the totalities we call selves, not only change, they have the unique capacity to be aware of states of transition. They are aware of their sociality. In other words, we are challenged by the environment, by the novel and unexpected. We change and find that we are not exactly who we thought we were. After many such episodes, we come to realize that we have lived and will live between past and future states, that we often live in sociality. This does not mean, of course, that all of the changes an individual is called on to make are particularly momentous. For example, in reaction to the manner in which someone else is playing a role, I may slightly modify the manner in which I take another role.

Now it is precisely this capacity for undergoing, and eventually learning to accept transformation—which is part and parcel of the early development of the child—that is thwarted in the individual who cannot tolerate differences or living in sociality. It has not been nurtured in an environment that strives to engage the new and different, that rewards the novel. This individual has come to see the novel, the other, as a threat to its established world, and not as an opportunity for learning and transformation. If a consciousness of this sort finds otherness within, it must be destroyed, as surely as if it finds it without. All otherness is suspect, for otherness brings with it the possibility of experiencing transition, sociality, with the dreaded danger of being transformed into something other to follow. The being (system) that I am must remain just as it is. One way of seeing to it that sociality is avoided is to become, in Freudian terms, one's ideal(s). Ideals, as all dogged Platonists well know, are unchanging.

One becomes solely ego ideal. Everything which does not meet this ideal is subject to attack, and this means all of one's other behaviors, impulses, and even biological life. This individual finds otherness everywhere, for even its own superego self came into being from the other and, hence, is permeated with (a past of) otherness. In some (subliminal) fashion, the superego self's dependence on its own biological life, as well as its need for the other, must have an impact; perhaps it makes the individual feel alienated from him/herself. However, the individual must deny the worth of life and its own needs, if it is to live up to its ideal (self).

The negating superego is not only willing to risk life, it must risk its life, for its being rests on the negation of all otherness. The ego ideal lives solely to be its own ideal, or what it believes to be its *own* ideal, and only when it is actualizing itself through the movement of negativity does it have any self at all. In other words, this consciousness comes to define itself as an oppositional consciousness, and the denial of specific differences gives way to a general denial of difference as it comes to feel at home only in negation. Its essence, its idea, is simply to not be the other. Under the claim of upholding rigid standards, it becomes a nihilistic consciousness, seeking to destroy difference itself. Self-consciousness "believes" that as pure negativity it can avoid the infiltration of otherness, so it maintains an attitude of perpetual negativity in order to obey its desire for self-sameness. It negates without arriving at the negation of the negation that would overcome its alienation. If it stopped to reflect on what it actually is, it would discover otherness.

The presentation of itself...as the pure abstraction of self-consciousness consists in showing itself as the pure negation of its objective mode, or in showing that it is not attached to any specific *existence*, not to the individuality common to existence as such, that it is not attached to life.[41]

Even if such a consciousness could avoid total self annihila-
tion, it would still have before it a further trauma from Freud's
perspective. Striving for complete independence, pure being-for-self,
entails a violation of the social authority that gave rise to superego
self-consciousness. Consciousness identified with external authority in order to overcome the other by making the other self. Superego
self-consciousness reproduces the authority "within" itself, but only,
paradoxically, so that it can overthrow the authority and be for self.
We could say that self-consciousness strives to identify with the
parental figure (for Freud, the father, of course), the authority in the
Freudian scheme of things, so that it will be able to kill him, by
becoming completely independent of him, by making him useless,
unnecessary. But one never fully escapes his/her father. (Should
self-consciousness succeed, as Aristotle might quip, such a one
would be either a beast or a god). We do not have to accept the
entire Oedipal dimension of the Freudian picture to see that children may very well have ambivalent feelings about taking over the
role of parent, because in so doing their parents' or caretakers'
power would be diminished. To take on the power of one's parents is
rather terrifying, since their power is used not only to control, but to
protect. And these fears and conflicts may very well follow one into
adult life.

However, by addressing the Freudian notion of the authority
figure in this manner, are we not begging the question as to how the
master arose? If we presuppose authority figures, such as fathers,
parents, or caretakes, etc., then do we not already have a master and
slave relationship (of sorts) between the authority and the child?
Hence, it would be the parent, not the child and the child's future
development, that requires explanation. One might wish to know
where the first authority figure came from and how it managed to
gain such power over the other.

Mead's account of the origin and development of self-
consciousness is superior to Freud's because he has a plausible
approach to the development of self-consciousness in the individual
and the species, while Freud's model of the superego's development
offers the rather unconvincing scenario of an "original" partricide.[42]
Freud appears to believe that he needs this account in order to avoid
an infinite regress with regard to how the superego originated and
became the internal representative of society's authority. For Mead,
the genesis of self and self-consciousness—and the corresponding
development of the generalized other and society's "influence"—is
linked to the incremental growth of language and social roles that
are part and parcel of the history of the species. We could criticize

Mead for not explaining in detail the historical sociology of this genesis, and then provide an account of it, but such a project is clearly beyond the scope of the present inquiry. We have, after all, been concentrating on the ontogenetic, not the phylogenetic. Here it is only necessary that his model of the development of the self through symbolic interaction be plausible, for both individuals and the species, since we are attempting to make sense of Hegel's dialectic through Mead, and not engaging in a detailed analysis and critique of Mead's work. From this perspective, the genesis of the role of parent as authority figure would be similar to other roles human beings take and have taken. Mead's position, then, does not require an original event to explain the existence of authority or why it is passed on to others, merely the assumption that there were historical conditions that required certain behaviors to be passed on, and that certain individuals came to be seen as models for these behaviors, with the most obvious, though by no means only, exemplars being parents or caretakers of children. His approach allows us to assume that different psychological, sociological, and/or historical conditions lead caretakers to exhibit varying degrees of "rigidity" in their responses. I might also add that the circularity mentioned above is only apparent because an authority figure cannot simply be equated with the master as described by Hegel. Hegel's master has some very unique characteristics, and we have been attempting to illuminate these.

While the very nature of self-consciousness implies a "splitting" or "othering" of the individual's consciousness, the split takes place in a social context; the manner in which it takes place, as well as its psychological impact, depends on this context. The mere birth of self-consciousness will not produce the type of consciousness Hegel describes, unless other factors are present, for example, a channeling of recognition that leaves an individual with a very narrow definition of self. Further, it must be noted that even being born into a highly authoritarian social structure is not sufficient in and of itself to produce the consciousness of the master, for such situations may result in different psychological stances in response to it depending on the presence of other factors. It has not been my aim to try to show that some one variable would give rise to Hegel's master. I have argued that a constellation of variables contributes to the development of the master. This constellation includes: the presence of authority figures(s); the recognition of the child for only a limited number or type of behaviors or qualities; distrust of that which is different or novel by the caretakers; and the refusal to allow the child to express his/her own impulses through saying *No* to the other. A correlate of the last point is that there may be individual differences in the experience of some impulses due to genetic endowment (for example, the need for food), and that this factor, when combined with certain social conditions, could also contribute to the genesis of the psychological stance of the master. I do not claim that this is an exhaustive list of the factors involved, nor that the influence of the variables can be plotted in a mathematically precise fashion. I do claim that the psychology of Hegel's master can be illuminated through their discussion.

That we cannot easily predict the development of the master, even if we were limited to the variables here discussed, is evident from the factors themselves. For example, suppose the caretakers of a child have a rather strict set of guidelines for what is deemed accept-able—in terms of the early impulsive behaviors of the child—but that they respect and recognize the child's *No*-saying in specific contexts. The self destructive rage that the master feels may not develop, although the individual may have little ability to tolerate a non-structured existence as an adult, and may show minimal flexibility in the face of the novel. (Such an individual may become a psychological slave, so to speak, to the world of the caretakers.) If one also considers that impulses are themselves open to some degree of intersubjective modification—and that, in addition to the issue of consistency in recognition, there is the issue of what one is recog-nized for as a child, as well as by whom (e.g., peers, older siblings)— one will step very lightly in predicting the rise of the master. Indeed, it must be said that the consciousness of Hegel's slave can be produced by emphasizing certain features of the factors we have discussed. But this should not be surprising, since the master and slave are shaped by similar forces, and can be seen as taking different turns depending on the manner in which these forces come together.[43]

This paper has appeared to focus on the rise of the individual master. But, of course, given the nature of Hegel's dialectic, we presume that in speaking of the master, we are speaking of a form of consciousness that would be found in more than one individual. Now Hegel makes the claim that the master and the slave dialectic occurred before human beings became civilized.[44] The present interpretation includes the "civilizing" of children, at least children in certain types of communities, who may very well live after what Hegel calls civilization has come into existence. Yet this is not a completely unHegelian move, since each child must be taken to the level of the spirit of the times for Hegel, and the spirit of the times includes the past, albeit in a superseded form. We have assumed that in order to have the master Hegel describes, there must be a burgeoning self-consciousness, which means that a certain level of social interaction must exist, at least enough for a degree of linguistic sophistication. In other words, we presuppose a level of social development in which there exists a relative degree of sophistication, as well as the presence of regulations and prohibitions. We may conclude, then, that masters of the sort Hegel describes can occur even after the world has become "civilized," if we presume that the master is actually an abstract "psychological type," and that features of this psychology can be called into existence by a confluence of social, interpersonal, and historical circumstances that are not limited to pre-history.

The master has taken the desire of self-consciousness to overcome otherness and has transformed it into a way of life. The master is willing to negate the other in order to be independent, yet its essence is in the other. It has come into being through the other, and depends on the other for recognition, but it cannot accept this (seeming) externality. If it could articulate its mode of being it might say: "I am the living idea of pure negativity. I am that which denies all difference from myself. Everything that is not my activity of negation is less than worthless. It is neither real, nor pure, for it is infested with otherness."

The master is not motivated by simple courage. It would be more accurate to say that s/he is raging against everything. The rage is the movement of pure unharnessed negativity, which self-consciousness continues to generate in attempting to be its ideal; it is a negativity that will destroy itself and those caught in its path. Some may view this self-consciousness as courageous because it risks death. The risking of one's life can indeed be a courageous act. Yet, this consciousness does not so much appear courageous, as it does driven and rash. Does not courage entail a certain independence of mind and an awareness of the stakes involved? But this consciousness, while claiming independence, is so unthinkingly threatened by otherness that it is willing to destroy itself to prove its purity.

However, as we know, life is necessary to self-consciousness if it is to prove itself by being recognized. Self-consciousness must live and allow the other(s) to live if it is to be recognized as an independent consciousness. Can our interpretation shed some insight into the reasons why self-consciousness allows the other to live?

Self-consciousness can never totally rid itself of its ties to the other, for it sees itself in the other. It is a being that has been born in responding to and in being recognized by the other, so that the other presents a familiar face, so to speak. One could deny this face, and continue in the destructive rampage that ends in death. There are mechanisms, however, for dealing with truths we cannot fully confront, but yet must live with, and the master appears to employ at least one of them. The otherness of the master is placed out there, in the world, at a distance, in the being of the slave, a being that is not fully human, but just human enough. The slave comes to embody all that the master cannot accept.

> A particular way is adopted of dealing with any internal excitations which produce too great an increase of unpleasure: there is a tendency to treat them as though they were acting, not from the inside, but from the outside, so that it may be possible to bring the shield against stimuli into operation as a means of defense against them. This is the origin of *projection*.[45]

The master finds otherness everywhere, even "within," so to speak. If the negation of otherness is not to be turned self-destructively inwards, it must be turned somewhere else. The slave prefers biological life to the life of confrontation. It is just this commitment that allows the master to displace in the direction of the slave negativity that would have been directed against itself. True, the master seems to care little for life, it even wishes to destroy life. But we know that it is not solely an independent self-consciousness, for its desire to be recognized depends on life. If it escapes this lesson, consciously or unconsciously, it loses what it has struggled to attain. It can save itself only through the other who helps rid the master's world of the otherness it so fears—who helps to channel and dampen the master's dangerous self-loathing by becoming an object of use and abuse.

The otherness of the world need never be encountered, for the slave serves up to the master all that s/he wishes ready made for consumption. The master can now negate that which is other without dealing with its otherness, because the slave has transformed the other to suit the master's wishes. Through the negating power of the slave, which the master takes as his/her own in "owning" the slave, the feared world of otherness is negated at a distance. In working on the world for the master, the slave is contaminated by otherness, while the master enjoys the rewards of the slave's work and thinks of the slave's power as his/her own.

The master lives under the illusion that s/he is completely independent because s/he has the slave to work upon the world. The slave recognizes the master as the ideal, the truly human, the independent one. The master now has someone to confirm, that is, to recognize, his unique status. The weight of the ideal that drove him/her to prove himself, through the activity of perpetual negation, is lessened by the recognition of the slave. The desire of self-consciousness, as channeled through the master, appears to have achieved satisfaction in and through the existence of the slave. Further, the master views the slave as antithetical to his/her own being, so if the slave loves life as the animal does, surely the master is above such needs. The master does not have to face his/her need for life.

The master, as we have seen, is actually far from independent. The master's truth lies in the slave, because its "truth is in reality the unessential consciousness and its unessential action."[46] This result is reflected in the psychology, for in order to escape self-negation, the master must come to see another in the place of its own "animal self." The other becomes its slave, and what would have been "self" abuse is then directed toward the other, and at the world through this other, who is expected both to tremble at the master's feet and negate the world in service of the lord. The power of the negative (seemingly) remains in the hands of the master, though it is directed at the world through the work of the slave.

Through fear and service, as well as in its work upon the world, the slave overcomes its living alienation from itself. It confronts the otherness of the world and transforms it, and in the transformed objects of the world the slave comes to see its own independence reflected. The master continues to depend on the slave in order to be recognized as the independent one, as a self-consciousness that is the ideal or essence of humanity. Only another self-consciousness, who has the capacity to recognize and to be recognized, could even begin to perform such a function. The master needs the slave in order to live as a master. The master exhibits the essentiality of the other in the very act of declaring the other a slave.

Notes and References

NOTES

1. John Dewey made this claim in his "Prefatory Remarks" to Mead's *Philosophy of the Present* (Chicago: University of Chicago Press, 1980). Whitehead concurred, "I regard the publication of the volumes [*Mind, Self, and Society; The Philosphy of the Present*] containing the late Professor George Herbert Mead's researches as of the highest importance for philosophy. I entirely agree with John Dewey's estimate, a seminal mind of the very first order." Whitehead's comments are quoted in David L. Miller's *George Herbert Mead: Self, Language, and the World* (Chicago: University of Chicago Press, 1973), p. ix.

2. Of course, there are exceptions to such sweeping claims; a notable one was Maurice Natanson, who had a background in phenomenology. See his, *The Social Dynamics of George H. Mead* (The Hague: Martinus Nijhoff, 1973; originally published Washington: Public Affairs Press, 1956).

3. See Habermas's contribution to this book.

4. Joas, *G. H. Mead. A Contemporary Re-examination of His Thought* (Cambridge, Mass.: MIT, 1985), p. 44, and in this book.

5. Randolph Collins takes this tack in his, "Toward a Neo-Meadian Sociology of Mind," *Symbolic Interaction* 12, no. 1 (Spring 1989). This article is followed by commentaries from fifteen Mead scholars, many whose work could not be included here due to space and thematic considerations.

6. Ernst Tugendhat, *Self-Consciousness and Self-Determination*, trans. Paul Stern (Cambridge, Mass.: MIT Press, 1986), see lectures 2, 13, and 14. Lectures 11 and 12 on Mead have been reprinted here. In the latter lecture Tugendhat notes the importance of Hegel's concept of recognition.

7. For a discussion of the differences between a functional and a behavioral reading of Mead, see Gary Cook, "G. H. Mead's Social Behaviorism," *Journal of the History of the Behavorial Sciences* 13 (1977): 307-316.

8. I know of only one book directed toward delineating Mead's potential contribution to feminism, Kathy E. Ferguson's, *Self, Society, and Womankind* (Westport: Greenwood, 1980). Rosalind Rosenberg, in her *Beyond Separate Spheres: Intellectual Roots of Modern Feminism* (New Haven, Conn.: Yale

University Press, 1982), discusses in some detail Mead's commitment to the rights of women.

9. I should also note that a number of authors in this book have written for the journal *Symbolic Interaction*.

10. Two authors attempting to address Mead and contemporary intellectual trends are Norman K. Denzin and R. S. Perinbanayagam. See Denzin's, "Act, Language, and Self in Symbolic Interactionist Thought," *Studies in Symbolic Interaction* 9 (1988): 51-80; and Perinbanayagam's, *Signifying Acts: Structure and Meaning in Everyday Life* (Carbondale and Edwardsville: Southern Illinois University Press, 1985).

INTRODUCTION

NOTES

1. *G. H. Mead. A Contemporary Re-examination of His Thought* (Cambridge, Mass.: MIT, 1985), by Hans Joas, is the best book-length developmental treatment of the Mead's thought to date; and David L. Miller's *George Herbert Mead: Self, Language, and the World* (Chicago: University of Chicago Press, Phoenix Edition, 1980), provides a very accessible and comprehensive interpretation of many of Mead's most important ideas.

2. It is fair to say that Mead's work is considerably more attuned to the ontogenetic, and I will concentrate on it in this introduction. See also the Habermas selection.

3. Mead, *Mind, Self, and Society: From the Standpoint of a Social Behaviorist* (Chicago: University of Chicago Press, 1934), p. 65. Henceforth, referred to as *MSS* .

4. *MSS*, p. 47.

5. *MSS*, p. 69

6. Mead's philosophy of the act is far richer than these few illustrative comments on the hand might suggest. See, for example, "Stages in the Act: Preliminary Statement," in *The Philosophy of the Act* (Chicago: University of Chicago Press, 1938), pp. 3-25; David L. Miller, *George Herbert Mead: Self, Language, and the World* , pp. 19, 60-65, 128-131; and Gary Cook's article in this book.

7. Mead, *MSS*, pp. 67-68.

8. See Habermas and Tugendhat in this book. Habermas attempts to augment Mead's position by introducing Wittgenstein's notion of rules, while claiming that Mead can be of assistance to Wittgenstein by providing the grounds for understanding the development of rules that govern symbols.

9. "Gestures may be either conscious (significant) or unconscious (non-significant). The conversation of gestures is not significant below the human level, because it is not conscious, that is, not *self*-conscious (though it is conscious in the sense of involving feelings or sensations)" (*MSS*, p. 81).

10. *MSS*, pp. 132-33

11. See the Lewis, Habermas, and Tugendhat papers for an interpretation of role of the term *attitude* in Mead's work.

12. Some interesting comparisons are to be made between Mead and Vygotsky on the role of inner speech. See, for example, Hans-Johann Glock, "Vygotsky and Mead on the Self, Meaning and Internalisation," *Studies in Soviet Thought* 31 (1986): 131-148. Also see, Jaan Valsiner and R. Van Der Veer, "On the Social Nature of Human Cognition: An Analysis of the Shared Intellectual Roots of George Herbert Mead and Lev Vygotsky." *Journal for the Theory of Social Behavior* 18 (March 1988): 117-136; and R. Van Der Veer, "Similarities between the Theories of G. H. Mead and L. S. Vygotskij: An Explanation?" In *Studies in the History of Psychology and the Social Sciences 3*, ed. S. Bem, H. Rappard, and W. van Hoorn (Leiden: Psychologisch Instituut van de Rijksuniversiteit, 1985).

13. See Habermas in this book.

14. *MSS*, p. 151.

15. *MSS*, pp. 149-159.

16. "The essence of the self, as we have said, is cognitive; it lies in the internalized conversation of gestures which constitutes thinking, or in terms of which thought or reflection proceeds. And hence the origin and foundations of the self, like those of thinking, are social" (*MSS*, p. 173).

17. *MSS*, p. 154.

18. I follow Mead's lead in employing the term *object* to describe the self, as well as in using (at times) the language of reflection and consciousness. But Mead also is quite critical of much that is entailed by this language, and this is evident in his emphasis on behavior and in his desire to avoid any form of ego-ology. See Tugendhat and Habermas in this book; also see Tugendhat's *Self-Consciousness and Self-Determination*. (I might add that I restrict the use of the term *object* to the "me" dimension of the self later, p. 10.)

19. *MSS*, p. 157.

20. *MSS*, pp. 260-261.

21. *MSS*, p. 265.

22. David L. Miller, in *George Herbert Mead: Self, Language, and the World*, tells us that, "Mead maintains that the generalized other is the social, cognitive, rational component of the self. It is invoked whenever a person

considers what he ought to do" (p. 53). He also claims that it "is flexible and may grow historically and for any particular community and for any individual member of a community. This depends on the character of the problems at hand, upon the developments in science and technology, and upon institutional structural changes. At the United Nations meetings we ask: What *is* the rational thing to do? But no one individual, say our best logician, is asked to come up with the answer. Rather, the attitudes of those involved in the dispute must first be known, and discussion must follow" (p. 55).

23. *MSS*, p. 334. Mead also tells us that, "Rationality is as large as the group which is involved; and that group could be, of course, functionally, potentially, as large as you like. It may include all beings speaking the same language" (*MSS*, pp. 334-335).

24. *MSS*, p. 337. Whether Freud has a more plastic notion of the instincts than he usually is credited with is another question. See Bruno Bettelheim, *Freud and Man's Soul* (New York: Knopf, 1983).

25. *MSS*, pp. 375-376. My own view is that Mead does not pay enough attention to the conflict that impulses give rise to and its repercussions for development. See my article in this book and my book, *The Mediating Self: Mead, Sartre, and Self-Determination* (New Haven, Conn.: Yale University Press, 1986).

26. For a discussion of the role of the Enlightenment and Romanticism in Pragmatism and Modernity, see Thelma Z. Lavine, "Modernity, Interpretation Theory, and American Philosophy," *Frontiers in American Philosophy*, ed. Robert Burch (College Station: Texas A & M University Press, forthcoming).

27. Mead, *Philosophy of the Present* (Chicago: University of Chicago Press, Phoenix edition, 1980), Chapters 1 and 2.

28. *MSS*, p. 175.

29. *MSS*, p. 173.

30. Mead, "The Mechanism of Social Consciousness," in *Selected Writings: George Herbert Mead*, ed. Andrew J. Reck (Chicago: University of Chicago Press, 1981), p. 141.

31. "The Social Self," in Reck, p. 142.

32. *MSS*, p. 174.

33. *MSS*, pp. 177-178. Here, the term *self-conscious* refers both to an awareness of meaning and more specifically to an awareness of self.

34. For example, I would argue that Mead's discussion on pp. 175-178 of *MSS* supports "the varying degrees of novelty" view. Note, for instance, the following: "The very taking of his expected steps [i.e., in walking] puts him in a certain situation which has a slightly different aspect from what is expected, which is in *a certain sense novel*" (p. 177, emphasis added).

35. For example, "The Social Self," in Reck, p. 142.

36. For example, *MSS*, p. 178.

37. "The Social Self," p. 144.

38. Ibid., p. 145.

39. Ibid., p. 145.

40. Ibid., p. 145.

41. *MSS*, pp. 352-353.

42. The word *reflection* is rather strikingly ambiguous in English: it refers to both a mirror image and several modes of thought. Both meanings are employed by Mead: there is the reflection (that is, the reflecting or mirroring) of significant symbols and role taking, and there is the reflection of problem solving. The former helps to produce the latter.

43. See, *The Mediating Self*, for a modification of Mead's position that allows for prereflective (self-)consciousness, and for an alternative presentation and critique of many of the points of this introduction.

44. *MSS*, p. 177. The phrase "a little different," I would argue, qualifies Mead's view in the direction of the degrees of novelty interpretation mentioned earlier. I also think the emphasis on novelty is exaggerated here, because "a little different," in reality, often turns out to mean functionally the same as prior responses. Lewis's piece bears on this point.

45. *MSS*, p. 201.

46. Mead, *Philosophy of the Present* (Chicago: University of Chicago Press, 1980) p. 1. Henceforth, referred to as *PP*.

47. *PP*, p. 47.

48. *PP*, p. 49.

49. Tugendhat alludes to the issue of recognition in his article and I raise it in my contribution as well.

50. Of course, this does not account for all of the features of Hegel's concept of recognition, especially the notion of mutual recognition, but it does shed light on how Mead's approach may be of service in grounding the insights of this tradition.

51. *PP*, p. 85.

52. Miller tells us that, "During the process of adjustment that takes place by reflective intelligence, the individual must occupy two systems at once—the old system, the world that was there and taken for granted, the generalized other or the Me, and that new order constructed by virtue of the activity of the creative I, an order which will lead to adjustment and enable the individual to continue in

a new system, a system (or order) to which the old must make an adjustment inasmuch as the Me and the generalized other are changed in the new order." Miller, *George Herbert Mead: Self, Language, and the World*, pp. 203-204.

CHAPTER 1

NOTES

1. This paper is part of a project on Progressivism and Chicago Sociology supported by a grant from the American Sociological Association's Committee on the Problems of the Discipline. The second section of the paper was presented at the annual meeting of the Midwest Sociological Society, Des Moines, 1986. I wish to thank my colleagues at Southern Illinois University for the generous responses they gave me during the discussion of this paper at the departmental seminar; Norbert Wiley for directing me to Mead's early publications in the *Oberlin Review;* Janet S. Belcove-Shalin for her help in deciphering some intractable passages from Mead's correspondence, as well as for her substantive comments; and three anonymous reviewers for their constructive criticism. Requests for reprints should be sent to Dmitri N. Shalin, Department of Sociology, Southern Illinois University at Carbondale, Carbondale, Illinois 62901.

2. One should also bear in mind that the articles by Mead gathered in a widely used volume edited by Reck (1964) sometimes appear there in an abridged form and that typically left out are the politically relevant sections.

3. The letters "MP" stand here and elsewhere in the text for the George H. Mead papers, a collection of letters and manuscripts by Mead in the Special Collections Department of the Joseph Regenstein Library, University of Chicago. The letters "b" and "f" followed by a number indicate, respectively, box number and folder number where a particular document is located. Mead's letters to Castle are gathered in box 1, folders 1-4. Editorial changes in the following excerpts from Mead's letters and manuscripts are limited to typographical errors and punctuation. Two of the letters pertaining to Mead's interests in socialism and reform have been transcribed by the author and are published in the Fall 1987 issue of *Symbolic Interaction* (see Shalin 1987).

4. In his senior year, Mead was elected an editor of the *Oberlin Review* and charged with the responsibility of assisting Henry Castle, his close friend and fellow editor, in the editorial department. Most of the editorials published during the academic year of 1882-83 were probably written by Castle, but some, judged by their style and other telltale signs, were penned by Mead, and virtually all must have had at least his tacit approval.

5. Mead's difficulties of those years were financial as much as intellectual. After college, Mead had to support himself and possibly his mother first by working as a schoolteacher and then as a member of a survey team of the Wisconsin Central Railroad Company. It does appear that Henry Castle, the son

of wealthy American missionaries in Hawaii, furnished Mead with some financial assistance during the latter's studies at Harvard and later in Germany. In 1891, Mead married Castle's sister, Helen, and eventually inherited, through her, part of the Castle family fortune. The influence of Henry Castle on Mead's personal and intellectual growth was great indeed, and one can only hope that the story of this beautiful friendship, which ended in 1895 with Castle's tragic death, will one day be told.

6. Mead's criticism of this period, and particularly his lamentations about the lack of a "national feeling" in America (MP October 19, 1890, b1, f1), bears a startling resemblance to the criticism of the American scene developed by the members of the Nationalist Club—a reform organization established by the followers of Bellamy, the author of the popular utopia, *Looking Backward,* which advocated the cause of socialism in the United States.

7. "The importance of social democracy here is tremendous, but not in the least alarming," wrote Castle ([1894] 1902, p. 784) to his parents while on a trip to Germany. "It simply stands as a protest against the existing conditions, not merely on their economical but also on their political side. The leaders are men of brains and education, whose influence is on the side of the general democratic movement after all, and as such useful and necessary."

8. Graham Taylor, a social worker with long experience in the Chicago reform movement, wrote to Mead's son on the death of his father, "More than he or any of us know the social settlement and city club movements owed much to his enlistment and guidance" (MP Taylor to Henry Mead, September 26, 1931, b1a, f7).

9. In a letter to his daughter-in-law, Mead, (MP March 10, 1919, b1, f16) refers to his duty as president of the City Club to nominate a few of its members as candidates for its leading positions: "Now I will spend hours on the phone securing the consent of five—well balanced between the radicals and conservatives—which means two reds, two blues and one Menshevik." Somehow, one gets the impression that Mead's sympathies were, at this time, with the Mensheviks, i.e., with the moderate social democrats committed to democracy, reform, and the rule of law.

10. Even in the heyday of Progressivism, teaching socialism in colleges was seen as a disloyal act. Here is a statement on the subject adopted in 1914 by the state of Wisconsin Republican Convention: "We favor the principle of *Lehrfreiheit.* The truth must and shall be taught. However, Socialism is not a demonstrated truth and we regard it as destructive of every principle of government that is dear to the American people and the mind of the student should be kept free from its misleading theories" (quoted in Mead 1915, p. 351).

11. One of Mead's letters to his wife contains an interesting reference to Veblen: "Had a pleasant call upon Veblen, who is pained because the Socialist Review says his doctrine is good socialism" (MP May 13, 1901, b1, f5). Veblen was no socialist, to be sure, but his precarious position at the University of Chicago must have made him sensitive to such suggestions.

12. In 1916, Mead wrote to his daughter-in-law, Irene Tufts Mead: "It is good that there is likely to be a popular majority for Wilson as well as the majority of the Electoral College, though I wish it had been larger, that is I wish that the country had swung further in the direction of progressivism..." (MP November 12, 1916, b1, f3).

13. In one place, Mead refers to "a real democracy in which the theoretical political power is not simply in the hands of a voting majority, but in which the community life expresses the interests of all..." (MP b2 addenda, f27).

14. "Human society, we have insisted, does not merely stamp the pattern of its organized social behavior upon any one of its individual members, so that this pattern becomes likewise the pattern of the individual's self; it also, at the same time, gives him a mind.... And his mind enables him in turn to stamp the pattern of his further developing self (further developing through his mental activity) upon the structure or organization of human society, and thus in a degree to reconstruct and modify in terms of his self the general pattern of social or group behavior in terms of which his self was originally constituted" (Mead 1934, p. 263). I have examined elsewhere (Shalin 1978) the macrosociological implications of this thesis.

15. There is an interesting parallel between the way pragmatists and contemporary German scholars searched for a proper mix of science and ethics. Thus, both Dewey and Weber expressed considerable regard for scientific procedures, both thought that objective knowledge is grounded in values, and both rejected the "ethic of ultimate ends" and opted for the "ethics of responsibility" or "ethics of means." Ultimately, however, Weber praised value neutrality as a stance befitting scientific workers, whereas Dewey and the pragmatists were more in tune with the idea of value tolerance.

REFERENCES

Aaron, D. 1951. *Men of Good Hope: A Story of American Progressives.* New York: Oxford University Press.

Addams, Jane. 1902. *Democracy and Social Ethics.* New York: Macmillan.

————. 1910. *Twenty Years at Hull-House.* New York: Macmillan.

Barnard, John. 1969. *From Evangelicalism to Progressivism at Oberlin College, 1866-1917.* Columbus: Ohio State University Press.

Bates, E. S. 1933. "John Dewey: America's Philosophic Engineer." *Modern Monthly* 7:387-96.

Bliss, W. D. P. (1890) 1970. "What to Do Now?" Pp. 350-54 in *Socialism in America: From the Shakers to the Third International*, edited by Albert Fried. Garden City, N.Y.: Doubleday.

Bourne, R. S. 1915. "John Dewey's Philosophy." *New Republic* 13:154-56.

Castle, Henry N. (1889) 1902. "Letter of Henry Castle to George H. Mead, February 3, 1899," pp. 578-81 in *Henry Northrup Castle: Letters.* London: Sands.

————. 1902. "Letter of Henry Castle to Mabel, Helen, and Mother, November 27, 1894." Pp. 783-85 in *Henry Northrup Castle: Letters.* London: Sands.

Conn, Peter. 1983. *The Divided Mind: Ideology and Imagination in America, 1898-1917.* Cambridge: Cambridge University Press.

Cremin, L. A. 1969. "John Dewey and the Progressive Education Movement." *Antioch Review* 67:160-73.

Croly, Herbert. 1909. *The Promise of American Life.* New York: Macmillan.

Debs, Eugene. 1912. "Sound Socialist Tactics." *International Socialist Review* 12:481-86.

Deegan, M. J., and J. S. Burger. 1978. "George Herbert Mead and Social Reform: His Work and Writings." *Journal of History of the Behavioral Sciences* 14:362-73.

Dewey, John (1888) 1969. "The Ethics of Democracy." Pp. 227-49 in *John Dewey, the Early Works, 1882-1889,* vol. 1. Carbondale: Southern Illinois University Press.

————. (1927) 1954. *The Public and Its Problems.* New York: Holt.

————. (1929) 1962. *Individualism, Old and New.* New York: Capricorn.

————. (1938) 1950. "What I Believe, Revised." Pp. 32-35 in *Pragmatism and American Culture,* edited by Gail Kennedy. Boston: Heath.

————. 1946. *The Problems of Men.* New York: Philosophical Library.

Dewey, John, and John L. Childs. 1933. "The Underlying Philosophy of Education." Pp. 287-319 in *The Educational Frontier,* edited by W. H. Kilpatrick. New York: Appleton-Century.

Diner, S. J. 1975. "Department and Discipline: The Department of Sociology at the University of Chicago, 1892-1920." *Minerva* 13:514-53.

————. 1980. *A City and Its Universities, Public Policy in Chicago, 1892-1919.* Chapel Hill: University of North Carolina Press.

Editorial. 1882. *Oberlin Review* 10:55

————. 1883. *Oberlin Review* 10:175-76.

Faris, Robert E. 1970. *Chicago Sociology, 1920-1932.* Chicago: University of Chicago Press.

Featherstone, J. 1972. "John Dewey." *New Republic* 8:27-32.

Fisher, Berenice M., and Anselm L. Strauss. 1978. "Introduction." Pp. 457-98 in *A History of Sociological Analysis*, edited by Tom Bottomore and Lewis A. Coser. New York: Basic.

Fried, Albert, ed. 1970. *Socialism in America: From the Shakers to the Third International*. Garden City, N.Y.: Doubleday.

Furner, Mary O. 1975. *Advocacy & Objectivity. A Crisis in the Professionalization of American Social Sciences, 1865-1905*. Lexington: University Press of Kentucky.

George, Henry. (1879) 1926. *Progress and Poverty*. New York: Doubleday, Page.

Giddens, Anthony. 1981. *A Contemporary Critique of Historical Materialism*, vol. 1. Berkeley and Los Angeles: University of California Press.

Goldman, Eric. 1956. *Rendezvous with Destiny: A History of Modern American Reform*. New York: Vintage.

Gouldner, Alvin A. 1973. "Romanticism and Classicism: Deep Structures in Social Science." Pp. 323-66 in *For Sociology: Renewal and Criticism in Sociology Today*, by Alvin A. Gouldner. New York: Basic.

Graham, Otis L. 1967. *An Encore for Reform: The Old Progressive and the New Deal*. New York: Oxford University Press.

Gutmann, Amy. 1983. "How Liberal is Democracy?" Pp. 25-50 in *Liberalism Reconsidered*, edited by Douglas MacLean and Claudia Mills. Totowa, N.J.: Rowman & Allanheld.

Habermas, Jürgen. 1981. *Theorie des Kommunikativen Handelns*. Band 2. Frankfurt: Suhrkamp.

Hofstadter, Richard. 1955. *The Age of Reform: From Byron to FDR*. New York: Knopf.

Janowitz, Morris. 1952. *The Community Press in an Urban Setting*. Chicago: University of Chicago Press.

————. 1970. "Preface." Pp. xi-xii in *Introduction to the Science of Sociology*, by Robert Park and Ernest W. Burgess. Chicago: University of Chicago Press.

————. 1978. *The Last Half-Century: Societal Change and Politics in America*. Chicago: University of Chicago Press.

Joas, Hans. 1985. *G. H. Mead: A Contemporary Reexamination of His Thought*. Cambridge: Polity.

Karier, C. J. 1975. "John Dewey and the New Liberalism." *History of Education Quarterly* 15:417-43.

Kolko, Gabriel. 1963. *The Triumph of Conservatism: A Reinterpretation of American History, 1900-1916.* New York: Free Press.

Lasch, Christopher. 1983. "Liberalism in Retreat." Pp. 105-16 in *Liberalism Reconsidered,* edited by Douglas MacLean and Claudia Mills. Totowa, N.J.: Rowman & Allanheld.

Laslett, John H. M., and Seymour Martin Lipset, eds. 1974. *Failure of a Dream? Essays in the History of American Socialism.* Garden City, N.Y.: Anchor.

Levine, D. 1969. "Randolph Bourne, John Dewey, and the Legacy of Liberalism." *Antioch Review* 29:234-44.

Lukes, Steven. 1985. *Morality and Marxism.* London: Oxford University Press.

Lynd, Staughton. 1974. "The Prospects of the New Left." Pp. 713-39 in *Failure of a Dream? Essays in the History of American Socialism,* edited by John H. M. Laslett and Seymour Martin Lipset. Garden City, N.Y.: Anchor.

McNaught, Kenneth. 1974. "Comment." Pp. 409-20 in *Failure of a Dream? Essays in the History of Socialism in America,* edited by John H. M. Laslett and Seymour Martin Lipset. Garden City, N.Y.: Anchor.

Marx, Karl. (1844) 1964. *The Economic & Philosophic Manuscripts of 1844.* New York: International.

————. (1846) 1963. *The German Ideology.* Parts 1 and 3. New York: International.

Mead, George H. (n.d.) George Herbert Mead Papers. University of Chicago Archives.

————. 1881. "The Relation of Art to Morality." *Oberlin Review* 9:63-64.

————. 1882a. "Charles Lamb." *Oberlin Review* 10:15-16.

————. 1882b. "De Quincey." *Oberlin Review* 10:50-52.

————. 1882c. "John Locke." *Oberlin Review* 10:217-19.

————. 1884. "Republican Persecution, Letter to the Editor." *Nation* 39:519-20.

————. 1899a. "The Working Hypothesis in Social Reform." *American Journal of Sociology* 5:367-71.

————. 1899b. "Review of Le Bon, Psychology of Socialism." *American Journal of Sociology* 5:404-12.

————. 1907. "Review of Jane Addams's *The Newer Ideals of Peace.*" *American Journal of Sociology* 13:121-28.

————. 1907-8. "The Educational Situation in the Chicago Public Schools." *City Club Bulletin* 1:131-38.

————. (1908) 1964. "The Philosophical Basis of Ethics." Pp. 82-93 in *Selected Writings: George Herbert Mead*, edited by A. J. Reck. New York: Bobbs-Merrill.

————. 1908. "Educational Aspects of Trade Unions." *Union Labor Advocate* 8:19-20.

————. 1908-9*a*. "Industrial Education, the Working Man, and the School." *Elementary School Teacher* 9:369-83.

————. 1908-9*b*. "Editorial Notes." *Elementary School Teacher* 9:156-57.

————. 1908-9*c*. "Editorial Notes." *Elementary School Teacher* 9:212-14.

————. 1909. "The Adjustment of Our Industry to Surplus and Unskilled Labor." *Proceedings of the National Conference of Charities and Corrections* 34:222-25.

————. 1912. "Remarks on Labor Night Concerning Participation of Representatives of Labor in the City Club." *City Club Bulletin* 5:214-15.

————. 1915. "Madison: The Passage of the University of Wisconsin through the State Political Agitation of 1914; the Survey by William H. Allen and His Staff and the Legislative Fight of 1915, with the Indications These Offer of the Place the State University Holds in the Community." *Survey* 35:349-61.

————. (1915) 1964. "Natural Rights and the Theory of the Political Institution." Pp. 150-70 in *Selected Writings: George Herbert Mead*, edited by A. J. Reck. New York: Bobbs-Merrill.

————. 1916-17. "Professor Hoxie and the Community." *University of Chicago Magazine* 9:114-17.

————. 1917*a*. "Germany's Crisis—Its Effect on Labor. Part I." *Chicago Herald*, Thursday, July 26.

————. 1917*b*. "Germany's Crisis—Its Effect on Labor. Part II." *Chicago Herald*, Friday, July 27.

————. 1917*c*. "War Issues to U.S. Forced by Kaiser." *Chicago Herald*, Thursday, August 2.

————. 1917*d*. "Democracy's Issues in the World War." *Chicago Herald*, August 4.

————. 1917*e*. "American Ideals and the War." *Chicago Herald*, Friday, August 3.

————. 1918. "Social Work, Standards of Living and the War." *Proceedings of the National Conference of Social Work* 45:637-44.

————. (1923) 1964. "Scientific Method and the Moral Sciences." Pp. 248-66 in *Selected Writings: George Herbert Mead*, edited by A. J. Reck. New York: Bobbs-Merrill.

————. (1924-25) 1964. "The Genesis of the Self and Social Control." Pp. 267-93 in *Selected Writings: George Herbert Mead*, edited by A. J. Reck. New York: Bobbs-Merrill.

————. (1925-26) 1964. "The Nature of Aesthetic Experience." Pp. 294-305 in *Selected Writings: George Herbert Mead*, edited by A. J. Reck. New York: Bobbs-Merrill.

————. (1930) 1964. "Philanthropy from the Point of View of Ethics." Pp. 392-407 in *Selected Writings: George Herbert Mead*, edited by A. J. Reck. New York: Bobbs-Merrill.

————. 1934. *Mind, Self, and Society*. Chicago: University of Chicago Press.

————. 1935-36. "The Philosophy of John Dewey." *International Journal of Ethics* 46:64-81.

————. 1936. *Movements of Thought in the Nineteenth Century*. Chicago: University of Chicago Press.

————. 1938. *The Philosophy of the Act*. Chicago: University of Chicago Press.

Niebuhr, Reinhold. (1932) 1960. *Moral Man and Immoral Society*. New York: Scribners.

Noble, David W. 1958. *The Paradox of Progressive Thought*. Minneapolis: University of Minnesota Press.

Novack, George. 1975. *Pragmatism versus Marxism*. New York: Pathfinder.

Orloff, Ann Shola, and Theda Skocpol. 1984. "Why Not Equal Protection? Explaining the Politics of Public Social Spending in Britain, 1900-1911, and the United States, 1880s-1920." *American Sociological Review* 49:726-50.

Pease, Otis, ed. 1962. *The Progressive Years: The Spirit and Achievement of American Reform*. New York: Braziller.

Purcell, Edward A., Jr. 1973. *The Crisis of Democratic Theory*. Lexington: University Press of Kentucky.

Raushenbush, Winifred. 1979. *Robert E. Park: Biography of a Sociologist*. Durham, N.C.: Duke University Press.

Reck, A. J., ed. 1964. *Selected Writings: George Herbert Mead*. New York: Bobbs-Merrill.

Resek, Carl. 1967. *The Progressives*. Indianapolis: Bobbs-Merrill.

Roosevelt, Theodore. 1909. "Socialism." *Outlook* 41:619:23.

_____. (1912) 1962. "A Confession of Faith." Pp. 310-41 in *The Progressive Years: The Spirit and Achievement of American Reform*, edited by Otis Pease. New York: Braziller.

Schwedinger, Herman, and Julia R. Schwedinger. 1974. *The Sociologists of the Chair*. New York: Basic.

Scott, A. M. 1959. "The Progressive Era in Perspective." *Journal of Politics* 21: 685-701.

Selsam, Howard. 1950. "Science and Ethics." Pp. 81-92 in *Pragmatism and American Culture*, edited by Gail Kennedy. Boston: Heath.

Shalin, D. N. 1978. "The Genesis of Social Interactionism and Differentiation of Macro- and Microsociological Paradigms." *Humboldt Journal of Social Relations* 6:3-38.

_____. 1979. "Between the Ethos of Science and the Ethos of Ideology." *Sociological Focus* 12:275-93.

_____. 1980. "Marxist Paradigm and Academic Freedom." *Social Research* 47:361-82.

_____. 1984. "The Romantic Antecedents of Meadian Social Psychology." *Symoblic Interaction* 7:43-65.

_____. 1986a. "Pragmatism and Social Interactionism." *American Sociological Review* 51:9-29.

_____. 1986b. "Romanticism and the Rise of Sociological Hermeneutics." *Social Research* 53:77-123.

_____. 1987. "Socialism, Democracy and Reform: A Letter and an Article by George H. Mead." *Symbolic Interaction*, vol. 10, no. 2.

Smith, T. V. 1931. "The Social Philosophy of George Herbert Mead." *American Journal of Sociology* 37:368–85.

Smith, Timothy L. 1957. *Revivalism and Social Reform in Mid-Nineteenth Century America*. New York: Abington.

Sombart, Werner (1909) 1968. *Socialism and Social Movement*. New York: Kelley.

White, Morton C. 1957. *Social Thought in America: The Revolt against Formalism*. Boston: Beacon.

Wilson, Woodrow. (1912) 1962. "Address at Duquesne Garden." Pp. 372-78 in *The Progressive Years: The Spirit and Achievement of American Reform*, edited by Otis Pease. New York: Braziller.

CHAPTER 2

NOTES

a. See Shalin's, "G. H. Mead, Socialism, and the Progressive Agenda," in this book.—ED.

1. See Mead's 'Review of C. L. Morgan, An Introduction to Comparative Psychology', *Psychological Review* 2 (1895), pp. 399-402.

2. The passage runs as follows: 'If the Pragmatic doctrine is a logical generalization of scientific method, it cannot merge the problem that engages thought with a larger problem which denies validity to the conditions that are the necessary tests of the solution which thought is seeking' (Mead, 'A Pragmatic Theory of Truth', in: A. Reck (ed.), *G. H. Mead: Selected Writings* [Indianapolis 1964], p. 334.)

3. As the worst example of the 'Marxist' (i.e. Stalinist) analysis of pragmatism, see the book by Wells, *Der Pragmatismus, eine Philosophie des Imperialismus* (Berlin [DDR] 1957).

4. Mead, *The Philosophy of Act,* edited by Charles W. Morris et al. (Chicago, 1938), pp. 97-98.

5. Peirce, *Collected Papers* (Harvard 1932), paragraph 5.412.

6. See 'A Pragamatic Theory of Truth', pp. 328-29; 'The Philosophies of Royce, James, and Dewey in Their American Setting', *International Journal of Ethics* 40 (1930), pp. 211-31 [A. Reck's *Selected Writings* reprints the latter article and Joas refers to p. 386 in it]; 'The Definition of the Psychical', *Decennial Publications of the University of Chicago,* First Series, Vol. III (Chicago 1903), pp. 77-112. [An abridged version of the latter appears in A. Reck.]

7. Only twice in 'The Philosophies of Royce, James, and Dewey in Their American Setting'.

8. See Mead papers, Chicago, Box X, Folder 26.

9. Lincourt conjectured that this was so in his dissertation *Precursors in American Philosophy of G. H. Mead's Theory of Emergent Selfhood* (Buffalo, New York 1972); see Chapter 5 [of Joas's *George Herbert Mead*] for a more detailed substantiation of this assertion.

10. Karl-Otto Apel, *Charles Sanders Peirce, From Pragmatism to Pragmaticism* (Amherst, Massachusetts 1981), p. 59.

11. Cf. C. W. Mills *Sociology and Pragmatism, The Higher Learning in America* (New York 1966), p. 155. It is also striking that Mead (e.g., *Movements of Thought in the Nineteenth Century,* edited by Merritt H. Moore [Chicago 1936], pp. 351-52 and elsewhere) refers to behaviourist psychology as a source of pragmatism and not as an application of it.

12. Cf. Jane M. Dewey, 'Biography of John Dewey', in: P. A. Schilpp (ed.), *The Philosophy of John Dewey* (New York 1951), pp. 1-45, particularly p. 26.

13. Scheler, *Erkenntnis und Arbeit* (Frankfurt 1977); *Horkheimer, Zur Kritik der instrumentellen Vernunft* (Frankfurt 1974).

14. See Apel, *Charles Sanders Peirce*; Habermas, 'Zu Nietzsches Erkenntnis Theorie', in: *Kultur und Kritik* (Frankfurt 1973), pp. 239-267; Heidegger had also attacked such a way of thinking in *Sein und Zeit* (Tübingen 1977), p. 101.

15. See Mead's article on Royce, James, and Dewey, pp. 388ff. [in Reck] and his arguments with Bergson in *Movements of Thought* and 'Review of Henri Bergson, L'Evolution créatrice', *Psychological Bulletin* 4 (1907), pp. 379-84.

16. Mead, 'Review of G. Le Bon, The Psychology of Socialism', *American Journal of Sociology* 5 (1899), pp. 404-12.

17. Because of their general relevance today, I would like to quote the beautiful and profound sentences in which Adorno criticizes Bergson (*Negative Dialectics* [London 1973], pp. 8-9): "A matter of urgency to the concept would be what it fails to cover, what its abstractionist mechanism eliminates, what is not already a case of the concept."

"Bergson and Husserl, carriers of philosophical modernism, both have innervated this idea but withdrawn from it to traditional metaphysics. Bergson, in a tour de force, created another type of cognition for nonconceptuality's sake. The dialectical salt was washed away in an undifferentiated tide of life; solidified reality was disposed of as subaltern, not comprehended along with its subalternity. The hater of the rigid general concept established a cult of irrational immediacy, of sovereign freedom in the midst of unfreedom. He drafted his two cognitive modes in as dualistic an opposition as that of the Cartesian and Kantian doctrines he fought had ever been; the causal-mechanical mode, as pragmatistic knowledge, was no more affected by the intuitive one than the bourgeois establishment was by the relaxed unself-consciousness of those who owe their privileges to that establishment."

"The celebrated intuitions themselves seem rather abstract in Bergson's philosophy; they scarcely go beyond the phenomenal time consciousness which even Kant had underlying chronological-physical time—spatial time, according to Bergson's insight. Although it takes an effort to develop, the intuitive mode of mental conduct does continue to exist in fact as an archaic rudiment of mimetic reactions. What preceded its past holds a promise beyond the ossified present. Intuitions succeed only desultorily, however. Every cognition including Bergson's own needs the rationality he scorns, and needs it precisely at the moment of concretion. Absolutized duration, pure becoming, the pure act—these would recoil into the same timelessness which Bergson chides in metaphysics since Plato and Aristotle. He did not mind that the thing he groped for, if it is not to remain a mirage, is visible solely with the equipment of cognition, by reflection upon its own means, and that it grows arbitrary in a procedure unrelated, from the start, to that of cognition."

18. Cf. texts by Manfred Reidel, Introduction to Dilthey's *Der Aufbau der geschichtlichen Welt in den Geisteswissenschaften* (Frankfurt 1970); Helmut, Johach, *Handelnder Mensch und objektiver Geist. Zur Theorie der Geistes- und Sozialwissenschaften bei Wilhelm Dilthey* (Meisenheim am Glan 1974); Jürgen Habermas, *Erkenntnis und Interesse* (Frankfurt 1968).

19. In my opinion, Riedel's interpretation of Dilthey's thought does not stress this point sufficiently.

20. Cf. Dilthey, *Der Aufbau der geschichtlichen Welt in den Geisteswissenschaften* (Frankfurt 1970); on the relationship between Dilthey and Husserl see their correspondence edited by Biemel, 'Briefwechsel Dilthey-Husserl', *Man and World* I (1968), pp. 428-46.

21. Karl-Otto Apel, *Charles Sanders Peirce*, p. 110.

22. I have great difficulty with the distinction between a psychological and a hermeneutic phase in the development of Dilthey's thought on which Gadamer and Habermas base their interpretations. It is my opinion that in this distinction several dimensions overlap one another: the merely empathic hermeneutics versus a hermeneutics directed to the understanding of meaning, and a relativist versus normative method of understanding. In addition, this distinction suggests that hermeneutics itself does not require more than a linguistic grounding, whereas it must also be grounded in philosophical anthropology. Helmuth Plessner saw this, and used it to justify his hermeneutics of non-linguistic expression. Habermas's *Erkenntnis und Interesse* opposes Peirce and Dilthey far too much on the basis of the distinction between instrumental and communicative action, which results in the slightly unjust treatment of both of them. See also R. Bernstein's critique of Habermas's interpretation of Peirce in his introduction to the German edition of *Praxis and Action* (Frankfurt 1975).

23. Husserl, *Philosophie als strenge Wissenschaft* (Frankfurt 1965).

24. Cf. Lucien Goldmann, *Lukács und Heidegger* (Darmstadt 1975) and Ernst Tugendhat, *Selbstbewusstsein und Selbstbestimmung. Sprachanalytische Interpretationen* (Frankfurt 1979).

25. On Gehlen's early philosophical writings, see Böhler 'Arnold Gehlen: Die Haudlung', in: Josef Speck (ed.), *Grundprobleme der grossen Philosophen, Philosophie der Gegenwart II* (Göttingen 1973); on his mature philosophical anthropology, see my article 'Intersubjektivität bei Mead und Gehlen', *Archiv für Rechts–und Sozialphilosophie* 65 (1979), pp. 105-21.

26. For a critique of Plessner from the standpoint of the theory of intersubjectivity, see Habermas's letter to Plessner, in: *Kultur und Kritik*, pp. 232-5; see also the chapter on Plessner in Axel Honneth and Hans Joas, *Soziales Handeln und menschliche Natur* (Frankfurt 1980), pp. 72ff.

27. I leave out of consideration the peculiar twist that Karl-Otto Apel gives to transcendental philosophy by making the motives for going beyond it, such as

corporeality and intersubjectivity, building blocks of a new 'transformed' transcendental philosophy.

28. As for French sociology, I recommend the article by Stone and Farberman on the difference and similarity between Durkheim and Mead, 'On the Edge of Rapprochement: Was Durkheim Moving Toward the Perspective of Symbolic Interaction', in: Stone and Farberman (eds), *Social Psychology through Symbolic Interaction* (Waltham, Massachusetts, 1970), pp. 100-112.

29. On Lukács, see my introduction to Agnes Heller, *Das Alltagsleben* (Frankfurt 1978); for a critique of an instrumentalist limitation implicit in Weber's concept of action, see Karl-Siegbert Rehberg, 'Rationales Handeln als grossbürgerliches Aktionsmodell. Thesen zu einigen handlungstheoretischen Implikationen der 'Soziologischen Grundbegriffe' Max Webers', in: *Kölner Zeitschrift für Soziologie und Sozialpsychologie* 31 (1979), pp. 199-236.

30. For an especially vivid account of this relationship, see Dewey's essay on Renan, 'Renan's Loss of Faith in Science', in: *The Early Works* 4 (Carbondale, Illinois 1971), pp. 11-18.

31. Charles Morris was the first to call for a study of this material by a historian of philosophy.

32. See Mead's lecture 'Rationalism and Empiricism', a copy of which is among his unpublished papers in Chicago.

33. Cf. Josiah Royce, *The Spirit of Modern Philosophy* (New York 1983).

34. Mead's course on Hume (Box VII, Folder 7-12).

35. *Movements of Thought* p. 67. I do not consider here Mead's extremely problematical concept of Romanticism and his assignment of post-Kantian idealism to Romanticism. Many of the simplifications in this book are undoubtedly due to the fact that the lectures on which it is based were given as an elementary introduction for undergraduate students.

36. *Movements of Thought*, pp. 85-110.

37. Ibid., p. 90.

38. Ibid., pp. 101ff. [my emphasis H. J.].

39. Ibid., pp. 91-92.

40. It is indeed no accident that Habermas, in his short but impressively concise interpretation of Fichte in *Erkenntnis und Interesse* (see p. 52), adduces Fichte as the forerunner of the second, non-Kantian moment in the concept of synthesis through social work.

41. See Lukacs's essay on Moses Hess, 'Moses Hess und die Probleme der idealistischen Dialektik', in: Lukács, *Werke*, Vol. 2 (Neuwied 1965), pp. 643-86.

42. Mead, 'The Objective Reality of Perspectives', in: Edgar S. Brightman (ed.), *Proceedings of the Sixth International Congress of Philosophy* (New York 1926), pp. 75-85; also in Mead, *The Philosophy of the Present*, edited by Arthur E. Murphy (LaSalle, IL.: 1932). [Joas specifically refers to p. 161 in *Philosophy of the Present.*]

43. See Apel on Peirce.

44. For qualifications of this assessment see chapter 2 [in Joas's *George Herbert Mead*].

45. See *Movements of Thought*, p. 472, where he posits a connection between German idealism and the early development of physiological psychology.

46. Ibid., p. 417.

47. This is particularly true of American sociologists, from some of whom I encountered an aggressive rejection of any connection between German idealism and Mead.

48. See Sidney Hook's review of 'Movements of Thought' in *The Nation* 143 (1936), pp. 220-21.

49. Cf. Dewey's assessment of Hegel in an autobiographical retrospect, quoted in R. Bernstein's *Praxis und Handeln* (Frankfurt 1975), p. 33.

50. Kurt Lasswitz, 'Die modern Energetik in ihrer Bedeutung für die Erkenntniskritik', *Philosophische Monatshefte* 29 (1893). See Mead's texts, 'Herr Lasswitz on Energy and Epistemology', *Psychological Review* 1 (1894), pp. 172-5; and 'Review of K. Lasswitz, Die moderne Energetik in ihrer Bedeutung für die Erkenntniskritik', *Psychological Review* 1 (1894), pp. 210-3.

51. Mead, 'Herr Lasswitz on Energy and Epistemology', *Psychological Review* 1 (1894), p. 173.

52. See the early text, 'The Problem of Psychological Measurement' (Abstract of a paper read to the second annual meeting of the American Psychological Association 1893). *Proceedings of the American Psychological Association* (New York 1894), pp. 22/23.

53. Schleiermacher, *Monologe.*

54. Mead, 'Review of G. Class, Untersuchungen zur Phänomenologie und Ontologie des menschlichen Geistes', *American Journal of Theology* 1 (1897), pp. 789-92. [Joas specifically refers to p. 789.]

55. Ibid., p. 790.

56. Ibid., p. 791.

57. Mead on D'Arcy, 'A New Criticism of Hegelianism: Is It Valid? (Review of C.F. D'Arcy, Idealism and Theology)', *American Journal of Theology* 5 (1901), pp. 87-96. [Joas specifically refers to pp. 94-95.]

58. Ibid., p. 92.

59. Ibid., p. 96.

60. Mead, 'Suggestions Towards a Theory of the Philosophical Disciplines', *Philosophical Review* 9 (1900), pp. 1-17. [Joas specifically refers to p. 2.]

61. See, for example, Piaget's book on the psychology of intelligence, *Psychologie der Intelligenz* (Munich 1974).

62. Mead, 'Suggestions', p. 13.

63. Ibid., p. 12.

CHAPTER 3

NOTES

1. Anselm Strauss, ed., *George Herbert Mead on Social Psychology* (Chicago: University of Chicago Press, Revised Edition 1964), p. xiii.

2. George Herbert Mead, *The Philosophy of the Present*. Edited, with an Introduction, by Arthur E. Murphy, and prefatory remarks by John Dewey (La Salle, Ill.: Open Court Publishing Company, 1932), pp. xxxvi-xxxvii.

3. Darnell Rucker, *The Chicago Pragmatists* (Minneapolis: University of Minnesota Press, 1969), pp. 59-60.

4. John Dewey, "The Reflex Arc Concept in Psychology," reprinted in John Dewey, *Philosphy, Psychology, and Social Practice*, ed. Joseph Ratner (New York: Capricorn Books, 1965), pp. 252-266.

5. Ibid., p. 260.

6. Ibid., p. 258.

7. Ibid., p. 254.

8. Ibid., pp. 254-255.

9. Ibid., p. 263.

10. Ibid., p. 265.

11. All the Mead essays discussed in this study are reprinted in George Herbert Mead, *Selected Writings*, ed. Andrew J. Reck (Indianapolis: Bobbs-Merrill, 1964). References to this volume will be indicated in the text by the abbreviation SW and the relevant page number.

12. In later years Mead preferred the term "impulse" when referring to the root tendencies of human conduct. "They are best termed 'impulses' and not 'instincts,' because they are subject to extensive modifications in the life-history of

individuals..." George Herbert Mead, *Mind, Self and Society*. Edited with an Introduction, by Charles W. Morris (Chicago: University of Chicago Press, 1934), p. 337.

13. Mead's use of the term "fictitious" in this passage is puzzling, but it may suggest that he was himself aware of the somewhat misleading character of the term "I" as applied to the immediate act. The "I," he says several lines earlier, is the transcendental self of Kant. But if this is so then the legitimacy of its right to be labelled by a personal pronoun is equally dubious.

14. *Mind, Self and Society*, p. 174.

15. "Now, it is this living act which never gets directly into reflective experience... It is that 'I' which we may be said to be continually trying to realize, and to realize through the actual conduct itself." *Mind, Self and Society*, p. 203. Also, "the act itself which I have spoken of as the 'I' in the social situation is a source of unity of the whole, while the 'me' is the social situation in which the act can express itself." Ibid., p. 279.

16. William L. Kolb, "A Critical Evaluation of Mead's 'I' and 'Me' Concepts," *Social Forces* (22 March 1944), p. 292. Reprinted in Jerome G. Manis and Bernard N. Meltzer, editors, *Symbolic Interaction: A Reader in Social Psychology* (Boston: Allyn and Bacon, 1967), pp. 241-250.

17. Charles Morris points out in his Introduction to *Mind, Self and Society*, p. xv, n. 6, that "A stenographic copy of the 1912 lectures on social psychology shows that his root ideas were already in mature form."

18. See Charles Morris, *The Pragmatic Movement in American Philosophy* (New York: George Braziller, 1970), p. 43, n. 2.

CHAPTER 4

NOTES

a. Lewis discusses covert behaviors in several places. They may be described as physiological processes that attend mental activity and remain outside of our awareness; for example, the movement of the lips or tongue that occurs when solving a problem. Lewis also tells us that a covert response (i.e., behavior) "may occur on an emotional or on a cognitive level," so that it "intervenes between the original attitude and the subsequent one," and in so doing allows us to be aware of the original attitude. "[F]requently it also takes the form of an image of the consequences of carrying through the overt response which the attitude prepares. For example, the chess player images the position which would be created by moving the pawn and may thereby discover a better move" p. 116.—ED.

1. A briefer version of this paper was read at the conference entitled "Social Behaviorism and Experimental Research: A Reconsideration of George Herbert

Mead," held at the University of North Carolina in 1976. I wish to thank the conference participants, especially Leonard S. Cottrell, Jr., Clark McPhail, and Richard L. Smith, for helpful comments. Lynn Stephens, Penelope Van Esterik, Andrew J. Weigert, and the anonymous referees [for the *American Journal of Sociology*] have also made valuable suggestions for which I am most grateful.

2. Interestingly, it is often during moments of emotional experiences that the representation of symbols which would normally be confined to inner speech burst out of the inner forum as loud exclamations. This is largely what we mean by "losing control" of oneself. This suggests that inner speech and outer speech might be profitably thought of as poles of a continuum rather than as a radical dichotomy. Muttering comments to oneself at a public gathering would represent the middle range of this continuum.

3. Unfortunately, the term "deterministically" is likely to connote many unwanted meanings in this context. I do not mean to imply an unfailing or direct causal connection. It is clear, e.g., that the significant symbol will have no effect on a receiver who is not paying attention, and there are intervening processes between the invocation of the symbol and the formation of the attitude (to be discussed below). Nevertheless, if the necessary physical and physiological conditions are satisfied, the representation of the symbol will call out the same attitude in both organisms, and this effect is regular and involuntary. As Swanson (1972, p. 31) observed, "Mead's account opposes the view that conduct is determined solely by the organism or by the environment. It is not opposed, in principle, to a deterministic view of behavior." If the connection between symbols and attitudes were not determinisitic in this sense, there could be no language other than that which occurs through what Mead called the "conversation of gestures" which goes on among lower animals.

4. It is indeed ironic that the psychological behaviorists profess to have elevated psychology beyond subjectivism, and yet their explanation of the source of meaning of verbal behavior on any given occasion would have the researcher delve into the peculiarities of the particular individuals engaged in such behavior. Chomsky (1959) has strongly challenged this theory of meaning on both theoretical and methodological grounds.

5. The theoretical and methodological subjectivism implied by the remedial interpretation of Mead is apparent in the work of Herbert Blumer (1969). Indeed, Coser (1976, p. 156) charges that "symbolic interactionism is at bottom an atheoretical sociological theory." During the 1970s, a number of theorists have pointed out the fundamental theoretical and methodological divergences between Blumerian symbolic interactionism and Meadian social behaviorism (e.g., Ropers 1973, pp. 52-53; Zeitlin 1973; Lewis 1977; Rubinstein 1977, pp. 212-13; McPhail and Rexroat 1979; Lewis and Smith, 1980).

6. But see List (1973) for a lucid statement of the social behaviorist interpretation of Mead's theory of meaning.

7. As a point of historical interest, it may be noted that Mead was aware of Jacobson's early work on the psychophysiology of relaxation and took an interest in the progress of his research (Smith, personal communication).

8. There is another type of feedback which Mead does not always adequately differentiate from the wholly symbolic or cognitive type. This is the "dialogue" between mind and body. We are sometimes frightened by our own thought; taking a certain attitude toward an object often stimulates emotive feedback which can influence the course of the act. Another type of body feedback occurs as distance runners monitor their fatigue level in order to adjust their running pace.

REFERENCES

Asch, S. E. 1955. "Opinions and Social Pressure." *Scientific American* 193:31-35.

Bassin, F. U., and E. S. Bein, 1961. "Application of Electromyography to the Study of Speech." Pp. 195-209 in *Recent Soviet Psychology*, edited by N. O'Connor. New York: Liveright.

Bateson, G. 1972. "Style, Grace, and Information in Primitive Art." Pp. 128-52 in *Steps to an Ecology of Mind*. New York: Ballantine.

Berger, H. 1929. "Über das Elektrenkephalogram des Menschen." *Archiv für Psychiatrie Nervenkrankheiten* 87:524-70.

Blumer, H. 1969. *Symbolic Interaction*. Englewood Cliffs, N.J.: Prentice-Hall.

Buckley, W. 1967. *Sociology and Modern Systems Theory*. Englewood Cliffs, N.J.: Prentice-Hall.
_____ , ed. 1968. *Modern Systems Research for the Behaviorial Scientist*. Chicago: Aldine.

Chomsky, N. 1959. "A Review of B. F. Skinner's *Verbal Behavior*." *Language* 35:26-58.

Coser, L.A. 1976. "Sociological Theory from Chicago Dominance to 1965." Pp. 145-60 in *Annual Review of Sociology*. Palo Alto, Calif.: Annual Reviews, Inc.

Cottrell, Leonard S., Jr. 1942a. "The Adjustment of the Individual to His Age and Sex Roles." *American Sociological Review* 7:617-20.

_____ . 1942b "The Analysis of Situational Fields in Social Psychology." *American Sociological Review* 7:370-82.

_____ . 1971. "Covert Behavior in Interpersonal Interaction." *Proceedings of the American Philosophical Society* 115:462-68.

_____ . 1978. "George Herbert Mead and Harry Stack Sullivan: An Unfinished Synthesis." *Psychiatry* 41:151-61.

Davis. R. C. 1966. "Response Patterns." Pp. 281-92 in *Thinking: Studies of Covert Language Processes,* edited by F. J. McGuigan. New York: Appleton-Century-Crofts.

Deetz, J. 1967. *Invitation to Archaeology.* Garden City, N.Y.: Natural History Press.

Foote, Nelson, and Leonard S. Cottrell, Jr. 1955. *Identity and Interpersonal Competence.* Chicago: University of Chicago Press.

Garfinkel, H. 1967. *Studies in Ethnomethodology.* Englewood Cliffs, N.J.: Prentice Hall.

Gillin, C. T. 1975. "Freedom and the Limits of Social Behaviorism: A Comparison of Selected Themes from the Works of G. H. Mead and Martin Buber." *Sociology* 9:29-47.

Hebb, D. O. 1969. "The Mind's Eye." *Psychology Today* 2 (12): 54-57, 67-68.

―――――. 1972. *Textbook of Psychology.* 3d ed. Philadelphia: Saunders.

Horowitz, M. J. 1970. *Image Formation and Cognition.* New York: Appleton-Century-Crofts.

Jacobson, Edmund. 1931. "Electrical Measurements of Neuromuscular States during Mental Activities. VII. Imagination, Recollection and Abstract Thinking Involving the Speech Musculature." *American Journal of Physiology* 97:200-209.

―――――. 1932. "Electrophysiology of Mental Activities." *American Journal of Psychology* 44:677-94.

―――――. 1973. "Electrophysiology of Mental Activities and Introduction to the Psychological Process of Thinking." Pp. 3-24 in McGuigan and Schoonover 1973.

Kolb. W. L. 1978. "A Criticial Evaluation of Mead's 'I' and 'Me' Concepts." Pp. 191-96 in *Symoblic Interaction: A Reader in Social Psychology,* edited by J. G. Manis and B. N. Meltzer. Boston: Allyn & Bacon.

Kuhn, M. H., and T. S. McPartland. 1954. "An Empirical Investigation of Self-Attitudes." *American Sociological Review* 19:68-77.

Lauer, R. H., and W. H. Handel. 1977. *Social Psychology: The Theory and Method of Symbolic Interactionism.* Boston: Houghton Mifflin.

Lehman, F. K. 1974. "Foreword." Pp. vii-xvii in *Mathematical Models of Social and Cognitive Structures,* edited by P. A. Ballonoff. Urbana: University of Illinois Press.

Lewis, J. D. 1977. "Reply to Blumer." *The Sociological Quarterly* 18:291-92.

Lewis, J. D., and R. L. Smith. 1908. *American Sociology and Pragmatism: Mead, Chicago Sociology, and Symbolic Interaction.* Chicago: University of Chicago Press.

Lindesmith, A. R., A. L. Strauss, and N. K. Denzin. 1977. *Social Psychology.* 5th ed. New York: Holt, Rinehart & Winston.

List, P. 1973. "Mead's Formulation of the Disposition Theory of Meaning." Pp. 107-33 in *The Philosophy of George Herbert Mead,* edited by W. R. Corti. Winterthur, Switzerland: Archiv für Genetische Philosophie.

McGuigan, F. J. 1967. "Feedback of Speech Muscle Activity during Silent Reading." *Science* 157:579-80.

————. 1970. "Covert Oral Behavior during the Silent Performance of Language Tasks." *Psychological Bulletin* 74:309-26.

————. 1971. "Covert Linguistic Behavior in Deaf Subjects during Thinking." *Journal of Comparative and Physiological Psychology* 75:417-20.

McGuigan, F. J., and S. C. Bailey. 1969. "Covert Response Patterns during the Processing of Language Stimuli." *Interamerican Journal of Psychology* 3:289-99.

McGuigan, F. J., B. Keller, and E. Stanton. 1964. "Covert Language Responses during Silent Reading." *Journal of Educational Psychology* 55:339-43.

McGuigan, F. J., and W. I. Rodier, III. 1968. "Effects of Auditory Stimulation on Covert Oral Behavior during Silent Reading." *Journal of Experimental Psychology* 76:649-55.

McGuigan, F. J., and R. A. Schoonover. 1973. *The Psychophysiology of Thinking.* New York: Academic Press.

McLuhan, M. 1964. *Understanding Media: The Extensions of Man.* New York: McGraw-Hill.

McPhail, C., and C. Rexroat. 1979. "The Methodological Perspectives of George H. Mead and Herbert Blumer: Divergence and Rapproachment." *American Sociological Review* 44:449-67.

Maines, D. R. 1977. "Social Organization and Social Structure in Symbolic Interactionist Thought." Pp. 235-59 in *Annual Review of Sociology.* Palo Alto, Calif.: Annual Reviews, Inc.

Max, L. W. 1937. "An Experimental Study of the Motor Theory of Consciousness. IV. Action-Current Responses in the Deaf during Awakening, Kinaesthetic Imagery and Abstract Thinking." *Journal of Comparative Psychology* 24:301-44.

Mead, G. H. 1934. *Mind, Self, and Society: From the Standpoint of a Social Behaviorist.* Edited with an introduction by C. W. Morris. Chicago: University of Chicago Press.

_____ . 1938. *The Philosophy of the Act.* Edited with an introduction by C. W. Morris. Chicago: University of Chicago Press.

_____ . 1964. *Selected Writings.* Edited with an introduction by A. J. Reck. Indiannapolis: Bobbs-Merrill.

Meltzer, B. N. 1978. "Mead's Social Psychology." Pp. 15-27 in *Symbolic Interaction: A Reader in Social Psychology,* edited by J. G. Manis and B. N. Meltzer. Boston: Allyn & Bacon.

Meltzer, B. N., and J. W. Petras. 1972. "The Chicago and Iowa Schools of Symbolic Interactionism." Pp. 43-57 in *Symbolic Interation: A Reader in Social Psychology,* edited by J. G. Manis and B. N. Meltzer. Boston: Allyn & Bacon.

Merton, R. K. 1968. *Social Theory and Social Structure.* New York: Free Press.

Morris, C. W. 1934. "Introduction." Pp. ix-xxxv in Mead 1934.

Novikova, L. A. 1961. "Electrophysiological Investigation of Speech." Pp. 210-26 in *Recent Soviet Psychology,* edited by N. O'Connor. New York: Liveright.

O'Toole, R., and R. Dubin. 1968. "Baby Feeding and Body Sway: An Experiment in George Herbert Mead's 'Taking the Role of the Other.'" *Journal of Personality and Social Psychology* 10:59-65.

O'Toole, R., R. L. Smith, and L. S. Cottrell. 1978. "Interpenetrative Interaction: Implications of a Neglected Approach." Paper read at the American Sociological Association Meetings, San Francisco.

Parsons, T. 1951. *The Social System.* New York: Free Press.

Polayni, M. 1958. *Personal Knowledge.* Chicago: University of Chicago Press.

Reynolds, V. 1976. *The Biology of Human Action.* San Francisco: Freeman.

Ropers, R. 1973. "Mead, Marx, and Social Psychology." *Catalyst,* no. 7 (Winter), pp. 42-61.

Rose, A. M. 1962. "A Systematic Summary of Symbolic Interaction Theory." Pp. 3-19 in *Human Behavior and Social Processes,* edited by A. M. Rose. Boston: Houghton Mifflin.

Rubinstein, D. 1977. "The Concept of Action in the Social Sciences," *Journal for the Theory of Social Behavior* 7:209-36.

Shibutani, T. 1961. *Society and Personality.* Englewood Cliffs, N.J.: Prentice-Hall.

Skinner, B. F. 1957. *Verbal Behavior*. New York: Appleton-Century-Crofts.

_____ . 1974. *About Behaviorism*. New York: Vintage.

Smith, R. L. 1971. "Reflexive Behavior: An Experimental Examination of George Herbert Mead's Treatment of Vocal Gestures." Master's thesis, University of South Carolina.

Strauss, A. 1964. "Introduction." Pp. vii-xxv in *George Herbert Mead: On Social Psychology*. Chicago: University of Chicago Press.

Swanson, G. 1972. "Mead and Freud: Their Relevance for Social Psychology." Pp. 23-43 in *Symbolic Interaction: A Reader in Social Psychology,* edited by J. G. Manis and B. N. Meltzer. Boston: Allyn & Bacon.

Thayer, H. S. 1968. *Meaning and Action*. Indianapolis: Bobbs-Merrill.

Varela, C. 1973. "The Crisis of Western Sociology: The Problem of Social Interaction, the Self and Unawareness for Sociological Theory." Ph.D. dissertation, New York University.

Watson, J. B. 1930. *Behaviorism*. New York: Norton.

Weigert, A. J. 1975. "Substantival Self: A Primitive Term for Sociological Psychology." *Philosophy of the Social Sciences* 5:43-62.

Wyczoikowska, A. 1913. "Theoretical and Experimental Studies in the Mechanism of Speech." *Psychological Review* 20:448-58.

Zeitlin, I. M. 1973. *Rethinking Sociology*. Englewood Cliffs, N.J.: Prentice-Hall.

CHAPTER 5

NOTES

a. Here and in a few other instances I have deleted a word or phrase in Habermas's text that refers to portions of his book not reprinted here.—ED.

b. Subsection E is not reprinted in this book.—ED.

c. Habermas tells us that, "Assertoric sentences express the speaker's belief that something is the case, intentional sentences the speaker's intention to perform an action so that something will be the case. Assertoric sentences can be true or false; because of this relation to truth, we can also say that they express the speaker's knowledge. It is only with respect to the feasibility and efficiency of intended actions that intentional sentences have a relation to truth. Teleological actions can be reconstructed in the form of intentional sentences that the agent could have uttered to himself; with these intentional sentences we give expression to the design of an action" (*The Theory of Communicative Action,* Vol. 2, p. 28).—ED.

d. Subsection E, "The Complementary Construction of the Social and Subjective Worlds," has been deleted at this juncture, as have the last two sentences of subsection D that allude to discussions that follow. The titles of subsection E and the following subsection have been drawn from the "Analytical Table of Contents" in the second volume of the *Theory of Communicative Action.*—ED.

e. The transition paragraph from the subsection that immediately precedes "Mead's Grounding of a Discourse Ethics" has been included here. In Habermas's text "Mead's Grounding of a Discourse Ethics" is in Section 3, whereas the previous excerpt is drawn from Section 1. In the intervening sixty or so pages Habermas not only addressed other aspects of Mead's work, but brought Durkheim into his analysis.—ED.

f. This is a key theme of the Section of Habermas's book from which this excerpt is drawn. The title of the Section is "The Rational Structure of the Linguistification of the Sacred."—ED.

1. Mead makes note of this on p. 2 of the methodological introduction to his lectures on social psychology, in *Mind, Self, and Society*, ed. C. Morris (Chicago, 1962): "Historically, behaviorism entered psychology through the door of animal psychology."

2. For an excellent account of his work as a whole, see H. Joas, *G. H. Mead: A Contemporary Re-Examination of His Thought* (Cambridge, Mass., 1985). See also N. Natanson, *The Social Dynamics of G. H. Mead* (Washington, D.C., 1956); A. H. Reck, "The Philosophy of G. H. Mead," *Tulane Studies in Philosophy* 12 (1963): 5-51; H. Blumer, "Sociological Implications of the Thought of G. H. Mead," *American Journal of Sociology* 71 (1966): 535-44; G. A. Cook, " The Self as Moral Agent," Ph.D. diss., Yale, 1966; K. Raiser, *Identität und Sozialität* (Munich, 1971). On Blumer's influential development of symbolic interactionism, see C. McPhail and C. Rexroat, *"Mead vs. Blumer,"* American Journal of Sociology 44 (1979): 449ff.; D. Miller, *G. H. Mead: Self, Language, and the World* (Chicago, 1980).

3. Mead, *Mind, Self, and Society*, p. 244; henceforth cited as *MSS*.

4. Ibid., p. 7.

5. Ibid.

6. Ibid., p. 6.

7. See vol. 1, chap. 3, this work *[The Theory of Communicative Action]*.

8. On the theory of singular terms, see E. Tugendhat, *Traditional and Analytical Philosophy: Lectures on the Philosophy of Language* (Cambridge, 1982).

9. *MSS*, p. 42-43. Elsewhere Mead explains gesture-mediated interaction between animals as follows: "There exists thus a field of conduct even among

animals below man, which in its nature may be classed as gesture. It consists of the beginning of those actions which call out instinctive responses from other forms. And these beginnings of acts call out responses which lead to readjustments of acts which have been commenced, and these readjustments lead to still other beginnings of response which again call out still other readjustments. Thus there is a conversation of gesture, a field of palaver within the social conduct of animals. Again the movements which constitute this field of conduct are themselves not the complete acts which they start out to become. They are the glance of the eye that is the beginning of the spring or the flight, the attitude of body with which the spring or flight commences, the growl or cry, or snarl with which the respiration adjusts itself to oncoming struggle, and they all change with the answering attitudes, glances of the eye, growls and snarls which are the beginnings of the actions which they themselves arouse." G. H. Mead, *Selected Writings*, ed. A. Reck (Chicago, 1964), p. 124.

10. *MSS*, p. 76.

11. Ibid., p. 47. L. S. Vygotsky takes a similar position in *Thought and Language* (Cambridge, Mass., 1962). Vygotsky's book first appeared in Moscow in 1934, a year after the death of its author, and at the same time as the posthumous publication of *Mind, Self, and Society*.

12. This is the point of departure for Ernst Tugendhat's treatment of Mead in *Self-Consciousness and Self-Determination* (Cambridge, Mass., 1986), pp. 219-62. [See Tugendhat in this book.]

13. *MSS*, p. 47.

14. Ibid., pp. 117-18.

15. Ibid., p. 100.

16. Mead, *Selected Writings*, p. 131.

17. Referring to the thought of Wilhelm von Humboldt, Arnold Gehlen emphasizes "the double givenness of the sound, which is both a motoric accomplishment of the language instrument and itself a sound that is returned and heard." *Der Mensch* (Bonn, 1950), p. 144; compare pp. 208-9.

18. See *MSS*, pp. 61ff., and Mead, *Selected Writings*, pp. 136-37.

19. Tugendhat, *Self-Consciousness and Self-Determination*, p. 228.

20. Ibid., pp. 229-30.

21. The only passage Tugendhat cites in support of its appears on pp. 108-9 of *MSS*.

22. Ibid., p. 108.

23. Ibid., p. 139. My emphasis.

24. Ibid., pp. 147-49.

25. D. S. Shwayder, *The Stratification of Behavior* (London, 1965), pp. 21ff.

26. Charles Morris, "Foundations of the Theory of Signs," in *International Encyclopedia of Unified Science*, vol. 1, no. 2 (Chicago, 1938); and idem, *Signs, Language and Behavior* (New York, 1946).

27. J. Habermas, *Zur Logik der Sozialwissenschaften* (Frankfurt, 1970), pp. 150ff. English trans. MIT Press, 1988.

28. L. Wittgenstein, *Philosophiche Grammatik II, Schriften* (Frankfurt, 1969), p. 272.

29. Cf. P. Winch, *The Idea of a Social Science and its Relation to Philosophy* (London: Routledge & Paul; N.Y.: Humanities Press, 1958), pp. 24ff.

30. L. Wittgenstein, *Philosophical Investigations* (New York, 1953), p. 81.

31. From this standpoint, Mead's efforts at reconstruction also serve to elucidate Wittgenstein's explication of the concept of a rule: the concept he develops holds, to start with, only for meaning conventions and not for norms of action. See 1:421-22, n. 37 [of *The Theory of Communicative Action*].

32. See E. W. Count, *Das Biogramm* (Frankfurt, 1970); E. Morin, *Das Rätsel des Humanen* (Munich, 1973).

33. *MSS*, p. 162.

34. G. H. Mead, "Fragments on Ethics," in *MSS*, pp. 379-89. See also G. Mead, "The Philosophical Basis of Ethics," in *George Herbert Mead: Selected Writings*, ed. Andrew Reck (Chicago, 1964), pp. 82-93. On this point see Gary A. Cook, "The Self as Moral Agent," Ph.D. diss., Yale, 1966, pp. 156ff.; and Hans Joas, *G. H. Mead: A Contemporary Re-examination of His Thought* (Cambridge, Mass., 1985), pp. 121ff.

35. On this point see R. Wimmer, *Universalisierung in der Ethik* (Frankfurt, 1980), which deals with the universalistic approaches of Kurt Baier, Marcus Singer, R. M. Hare, John Rawls, Paul Lorenzen, Fr. Kambartel, K.-O. Apel, and myself.

36. *MSS*, pp. 381-82.

37. Ibid., p. 379.

38. G. H. Mead, "Philanthropy from the Point of View of Ethics," in *Selected Writings*, p. 404.

39. *MSS*, p. 380.

40. Ibid.

41. Ibid., 388-89.

42. Ibid., p. 386.

43. Mead, "Philanthropy," pp. 404-5.

44. *MSS*, p. 387.

45. Ibid., p. 384.

46. Ibid., p. 385.

47. Ibid., p. 381.

48. G. H. Mead, "Scientific Method and the Moral Sciences," in *Selected Writings*, pp. 257ff.

CHAPTER 6

NOTES

a. It is impossible in a note to do justice to Tugendhat's understanding of the phrase "one's own to-be." Tugendhat dedicates three lectures to Heidegger in *Self-Consciousness and Self-Determination,* and the question of how we should understand the relation of the being of human beings to the being of that which is present-at-hand, e.g., material objects, is the focus of an entire lecture. In an earlier lecture in which he formulates the themes for the book, Tugendhat provides a preliminary statement of the meaning of the term *to-be:* "According to Heidegger, I am not related to my being in the 'I am' statement 'aesthetically,' that is, in the mode of looking or contemplating. I do not describe my being as something present-at-hand (*Vorhandenes*), but I relate myself to it in the mode of 'self concern' (*Selbstbekümmerung*) [1]; this being thereby does not have the sense of being-present-at-hand, but I relate myself to my being as something that I, as he says in *Being and Time,* have to be'.... [2] What Heidegger means by this to-be can be made evident most simply by recalling Hamlet's question: 'To be or not to be—that is the question.' It is a question that is obviously not theoretical. Someone who poses it is not asking whether something can be asserted, that is, whether it (he himself) is or is not, or more precisely, will or will not be. On the contrary, this question concerns the issue of whether the questioner says yes or no in a practical sense to the being that impends at every moment; and this means he either wants to prepare an end to this being or he is willing to continue with it. We are beings, according to Heidegger, who only are insofar as they relate themselves to this being—to the accomplishment of life that impends at any given time. This relating of oneself to this being is indeed not a representing, and it also cannot be understood as a consciousness of something; rather, this relation consists in the fact that we can say yes or no to our to-be, or, more accurately, we always have to say yes or no to it" (*Self-Consciousness and Self-Determination,* p. 27). [The following are Tugendhat's references: 1. "Anmerkungen zu Karl Jaspers 'Psychologie der Weltanschauungen'," in H. Saner, ed., *Karl Jaspers in der Diskussion,*

Munich, 1973, p. 93. 2. *Being and Time,* trans. J. Macquarrie and E. Robinson, New York, 1962, p. 67.]—ED.

b. In several places in his text Tugendhat refers to portions of his book not reprinted here. When this occurs words and phrases have been deleted, and at times added, in order to avoid confusion. Aside from these and typographical corrections, no other changes have been made in the body of the text.—ED.

c. Tugendhat's discussion of *identity* has not been reprinted here.—ED.

d. A large portion of *Self-Consciousness and Self-Determination* is concerned with the propositional character of states in which we are conscious of sensations, beliefs, intentions, and actions (pp. 118–119.) These are gathered together by Tugendhat under the rubric: *immediate* epistemic self-consciousness. "It has the form 'I know: I ϕ,' where 'ϕ' is a predicate that designates a state of consciousness" (p. 39). For instance, I know that I have a toothache (a pain). Immediate epistemic self-consciousness should be distinguished "from a wider concept of epistemic self-consciousness that includes all knowledge that is expressed in sentences of the form 'I know that I....' For naturally there are sentences of this form in which the predicate does not stand for a conscious state, that is, for a state of which the person concerned has an immediate knowledge. Such sentences may pertain to my physical properties—for example, 'I know that I was born in Berlin,' or 'I know that I am six feet tall'—as well as to my character and modes of behavior, for example, 'I know that I am a coward' " (p. 18).—ED.

e. Although Tugendhat tells us in his Preface to *Self-Consciousness and Self-Determination* that he thoroughly revised the Mead sections of his book, he also informs us that he originally gave them as lectures: hence, the reference to faces.—ED.

f. Tugendhat provides a brief definition of self-determination in the paragraph immediately following the next one.—ED

g. The appendix to Tugendhat's Mead lecture, "The Concept of Identity in Social Psychology," has not been reprinted here.—ED.

1. *Politics,* I, 2, 1253a9ff.

2. Mead's statements on this topic are definitely clearer in the third supplementary essay, pp. 354ff., which is part of an original manuscript, than they are in paragraphs 8-9 of the compilation of lectures.

3. *Selected Writings,* ed. A. J. Reck, New York, 1964, p. 244 (my emphasis).

4. Cf. my *Traditional and Analytical Philosophy: Lectures on the Philosophy of Language,* trans. P. A. Gorner, Cambridge, 1982, especially, pp. 223ff.

5. *Politics,* I, 1-2.

6. H. L. A. Hart, *The Concept of Law,* Oxford, 1961, pp. 54ff.

7. That is, the colloquial meaning of the German *Selbstbewusstsein* (Trans.).

8. *Nicomachean Ethics*, I, 6.

9. Cf. G. H. von Wright, *The Varieties of Goodness*, London, 1963, chapter 2, which deals with this sense of *good* under the title "technical goodness."

10. *Nicomachean Ethics*, I, 6.

11. Ibid., III, 6.

12. Ibid., II, 4-5.

13. There are good reasons here to suspect a mistake in the lecture notes. Mead probably simply said "adjusting oneself."

CHAPTER 7

NOTES

a. Susan Hales is the editor referred to here. She was the editor of a special issue of the *Journal for the Theory of Social Behavior,* entitled "The Rediscovery of the Self in Social Psychology: Theoretical and Methodological Implications," in which Swanson's article originally appeared.—ED.

1. Mead talks about athletic teams and Freud about families, but their formulations turn on properties of any collectivity and are therefore generalizable to collective relations of any scope or form (e.g., Swanson, forthcoming).

2. This last point is one reason for my preferring to treat each individual as having one self, not many (contra, e.g., Brim, 1960). He will, of course, see his behavior and desires differently in different social contexts—in his capacity, say, as a husband as contrasted with his position as a parent or employee or citizen.

3. A related point: Mead's analysis, and Freud's, employ as necessary independent variables some properties, distinctive to social and collective relations and they relate these to properties distinctive of people as selves. Thus, Mead's is not an explanation of cognitive complexity as such but of the form of such complexity—the evaluation of one's action from several points of view as integrated by a superordinate point of view—that he thinks characteristic of human persons and he suggests that training for such evaluations comes to the degree one participates in groups having roles that are differentiated (therefore embodying special perspectives) yet integrated under a regnant collective purpose. Similarly, Freud's is not an account of responses to a pattern of attractions and threats but of a particular pattern of self-regulation; one he sees as determined specifically by normatively prescribed relations of participants to the persons mainly responsible for, respectively, the nurture and authority afforded by a group.

Because they are at this "level of analysis," it is possible to integrate Mead's and Freud's accounts with systematic treatments of further aspects of selves and social/collective relations. By contrast, the propositions in many accounts that employ "social" terminology do not turn necessarily on properties distinctive to selves and social relations and are therefore of limited theoretical usefulness when such properties are the ones of interest.

This is so common a difficulty in analyses that a brief example is warranted. Stryker (1981: 24) offers the following hypothesis: "The greater the commitment premised on an identity, the higher that identity will be in the salience hierarchy." By commitment he means "the degree to which the individual's relationships to specified sets of other persons depends on his or her being a particular kind of person." Identities are (1981: 23) "internalized positional designations that exist insofar as the person participates in structured role relationships ..." As for "salience," identities are ... organized into a hierarchy of salience defined by the probability of various identities being invoked in a given situation or over many situations." Despite all the "social" concepts in these definitions, Stryker's hypothesis appears to be an instance of another in which social terms need not appear: "The more comprehensive the situational demands, the more likely it is that expectations based upon earlier encounters with those demands will be aroused." And some such hypothesis probably applies to the behavior of all animals; not distinctively to humans acting as selves.

4. Note that this is not Parsons' (1959: 637) distinction between self and collectivity. It is, I think, a more useful way than Mead's "I" and "Me" for dealing with the problems for which Mead (1934: 173-178, 192-222) chose those terms. For a different formulation, see Lewis, 1979. [Reprinted in this book.]

5. This finding on active trance may clarify a suggestion of Mary Douglas' (1970: 74).

REFERENCES

Atkinson, John W., and David Birch (1970). *The Dynamics of Action*. New York: Wiley.

Baldwin, James Mark, and G. S. Stout (1902). Self. Pp. 507-508 in James Mark Baldwin (ed.), *Dictionary of Philosophy and Psychology*. Vol. 2. New York: Macmillan.

Bales, Robert F. (1968). Interaction process analysis. Pp. 465-470 in David L. Sills (ed.), *International Encyclopedia of the Social Sciences*. Vol. 7. New York: Macmillan.

———— (1970). *Personality and Interpersonal Behavior*. New York: Holt, Rinehart and Winston.

Bandura, Albert (1971). *Psychological Modeling: Conflicting Theories*. Chicago: Aldine/Atherton.

_____ (1977a). Self efficacy: Toward a unifying theory of behavioral change. *Psychological Review* 84 (March): 191-95.

_____ (1977b). *Social Learning Theory.* Englewood Cliffs: Prentice-Hall.

Bandura, Albert, Dorothea Ross, and Sheila A. Ross (1963). A comparative test of the status, envy, social power, and secondary reinforcement theories of identificatory learning. *Journal of Abnormal and Social Psychology* 67 (December): 527-534.

Bellah, Robert N. (1964). Religious evolution. *American Sociological Review* 29 (June): 358-374.

Bem, Daryl J., and Andrea Allen (1972). On predicting some of the people some of the time: The search for cross-situational consistencies in behavior. *Psychological Review* 81 (November): 506-520.

Berndt, Thomas J., and Emily G. (1975). Children's use of motives and intentionality in person perception and moral judgement. *Child Development* 46 (December): 904-912.

Block, Jack, and Norma Haan (1971). *Lives through Time.* Berkeley: Bancroft.

Bourguignon, Erika (1976). *Possession.* San Francisco: Chandler and Sharp.

Brim, Orville G., Jr. (1960). Personality development as role-learning. Pp. 127-159 in Ira Iscoe and Harold Stevenson (eds.), *Personality Development in Children.* Austin: University of Texas Press.

Conte, Hope R., and Robert Plutchik (1981). A circumplex model for interpersonal personality traits. *Journal of Personality and Social Psychology* 40 (April): 701-711.

Couch, Arthur S. (1960). *Psychological Determinants of Interpersonal Behavior.* Doctoral dissertation. Department of Social Relations, Harvard University.

Danto, Arthur C. (1967). Persons. Pp. 110-114 in P. Edwards (ed.), *Encyclopedia of Philosophy.* Vol. 6. New York: Macmillan-Free Press.

Dewey, John, and Others (1903). *Studies in Logical Theory.* Chicago: University of Chicago Press.

Douglas, Mary (1970). *Natural Symbols, Explorations in Cosmology.* New York: Pantheon.

Durkheim, Emile (1912). *The Elementary Forms of the Religious Life.* Joseph W. Swain, translator. Glencoe: Free Press, 1954.

Eichorn, Dorothy H. and Others (eds.) (1981). *Present and Past in Middle Life.* New York: Academic.

Flavell, John H., and Others (1968). *The Development of Role-taking and Communication Skills in Children.* New York: Wiley.

Foa, Edna B. and Uriel, G. (1974). *Societal Structures of the Mind*. Springfield: Charles Thomas.

_____ (1980). Resource theory: Interpersonal behavior as exchange. Pp. 77 in Kenneth J. Gergen, Martin S. Greenberg and Richard H. Willis (eds.), *Social Exchange: Advances in Theory and Research*. New York: Plenum.

Freud, Sigmund (1933). *New Introductory Lectures on Psycho-Analysis*. James Strachey, translator. New York: Norton, 1965.

Gedo, John E. (1979). *Beyond Interpretation: Toward a Revised Theory of Psychoanalysis*. New York: International Universities Press.

Gedo, John E., and Arnold Goldberg (1973). *Models of the Mind*. Chicago: University of Chicago Press.

Gordon, Steven L. (1981). The sociology of sentiments and emotion. Pp. 562-592 in Morris Rosenberg and Ralph H. Turner (eds.), *Social Psychology, Sociological Perspective*. New York: Basic Books.

Greenblatt, Stephen J. (1980). *Renaissance Self-Fashioning from More to Shakespeare*. Chicago: University of Chicago Press.

Hales, Susan (1980). *A Developmental Model of Self-Esteem Based on Competence and Moral Behavior, a Longitudinal and Cross-Sectional Anaylsis*. Doctoral dissertation. Department of Psychology, University of California, Berkeley.

Heidbreder, Edna (1933). *Seven Psychologies*. New York: D. Appleton-Century.

Hilgard, Josephine R. (1970). *Personality and Hypnosis, A Study of Imaginative Involvement*. Chicago: University of Chicago Press.

Hirschman, Albert O. (1977). *The Passions and the Interests, Political Arguments for Capitalism before Its Triumph*. Princeton: Princeton University Press.

Hochschild, Arlie R. (1979). Emotion work, feeling rules, and social structure. *American Journal of Sociology* 85 (November): 551-575.

Inhelder, Barbel, and Jean Piaget (1955). *The Growth of Logical Thinking from Childhood to Adolescence*. Anne Parsons and Stanley Milgram, translators. New York: Basic Books, 1958.

James, William (1904). The Chicago School. *Psychological Bulletin* 1 (January): 1-5.

Kemper, Theodore (1978). *A Social Interactional Theory of Emotions*. New York: Wiley.

Lamb, Michael E., and Brian Sutton-Smith (eds.) (1982). *Sibling Relationships, Their Nature and Significance across the Lifespan*. Hillsdale: Erlbaum.

Langer, Ellen, J., Arthur A. Blank, and Benzion Chanowitz (1978). The mindlessness of ostensibly thoughtful action: The role of "placebic" information in interpersonal interaction. *Journal of Personality and Social Psychology* 36 (June): 635-642.

Leary, Timothy (1957). *Interpersonal Diagnosis of Personality.* New York: Ronald.

Lerner, Max (1934). Social process. Pp. 148-151 in Edwin R. A. Seligman (ed.), *International Encyclopaedia of the Social Sciences.* Vol. 14. New York: Macmillan.

Lewis, J. David (1979). A social behaviorist interpretation of the Meadian "I." *American Journal of Sociology* 85 (September): 261-287.

Liem, Joan H. (1980). Family studies of schizophrenia: An update and commentary. *Schizophrenia Bulletin* 6, No. 3: 429-455.

Longabaugh, Richard (1966). The structure of interpersonal behavior. *Sociometry* 29 (December): 441-460.

Mannheim, Karl (1929-1931). *Ideology and Utopia.* Louis Wirth and Edward Shils, translators. New York: Harcourt Brace, 1954.

Mead, George H. (1930). The philosophies of Royce, James and Dewey in their American setting. *International Journal of Ethics* 40 (January): 211-231.

————— (1934). *Mind, Self and Society.* Chicago: University of Chicago Press.

Mills, C. Wright (1964). *Sociology and Pragmatism: The Higher Learning in America.* New York: Paine-Whitman.

Mischel, Walter (1968). *Personality and Assessment.* New York: Wiley.

————— (1973). Toward a cognitive social learning reconceptualization of personality. *Psychological Review* 80 (July): 252-283.

Misiak, Henryk, and Virginia S. Sexton (1966). *History of Psychology, An Overview.* New York: Grune and Stratton.

Morse, David (1981). *Perspective on Romanticism, A Transformational Analysis.* London: Macmillan.

Newcomb, Theodore M. (1950). *Social Psychology.* New York: Dryden.

Ofshe, Richard J., and Kenneth Christman (1986). Two process theory: A model of behavior prediction. In Anthony Harris (ed.), *Rationality and Collective Behavior.* New York: Ablex.

Parsons, Talcott (1955a). Family structure and the socialization of the child. Pp. 35-131 in Talcott Parsons and Robert F. Bales (eds.), *Family, Socialization and Interaction Process.* Glencoe: Free Press.

_____ (1955b). The organization of personality as a system of action. Pp. 133-186 in Talcott Parsons and Robert F. Bales (eds.), _Family, Socialization and Interaction Process_. Glencoe: Free Press.

_____ (1959). An approach to psychological theory in terms of the theory of action. Pp. 612-711 in Sigmund Koch (ed.), _Psychology: A Study of a Science_. Vol. 3. New York: McGraw-Hill.

Parsons, Talcott, Robert F. Bales, and Edward A. Shils (1953). Phase movement in relation to motivation, symbol formation, and role structure. Pp. 163-269 in their _Working Papers in the Theory of Action_. Glencoe: Free Press.

Parsons, Talcott, and James Olds (1955). The mechanisms of personality functioning with special reference to socialization. Pp. 187-257 in Talcott Parsons and Robert F. Bales (eds.), _Family, Socialization and Interaction Process_. Glencoe: Free Press.

Parsons, Talcott, and Neil J. Smelser (1956). _Economy and Society, A Study in the Integration of Economic and Social Theory_. Glencoe: Free Press.

Peckham, Morse (1962). _Beyond the Tragic Vision: The Quest for Identity in the Nineteenth Century_. New York: Braziller.

Petras, John W. (ed.) (1968). _George Herbert Mead, Essays on His Social Philosophy_. New York: Teachers College Press.

Rapaport David (1959). A historical survey of psychoanalytic ego psychology. _Psychological Issues_ 1, No. 1: 5-17.

Rawls, John (1979). _A Theory of Justice_. Cambridge: Harvard University Press.

Reiss, David (1981). _The Family's Construction of Reality_. Cambridge: Harvard University Press.

Rosenberg, Morris (1979). _Conceiving the Self_. New York: Basic Books.

Rosenblatt, Allan D., and James T. Thickstun (1978). Modern psychoanalytic concepts in a general psychology. Part Two: Motivation. _Psychological Issues_ Nos. 42-43.

Russell, James A. (1980). A circumplex model of affect. _Journal of Personality and Social Psychology_ 39 (December): 1161-1178.

Sarbin, Theodore, R. (1950). Contributions to role-taking theory. I. Hypnotic behavior. _Psychological Review_ 57 (September): 255-270.

_____ (1952). A preface to a psychological analysis of the self. _Psychological Review_ 59 (January): 11-22.

_____ (1954). Role theory. Pp. 223-258 in Gardner Lindzey (ed.), _Handbook on Social Psychology_. Vol. 1. Cambridge: Addison-Wesley.

Sarbin, Theordore R., and Vernon L. Allen (1968). Role theory. Pp. 488-567 in Gardner Lindzey and Elliott Aronson (eds.), *Handbook of Social Psychology*. Vol. 1. Reading: Addison-Wesley.

Schacter, Stanley, and Jerome E. Singer (1962). Cognitive, social and physiological determinants of emotional state. *Psychological Review* 69 (September): 379-399.

Schaefer, Earl S., and Nancy Bayley (1963). *Maternal behavior, child behavior, and their intercorrelations from infancy through adolescence.* Monographs of the Society for Research in Child Development, 28, No. 3.

Schafer, Roy (1976). *A New Language for Pscyhoanalysis.* New Haven: Yale University Press.

———— (1978). *Language and Insight.* New Haven: Yale University Press.

———— (1981). Action, language and the psychology of the self. *The Annals of Psychoanalysis* 8: 83-92.

Schorske, Carl E. (1980). *Fin-de-Siecle Vienna: Politics and Culture.* New York: Knopf.

Schranger, J. Sidney, and Thomas J. Schoeneman (1979). Symbolic interactionist view of self-concept: Through the looking glass darkly. *Psychological Bulletin* 86 (May): 549-573.

Schutz, William C. (1960). *FIRO: A Three-Dimensional Theory of Interpersonal Behavior.* New York: Holt, Rinehart and Winston.

Scott, Marvin B., and Stanford M. Lyman (1968). Paranoia, homosexuality, and game theory. *Journal of Health and Social Behavior* 9 (September): 179-187.

Selman, Robert (1980). *The Growth of Interpersonal Understanding: Developmental and Clinical Analysis.* New York: Academic.

Selznick, Gertrude J. (1960). *Functionalism, the Freudian Theory, and Philosophy of Value.* Doctoral dissertation, Department of Philosophy. University of California, Los Angeles.

Shibutani, Tamotsu (1968). George Herbert Mead. Pp. 83-87 in David L. Sills (ed.), *International Encyclopedia of the Social Sciences.* Vol. 10. New York: Macmillan and Free Press.

Stryker, Sheldon (1980). *Symbolic Interactionism: A Social Structural Version.* Menlo Park: Benjamin/Cummings.

———— (1981). Symbolic interactionism: themes and variations. Pp. 3-29 in Morris Rosenberg and Ralph H. Turner (eds.), *Social Psychology, Sociological Perspectives.* New York: Basic Books.

Swanson, Don R. (1977). A critique of psychic energy as an explanatory concept. *Journal of the American Psychoanalytic Association 25, No. 3: 603-633.*

Swanson, Guy E. (1960). *The Birth of the Gods, Origins of Primitive Beliefs.* Ann Arbor: Unviersity of Michigan Press.

_____ (1967). *Religion and Regime, A Sociological Account of the Reformation.* Ann Arbor: University of Michigan Press.

_____ (1968). To live in concord with a society: Two empirical studies of primary relations. Pp. 87-150 in Albert J. Reiss (ed.), *Cooley and Sociological Analysis.* Ann Arbor: University of Michigan Press.

_____ (1969). Rules of descent: Studies in the sociology of parentage. *Anthropological Papers,* Museum of Anthropology, University of Michigan, No. 39.

_____ (1970). Toward corporate action: A reconstruction of elementary collective processes. Pp. 124-144 in Tamotsu Shibutani (ed.), *Human Nature and Collective Behavior.* Englewood Cliffs: Prentice-Hall.

_____ (1971a). An organizational analysis of collectivities. *American Sociological Review* 36 (August): 607-624.

_____ (1971b). Interpreting the Reformation. *Journal of Interdisciplinary History* 1 (Spring): 419-446.

_____ (1974a). Family structure and the reflective intelligence of children. *Sociometry* 37 (December): 459-490.

_____ (1974b). The primary process of groups, its systematics and representation. *Journal for the Theory of Social Behaviour* 4 (April): 53-70.

_____ (1976). Orpheus and Star Husband: Meaning and structure of myths. *Ethnology* 15 (April): 115-133.

_____ (1978a). Trance and possession: Studies of charismatic influence. *Review of Religious Research* 19 (Spring): 253-275.

_____ (1978b). Travels through inner space. *American Journal of Sociology* 83 (January): 890-919.

_____ (1980). A basis of authority and identity in post-industrial society. Pp. 190-217 in Roland Robertson and Burkart Holzner (eds.), *Identity and Authority, Explorations in the Theory of Society.* New York: St. Martin's.

_____ (1988). *Ego Defenses and the Legitimation of Behavior.* New York: Cambridge University Press.

_____ Forthcoming. Tricksters in myths and families: Studies on the meaning and sources of "pregenital" relations. In Leland Donald and Joseph G. Jorgensen (eds.), *Kinship and Personality.* New Haven: HRAF Press.

Swanston, Hamish F. G. (1982). Luther and the structure of Catholicism. Pp. 51-63 in J. Davis (ed.), *Religious Organization and Religious Experience.* New York: Academic Press.

Turner, Ralph H. (1978). The role and the person. *American Journal of Sociology* 84 (July): 1-23.

Weiner, Bernard (1980). *Human Maturation.* New York: Holt, Rinehart and Winston.

White, Morton G. (1943). *The Origin of Dewey's Instrumentalism.* New York: Columbia University Press.

Whiting, John W. M. (1960). Resource mediation and learning by identification. Pp. 112-123 in Ira Iscoe and Harold Stevenson (eds.), *Personality Development in Children.* Austin: University of Texas Press.

Wiggins, Jerry S. (1979). A psychological taxonomy and trait-descriptive terms: The interpersonal domain. *Journal of Personality and Social Psychology* 37 (March): 395-412.

Wrong, Dennis (1961). The oversocialized conception of man. *American Sociological Review* 26 (April): 183-193.

Wylie, Ruth C. (1974). *The Self-Concept.* 2 Vols. Lincoln: University of Nebraska Press.

CHAPTER 8

NOTES

a. Although a number of corrections and minor changes have been made in this article, the last few sentences stand as they were originally published. In light of the alternative readings of Mead that have graced the pages of this book, I should note that this article emphasizes those elements in Mead that most naturally suit Hegel's vantage point; viz., the self as a cognitive phenomenon and the language of reflection.—ED.

b. Much rides here on the meaning of the "as if," in the phrase "as if they were the other," and it is not clear that Mead adequately deals with this issue. See, for example, the selection by Tugendhat in this volume.—ED.

c. See Swanson pp. 281–82 and note #3. —ED.

1. Jean Hyppolite, *Genesis and Structure of Hegel's Phenomenology of Spirit,* trans. S. Cherniak and J. Heckman (Evanston: Northwestern University Press, 1974), p. 172.

2. Its plausibility rests in part on the fact that Hegel sees the master and slave at a pre-rational stage of development. "Slavery occurs in man's transition

from the state of nature to genuinely ethical conditions; it occurs in a world where a wrong is still right. At that stage wrong has validity and so is necessarily in place." *Philosophy of Right*, trans. T. M. Knox (Oxford: Oxford University Press, 1967), p. 239, paragraph 57, addition to remark. Also, see note 44 below.

3. *Genesis and Structure of Hegel's Phenomenology*, p. 166.

4. G. W. F. Hegel, *Phenomenology of Spirit*, trans., A. V. Miller (Oxford: Oxford University Press, 1977), p. 110.

5. *Genesis and Structure of Hegel's Phenomenology*, pp. 160-63.

6. *Phenomenology of Spirit*, p. 110; original emphasis.

7. Ibid., p. 113, original emphasis, translator's brackets.

8. Ibid., p. 113.

9. Ibid., p. 114.

10. Alexandre Kojève translates and interprets part of the previous quoted passage as follows (Kojève's remarks are in brackets): "His esential reality [which is his recognized, human reality and dignity] manifests itself to him as an other-entity [or another man, who does not recognize him and is therefore independent of him.] He is outside of himself [insofar as the other has not 'given him back' to himself by recognizing him, by revealing that he has recognized him, and by showing him that he (the other) depends on him and is not absolutely other than he]." *Introduction to the Reading of Hegel*, Assembled by Raymond Queneau, ed. Allan Bloom, trans. J. Nichols, Jr. (New York: Basic Books, 1969), p. 13.

11. *Phenomenology of Spirit*, p. 114; original emphasis.

12. Ibid., p. 115.

13. *Introduction to the Reading of Hegel*, p. 8.

14. Ibid., p. 8.

15. *Genesis and Structure of Hegel's Phenomenology*, pp. 170-71.

16. Ibid., p. 173.

17. Ibid., p. 175.

18. Ibid., p. 169; original emphasis.

19. George Herbert Mead, *Mind, Self, and Society*, ed. Charles W. Morris (Chicago: University of Chicago Press, 1934), p. 173. This work will be referred to as *MSS*.

20. Mead is well aware of the possibility that a hand sign language may be substituted for the spoken word.

21. *MSS*, p. 69.

22. *MSS*, p. 134.

23. *MSS*, p. 154.

24. *MSS*, p. 158.

25. With the exception of some comments in section 26 of *MSS*, Mead does not employ the term *recognition* in this fashion, although there is a connection to his use of the term in discussing universals; see his discussion of recognition and universals, *MSS*, pp. 82-85. In any case, my use of the term in this fashion does not violate the essence of Mead's approach. See Tugendhat in this book, p. 191.

26. For discussion of this issue and a more detailed summary and criticism of Mead's position, see my *The Mediating Self: Mead, Sartre, and Self-Determination* (New Haven: Yale University Press, 1986).

27. According to Mead, "An impulse is a congenital tendency to react in a specific manner to a certain sort of stimulus, under certain organic conditions. Hunger and anger are illustrations of such impulses. They are best termed 'impulses,' and not 'instincts,' because they are subject to extensive modifications in the life-history of individuals" (*MSS*, p. 337).

28. *MSS*, p. 375.

29. *MSS*, pp. 375-76.

30. *Genesis and Structure of Hegel's Phenomenology of Spirit*, p. 158.

31. *Phenomenology of Spirit*, p. 110; original emphasis.

32. Sigmund Freud, *Civilization and its Discontents*, trans. and ed. James Strachey (New York: W. W. Norton, 1962), p. 15.

33. Ibid., p. 76.

34. Sigmund Freud, *Group Psychology and the Analysis of the Ego*, trans. J. Strachey (New York: W. W. Norton, 1959), pp. 41-42.

35. Freud follows this sentence with what is perhaps a warning to unrepentant Hegelians (or Freudians for that matter): "This must have something to do with the characteristic tendency of paranoiacs to form speculative systems." "On Narcissism: An Introduction," in *Collected Papers, Volume 4*, trans. Joan Riviere (New York: Basic Books, 1959), pp. 53-54. In a footnote on p. 55, Freud hedges on whether conscience should be equated with self-consciousness. "I cannot here determine whether the differentiation of the censorial function from the rest of the ego is capable of forming the basis of the philosophic distinction between consciousness and self-consciousness." I would argue that based on a later comment, Freud did continue to equate the two, or at least continued to think there were good grounds for comparison. In *Group Psychology and the Analysis of the Ego*, a work written after his paper "On

Narcissism," he says "On previous occasions—In my paper on narcissism (1914c) and in 'Mourning and Melancholia,' (1917e) [S.E., **14,** 95, and 249]—we have been driven to the hypothesis that some such agency develops in our ego which may cut itself off from the rest of the ego and come into conflict with it. We have called it the 'ego ideal,' and by way of functions we have ascribed to it self-observation, the moral conscience, the censorship of dreams, and the chief influence in repression" (pp. 41-42). The key term here is *self-observation.* If we can assume a connection between self-observation and conscience, and combine this with the fact that conscience can be viewed as either conscious or unconscious, then self-observation would appear to be capable of including a conscious as well as an unconscious dimension from Freud's perspective. Given this, and Freud's other comments, ascribing the source of self-consciousness to the ego ideal (superego) seems reasonable.

36. For definition of *impulse* see note #27.

37. "On Narcissism," p. 51.

38. *Phenomenology of Spirit,* p. 114.

39. The generalized other can be conceived of in terms of the social group that is called a nation, but this is not the only group that can have a generalized other. "Some of them are concrete social classes or subgroups, such as political parties, clubs, corporations, which are all actually functional social units, in terms of which their individual members are directly related to one another. The others are abstract social classes or subgroups, such as the class of debtors and the class of creditors, in terms of which their individual members are related to one another only more or less indirectly" (*MSS,* p. 157). See the Introduction in this anthology.

40. George Herbert Mead, *Philosophy of the Present,* ed. Arthur E. Murphy (Chicago: Open Court, 1932; rpt. Chicago, University of Chicago Press, Phoenix Edition, 1980), p. 85.

41. *Phenomenology of Spirit,* p. 113.

42. "But if the human sense of guilt goes back to the killing of the primal father, that was after all a case of 'remorse'.... [W]here...did the remorse come from?...This remorse was the result of the primodrial ambivalence of feeling towards the father. His sons hated him, but they loved him, too. After their hatred had been satisfied by their act of aggression, their love came to the fore in their remorse for the deed. It set up the super-ego by identification with the father."

43. See, *The Mediating Self,* Chapter Five, for a discussion of the slave's development.

44. "To prevent any possible misunderstandings...the fight for recognition pushed to the extreme here indicated can only occur in the natural state, where men exist only as single, separate individuals; but it is absent in civil society and the State because here the recognition for which the combatants

fought already exists." G. W. F. Hegel, *Philosophy of Mind, Being Part Three of the Encyclopaedia of the Philosophical Sciences*, trans., William Wallace and A. V. Miller (Oxford: Oxford University Press, 1971), p. 172, paragraph 432, Zusatz. In the *Philosophy of Right* Hegel states, "This false, comparatively primitive, phenomenon of slavery is one which befalls mind when mind is only at the level of consciousness. The dialectic of the concept and of the purely immediate consciousness of freedom brings about at that point the fight for recognition and the relationship of master and slave" (p. 48, paragraph 57, Zusatz).

45. Sigmund Freud, *Beyond the Pleasure Principle*, trans. J. Strachey (New York: W. W. Norton, 1961), p. 23; original emphasis.

46. *Phenomenology of Spirit*, p. 117.

A Bibliography of Recent Secondary Literature on G. H. Mead

With the exception of a few well-established books, this bibliography of secondary literature is composed of material published from 1978 to early 1989 (with some forthcoming titles also included). A number of good bibliographies are widely available. Hans Joas's, *G. H. Mead. A Contemporary Re-examination of His Thought*, contains an extensive listing of primary and secondary sources, as does David L. Miller's, *George Herbert Mead: Self, Language, and the World*. The volume edited by Walter R. Corti, *The Philosophy of George Herbert Mead*, contains a bibliography of Mead's writings compiled by John Albin Broyer; whereas the most extensive list of secondary materials, "George Herbert Mead: A Bibliography of the Secondary Literature with Relevant Symbolic Interactionist References," was developed by Richard Lowy and published in 1986 in *Studies in Symbolic Interaction*. Also helpful are Lester R. Kurtz's more general, *Evaluating Chicago Sociology*—which contains short descriptions of articles and books on Mead—and the bibliography in Maurice Natanson's *The Social Dynamics of George H. Mead*. All of these are listed in this bibliography.

Aboulafia, Mitchell. *The Mediating Self: Mead, Sartre, and Self-Determination*. New Haven, Conn.: Yale University Press, 1986.

_____. "Mead, Sarte: Self, Object, and Reflection." *Philosophy and Social Criticism* 11 (Winter 1986): 63-86.

_____. "Mead and the Social Self." In *Frontiers in American Philosophy*, edited by Robert Burch. College Station:Texas A & M University Press, forthcoming. [The Introduction to this book expands on several of the themes found in this paper.]

Baldwin, John D. "George Herbert Mead and Modern Behaviorism." *Pacific Sociological Review* 24 (October 1981): 411-440.

_____. "Comment on Denzin's 'Note on Emotionality, Self, and Interaction'." *American Journal of Sociology* 90 (September 1984): 418-422.

_____. "Social Behaviorism on Emotions: Mead and Modern Behaviorism Compared." *Symbolic Interaction* 8 (Fall 1985): 263-289.

_____. *George Herbert Mead: A Unifying Theory for Sociology*. Newbury Park, Calif.: Sage Publications, 1986.

_____. "The Matter of Habit and G. H. Mead: Comment on Camic." *American Journal of Sociology* 93 (January 1988): 952-957.

————. "Mead's Solution to the Problem of Agency." *Sociological Inquiry* 58 (Spring 1988): 139-162.

————. "Mead and Skinner: Agency and Determinism." *Behaviorism* 16 (Fall 1988): 109-127.

Batiuk, Mary Ellen, and Howard L. Sacks. "George Herbert Mead and Karl Marx: Exploring Consciousness and Community." *Symbolic Interaction* 4 (Fall 1981): 207-223.

Bergmann, Werner. "Zeit, Handlung und Sozialität bei G. H. Mead." *Zeitschrift für Soziologie* 10 (October 1981): 351-363.

Bergmann, Werner, and Gisbert Hoffmann. "Mead und die Tradition der Phänomenologie." In *Das Problem der Intersubjektivität. Neuere Beiträge zum Werk George Herbert Meads*, edited by Hans Joas, pp. 93-130. Frankfurt am Main: Suhrkamp, 1985.

Bhattacharya, Nikhil. "Pyschology and Rationality: The Structure of Mead's Problem." *Philosophical Forum* 10 (Fall 1978): 112-138.

Blumer, Herbert. "George Herbert Mead." In *The Future of the Sociological Classics*, edited by Buford Rhea, pp. 136-169. London: George Allen & Unwin, 1981.

Bolton, Charles D. "Some Consequences of the Meadian Self." *Symbolic Interaction* 4 (Fall 1981): 245-259.

Bonk, Ludwig. "Das 'Uber-Ich' bei Sigmund Freud und das 'Me' bei George Herbert Mead: Ein Vergleich der wissenschaftlichen Zugänge und der inhaltlichen Quellen." *Soziologenkorrespondenz* 5 (July 1978): 29-66.

Bouton, Clark. "Self and Society: A Critique of Symbolic Interaction." *Papers in the Social Sciences* 4 (1984): 107-117.

Boyle, Richard P. "The Dark Side of Mead: Neuropsychological Foundations for Immediate Experience and Mystical Consciousness." *Studies in Symbolic Interaction* 6 (1985): 59-78.

Broyer, John Albin. "George Herbert Mead: Contributions toward a Theory of Creativity and Social Life." *Dialectics and Humanism* 5 (Fall 1978): 27-32.

————. "George Herbert Mead: Contributions toward a Theory of Universal Humanism." *Religious Humanism* 15 (Summer 1981): 126-132.

Burger, John S., and Mary Jo Deegan. "George Herbert Mead on Internationalism, Democracy, and War." *Wisconsin Sociologist* 18 (Spring-Summer 1981): 72-83.

Callero, Peter L., Judith A. Howard, and Jane A. Piliavin. "Helping Behavior as Role Behavior: Disclosing Social Structure and History in the Analysis of

Prosocial Action." *Social Psychology Quarterly* 50 (September 1987): 247-256.

Campbell, James. "George Herbert Mead on Intelligent Social Reconstruction." *Symbolic Interaction* 4 (Fall 1981): 191-205.

_____. "George Herbert Mead and the Pragmatic Self." In *American Philosophy*, edited by Marcus G. Singer, pp. 91-114. Cambridge: Cambridge University Press, 1985.

_____. "Optimism, Meliorism, Faith." *History of Philosophy Quarterly* 4 (January 1987): 93-113.

_____. "George Herbert Mead on Social Fusion and the Social Critic." In *Frontiers in American Philosophy*, edited by Robert Burch. College Station: Texas A & M University Press, forthcoming.

Carabaña, Julio, and Emilio Lamo de Espinosa. "La teoria social del interaccionismo simbolico: analisis y valoracion critica." *Revista Española de Investigaciones Sociologicas* 1 (January 1978): 159-203.

Civelli, Ester Monti. "G. H. Mead ed il concetto di comunicazione." *Sociologia* 12 (January-April 1978): 3-12.

Clagett, Arthur F. "Theories of Self: William James, George Herbert Mead and Manford Kuhn." *Quarterly Journal of Ideology* 7 (1983): 9-19.

Collins, Randall. "Toward a Neo-Meadian Sociology of Mind." *Symbolic Interaction* 12 (Spring 1989): 1-32. [This article is followed by comments from: Eugene Rochberg-Halton, Dmitri N. Shalin, Clark McPhail, John D. Baldwin, Carl J. Couch, Hans Joas, P. K. Manning, Arthur W. Frank, Norbert Wiley, George Ritzer, Mitchell Aboulafia, Deirdre Boden, Gary Alan Fine, David D. Franks, Anne Warfield Rawls, and a response by Randall Collins.]

Cook, Gary Allan. "Whitehead's Influence on the Thought of G. H. Mead." *Transactions of the Charles S. Peirce Society* 15 (Spring 1979): 107-131.

_____. "Moralität und Sozialität bei Mead." In *Das Problem der Intersubjektivität. Neuere Beiträge zum Werk George Herbert Meads*, edited by Hans Joas, pp. 131-155. Frankfurt am Main: Suhrkamp, 1985.

Corti, Robert Walker (ed.). *The Philosophy of George Herbert Mead*. Winterthus, Switzerland: Amriswiler Bücherei, 1973.

Cottrell, Leonard S., Jr. "George Herbert Mead and Harry Stack Sullivan: An Unfinished Synthesis." *Psychiatry* 41 (May 1978): 151-62.

_____. "George Herbert Mead: The Legacy of Social Behaviorism." In *Sociological Traditions from Generation to Generation: Glimpses of the American Experience*, edited by Robert K. Merton and Matilda White Riley, pp. 45-65. Norwood, N.J.: Ablex, 1980.

Das, Robin, and E. Doyle McCarthy. "The Cognitive and Emotional Significance of Play in Child Development: G. H. Mead and D. W. Winnicott." In *Sociological Studies of Child Development: A Research Annual*, vol. 1, edited by P. A. Adler and P. Adler, pp. 35-53. Greenwich, Conn.: JAI Press, 1986.

Deegan, Mary Jo, and John S. Burger. "George Herbert Mead and Social Reform: His Work and Writings." *Journal of the History of the Behavioral Sciences* 14 (1978): 362-72.

Dennis, Lawrence J., and George W. Stickel. "Mead and Dewey: Thematic Connections on Educational Topics." *Educational Theory* 31 (Summer-Fall 1981): 319-331.

Denzin, Norman K. "Reply to Baldwin." *American Journal of Sociology* 90 (September 1984): 422-427.

_____. "Act, Language, and Self in Symbolic Interactionist Thought." *Studies in Symbolic Interaction* 9 (1988): 51-80.

Diner, Steven J. "George Herbert Mead's Ideas on Women and Careers: A Letter to His Daughter-in-Law, 1920." *Signs: Journal of Women in Culture and Society* 4 (Winter 1978): 407-409.

Durbin, Paul T. "Toward a Social Philosophy of Technology." In *Research in Philosophy and Technology: An Annual Compilation of Research*, vol. 1, edited by Paul T. Durbin, pp. 67-97. Greenwich, Conn.: JAI Press, 1978.

Elliot, Rodney D., and Bernard N. Meltzer. "Symbolic Interactionism and Psychoanalysis: Some Convergences, Divergences, and Complementarities." *Symbolic Interaction* 4 (Fall 1981): 225-244.

Falding, Harold. "G. H. Mead's Orthodoxy." *Social Forces 60* (March 1982): 723-737.

Farberman, Harvey A. "The Foundations of Symbolic Interaction: James, Cooley, and Mead." In *Foundations of Interpretive Sociology: Original Essay in Symbolic Interaction, Studies in Symbolic Interaction*, Supplement 1, edited by Harvey A. Farberman and R. S. Perinbanayagam, pp. 13-27. Greenwich, Conn.: JAI Press, 1985.

Farberman, Harvey A., and R. S. Perinbanayagam (eds.). *Foundations of Interpretive Sociology: Original Essays in Symbolic Interaction, Studies in Symbolic Interaction*, Supplement 1. Greenwich, Conn.: JAI Press, 1985.

Ferguson, Kathy E. *Self, Society, and Womankind: The Dialectic of Liberation.* Westport, Conn.: Greenwood Press, 1980.

Fine, Gary Alan. "The Diffusion Structure of Common Knowledge: Comments on Haferkamp's 'Mead und das Problem des gemeinsamen Wissens'." *Zeitschrift für Soziologie* 15 (August 1986): 302-303.

Fine, Gary Alan, and Sherryl Kleinman. "Interpreting the Sociological Classics: Can There Be a 'True' Meaning of Mead?" *Symbolic Interaction* 9 (Spring 1986): 129-146.

Fisher, Berenice M., and Anselm L. Strauss. "George Herbert Mead and the Chicago Tradition of Sociology." Part One in *Symbolic Interaction* 2 (Spring 1979): 9-26. Part Two in *Symbolic Interaction* 2 (Fall 1979): 9-20.

Franks, David. "The Self in Evolutionary Perspective." In *Foundations of Interpretive Sociology: Original Essays in Symbolic Interaction, Studies in Symbolic Interaction*, Supplement 1, edited by Harvey A. Farberman and R. S. Perinbanayagam, pp. 29-61. Greenwich, Conn.: JAI Press, 1985.

Franks, David D., and Francis F. Seeburger. "The Person behind the Word: Mead's Theory of Universals and a Shift of Focus in Symbolic Interactionism." *Symbolic Interaction* 3 (Spring 1980): 41-58.

Franzosa, Susan Douglas. "The Texture of Educational Inquiry: An Exploration of George Herbert Mead's Concept of the Scientific." *Journal of Education* 166 (Fall 1984): 254-272.

Frings, Manfred S. "Social Temporality in George Herbert Mead and Scheler." *Philosophy Today* 27 (Winter 1983): 281-289.

Gallant, Mary J., and Sherryl Kleinman. "Symbolic Interactionism vs. Ethnomethodology." *Symbolic Interaction* 6 (Spring 1983): 1-18.

Glock, Hans-Johann. "Vygotsky and Mead on the Self, Meaning and Internalisation." *Studies in Soviet Thought* 31 (1986): 131-148.

Goff, Tom W. *Marx and Mead: Contributions to a Sociology of Knowledge.* London and Boston: Routledge & Kegan Paul, 1980.

Grathoff, Richard. "Zur gegenwärtigen Rezeption von Georg Herbert Mead." *Philosophische Rundschau. Eine Zeitschrift für Philosophische Kritik. Sonderdruck* (1987): 131-145.

Haas, David F., and William W. Falk. "Theory and Method in Status Attainment Research." *Symbolic Interaction* 4 (Spring 1981): 59-73.

Habermas, Jürgen. "Individuierung durch Vergesellschaftung. Zu G. H. Meads Theorie der Subjektivität." In *Nachmetaphysisches Denken*, pp. 187-241. Frankfurt am Main: Suhrkamp, 1988. [MIT Press plans to publish an English translation of Habermas's book.]

Hanson, Karen. *The Self-Imagined: Philosophical Reflections on the Social Character of the Psyche.* New York and London: Routledge & Kegan Paul, 1986.

Hardin, Joseph B., Martha Bauman Power, and Noreen M. Sugrue. "The Progressive Concretization of Phenomenological Sociology." *Studies in Symbolic Interaction* 7, Part A (1986): 49-74.

Hoover, Michael C. "Adorno and Mead: Toward an Interactionist Critique of Negative Dialectics." *Sociological Focus* 2 (April 1986): 189-205.

Hurvitz, Nathan. "The 'Significant Other' in Marital and Family Therapy." *Journal of Sociology and Social Welfare* 6 (January 1979): 122-143.

Isobe, Takuzo. "Two Models of Moral Socialization—S. Freud and G. H. Mead." *Shakaigaku Hyoron* 30, No. 1 (1979): 80-87.

Joas, Hans. "Intersubjektivität bei Mead und Gehlen." *Archiv für Rechts- und Sozialphilosophie* 65 (1979): 105-121.

_____. "George Herbert Mead and the 'Division of Labor': Macro-sociological Implications of Mead's Social Psychology." *Symbolic Interaction* 4 (Fall 1981): 177-90.

_____. *G. H. Mead. A Contemporary Re-examination of His Thought.* Translated by Raymond Meyer. Cambridge, Mass.: MIT Press, 1985.

_____ (ed.). *Das Problem der Intersubjektivität. Neuere Beiträge zum Werk George Herbert Meads.* Frankfurt am Main: Suhrkamp, 1985. [This anthology includes essays by Harald Wenzel, Karl-Siegbert Rehberg, Werner Bergmann/and Gisbert Hoffmann, Gary Allan Cook, Lothar Krappmann, and Friedrich H. Tenbruck. The titles appear in separate listings here.]

Johnson, G. David, and Peggy A. Shifflet. "George Herbert Who? A Critique of the Objectivist Reading of Mead." *Symbolic Interaction* 4 (Fall 1981): 143-55.

Kammhuber, Siegfried. "Der soziale Akt und das 'self' in der Sozialpsychologie von George Herbert Mead." *Soziologenkorrespondenz* 5 (July 1978): 1-28.

Karier, Clarence J. "In Search of Self in a Moral Universe: Notes on George Herbert Mead's Functionalist Theory of Morality." *Journal of the History of Ideas* 45 (January-March 1984): 153-161.

Karim, Manjur E. "George Herbert Mead and Pragmatic Socialism." *Transformations* 3 (1988): 3-19.

Katovich, Michael A. "A Radical Critique of Behaviorism: Mead versus Skinner." *Studies in Symbolic Interaction* 8 (1987): 69-90.

Kohout, Frank J. "George Herbert Mead and Experimental Knowledge." *Studies in Symbolic Interaction* Supplement 2, Part A (1986): 7-24.

Krappmann, Lother. "Mead und die Sozialisationsforschung." In *Das Problem der Intersubjektivität. Neuere Beiträge zum Werk George Herbert Meads,* edited by Hans Joas, pp. 156-178. Frankfurt am Main: Surhkamp, 1985.

Krzeminski, Ireneusz. "Interactionist Interpretations of the Theory of G. H. Mead." *Polish Sociological Bulletin* 2 (46), (1979): 67-82.

Kurtz, Lester R. *Evaluating Chicago Sociology: A Guide to the Literature, with an Annotated Bibliography.* Chicago and London: University of Chicago Press, 1984.

Lee, Donald S. "The Pragmatic Origins of Concepts and Categories: Mead and Piaget." *Southern Journal of Philosophy* 21 (Summer 1983): 211-228.

Lewis, J. David. "G. H. Mead's Contact Theory of Reality: The Manipulatory Phase of the Act in the Constitution of Mundane, Scientific, Aesthetic, and Evaluative Objects." *Symbolic Interaction* 4 (Fall 1981): 129-141.

Lewis, J. David, and Richard L. Smith. *American Sociology and Pragmatism: Mead, Chicago Sociology, and Symbolic Interaction.* Chicago: University of Chicago Press, 1980.

_____. "Putting the Symbol in Symbolic Interaction: A Rejoinder." *Symbolic Interaction* 6 (Spring 1983): 165-174. [This piece is a response to criticisms of Lewis and Smith's, *American Sociology and Pragmatism*, made by Herbert Blumer, Eugene Rochberg-Halton, and James Campbell in the same issue of *Symbolic Interaction*, pp. 127-164.]

Lowy, Richard. "George Herbert Mead: A Bibliography of the Secondary Literature with Relevant Symbolic Interactionist References." *Studies in Symbolic Interaction* 7, Part B (1986): 459-521.

McCarthy, E. Doyle. "Toward a Sociology of the Physical World: George Herbert Mead on Physical Objects." *Studies in Symbolic Interaction* 5 (1984): 105-121.

_____. "In the Beginning Was the Act..." Review of R. S. Perinbanayagam's *Signifying Acts: Structure and Meaning in Everyday Life. Contemporary Sociology* 14, No. 6 (1985): 690-693.

McPhail, Clark, and Cynthia Rexroat. "Mead vs. Blumer: The Divergent Methodological Perspectives of Social Behaviorism and Symbolic Interactionism." *American Sociological Review* 44 (June 1979): 449-467.

Maines, David R., Noreen M. Sugrue, and Michael A. Katovich. "The Sociological Import of G. H. Mead's Theory of the Past." *American Sociological Review* 48 (April 1983): 161-173.

Malhotra, Valerie Ann. "Research as Critical Reflection: A Study of Self, Time, and Communicative Competency." *Humanity and Society* 8 (November 1984): 468-477.

_____. "A Comparison of Mead's 'Self' and Heidegger's 'Dasein': Toward a Regrounding of Social Psychology. *Human Studies* 10 (October 1987): 357-382.

_____. "From 'Self' to 'Dasein': A Heideggerian Critique of Mead's Social Psychology." *Studies in Symbolic Interaction* 8 (1987): 23-42.

Miller, David L. *George Herbert Mead: Self, Language, and the World.* Austin: University of Texas Press, 1973. Reprint, Chicago: University of Chicago Press, Phoenix Edition, 1980.

_____. "The Meaning of Role-Taking." *Symbolic Interaction* 4 (Fall 1981): 167-175.

_____. "The Meaning of Freedom from the Perspective of G. H. Mead's Theory of the Self." *Southern Journal of Philosophy* 20 (1982): 453-463.

Moehle, Natalia R. *The Dimensions of Evil and of Transcendence: A Sociological Perspective.* Washington, D. C.: University Press of America, 1978.

Moran, Jon S. "Mead, Gadamer, and Hermeneutics." In *Frontiers in American Philosophy*, edited by Robert Burch. College Station: Texas A & M University Press, forthcoming.

Müller, Horst. "Marx, Mead und das Konzept widersprüchlicher Praxis." *Zeitschrift für Soziologie* 12 (April 1983): 119-138.

Natanson, Maurice. *The Social Dynamics of George H. Mead.* The Hague: Martinus Nijhoff, 1973 (Originally published: Washington, D.C.: Public Affairs Press, 1956).

Natsoulas, Thomas. "George Herbert Mead's Conception of Consciousness." *Journal for the Theory of Social Behavior* 15 (March 1985): 60-75.

Noble, William G. "Gibsonian Theory and the Pragmatist Perspective." *Journal for the Theory of Social Behavior* 11 (March 1981): 65-85.

O'Meara, William M. "The Social Nature of Self and Morality for Husserl, Schutz, Marx, and Mead." *Philosophy Research Archives* 12 (1986-87): 329-355.

_____. "Marx and Mead on the Social Nature of Rationality and Freedom." In *Frontiers in American Philosophy*, edited by Robert Burch. College Station: Texas A & M University Press, forthcoming.

Perinbanayagam, R. S. *Signifying Acts: Structure and Meaning in Everyday Life.* Carbondale and Edwardsville: Southern Illinois University Press, 1985.

Powell, R. P., and A. W. Still. "Behaviorism and the Psychology of Language: An Historical Reassessment." *Behaviorism* 7 (Spring 1979): 71-89.

Reck, Andrew J. "Society and Self in the Philosophy of George Herbert Mead." *Rice Unviersity Studies* 66 (Fall 1980): 55-74.

Rehberg, Karl-Siegbert. "Die Theorie der Intersubjektivität als eine Lehre vom Menschen. George Herbert Mead und die deutsche Tradition der 'Philosophischen Anthropologie'." In *Das Problem der Intersubjektivität. Neuere Beiträge zum Werk George Herbert Meads*, edited by Hans Joas, pp. 60-92. Frankfurt am Main: Suhrkamp, 1985.

Renger, Paul, III. "The Historical Significance of George Herbert Mead's Philosophy of Education." In *Critical Issues in Philosophy of Education*, edited by Creighton Peden and Donald Chipman, pp. 42-53. Washington, D.C.: University Press of America, 1979.

_____. "George Herbert Mead's Contribution to the Philosophy of American Education." *Educational Theory* 30 (Spring 1980): 115-133.

Ritsert, Jürgen. "Die gesellschaftliche Basis des Selbst: Entwurf einer Argumentationslinie im Anschluss an Mead." *Soziale Welt* 31 (1980): 288-310.

_____. "Anerkennung, Selbst und Gesellschaft: Zur gesellschaftlichen Konstitution von Subjektivität in Hegels 'Jenaer Realphilosophie'," *Soziale Welt* 32 (1981): 275-311.

Rosenberg, Rosalind. *Beyond Separate Spheres: Intellectual Roots of Modern Feminism.* New Haven, Conn.: Yale University Press, 1982.

Rosenthal, Sandra B., and Patrick I. Bourgeois. "Meaning and Human Behavior: Mead and Merleau-Ponty." *Southern Journal of Philosophy* 26 (Fall 1988): 339-349.

Ruszkowski, Piotr. "Critical Evaluation of Mead's Conception of the Self: An Attempt at Reinterpretation." *Polish Sociological Bulletin* 3 (51), (1980): 51-59.

Schwalbe, Michael L. "Language and the Self: An Expanded View from a Symbolic Interactionist Perspective." *Symbolic Interaction* 6 (Fall 1983): 291-306.

_____. "Mead among the Cognitivists: Roles as Performance Imagery." *Journal for the Theory of Social Behavior* 17 (July 1987): 113-133.

Shalin, Dmitri N. "The Romantic Antecedents of Meadian Social Psychology." *Symbolic Interaction* 7 (Spring 1984): 43-65.

_____. Review of Hans Joas's *G. H. Mead. A Contemporary Re-examination of His Thought. Symbolic Interaction* 9 (Fall 1986): 273-276.

_____. "Socialism, Democracy and Reform: A Letter and an Article by George H. Mead." *Symbolic Interaction* 10 (Fall 1987): 267-278.

Singer, Beth J. "Rights and Norms." In *Frontiers in American Philosophy,* edited by Robert Burch. College Station: Texas A & M University Press, forthcoming.

Sixel, Friedrich W. "Motivation und Wissen." *Kölner Zeitschrift für Soziologie und Sozialpsychologie. Supplement* 22 (1980): 246-267.

Smith, Charles W. *A Critique of Sociological Reasoning: An Essay in Philosophical Sociology.* Oxford: Basil Blackwell, 1979. [See Part I.]

Stewart, Robert L. "What George Herbert Mead Should Have Said: Exploration of a Problem of Interpretation." *Symbolic Interaction* 4 (Fall 1981): 157-166.

Sykes, Richard E. "Toward a Sociology of Religion Based on the Philosophy of George Herbert Mead." In *Sociology and Human Destiny: Essays on Sociology, Religion and Society*, edited by Gregory Baum, pp. 167-182. New York: A Crossroad Book, The Seabury Press, 1980.

Tanaka, Shigeru. "A Logical Structure of 'the Other'—Towards a Dialogue between the Theory of Reification and Role Theory." *Shakaigaku Hyoron (Japanese Sociological Review)* 35 (December 1984): 103-119. [This article is in Japanese. There is an English abstract in the journal.]

Tenbruck, Friedrich H. "George Herbert Mead und die Ursprünge der Soziologie in Deutschland und Amerika. Ein Kapitel über die Gültigkeit und Vergleichbarkeit soziologischer Theorien." In *Das Problem der Intersubjektivität. Neuere Beiträge zum Werk George Herbert Meads*, edited by Hans Joas, pp. 179-243. Frankfurt am Main: Suhrkamp, 1985.

Travisano, Richard V. "The Sociology of the Is: The Self as Social Force." *Free Inquiry in Creative Sociology* 13 (November 1985): 187-189.

Turner, Jonathan H. "Returning to 'Social Physics': Illustrations from the Work of George Herbert Mead." *Current Perspectives in Social Theory* 2 (1981): 187-208.

————. "A Note on George Herbert Mead's Behavioral Theory of Social Structure." *Journal for the Theory of Social Behavior* 12 (July 1982): 213-222.

————, Leonard Beeghley, and Charles H. Powers. *The Emergence of Sociological Theory*, 2d ed. pp. 407-469. Belmont, CA.: Wadsworth, 1989.

Ule, Mirjana. "The Dialectic Basis of Symbolic Interactionism in the Comprehension of Interhuman Relations and Human Activity." *Anthropos* (Yugoslavia) No. 4-6 (1983): 385-396. [In Slovak.]

Valsiner, Jaan, and R. Van Der Veer, "On the Social Nature of Human Cognition: An Analysis of the Shared Intellectual Roots of George Herbert Mead and Lev Vygotsky." *Journal for the Theory of Social Behavior* 18 (March 1988): 117-136.

Van Der Veer, R. "Similarities between the Theories of G. H. Mead and L. S. Vygotskij: An Explanation?" In *Studies in the History of Psychology and the Social Sciences* 3, edited by S. Bem, H. Rappard, and W. van Hoorn. Leiden: Psychologisch Instituut van de Rijksuniversiteit, 1985.

Vaughn, Ted R., and Gideon Sjoberg. "The Individual and Bureaucracy: An Alternative Meadian Interpretation." *Journal of Applied Behavorial Science* 20 (1984): 57-69.

Wandschneider, Dieter. "Selbstbewusstsein als sich selbst erfüllender Entwurf." *Zeitschrift für Philosophische Forschung* 33 (October-December 1979): 499-520.

Warshay, Leon H., and Diana W. Warshay. "The Individualizing and Subjectiv- izing of George Herbert Mead: A Sociology of Knowledge Interpretation." *Sociological Focus* 19 (April 1986): 177-188.

Wenzel, Harald. "Mead und Parsons. Die emergente Ordnung des sozialen Handelns." In *Das Problem der Intersubjektivität. Neuere Beiträge zum Werk George Herbert Meads*, edited by Hans Joas, pp. 26-59. Frankfurt am Main: Suhrkamp, 1985.

Wiley, Norbert. "Notes on Self Genesis: From Me to We to I." *Studies in Symbolic Interaction: A Research Annual* 2, edited by Norman K. Denzin, pp. 87-105. Greenwich, Conn.: JAI Press, 1979.

Wood, Michael, and Mark L. Wardell. "G. H. Mead's Social Behaviorism vs. The Astructural Bias of Symbolic Interactionism." *Symbolic Interaction* 6 (Spring 1983): 85-96.

Yasukawa, Hajime. "The Nature and the Task of Meadian 'Social Psychology'— Social Practice and Social Psychology." *Shakaigaku-Hyoron (Japanese Sociological Review)* 36 (September 1985): 71-85. [This article is in Japanese. There is an English abstract in the journal.]

Yoels, William C. and David A. Karp. "A Social Psychological Critique of 'Oversocialization': Dennis Wrong Revisted." *Sociological Symposium* 24 (Fall 1978): 27-39.

Zito, George V., and Jerry Jacobs. "Attribution and Symbolic Interaction: An Impasse at the Generalized Other." *Human Relations* 32 (July 1979): 571-578.

Index